A-Z NORTHAMPTONSHIRE

CONTENTS

Key to Map Pages	2-5
Map Pages	6-130
Large Scale Town Centre	131

Road Map Pages (1:200,000 / 3.156miles to 1inch) (Reference - Inside Back Cover Flap)	132-141
Index to Streets etc.	142-175
Index to Hospitals etc.	176

REFERENCE

Motorway — M1

Primary Route — A14

  Proposed

A Road — A510

  Proposed

B Road — B573

Dual Carriageway

One-way Street
Traffic flow on A Roads is also indicated by a heavy line on the driver's left.

Restricted Access

Pedestrianized Road

Track / Footpath

Residential Walkway

Railway — Station / Heritage Station / Level Crossing / Tunnel

Built-up Area — ROMAN WY

Local Authority Boundary

Posttown Boundary

Postcode Boundary (within Posttown)

Map Continuation — 129 / Large Scale Centre 131 / Road Map Pages 132

Car Park (Selected) — P

Church or Chapel — †

Cycleway (Selected)

Fire Station — ■

Hospital — H

House Numbers (A & B Roads only) — 298 / 77

Information Centre — ℹ

National Grid Reference — 405

Police Station — ▲

Post Office — ★

Safety Camera with Speed Limit
Fixed cameras and long term road works cameras Symbols do not indicate camera direction — 30

Toilet:
  without facilities for the Disabled — ▽
  with facilities for the Disabled — ▽
  for the Disabled only — ▽

Educational Establishment

Hospital or Healthcare Building

Industrial Building

Leisure or Recreational Facility

Place of Interest

Public Building

Shopping Centre or Market

Other Selected Buildings

SCALE

Map Pages 6-130	Map Page 131
1:16,896 3¾ inches (9.52 cm) to 1 mile 5.9 cm to 1km	1:8,448 7½ inches (19.05 cm) to 1 mile 11.8 cm to 1km
0 ¼ ½ Mile	0 ⅛ ¼ Mile
0 250 500 750 Metres	0 100 200 300 400 Metres

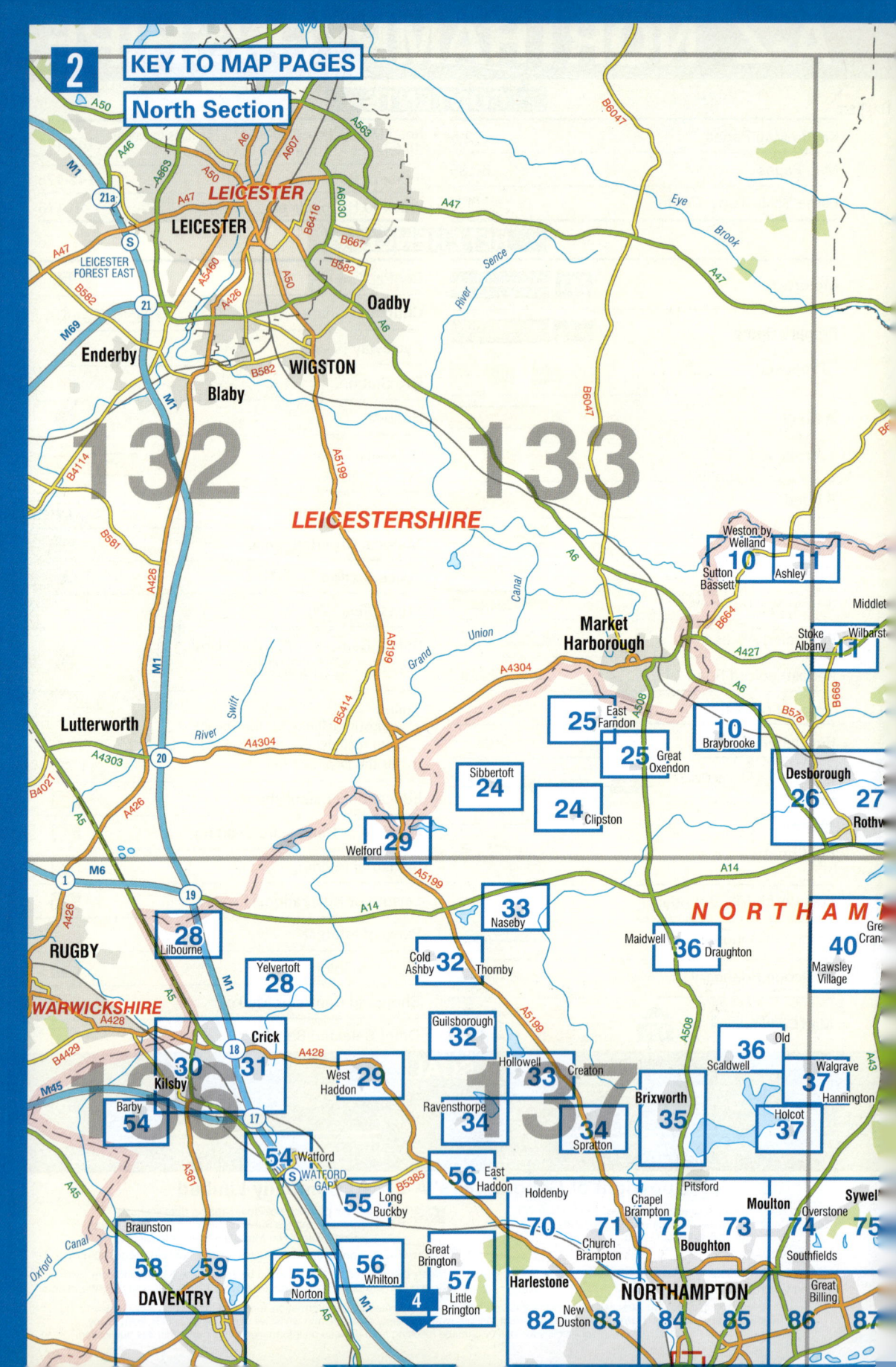

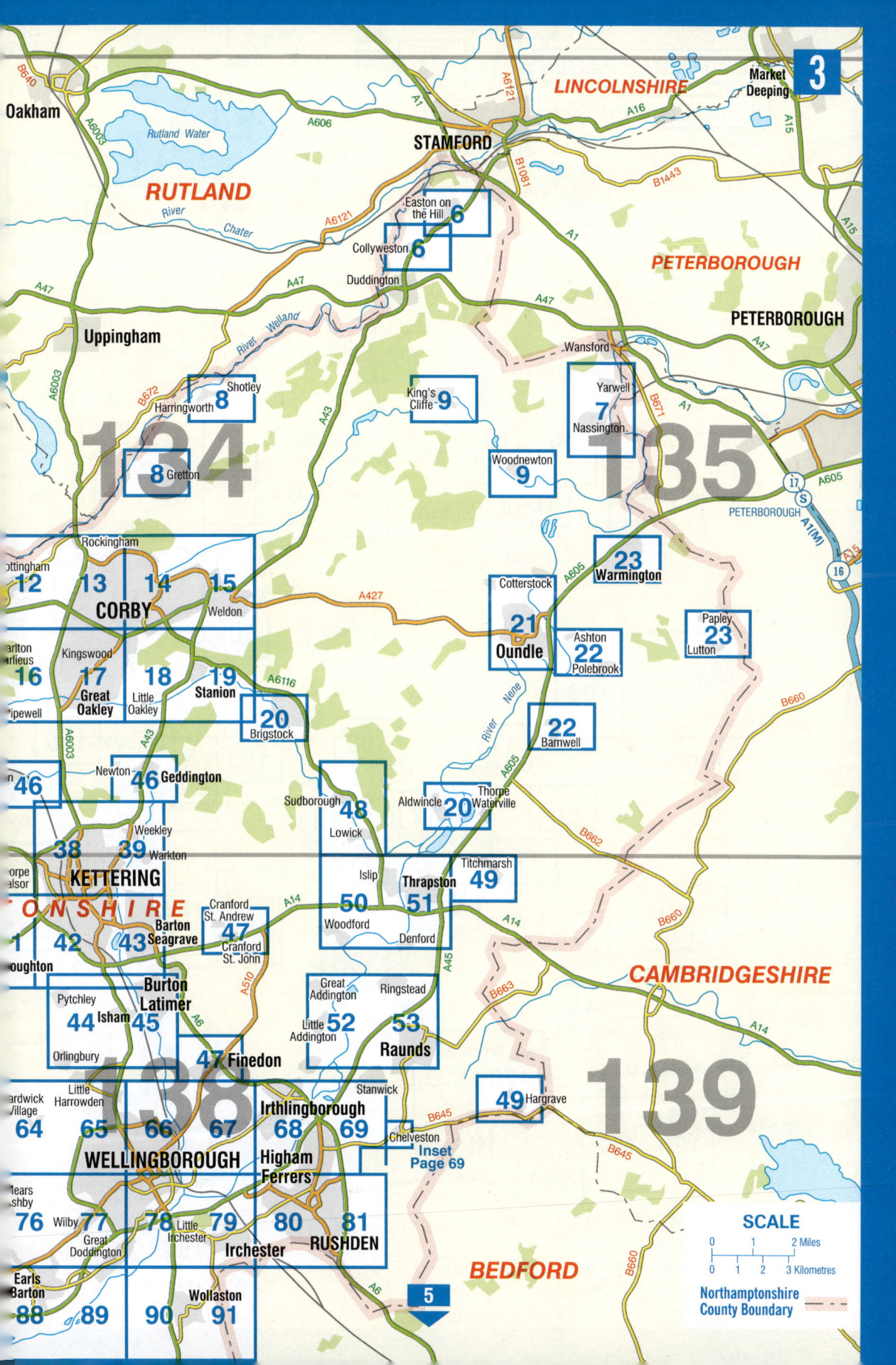

LINCOLNSHIRE

Market Deeping

Oakham

Rutland Water

RUTLAND

River Chater

STAMFORD

Easton on the Hill **6**

Collyweston **6**

Duddington

PETERBOROUGH

PETERBOROUGH

Uppingham

River Welland

Wansford

Shotley **8**

Harringworth

King's Cliffe **9**

Yarwell **7**
Nassington

Woodnewton **9**

8 Gretton

134

135

PETERBOROUGH

Rockingham

12 **13** **14** **15**

CORBY

Weldon

Cotterstock

23 Warmington

Papley **23**
Lutton

ottingham

arlton arlieus

Kingswood

16 **17** **18** **19** Stanion

Great Oakley

Little Oakley

A6116

21 Oundle

Ashton **22**
Polebrook

ipewell

20
Brigstock

46 Newton **46** Geddington

22
Barnwell

River Nene

48 Sudborough

Lowick

Aldwincle **20**

Thorpe Waterville

n **46**

Weekley

38 **39** Warkton

KETTERING

orpe alsor

Islip

Titchmarsh

Thrapston **49**

Cranford St. Andrew **47**

50 **51**

Woodford

Denford

CAMBRIDGESHIRE

Cranford St. John

ONSHIRE

1 **42** **43**

Barton Seagrave

Burton Latimer

Pytchley

44 Isham **45**

Orlingbury

Great Addington

Ringstead

Little Addington **52** **53**

Raunds

oughton

47 Finedon

Stanwick

49 Hargrave

138

139

ardwick illage

Little Harrowden

64 **65** **66** **67** **68** **69**

WELLINGBOROUGH

Higham Ferrers

Chelveston

Inset Page 69

ears shby

76 Wilby **77** **78** Little Irchester **79** **80** **81**

Great Doddington

RUSHDEN

Irchester

BEDFORD

Earls Barton

Wollaston

88 **89** **90** **91**

5

SCALE

0   1   2 Miles

0   1   2   3 Kilometres

Northamptonshire County Boundary

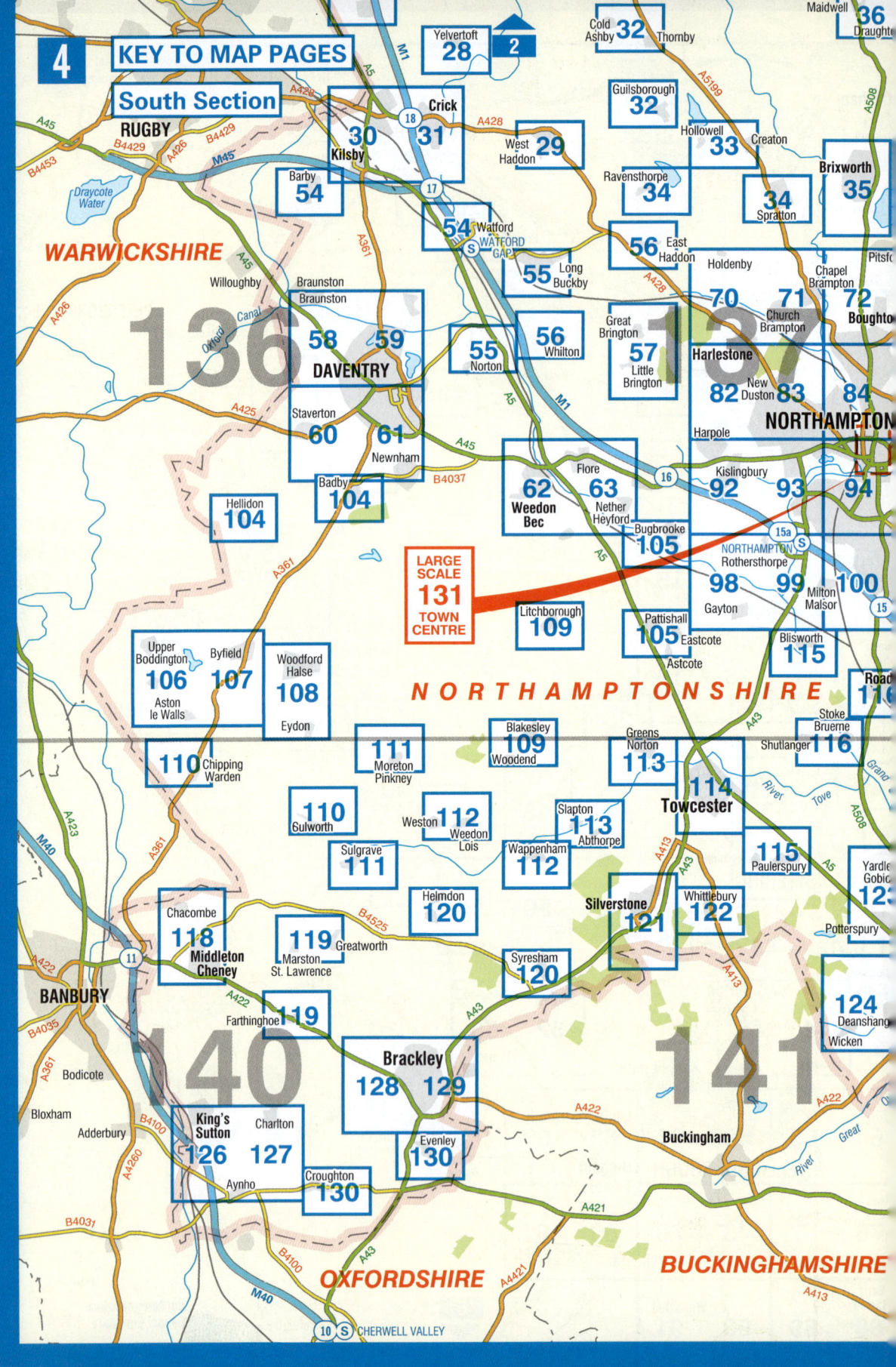

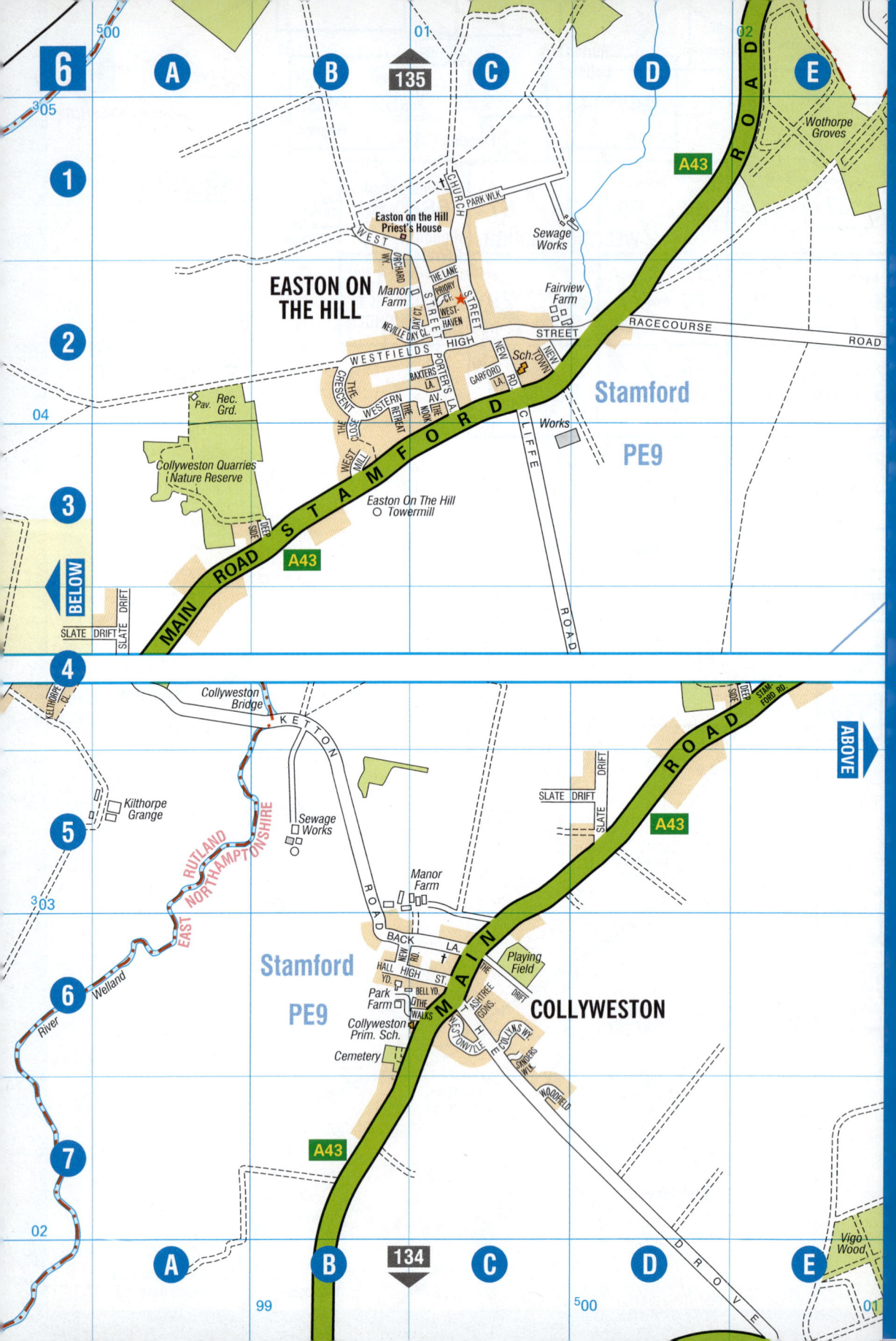

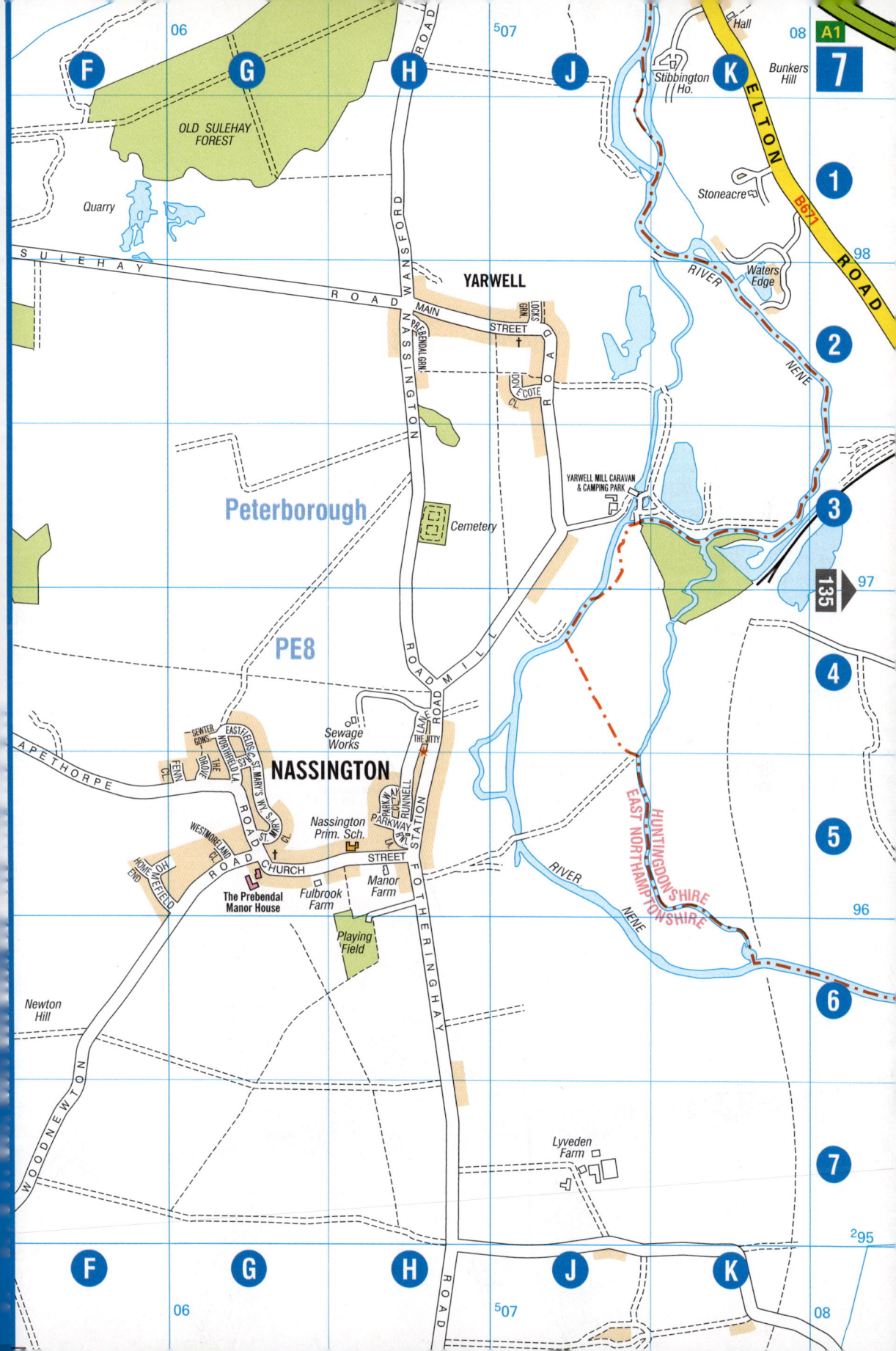

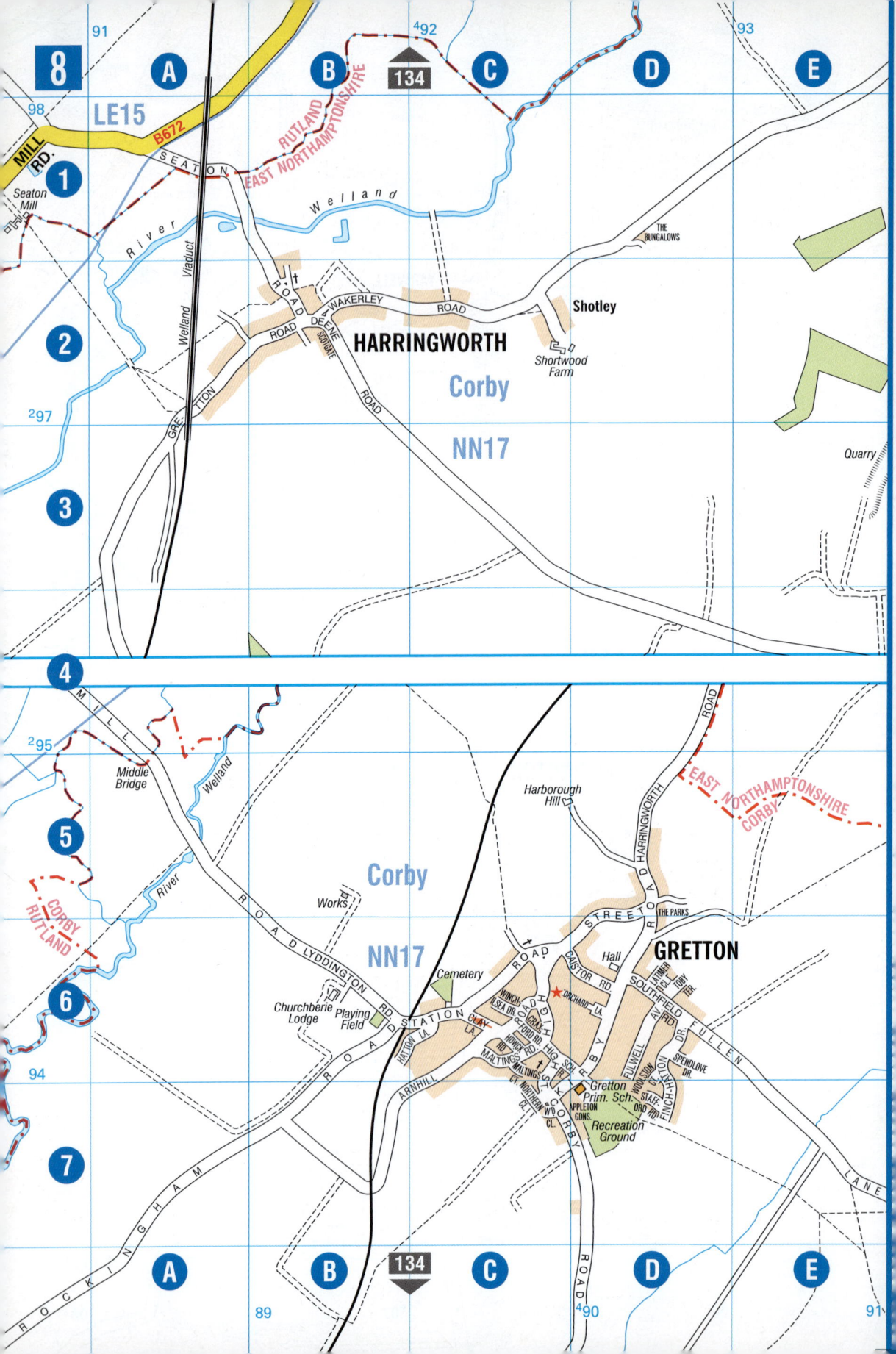

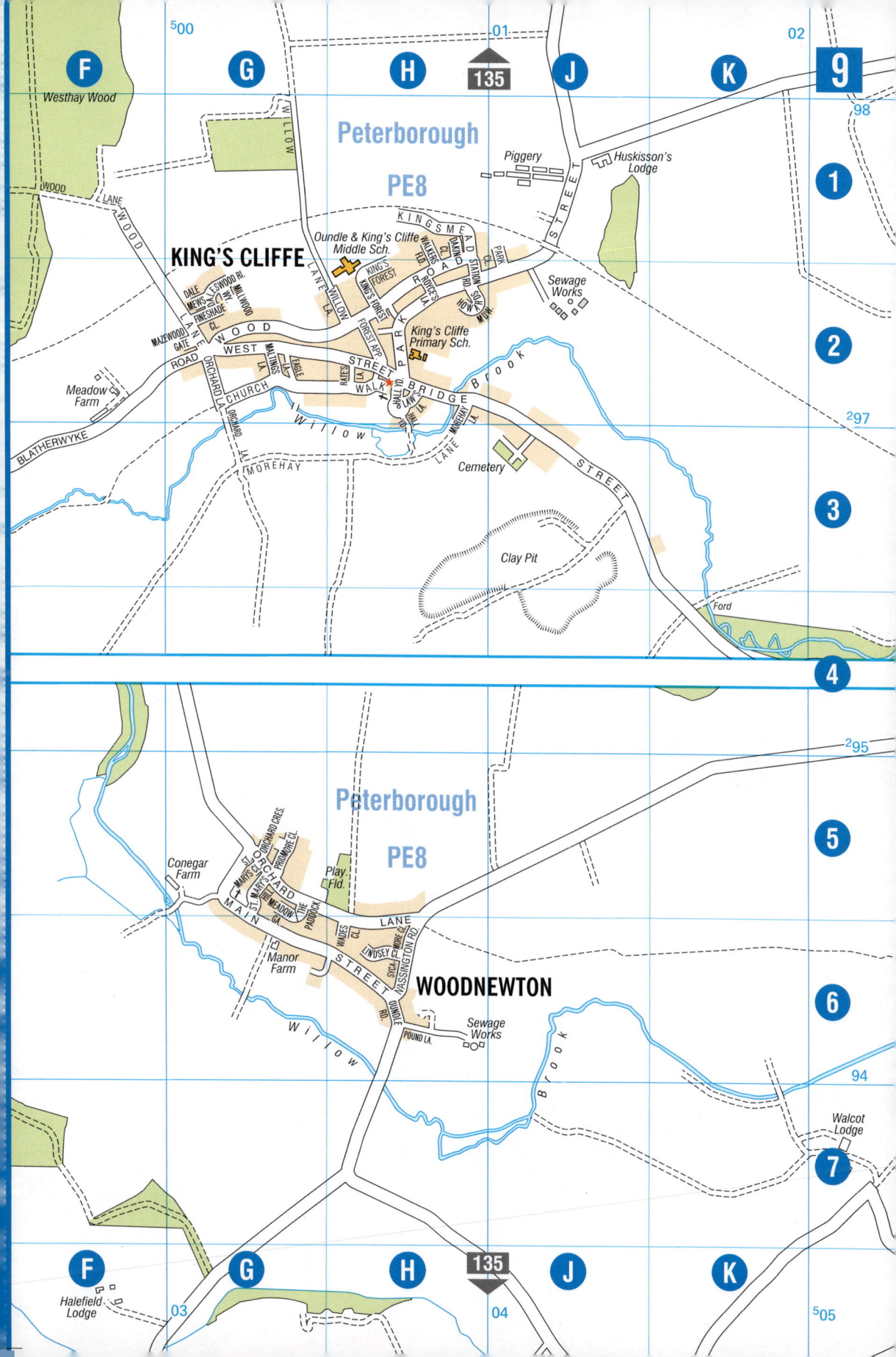

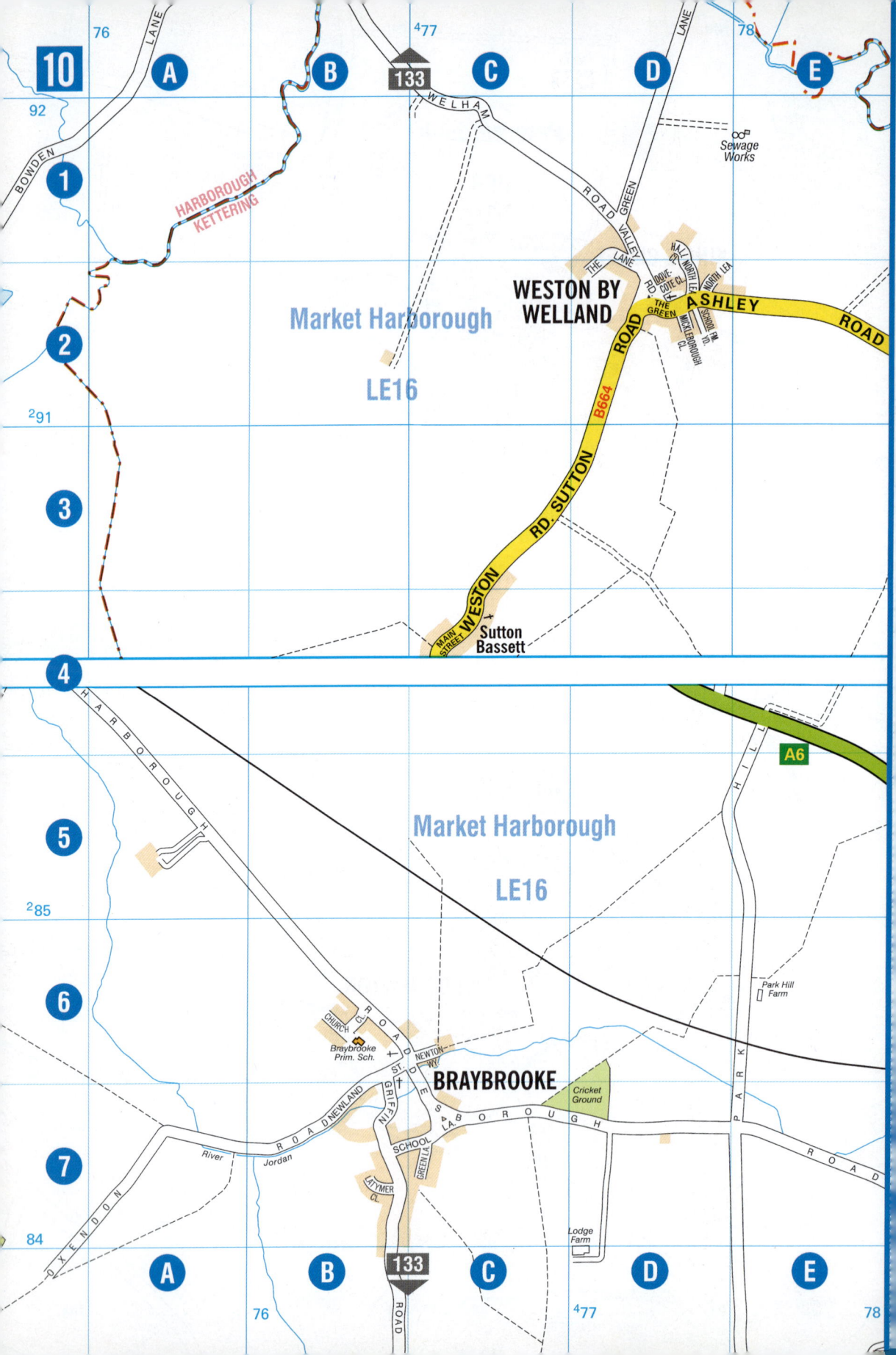

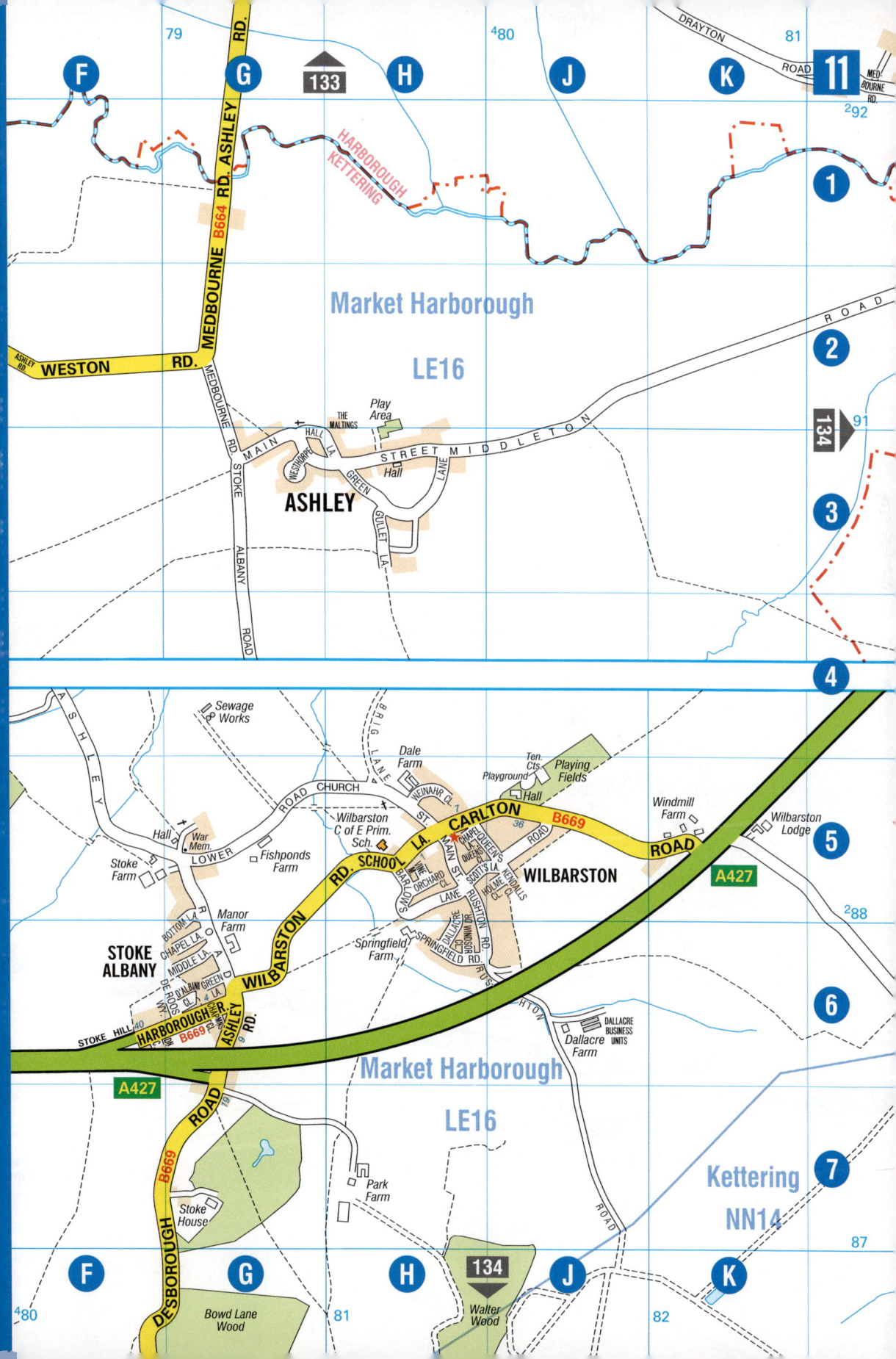

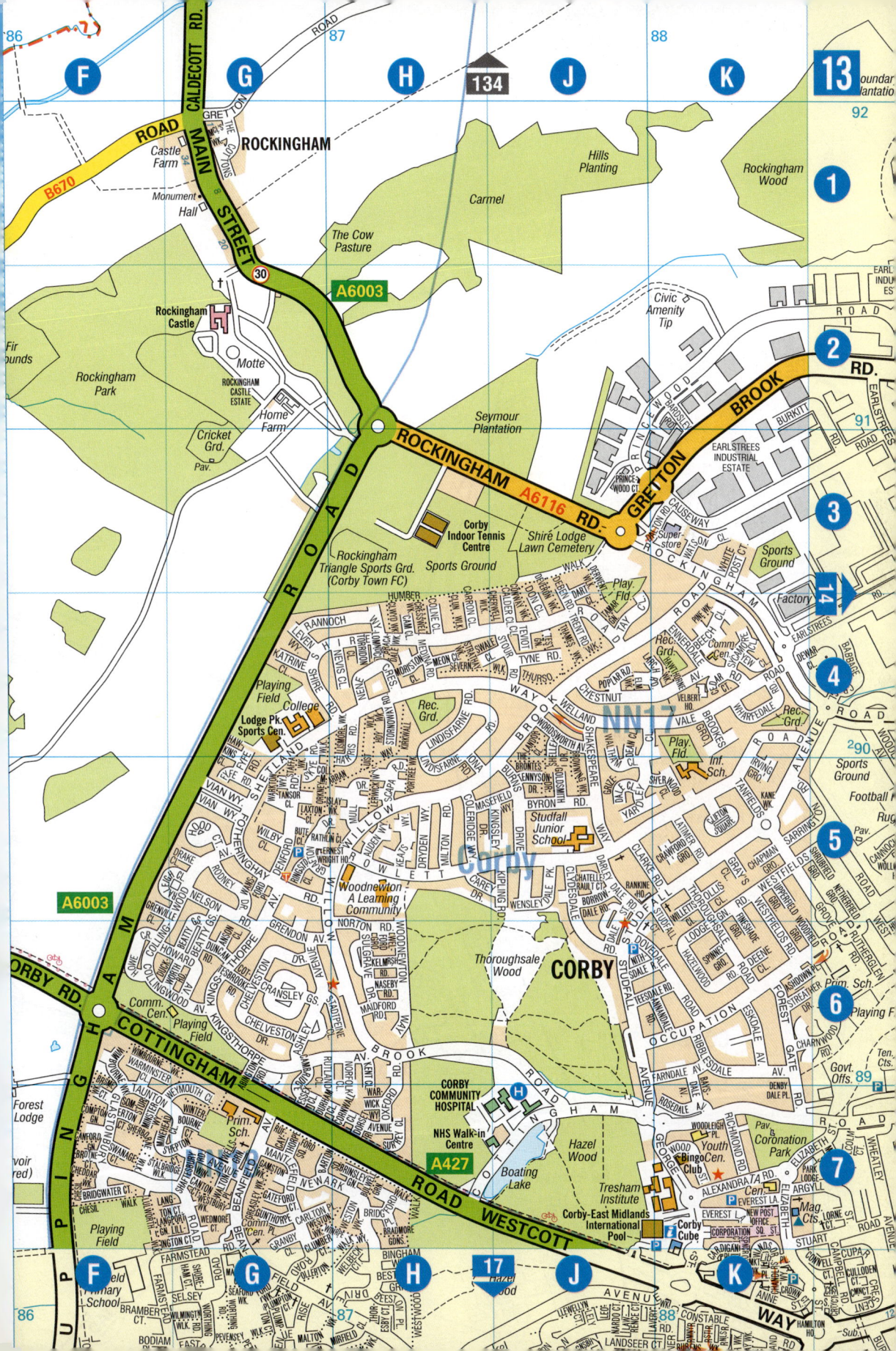

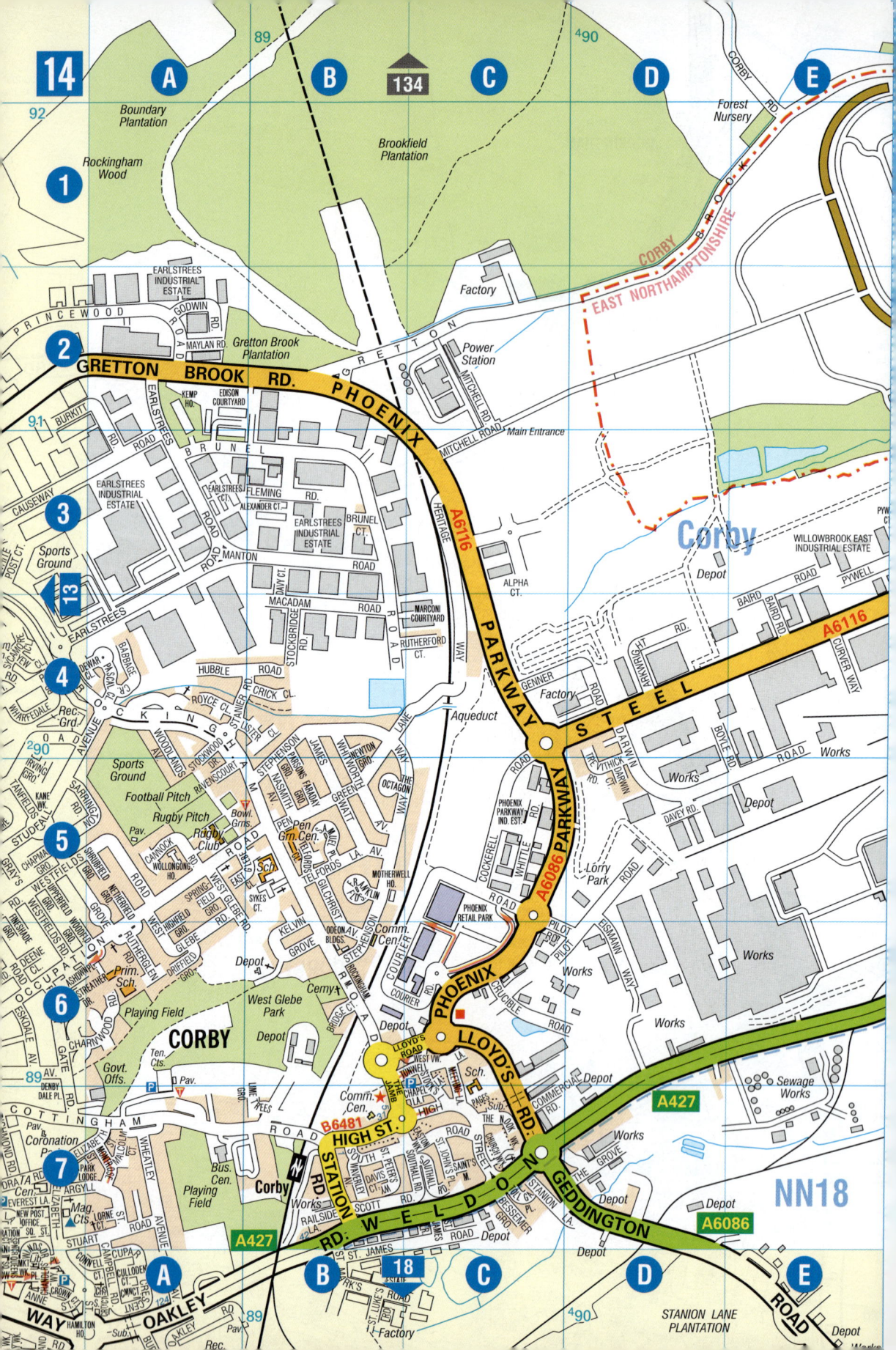

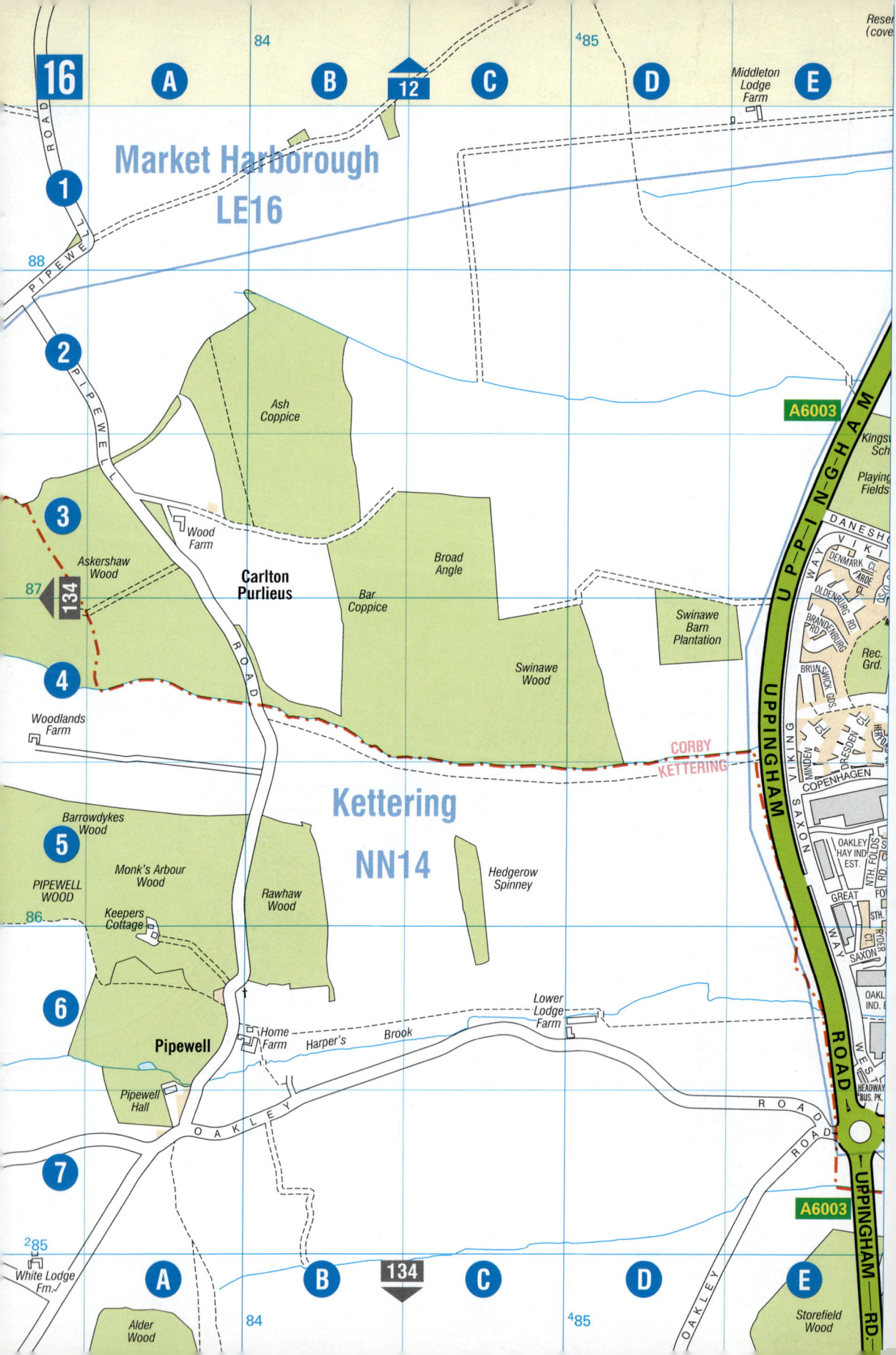

16

Market Harborough
LE16

Kettering

NN14

A6003

CORBY
KETTERING

A6003

Reservoir (covered)

Middleton Lodge Farm

UPPINGHAM WAY

Kingsw... Sch...

Playing Fields

DANESH...

DENMARK CL.
AROE CL.

VIKI...

OLDENBURG RD.

BRANDENBURG RD.

BRUNSWICK GDNS.

DRESDEN

Rec. Grd.

MINDEN

HER...

COPENHAGEN

VIKING

SAXON WAY

OAKLEY HAY IND. EST.

NTH. FOL...

RYDER CT.

STH.

GREAT

OAKL IND. EST.

WEST...

HEADWAY BUS. PK.

Ash Coppice

Wood Farm

Carlton Purlieus

Askershaw Wood

134

Bar Coppice

Broad Angle

Swinawe Wood

Swinawe Barn Plantation

Woodlands Farm

Barrowdykes Wood

Monk's Arbour Wood

Rawhaw Wood

Hedgerow Spinney

PIPEWELL WOOD

Keepers Cottage

Lower Lodge Farm

Pipewell

Home Farm

Harper's Brook

Pipewell Hall

OAKLEY

ROAD

ROAD

UPPINGHAM RD.

White Lodge Fm.

Storefield Wood

Alder Wood

PIPEWELL ROAD

88

87

86

85

84

485

12

A B C D E

1

2

3

4

5

6

7

A B C D E

134

134

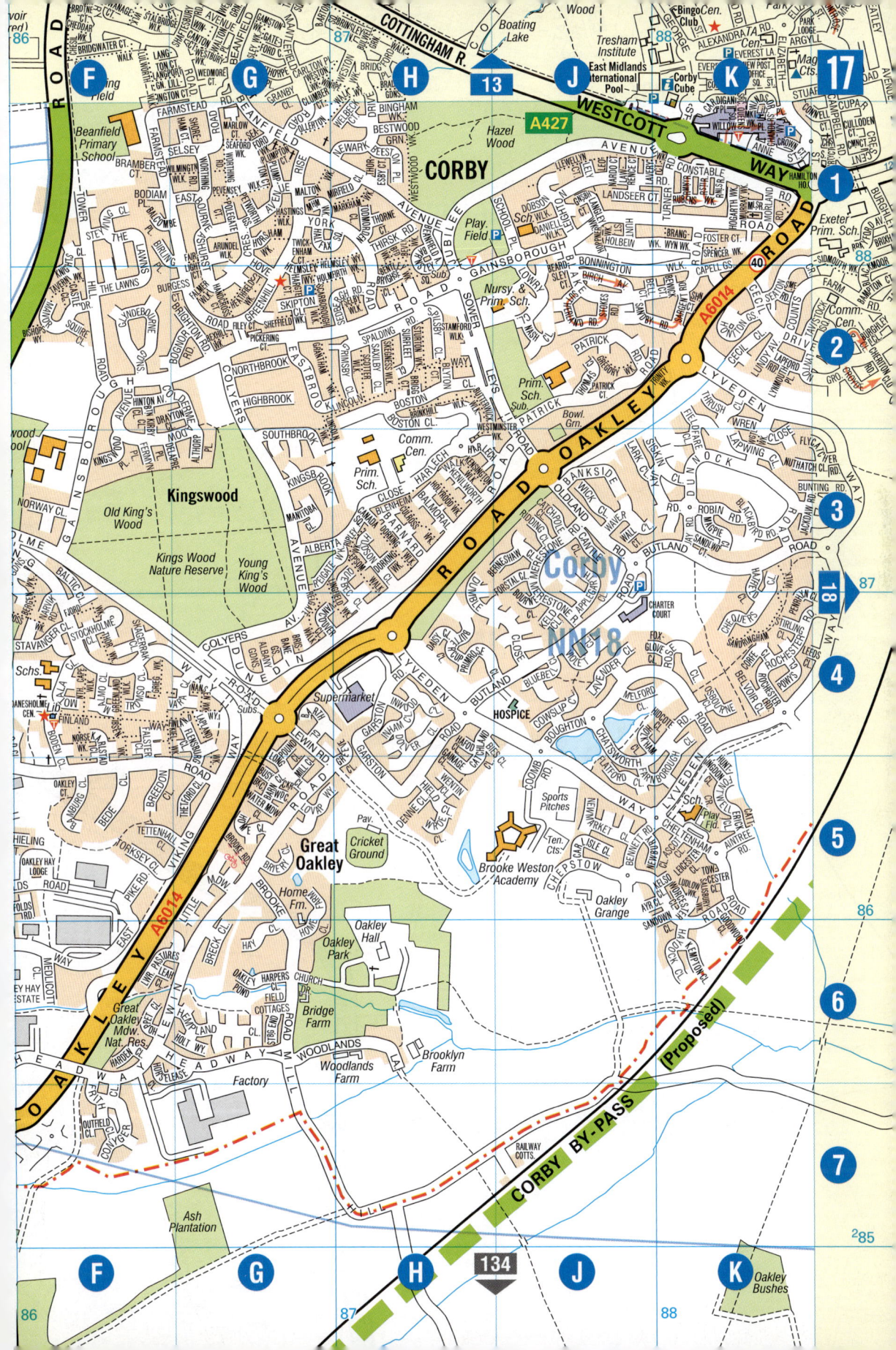

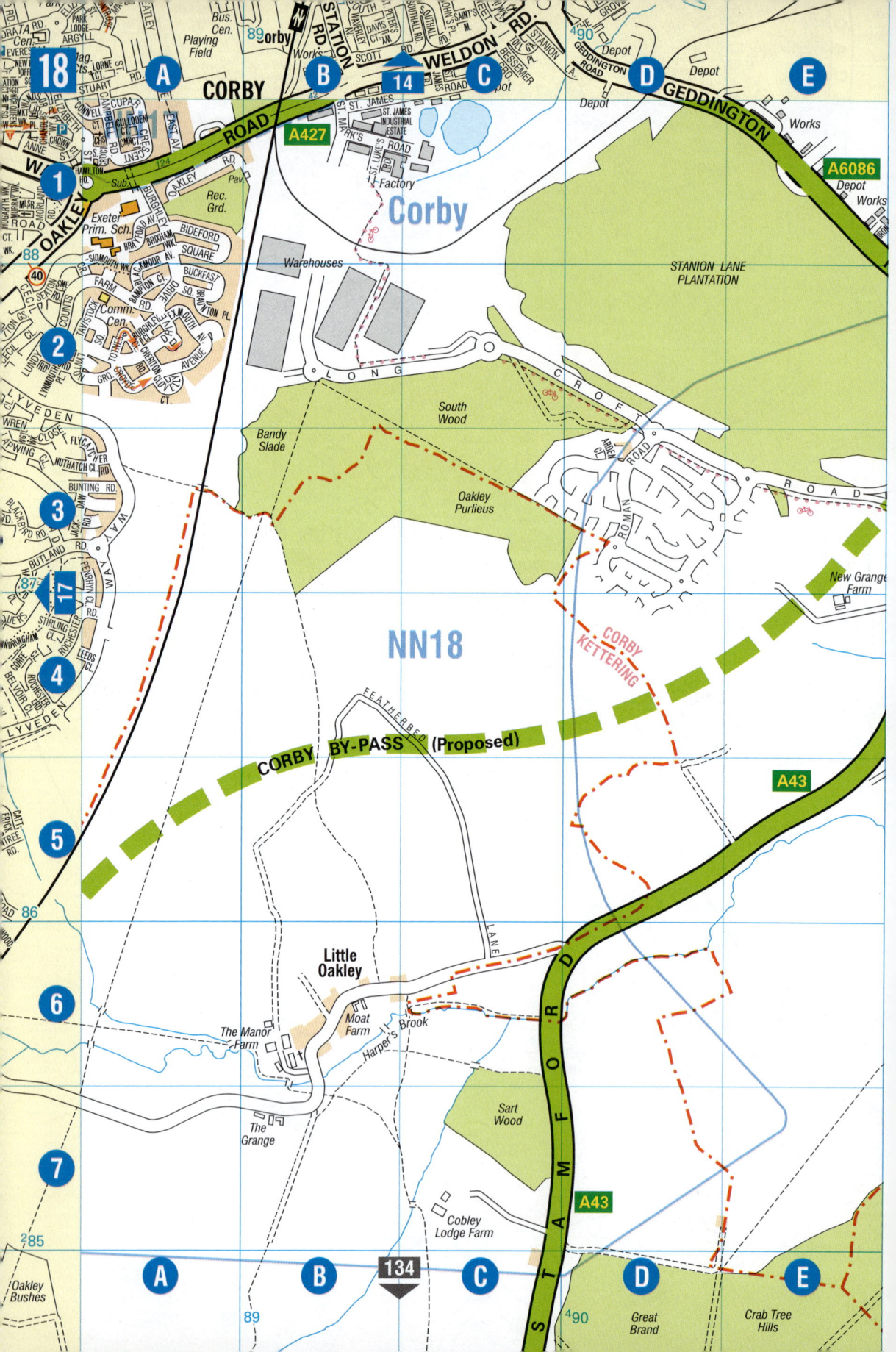

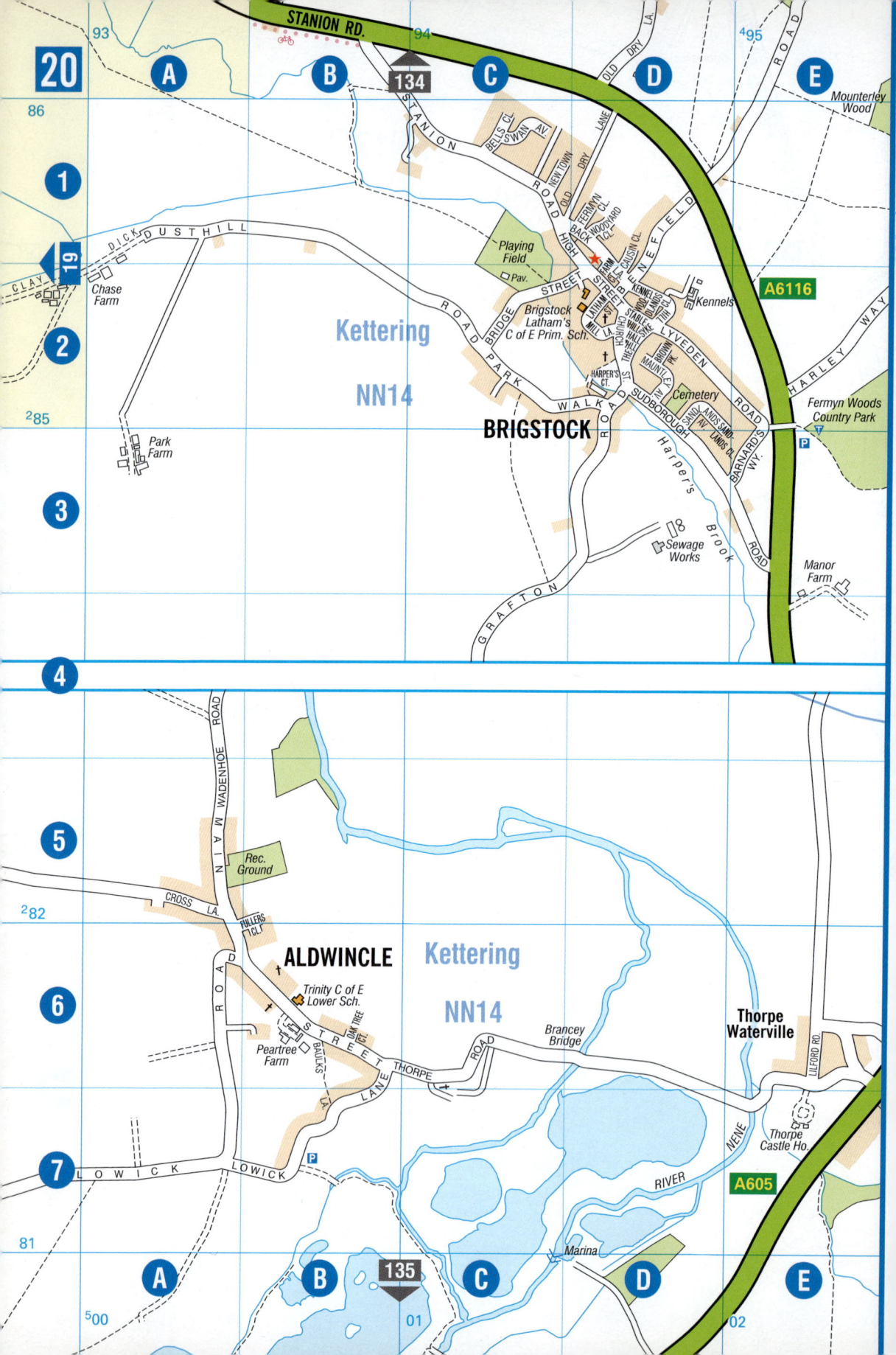

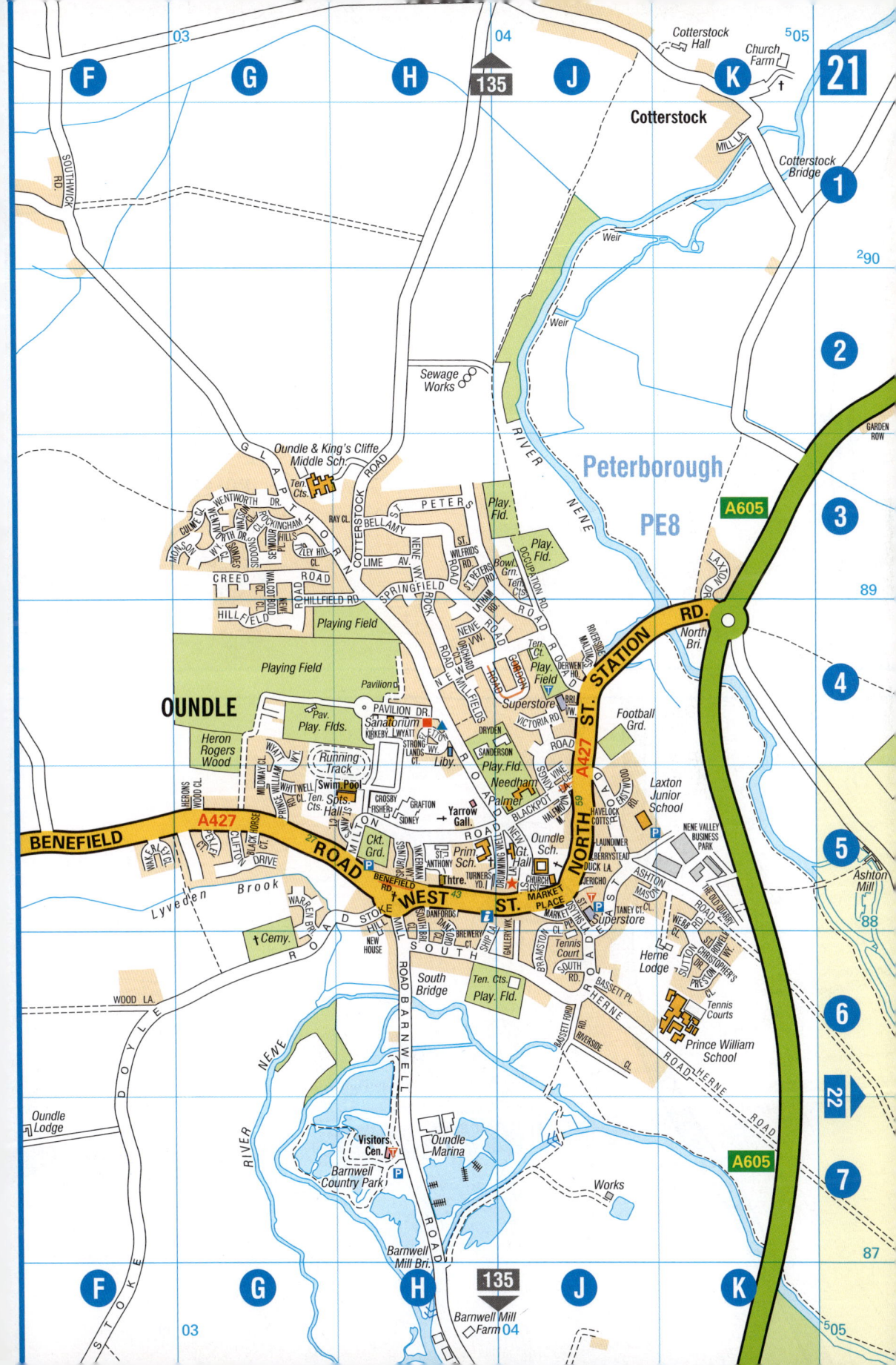

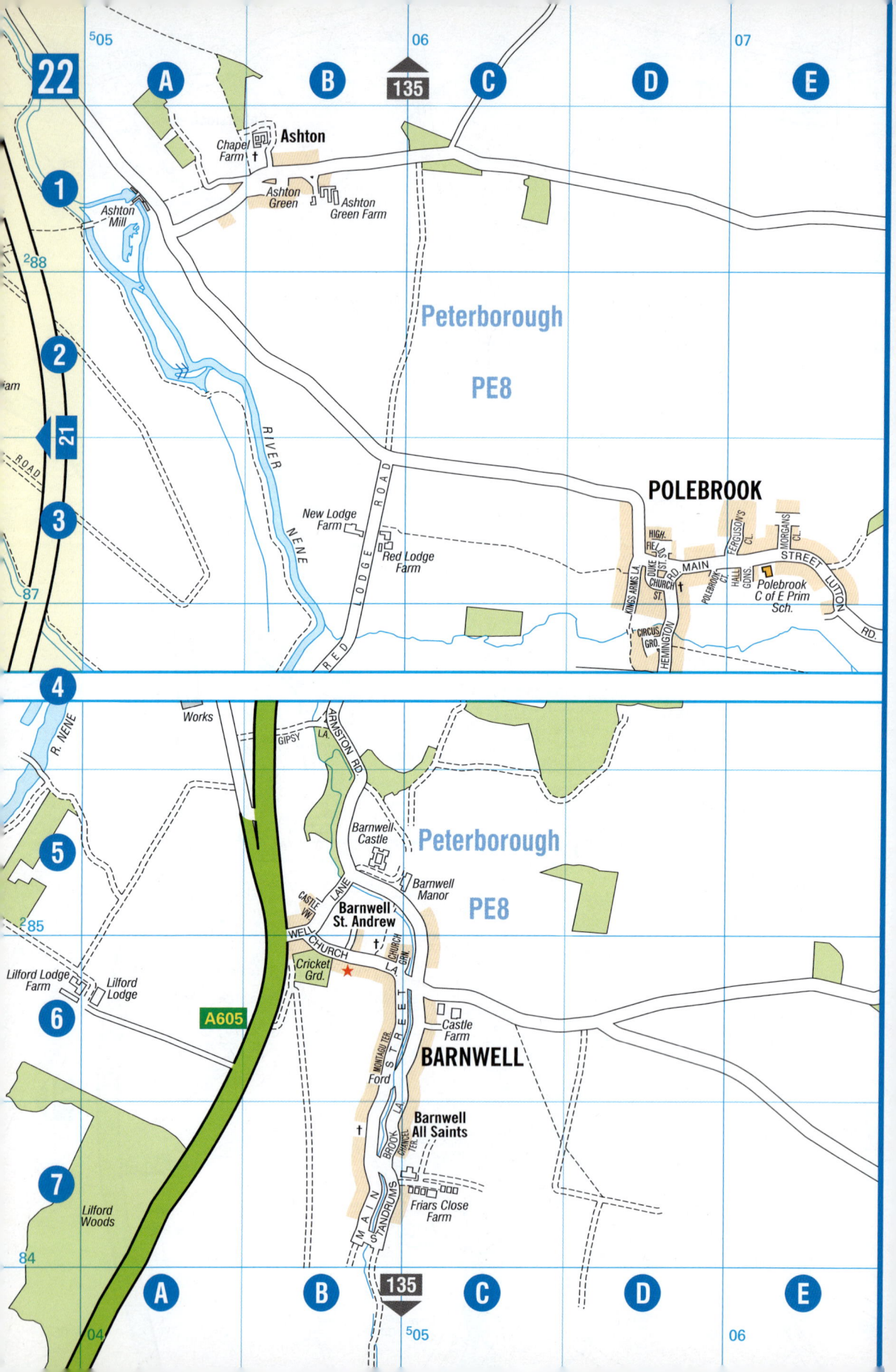

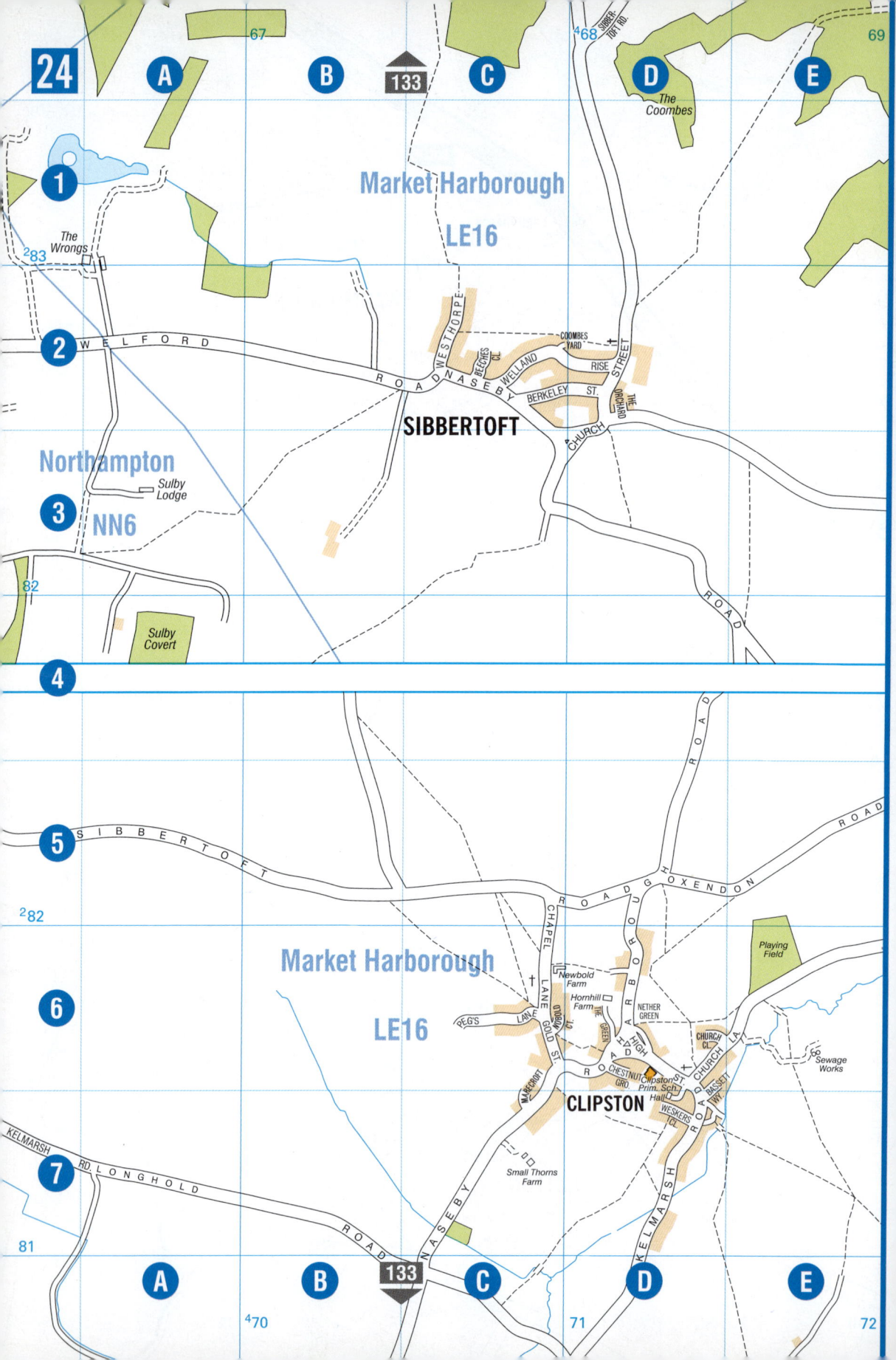

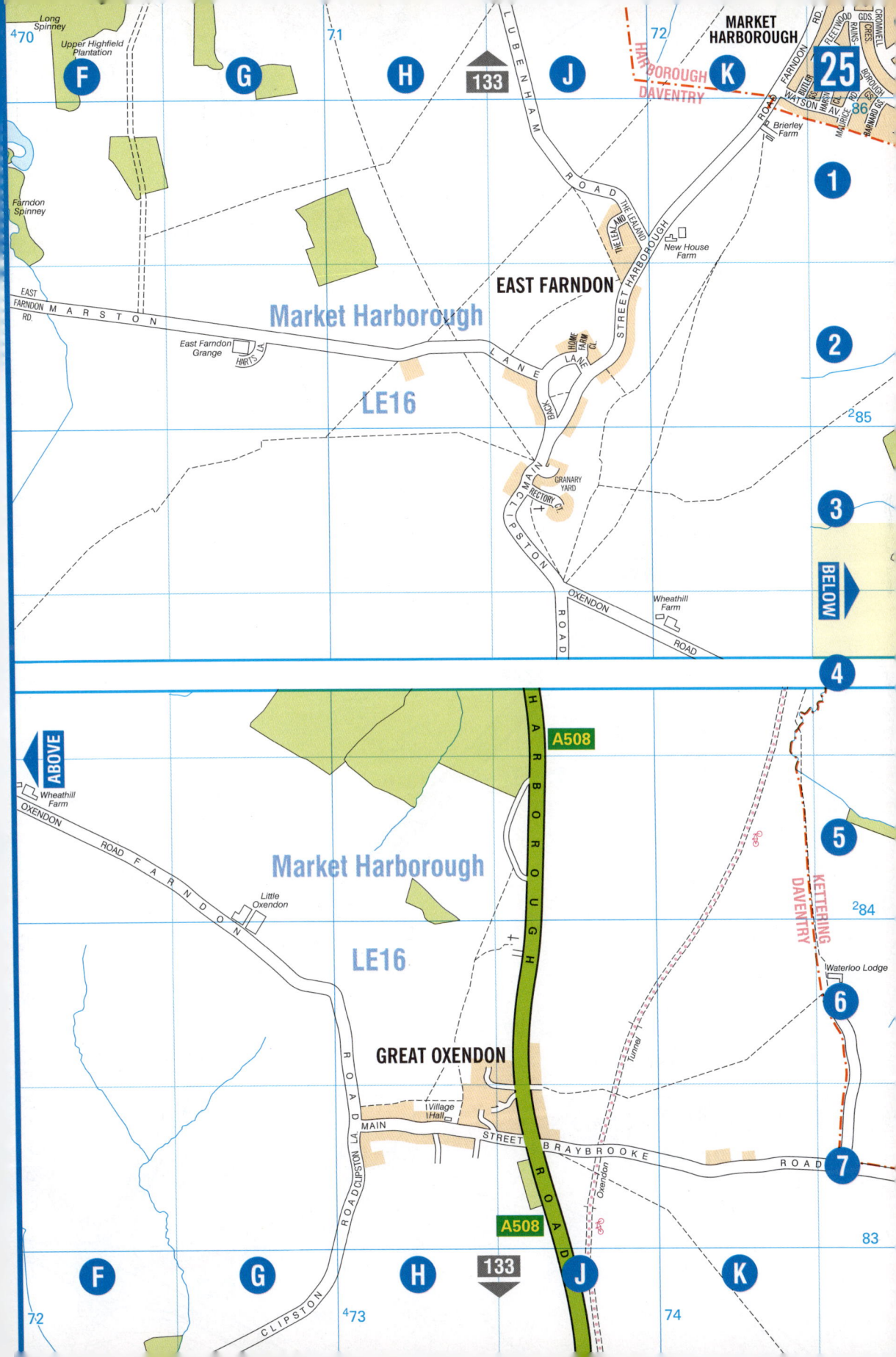

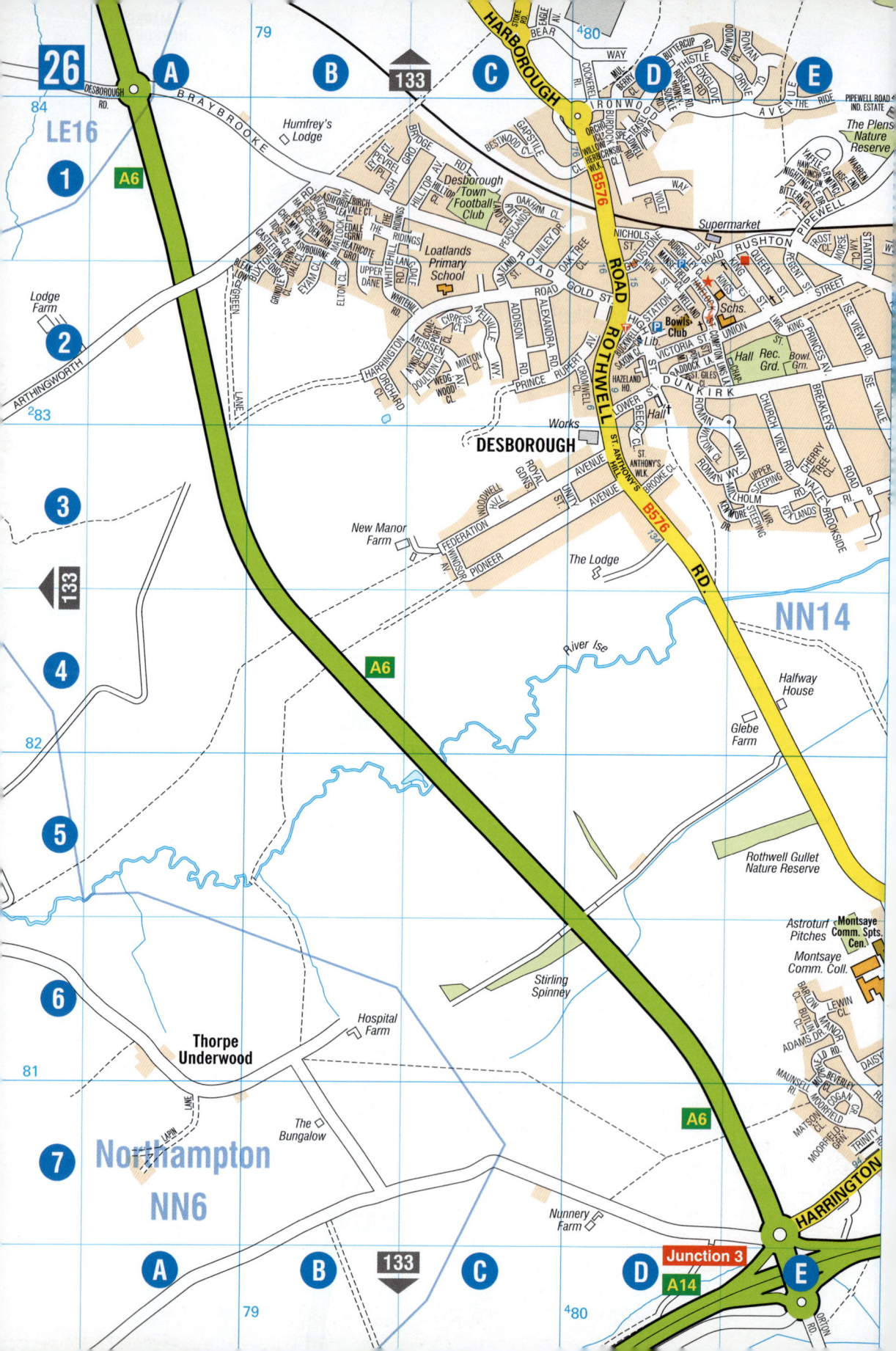

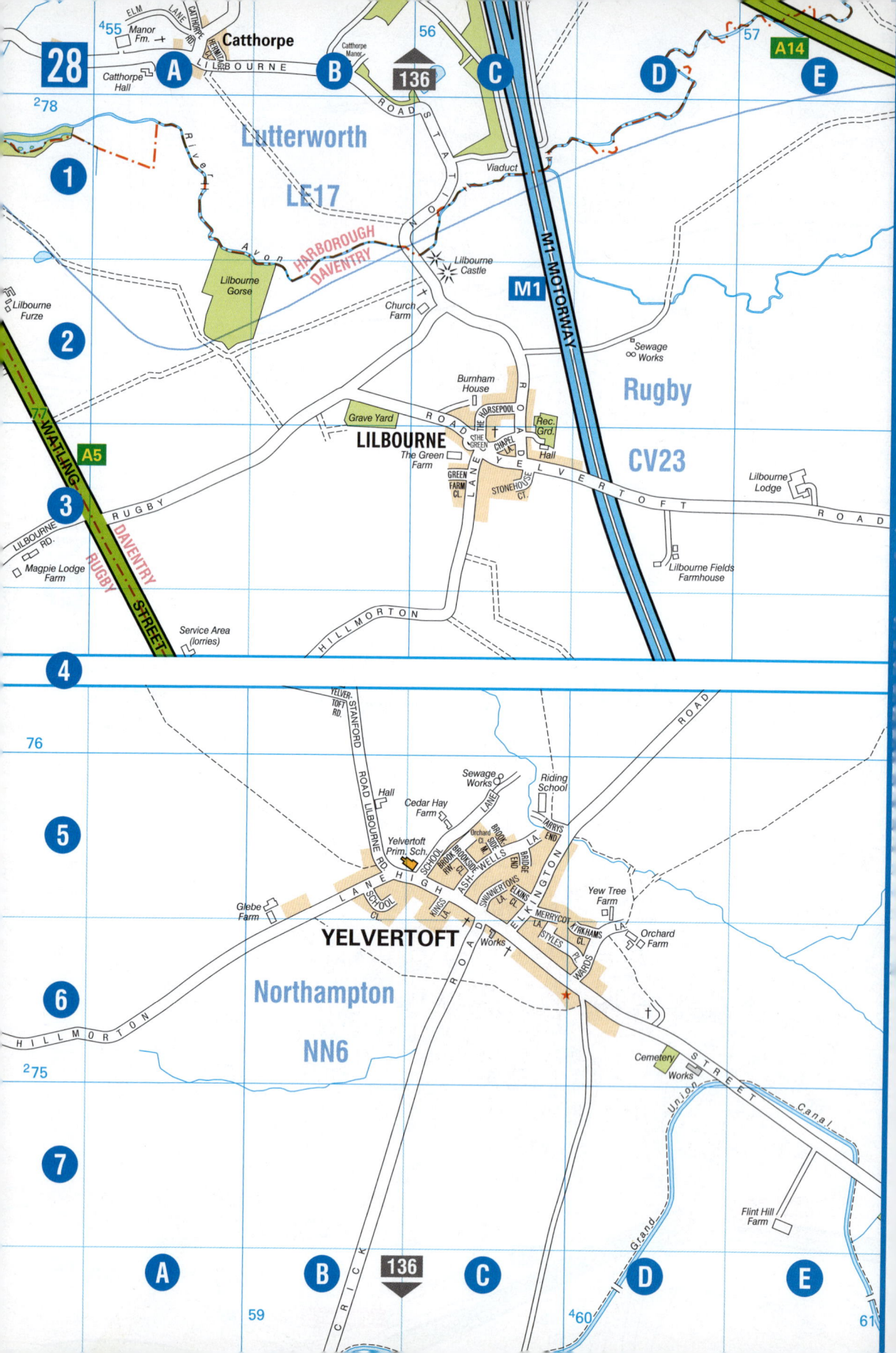

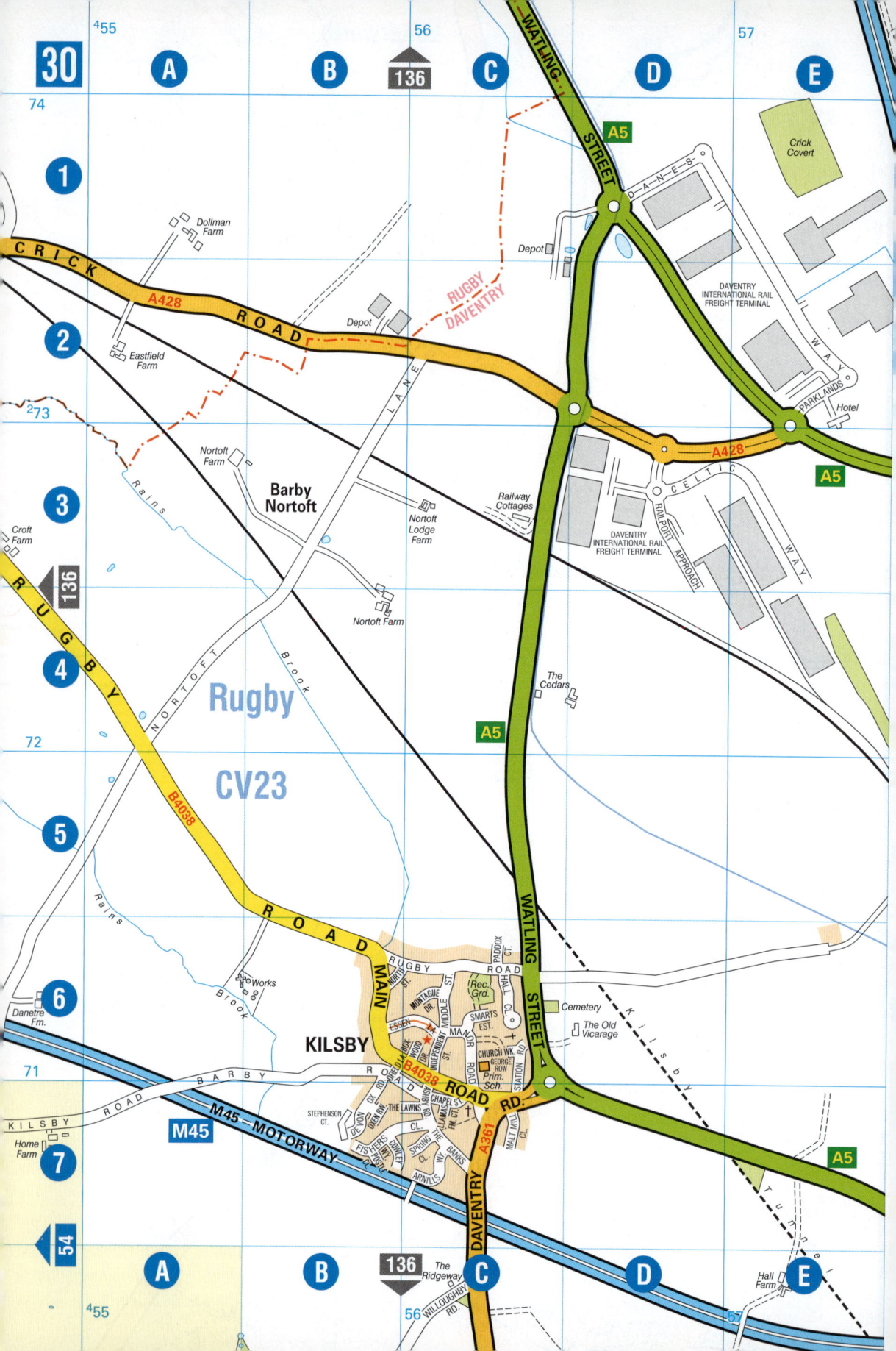

F   G   H   136   J   K

Junction 18

CRICK

A428

Northampton

NN6

WEST HADDON ROAD

136

M1 MOTORWAY

M1

Industrial Estate

Industrial Estate

Hotel

CRICK MOTORWAY ESTATE

Sewage Works

Factory

Nursery

Pappillion Fields

The Bungalow

Crack's Hill

CRICK RD

Grand Union Canal

Crick Wharf

Cottage Farm

Woolcombe Adams Fm.
Highfield Ho. Fm.

Pav'd Playing Field

KING CL
KLEN
BUCKNILLS

STYLE
PORTION
CL

CLOSE
CHURCH
STREET
RECTORY CL

THE DERRY
THE PADDOCK

BARLEY CFT
DRAYSON LA
OAK ALCE.
CLA
LA

EVERTOFT

DUNN CL
LALLOW
JURY DYKE
MONKS

HIGH
MARSH
LA
CHAPEL
CL
LAUD'S
SOUTH-
FIELDS DR.

THE MARSH

ROAD

BOAT HORSE LA

MARSONS DR.
WELL
HILL
ASHBY DR.
THE HIGH LEYS

WATFORD ROAD

WATFORD ROAD

KILSBY

Subway

Tunnel Farm

Bungalow Farm

Bellgarie

Field House Farm

Haycocks Farm

Tunnel

Grand Union Canal

Crick

Limes Fm.

Crick Prim. Sch.

1

2

²73

3

4

72

5

6

71

7

58   G   H   136   J   K   ⁴60

M1 MOTORWAY

M1

Junction 17

136

Kilsby Grange

Weir

59

58

31

74

⁶0

59

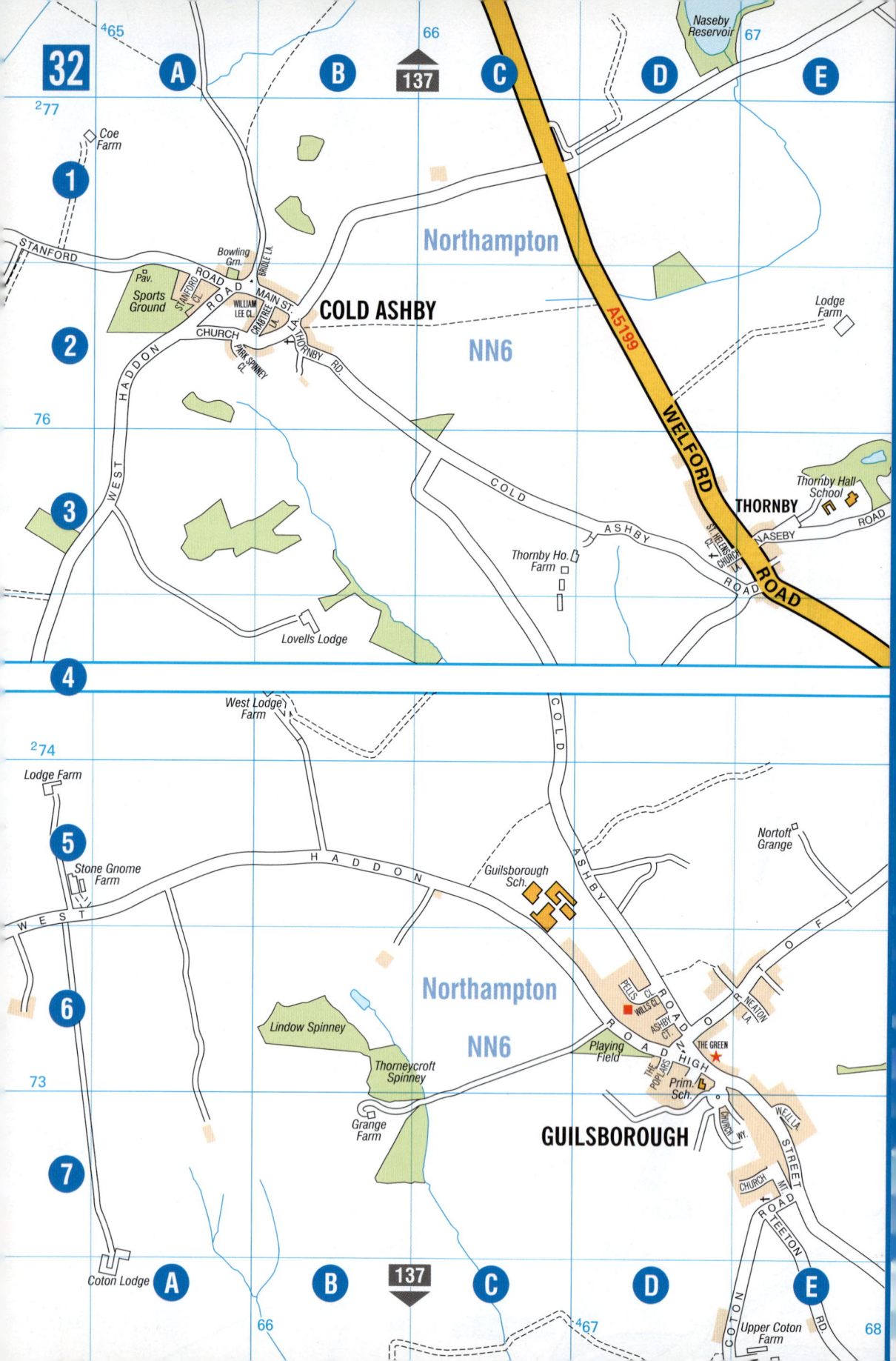

32

²77

A B 137 C D E

65 66 67

Coe Farm

1

STANFORD

Bowling Grn.

Northampton

2 Pav.
Sports Ground

STANFORD CL.
ROAD
WILLIAM LEE CL.
CRABTREE LA.
MAIN ST.
BRIDLE LA.

COLD ASHBY

CHURCH
PARK SPINNEY CL.
LA. THORNBY RD.

NN6

A5199

Lodge Farm

WELFORD

3

WEST
HADDON

COLD

ASHBY

Thornby Ho. Farm

Thornby Hall School

THORNBY

ST. HELENS CL.
CHURCH
NASEBY

ROAD

ROAD

Lovells Lodge

4

West Lodge Farm

COLD

²74

Lodge Farm

5

Stone Gnome Farm

HADDON

Guilsborough Sch.

ASHBY

Nortoft Grange

WEST

Northampton

Lindow Spinney

NN6

Thorneycroft Spinney

6

ROAD

FELS CL.
WILLS CL.

THE POPLARS
Playing Field

THE GREEN

HIGH
ASHBY
ROAD
NEATON LA.

ROAD

NORTOFT

WELLA LA.

7

Grange Farm

GUILSBOROUGH

Prim. Sch.

CHURCH WY.

STREET

CHURCH
ROAD
TEETON

Coton Lodge

COTON RD.

Upper Coton Farm

A B 137 C D E

66 ²467 68

Naseby Reservoir

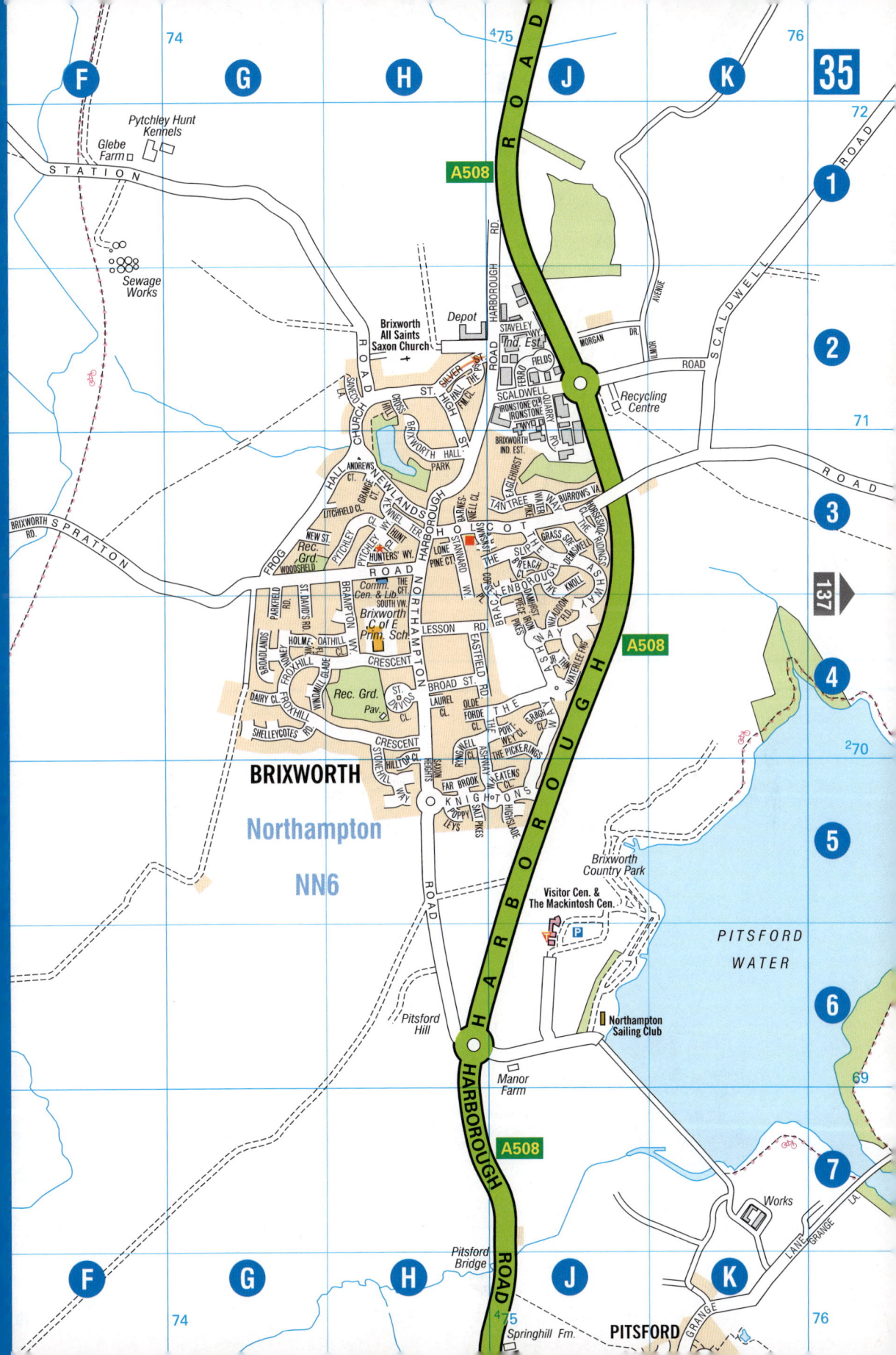

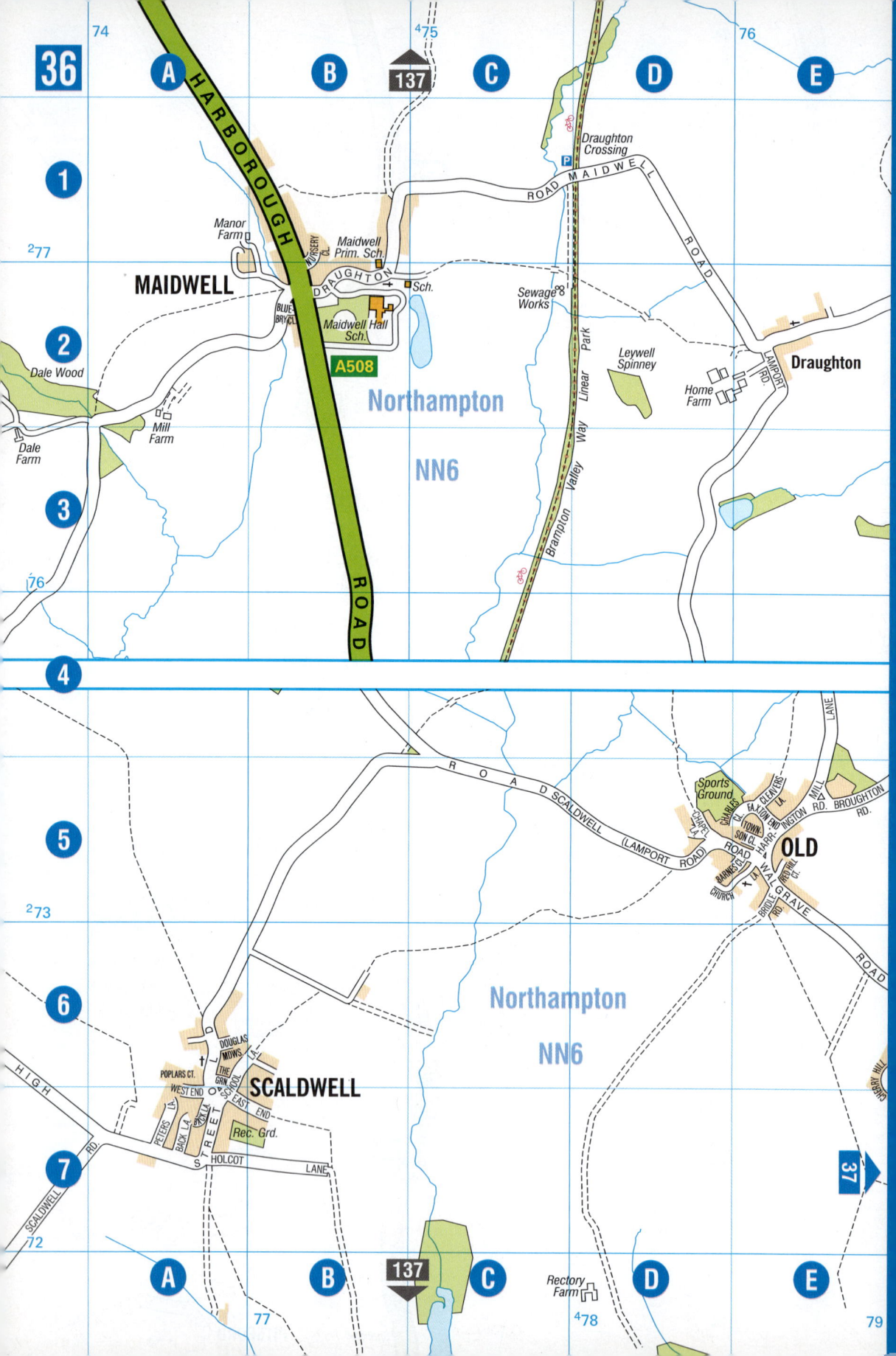

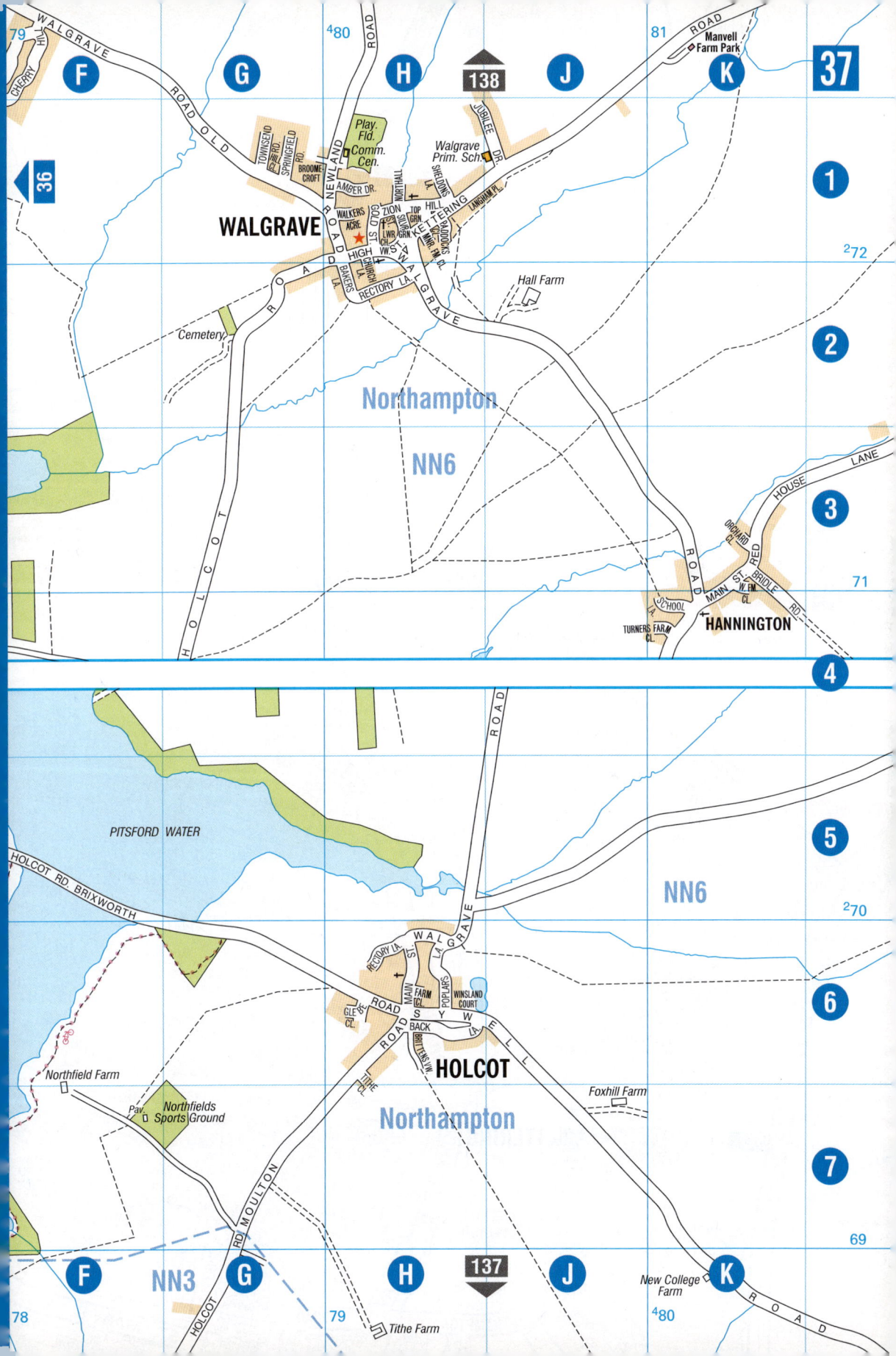

40

Three Chimneys

1

Uplands Farm

STERLING CT.

The Grove

Prim Sch.

PARK LANDS CL.

LODDINGTON HALL

STABLE YARD

MAIN STREET

ORTON RD.

RICHARD SONS LA.

CRANSLEY ROAD

LODDINGTON

HALL GARDENS

78

HARRINGTON

LANE

Pav. Playing Field

2

Mawsley Furze

Loddington Grange

MAWSLEY

Hall Farm

Mill Farm

3

77

◄ 137

Ragsdale Spinney

Cransley Wood

4

Birch Spinney

Cransley Lodge

Cemetery

Mawsley Wood

5

76

LONG BEECH WY.

ROSE HILL

HAWTHORN AV.

PASTURE END

HEDGE ROW LA.

CHASE VW.

SIDE LA.

AVENUE VI.

BADGERS WY.

HARES

New Lodge

COWSLIP

R. WOOD

HAWTHORN ROAD

Hall

SPINNEYS

Sch.

GREEN

BARNWELL CT.

THE RING

MAWSLEY VILLAGE

Old Lodge

CRANSLEY RD.

SIDNEY FIELDS CL.

LENS WAY

MAWSLEY WAY

6

WARREN END

FOX COVERTS

BIRCH SPINNEY

MALAS

LEA

RISE

SCHOOL CL.

ELLIS LA.

CHAMBERS

LINK WY.

PADDOCK END

MAIN RD.

THE JITTY

WAY

O-D-D-I-N-G-T-O-N

OLD GORSE

THE ROUND

BROWNING CL.

GORSE CL.

KEMPS CL.

HILL

WAY

CRANSLEY CT.

Old Poor's Gorse

7

BROUGHTON

Mawsley Lodge

Northampton

NN6

KETTERING

DAVENTRY

275

480

81

82

Red Lodge

A 86 B ⬆42 C 87 D **Junction 9** E A14

A509

1

²75

Depot

PYTCHLEY GOLF LODGE

Pytchley Lodge

Northfield House

Elbow Spinney

Manor Ho.

2

Pinwell Spinney

BROUGHTON

Pytchley Ho.

GLEBE FM

Cemy.

The Elms

Pond Coppice

Mill Beds

Kettering

PYTCHLEY

Sch.

Home Farm

Cemy.

Pav.

Play Fld.

Cricket Grd.

CHURCH

3

Sewage Farm

Foxhill Spinney

74 ◄ 138

NN14

4

North Lodge

Pytchley Grange

Ryehill Farm

5

73

PYTCHLEY

Lodge Farm

Big Covert

6

Pav.

Sports Ground

ORLINGBURY

7

ORLINGBURY

Orlingbury Hall

72 REDHOUSE

NORTHAMPTON RD.

THE PADDOCKS

Lammas Spinney

A 86 B 138 ⬇ C D **MAIN ST.** HILL B574 TOP E

Roadside Spinney

ORLINGBURY RD.

Little Harrowden Comm. Prim. Sch.

87

Grave Yard

BARN CT.

Proposed

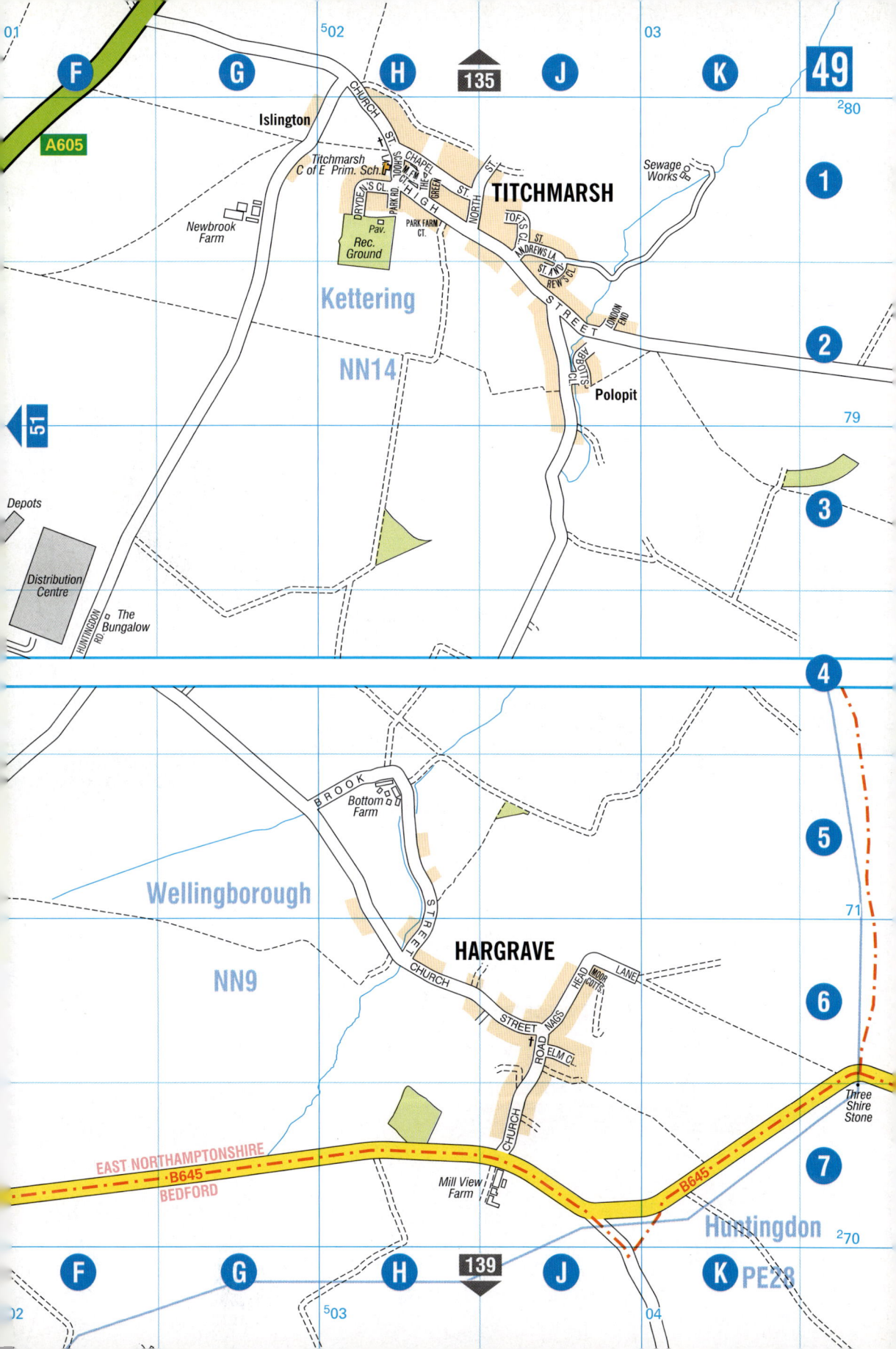

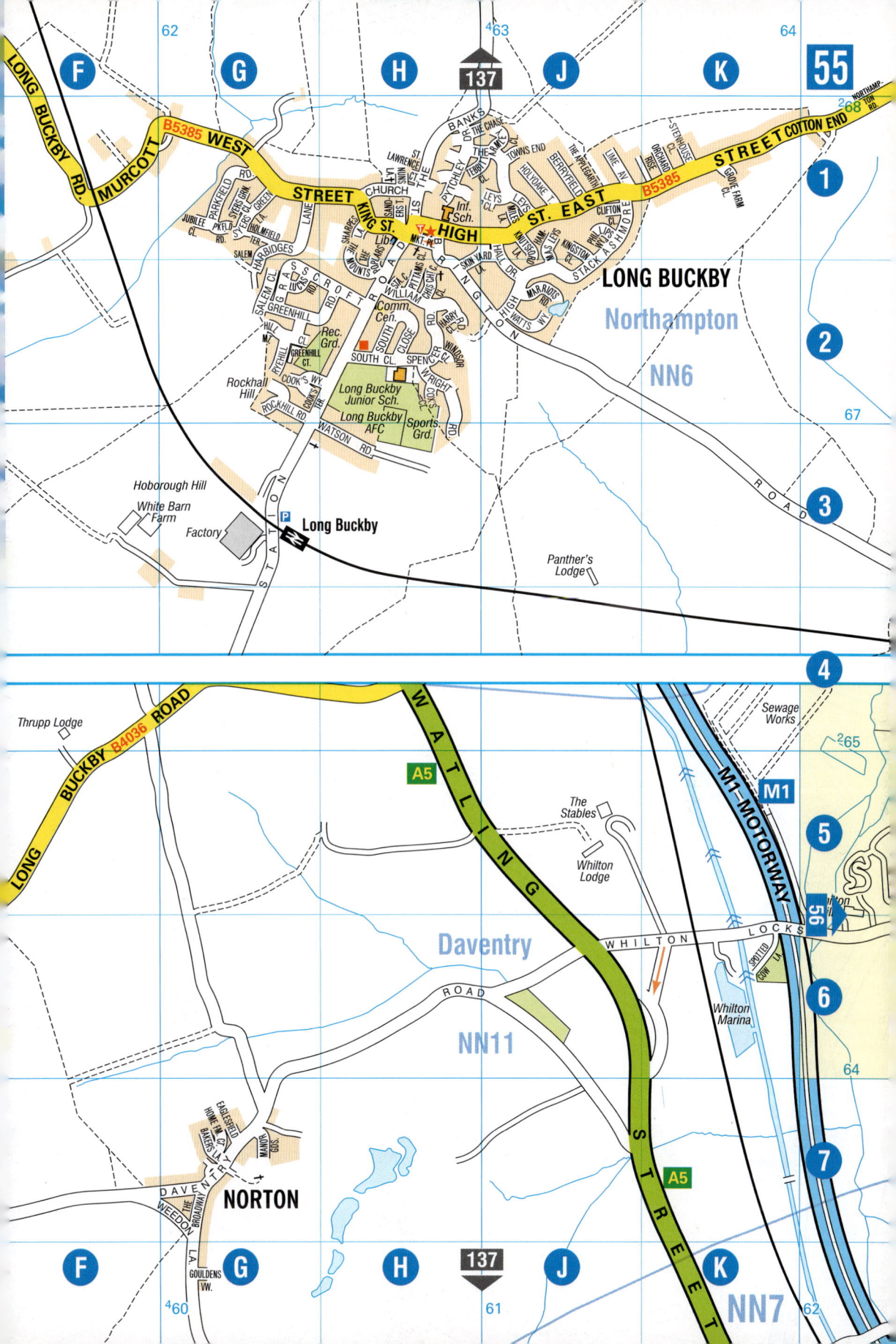

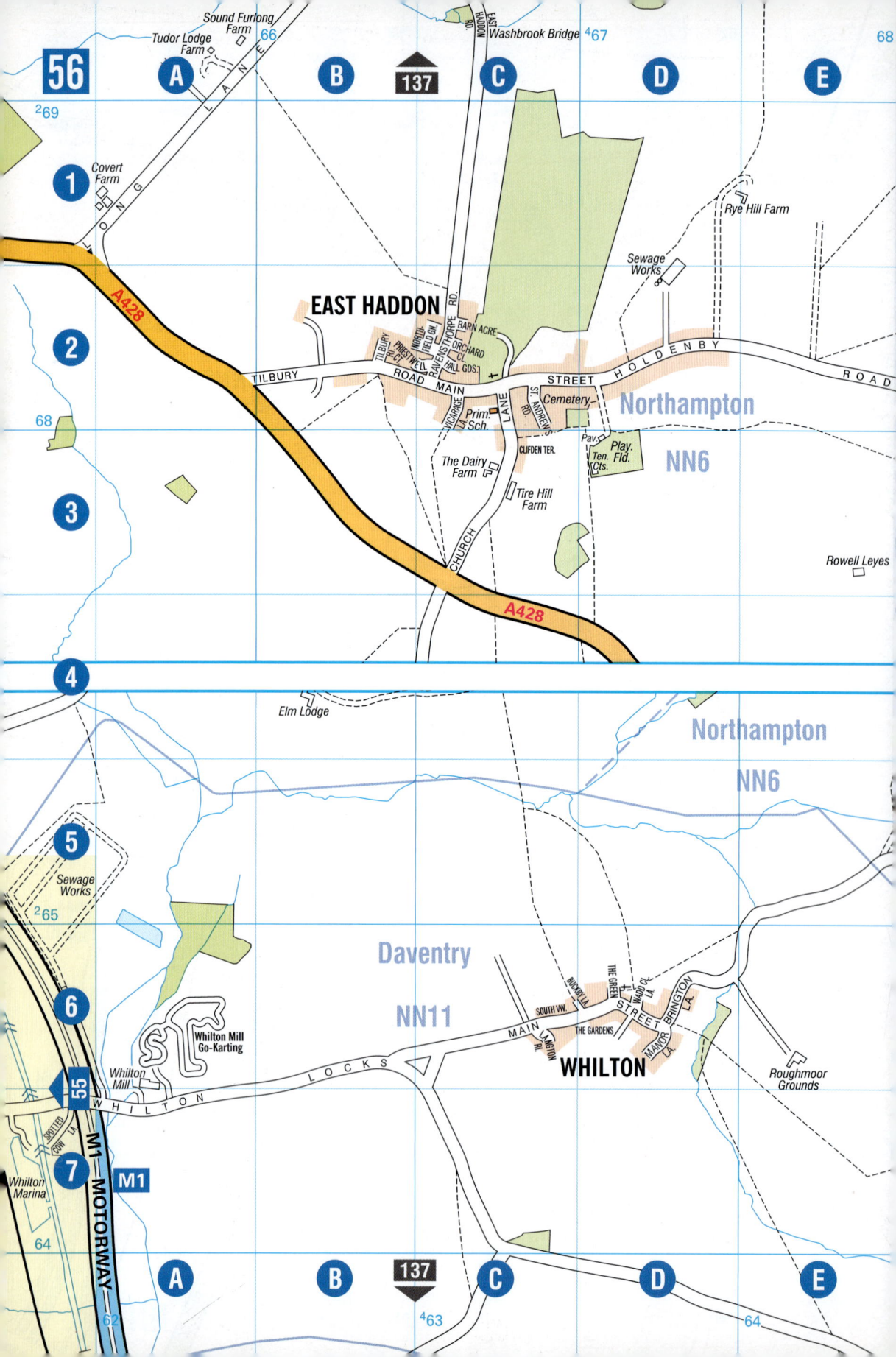

Works 68

A428

66

1

Glebe
Farm

Sewage
Works

Sir John's Wood

2

Brickfield
Spinney

Thornburrow
Hill

**GREAT
BRINGTON**

Althorp Park

Althorp

WHILTON

ROAD

BACK

STREET

WHITE'S CL.

THE
POUND

MAIN

THE
GREEN

65

THE
PADDOCKS

WALTON CL.

Chinkwell
Spinney

3

137

Northampton

4

64

NN7

Bringston
Prim. Sch.

SWEDISH
HOUSES

PYKE CT.

5

JOLLY LA.

FERMOY
CT.

STREET

**LITTLE
BRINGTON**

BLACKSMITHS LA.

Church
Farm

Nobottle Wood

6

MAIN

BRINGTON

63

Nobottle

Townsend
Farm

ROAD

Grange
Farm

Nobottle
House

7

F   G   H   J   K

66   467   68

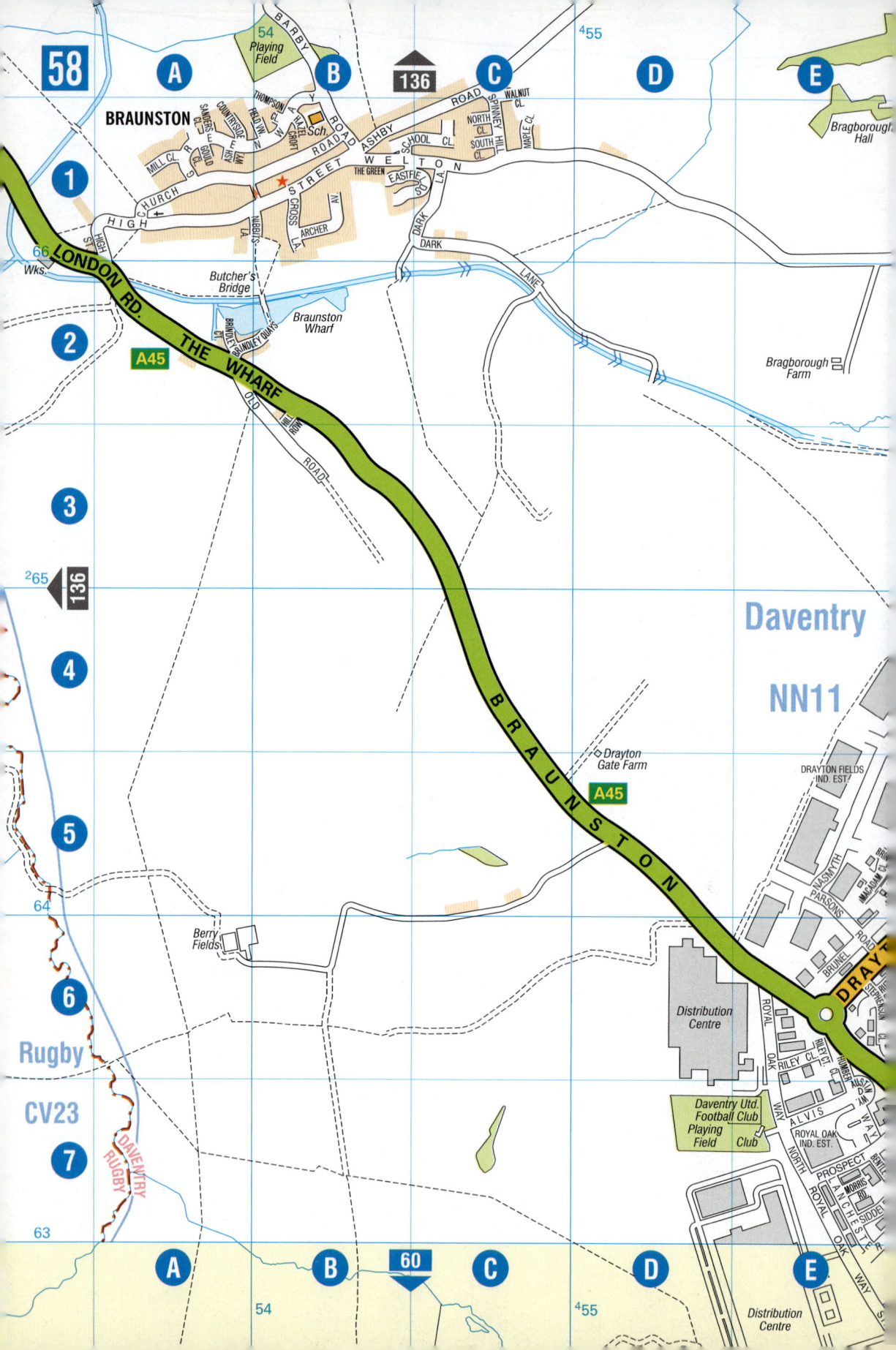

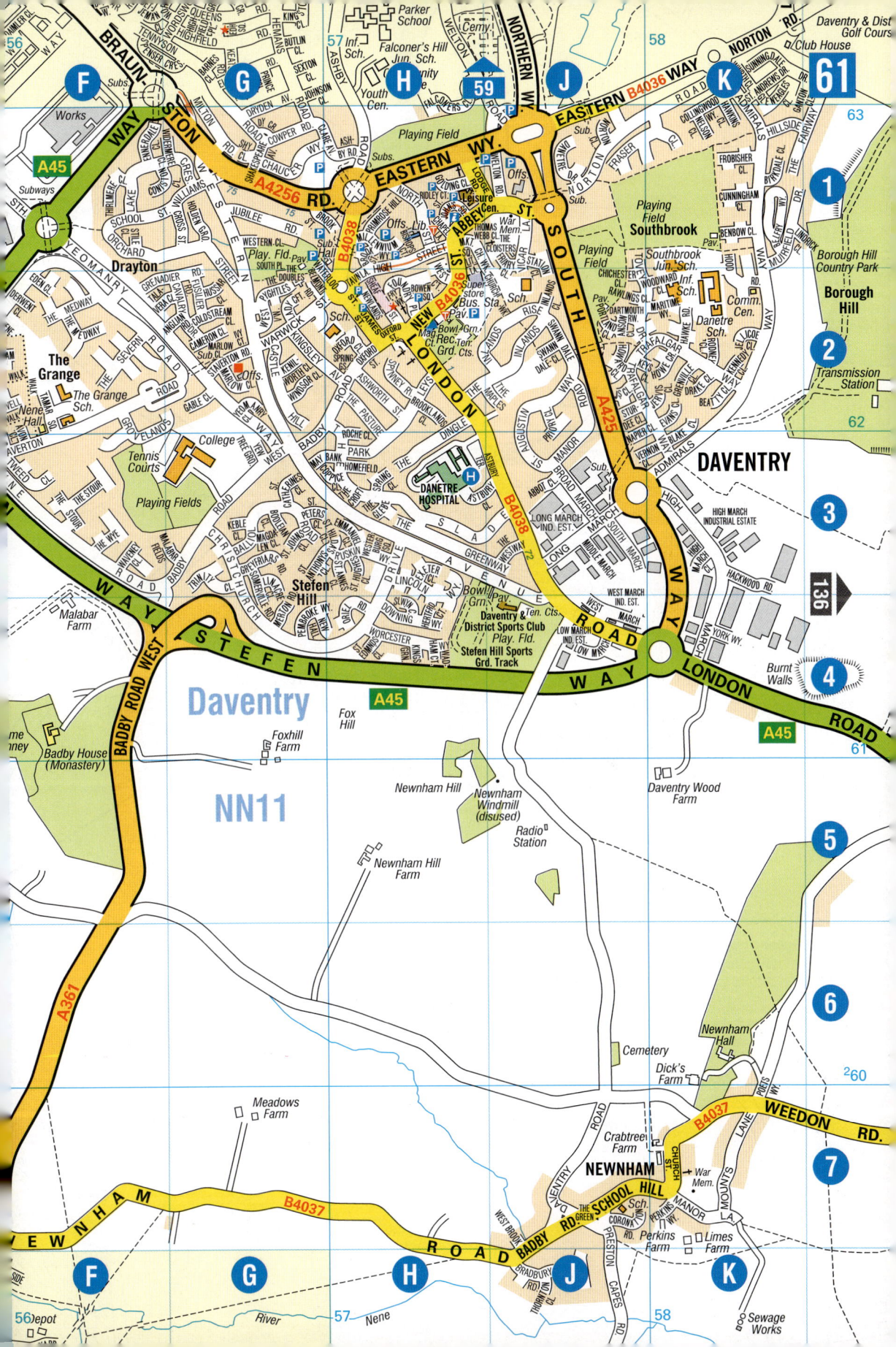

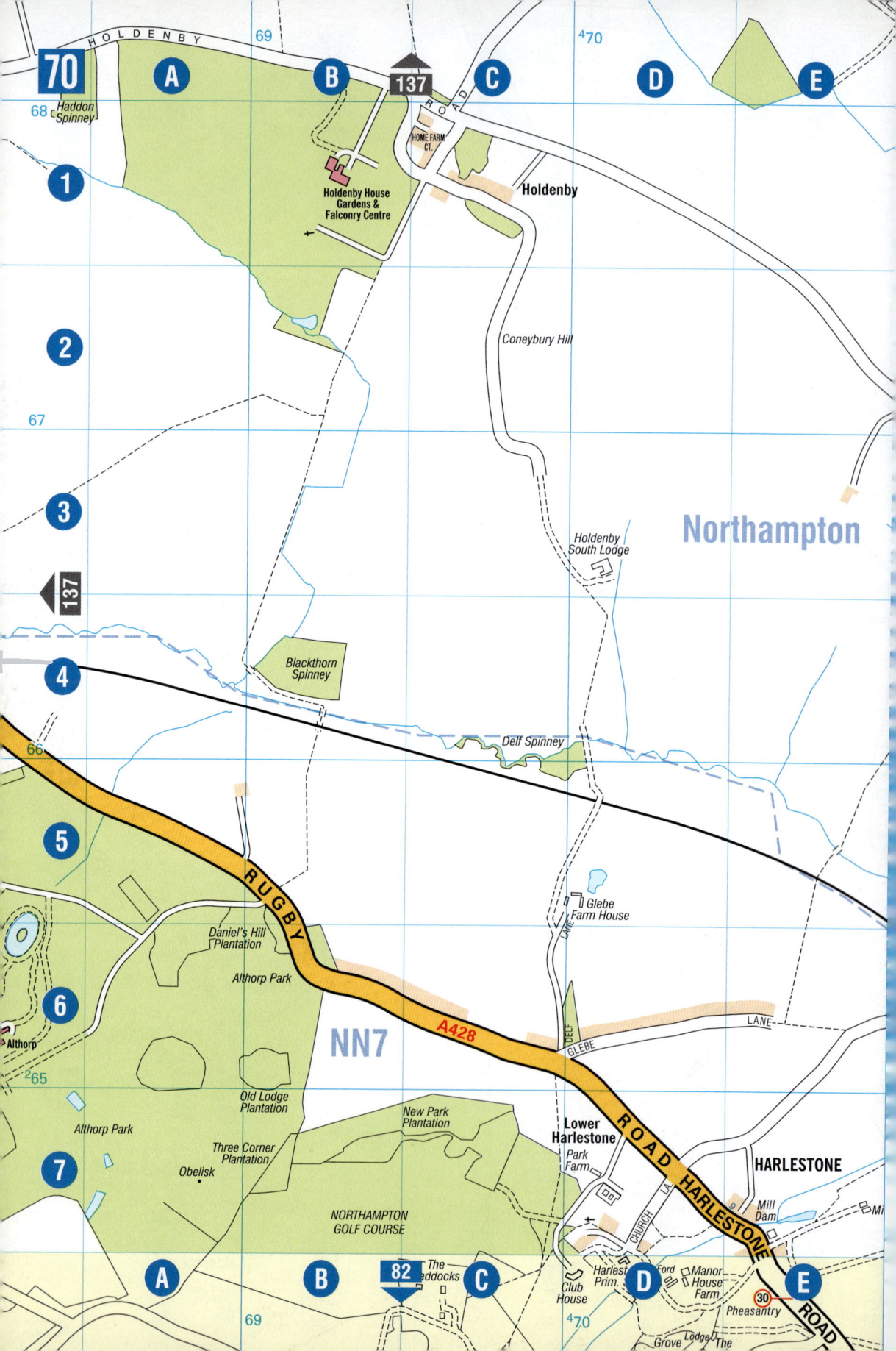

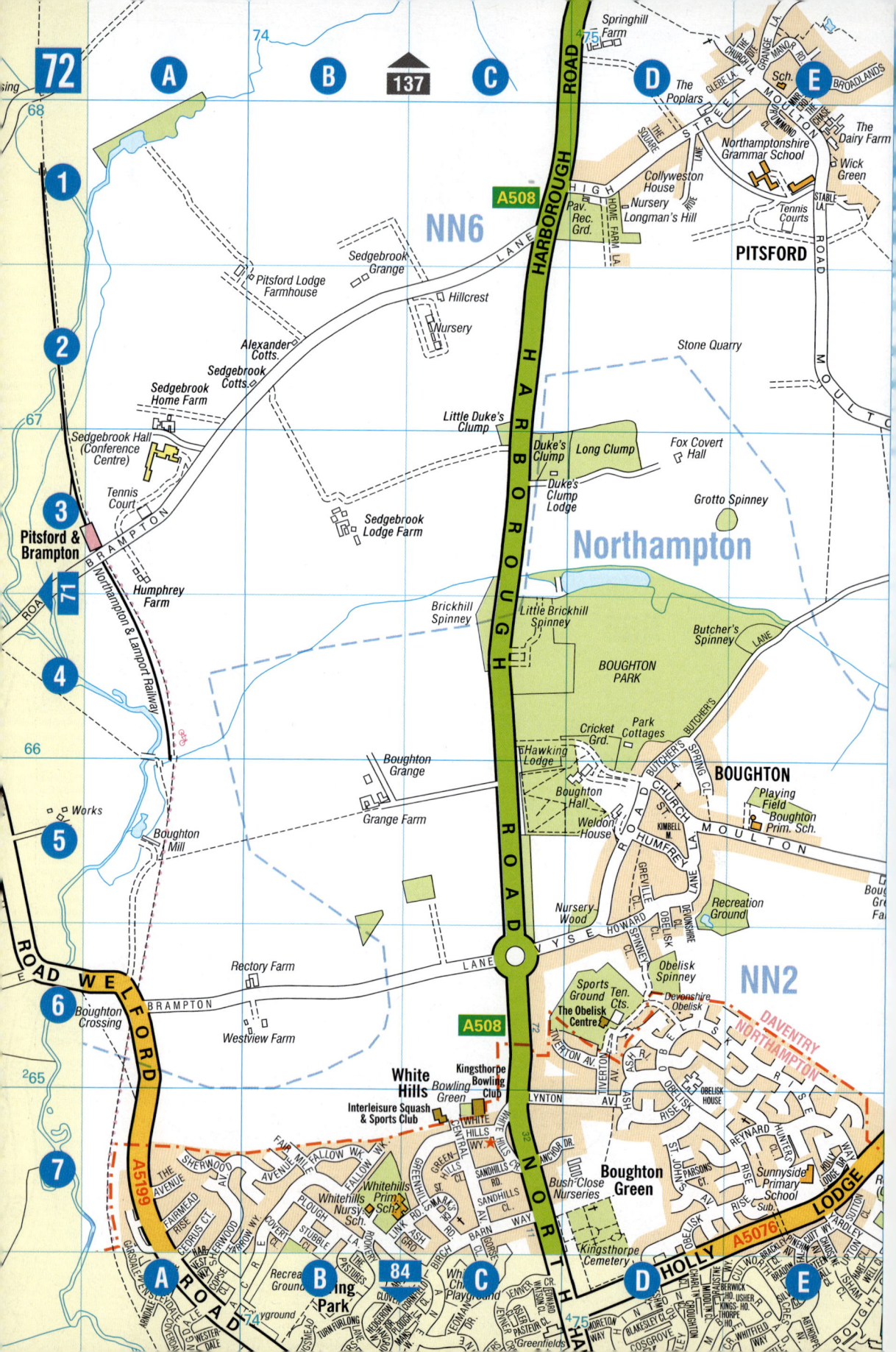

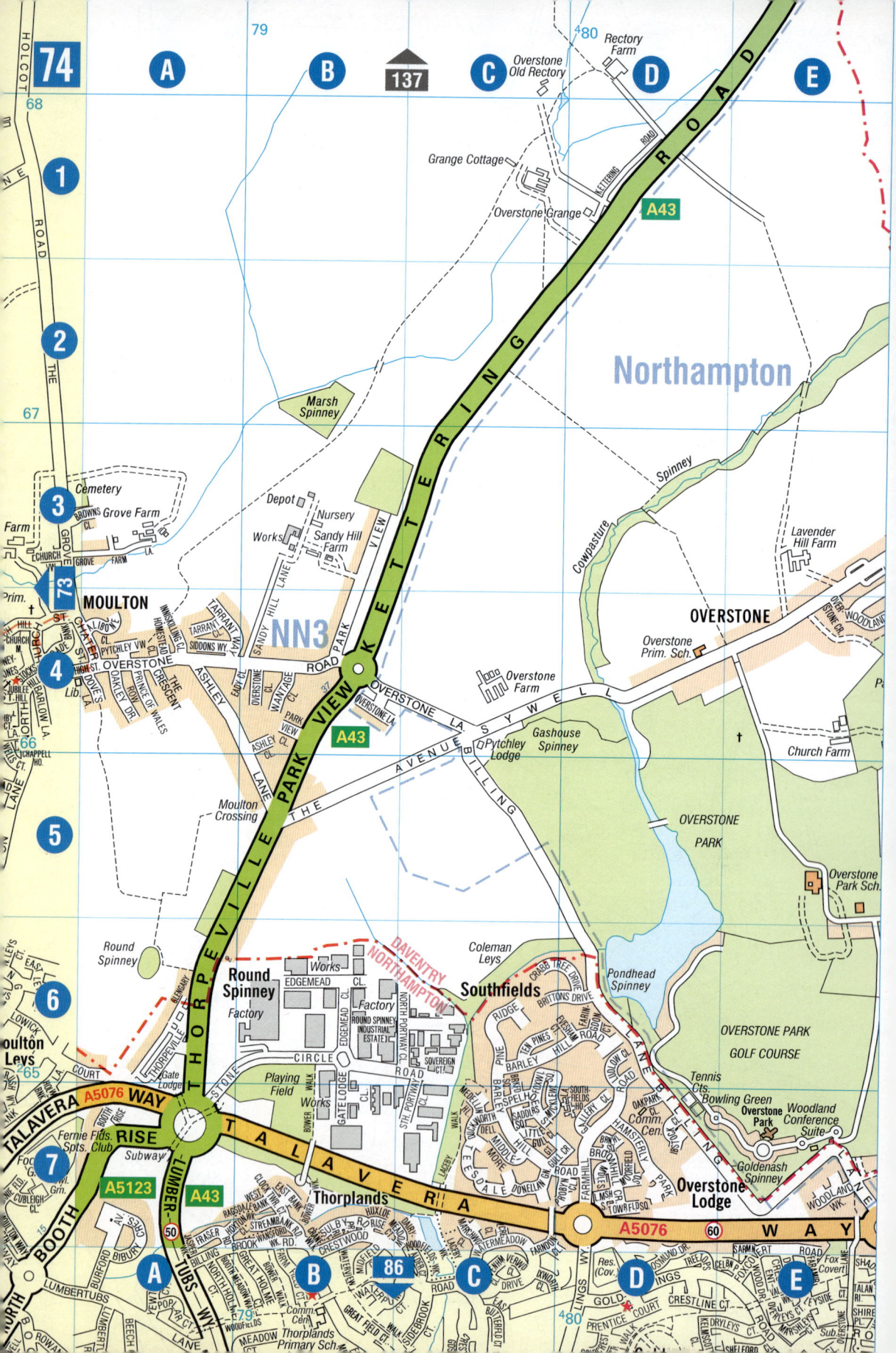

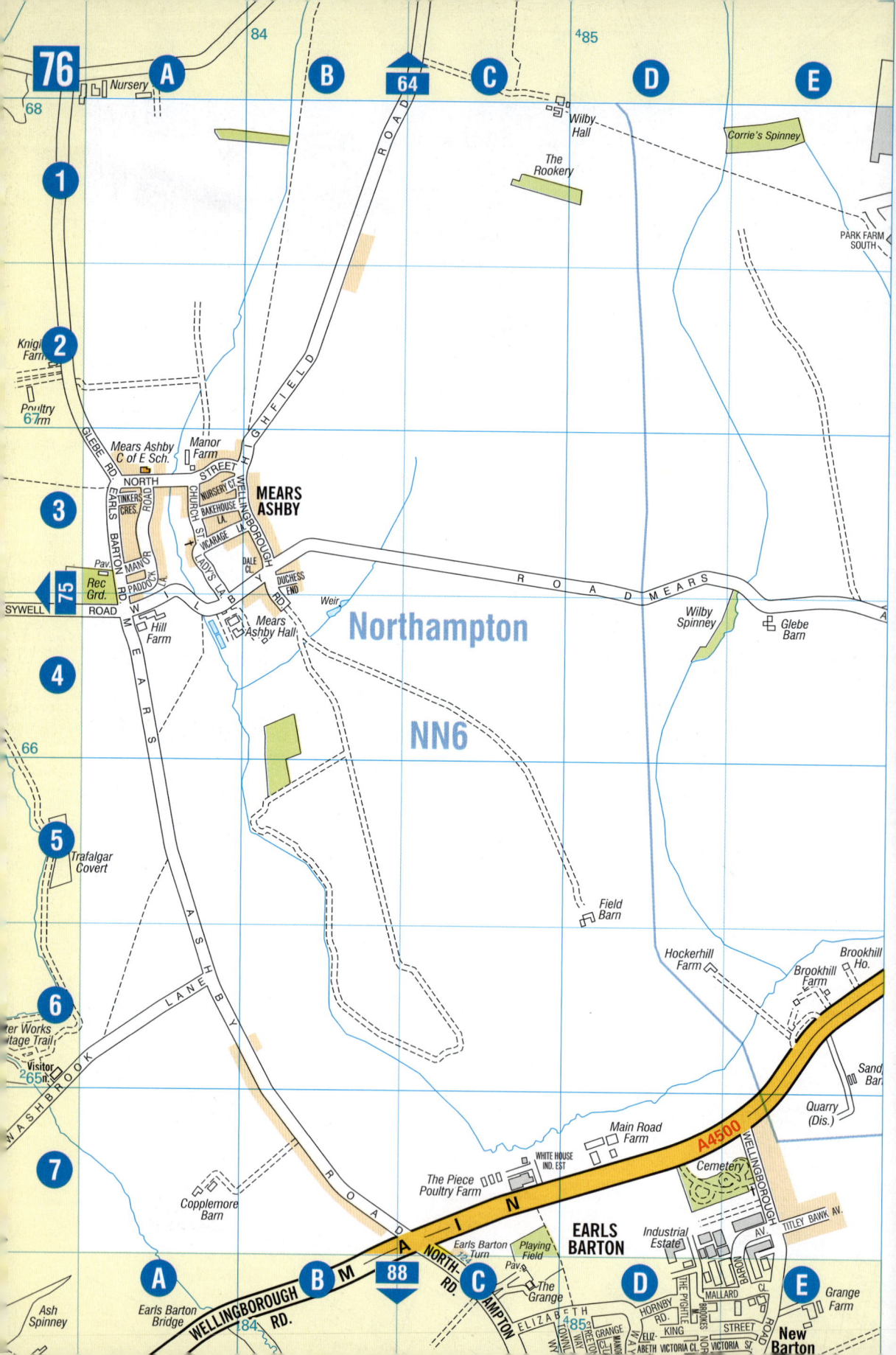

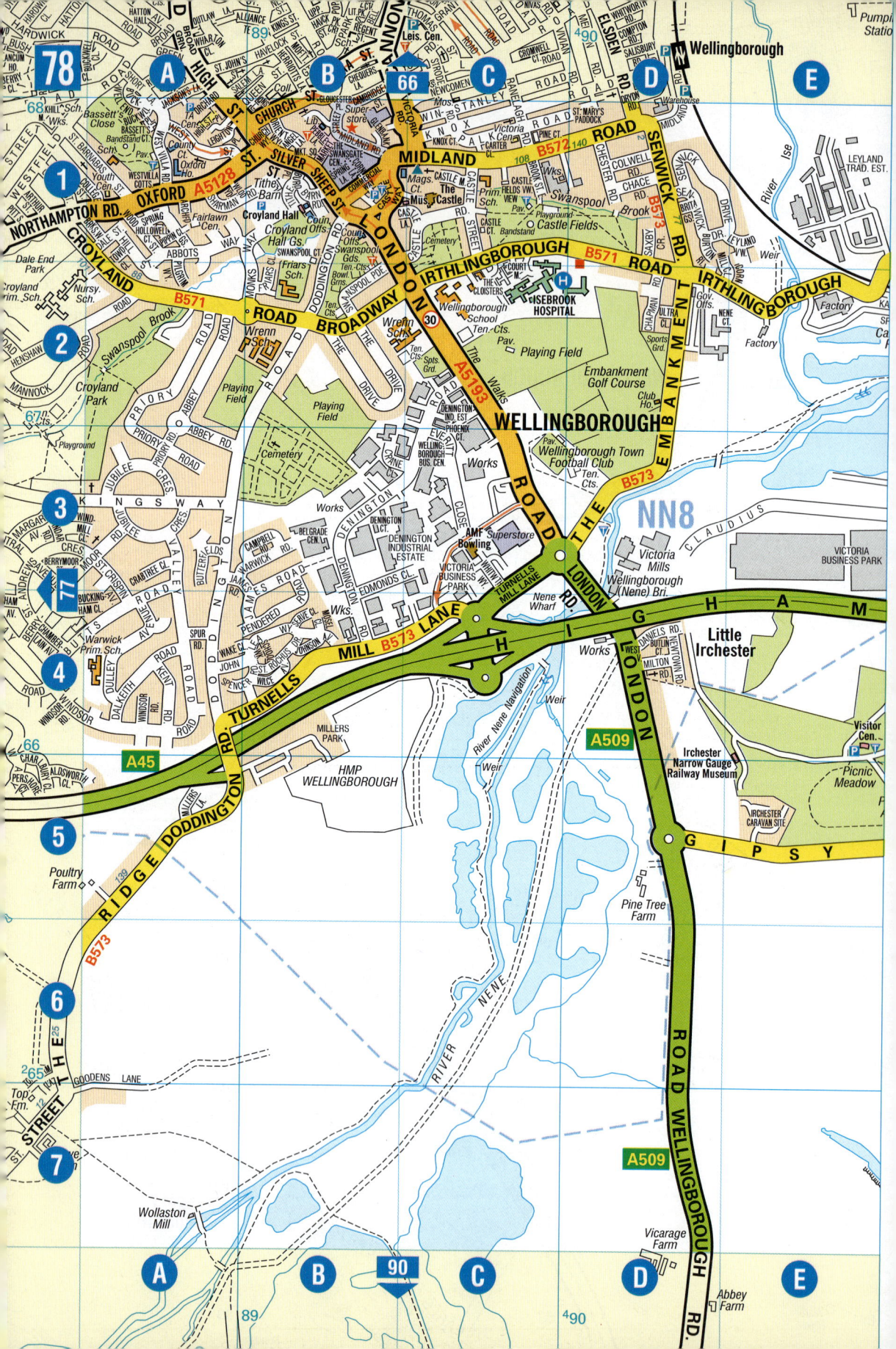

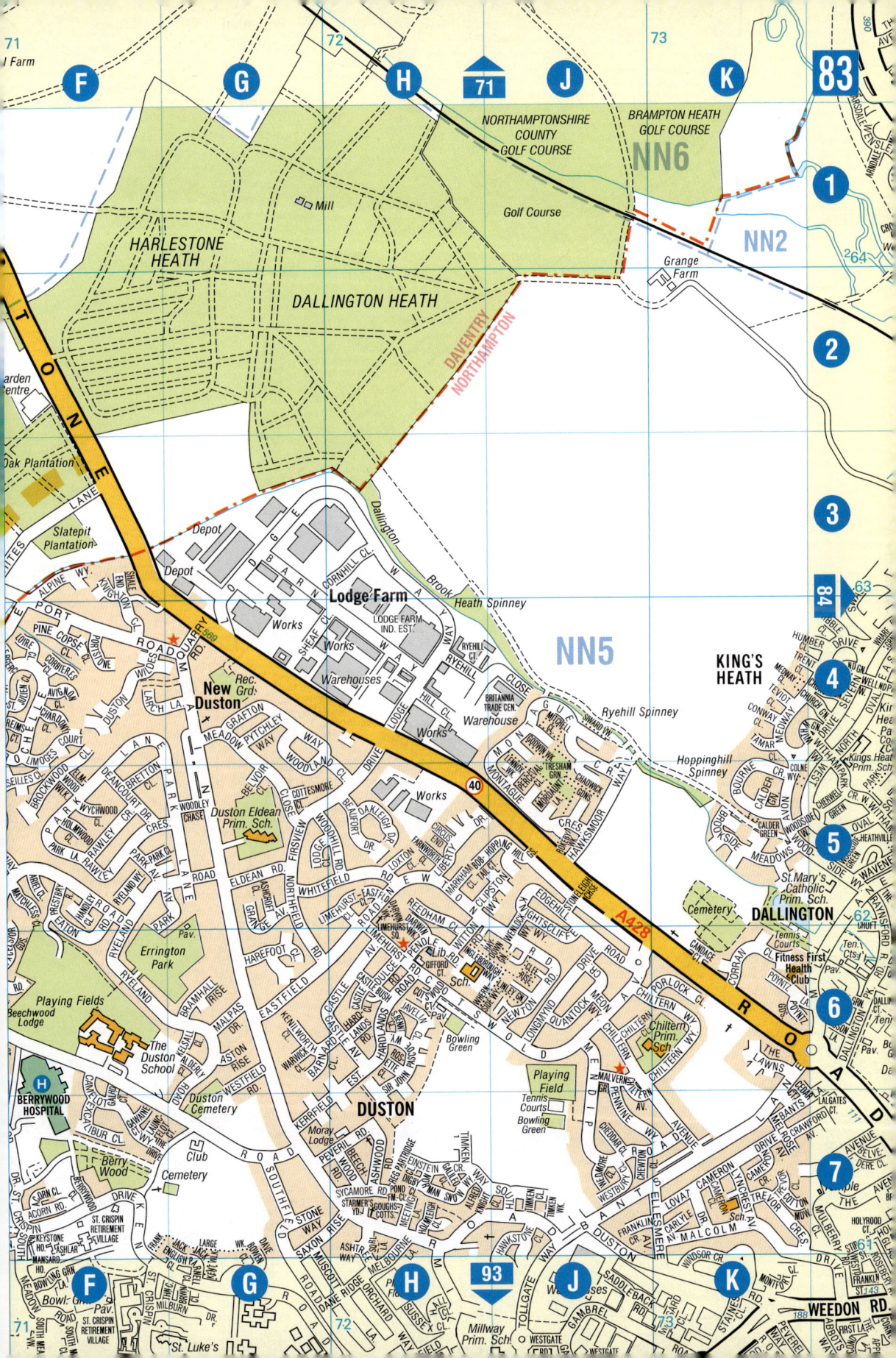

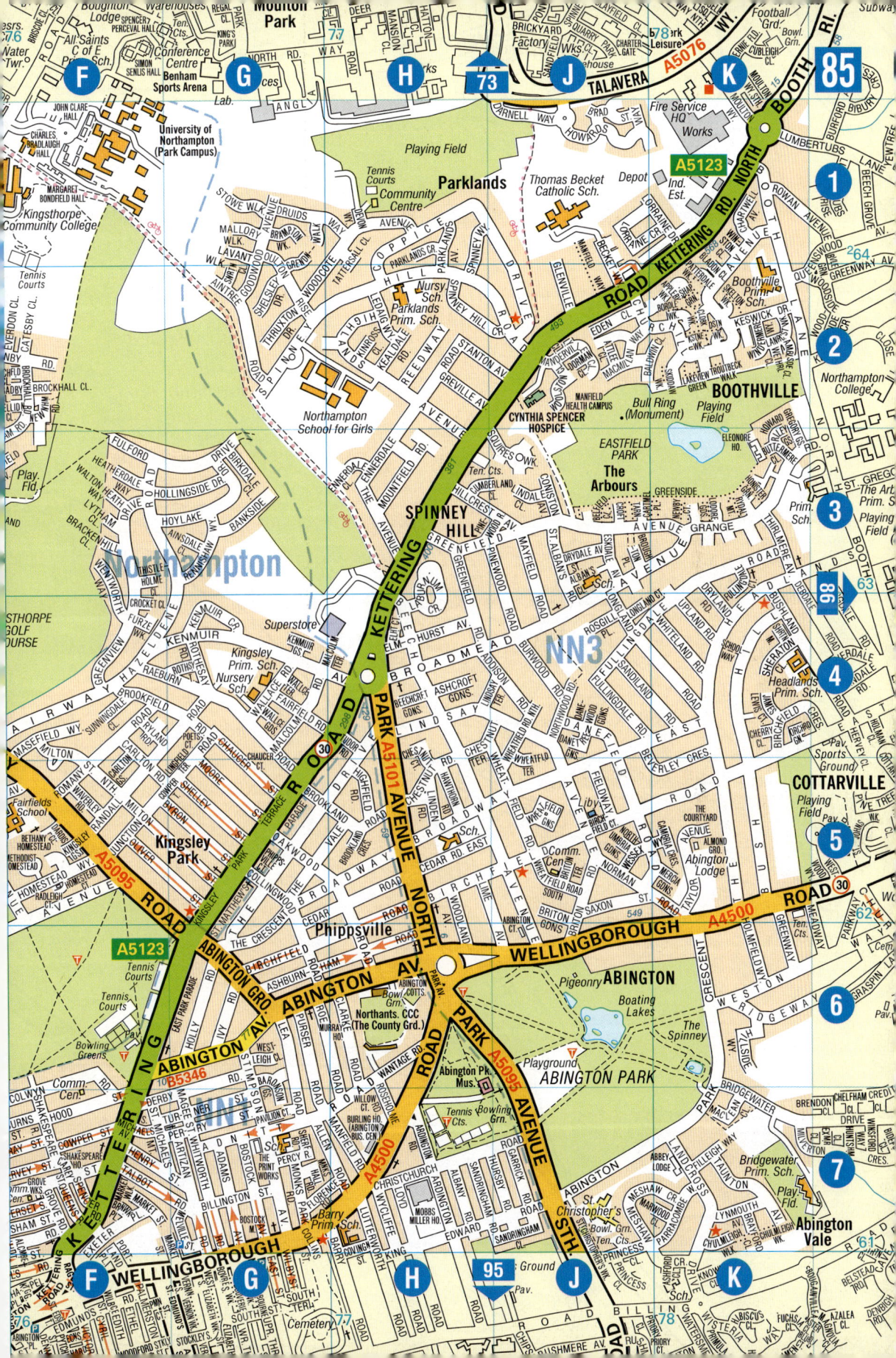

Wellingborough

NN29

Farndish

Grange Farm

Manor Farm

IRCHESTER

Long Plantation

ox Covert

Wollaston Hall

Water Tower

Tower Farm

TOWER CT.

Francis Dickins Ct.

Ten Ct.

Wollaston School

Ten Ct.

CHESTER

HOOKHAMS

MILL RI.

WNDML CL.

THE SQ.

ROAD

THE

PARK

KE RD.

ROAD

ST. MARYS RD

GREEN ST.

POPLAR PL.

STREET

WILLIAM'S

PATH

WICK

RAYMOND

WILLIAM'S WY.

WOLLASTON IND. EST.

SHEPHERDS

Shepherds Hill Farm

WELLINGBOROUGH

BEDFORD

ROAD

Hinwick Hall College

Lodge Farm

HILL

Poplars Farm

Trendeland Spinney

Hinwick

Fordlands

The Croft

Slade Plantation

Longleys Bushes

ROMAN

ROAD

WOLLASTON RD.

FARNDISH RD.

B569

79

138

138

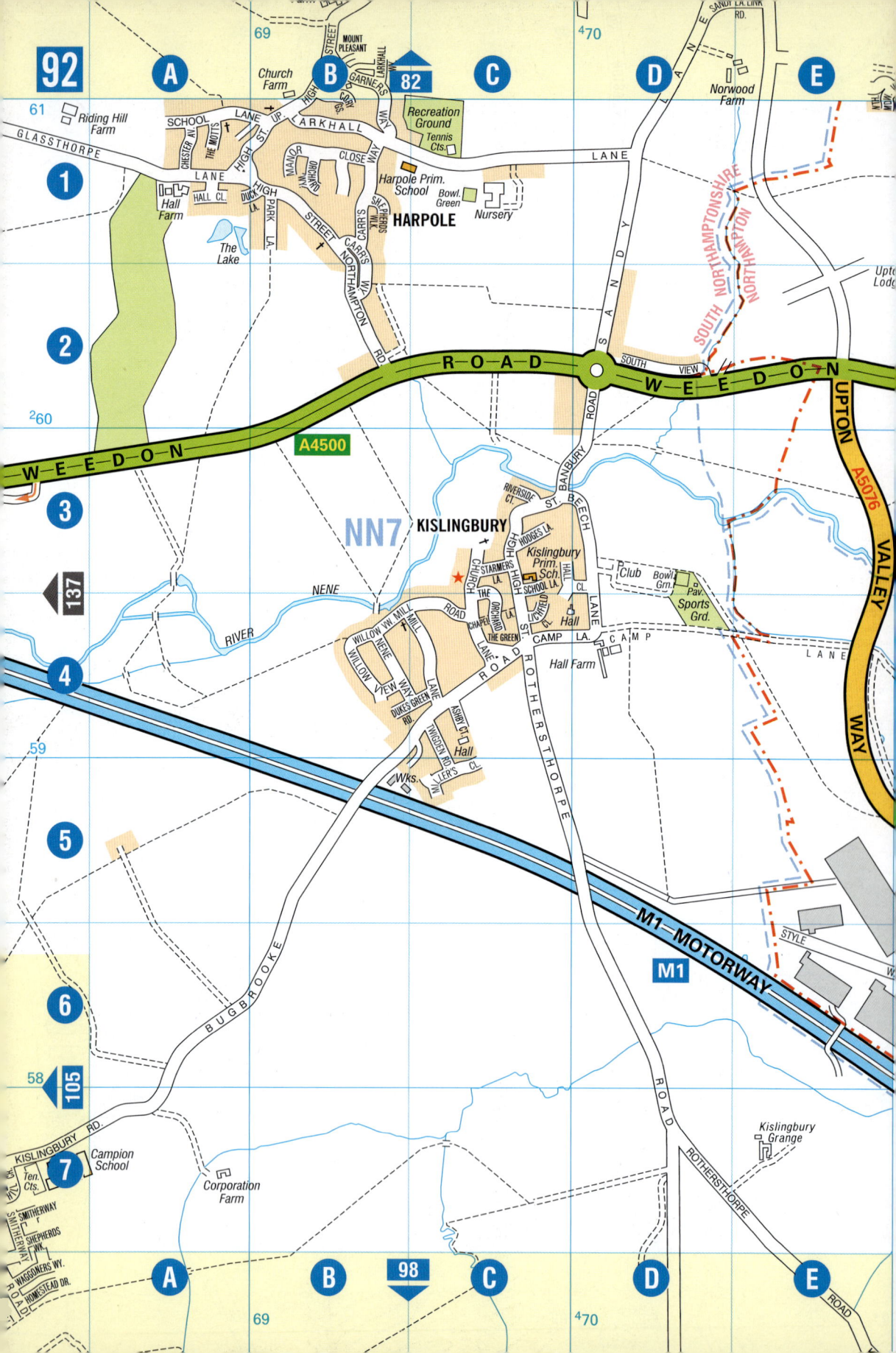

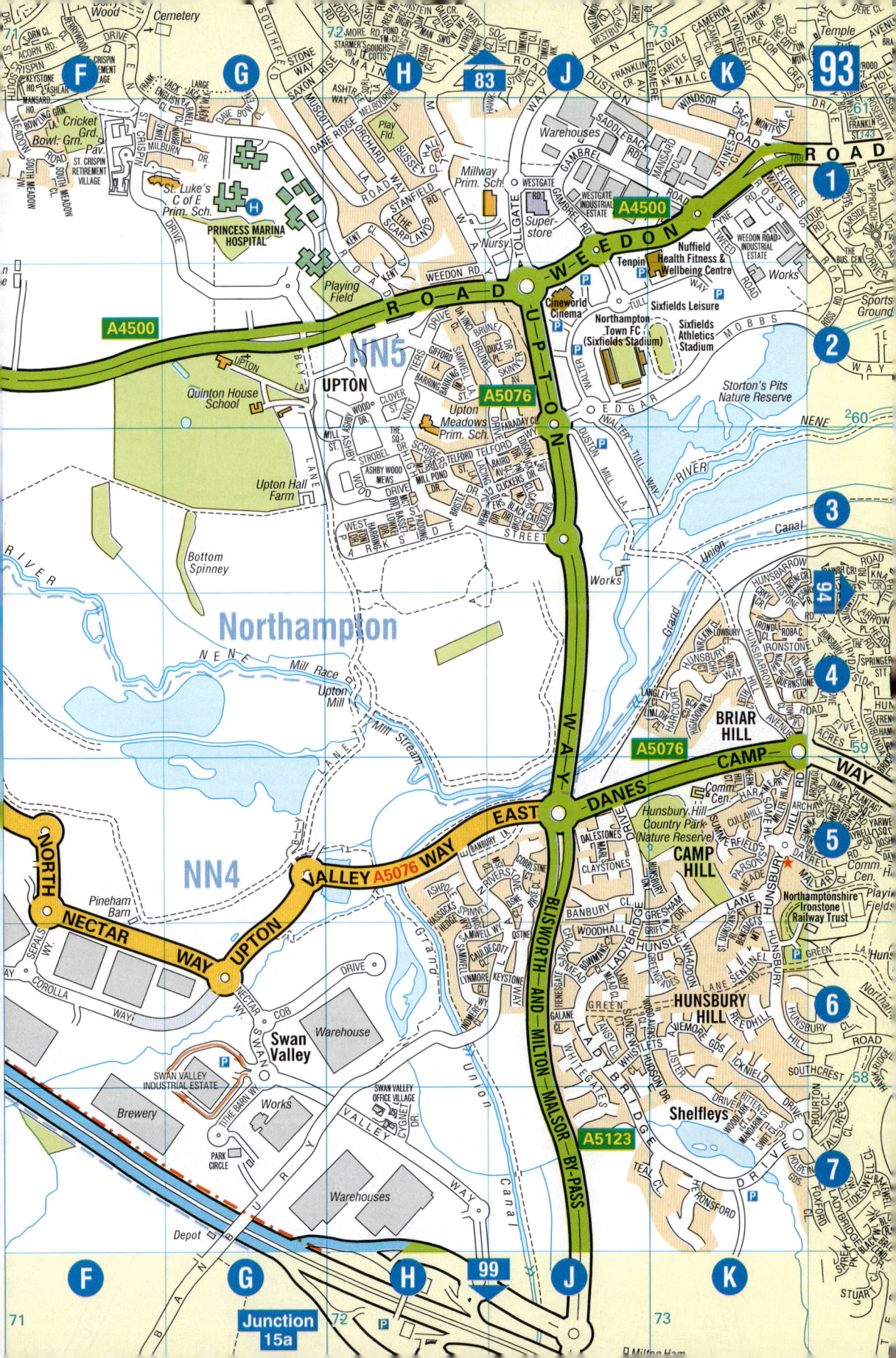

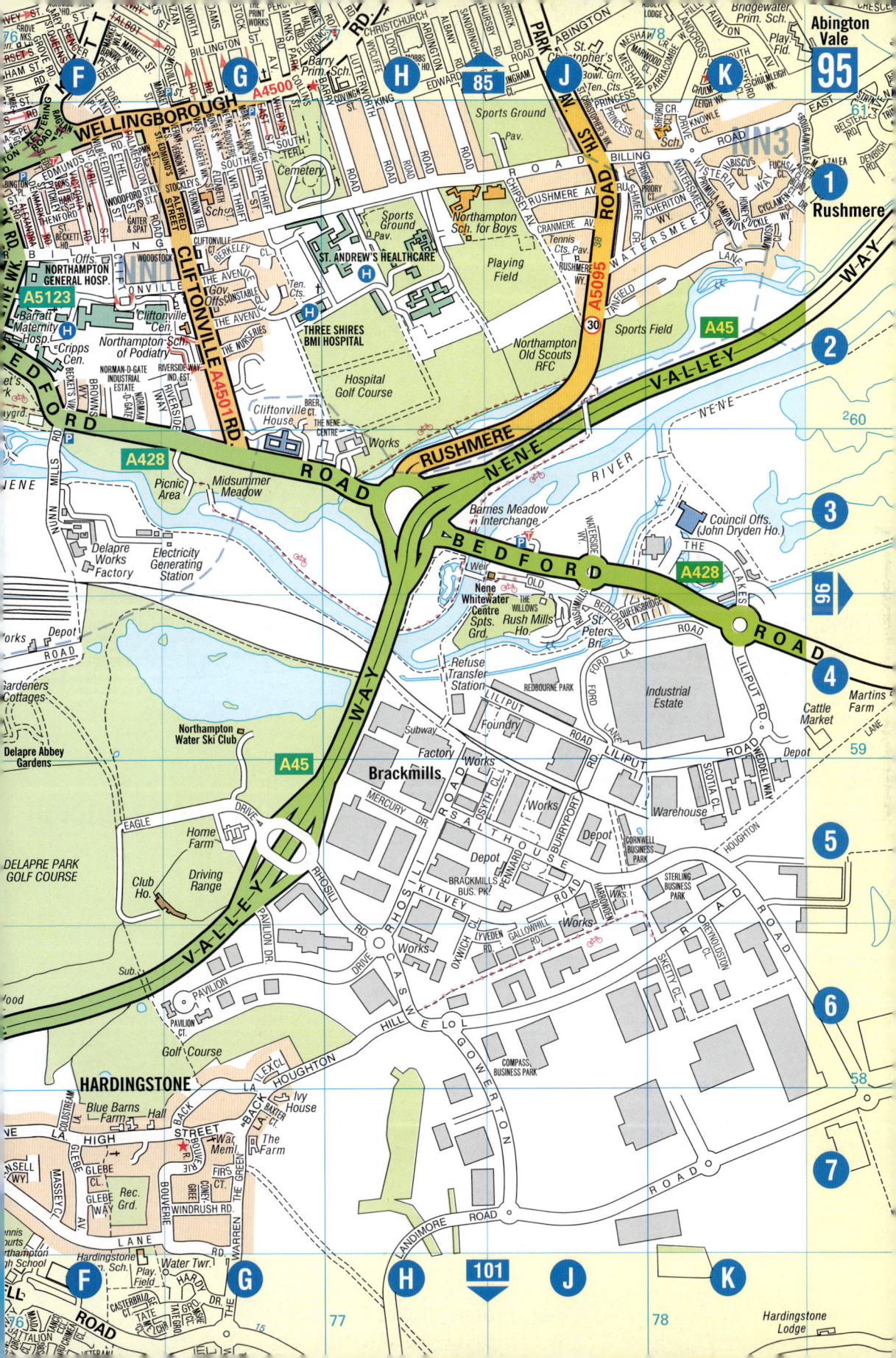

A   B   C   D   E

92

1

57   105

Football Grd.

2

Depot

3

56   Bugbrooke Downs

NN7

4

Scurf Barn   137

5

2 55

6

Towcester

7

54   105

A   B   137   C   D   E

School
Corporation Farm   69
470

Hill Farm
ROTHERSTHORPE ROAD
KIS

LANE BANBURY
WRIGHTS
Grand Union

Lower Downes Farm
Anchor Farm
Headlands Farm
BUGBROOKE
BANBURY

Sewage Works

GAYTON
PARK ST   DEANS ROW   ST MARYS CT   STREET   MILTON   BLISWORTH   LANE
HIGH   BAKER   ROAD   BACK   LANE
Glebe Farm   Sch
HILL CREST RD.   ROAD   OTTFIELD

Dalscote
ANNA'S
NWAY
Manor Farm

NN12

Cricket Ground

EASTCOTE
ROAD

Goggs Farm

69   470

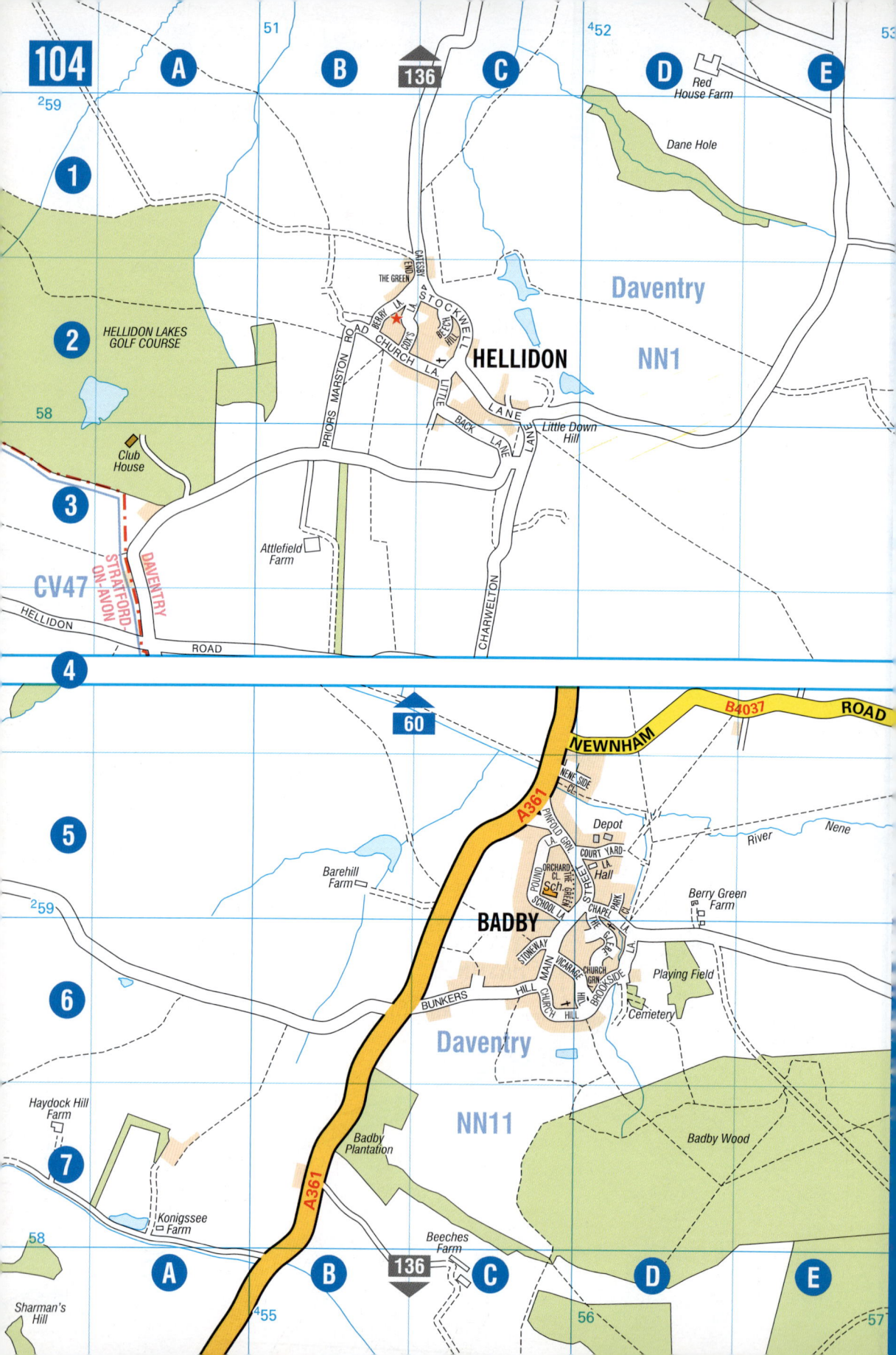

A B C D E

1

2

3

4

5

6

7

A B C D E

51 136 52 53

Daventry

NN1

THE GREEN

CHESBY END

STOCKWELL

BERRY LA.

S. CL.

A361 HILL

CHURCH LA.

PRIORS MARSTON ROAD

LITTLE LANE

BACK LANE

HELLIDON

Little Down Hill

58

Club House

CV47

STRATFORD ON-AVON

DAVENTRY

HELLIDON ROAD

Attlefield Farm

CHARWELTON

Red House Farm

Dane Hole

HELLIDON LAKES GOLF COURSE

60

NEWNHAM

B4037 **ROAD**

A361

NENE SIDE CL.

PINFOLD GRN.

POUND LA.

THE GREEN

ORCHARD CL.

Sch.

SCHOOL LA.

COURT YARD

Depot

LA.

Hall

STREET

CHAPEL

THE GLEBE

BANK LA.

BADBY

STONEWAY

VICARAGE

MAIN

CHURCH HILL

BUNKERS HILL

BROOKSIDE

CHURCH GRN.

HILL

Barehill Farm

Berry Green Farm

Playing Field

Cemetery

River Nene

Daventry

NN11

259

Haydock Hill Farm

Konigssee Farm

Badby Plantation

A361

Beeches Farm

136

Badby Wood

Sharman's Hill

58

55 56 57

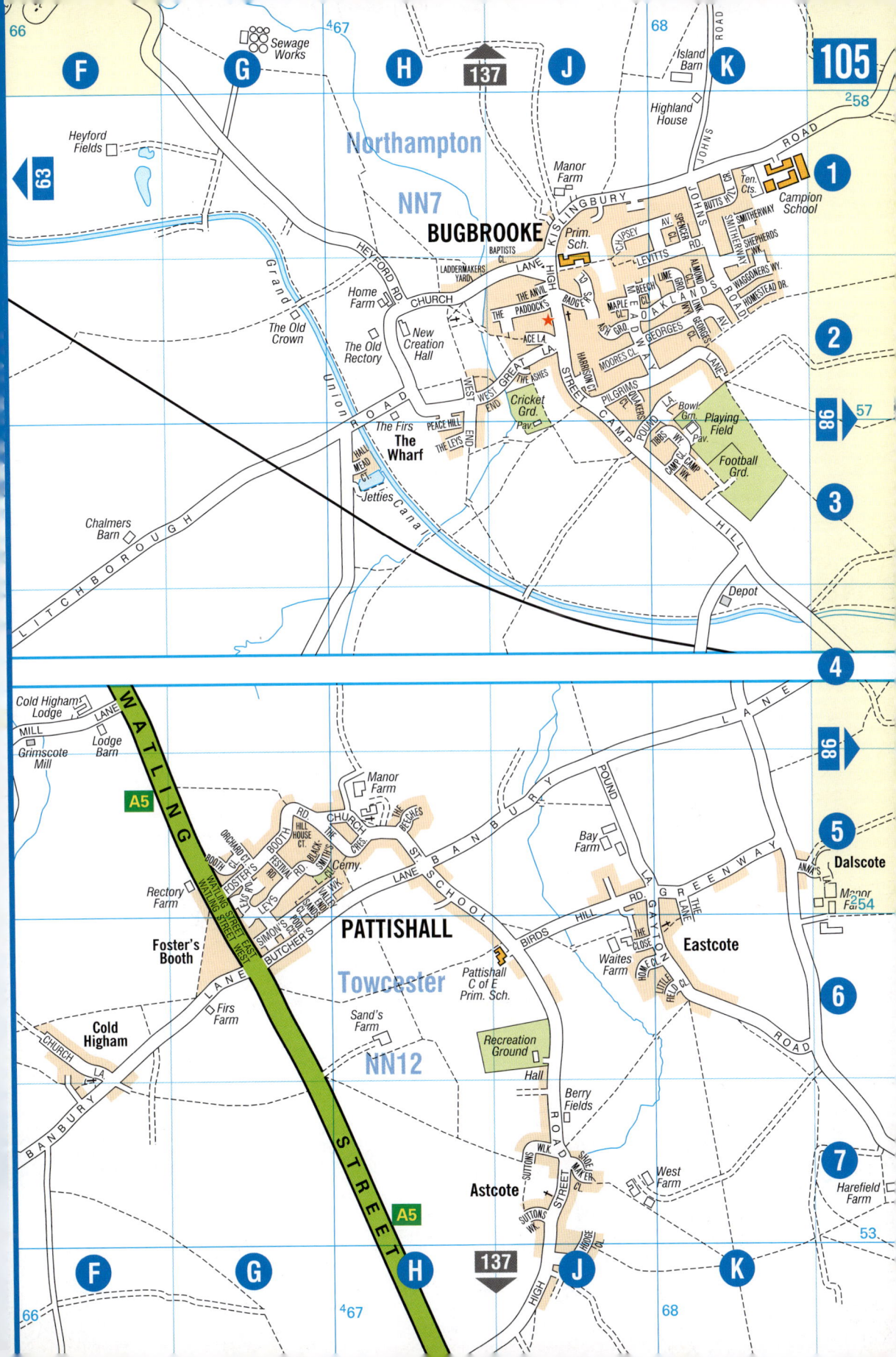

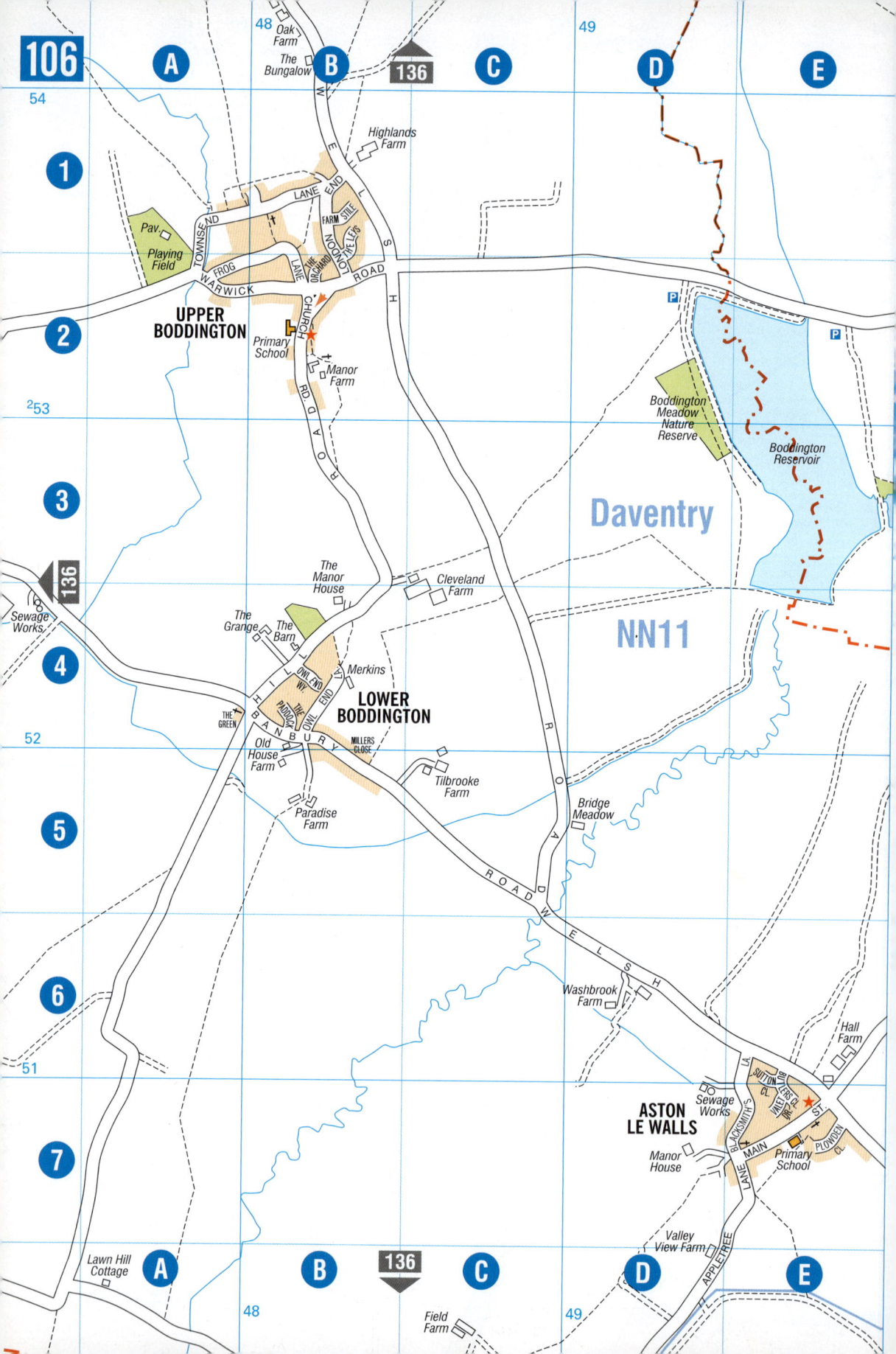

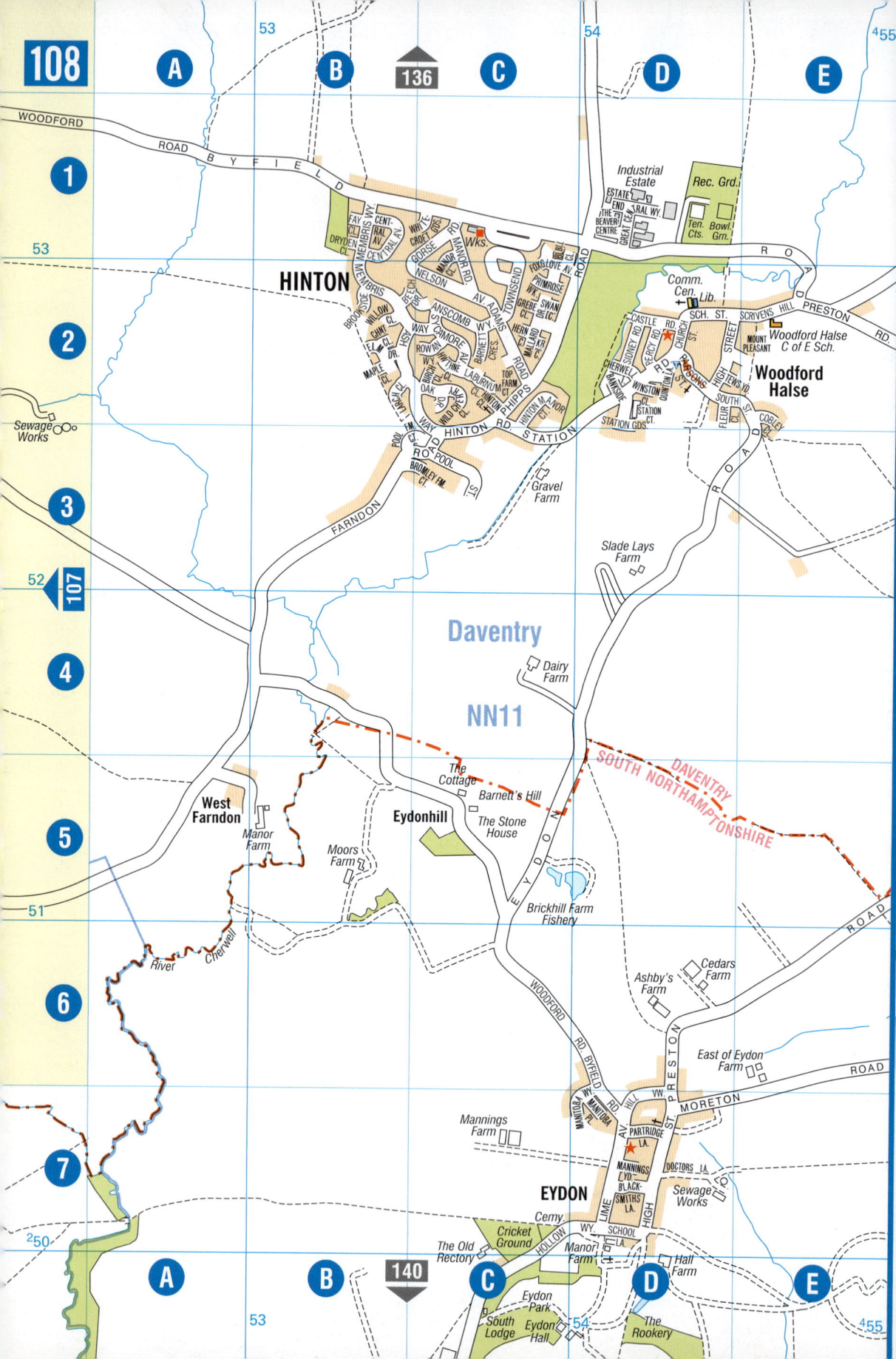

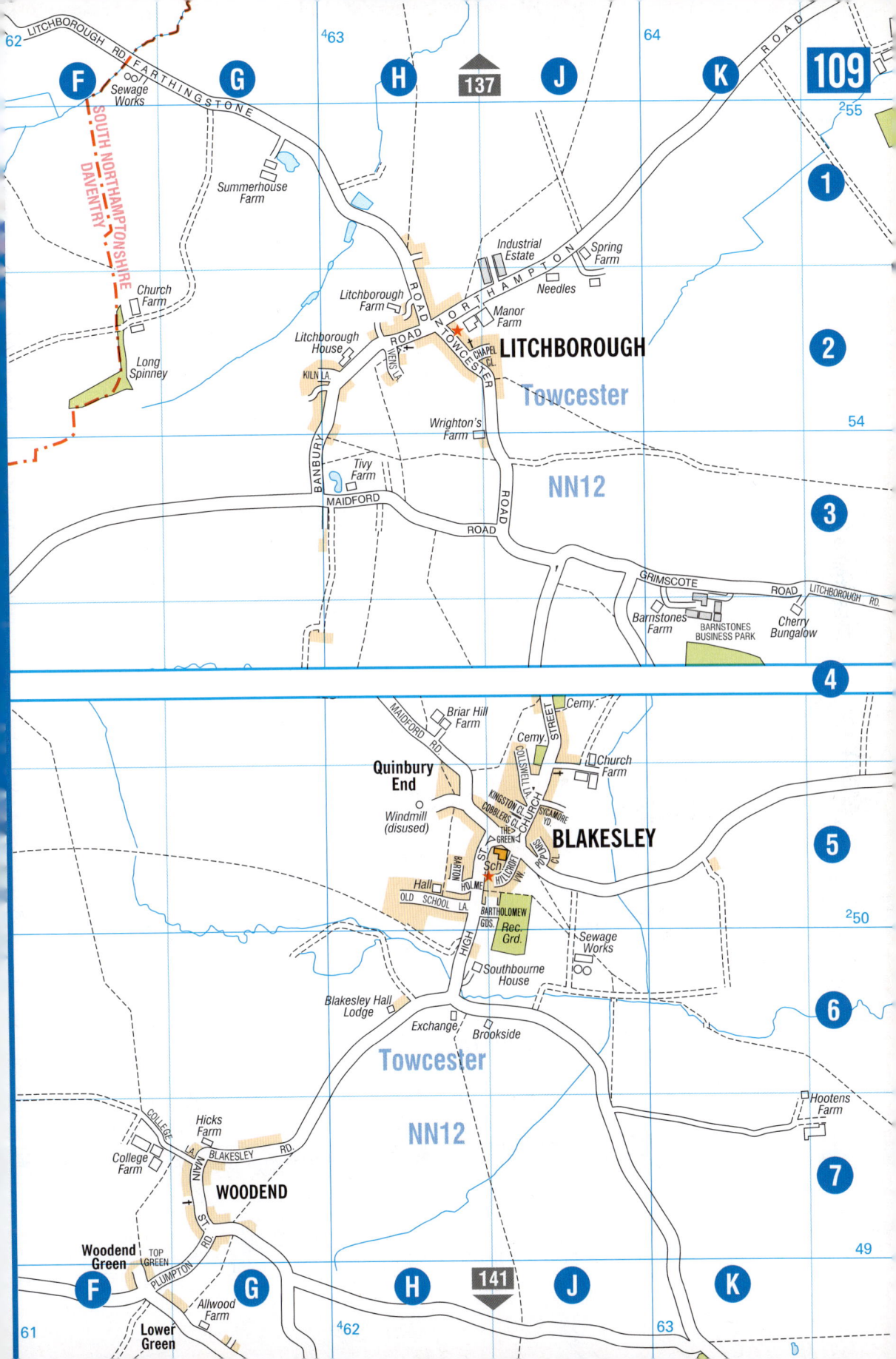

LITCHBOROUGH

Towcester

NN12

BLAKESLEY

Quinbury End

Towcester

NN12

WOODEND

Woodend Green

Lower Green

SOUTH NORTHAMPTONSHIRE DAVENTRY

LITCHBOROUGH RD FARTHINGSTONE

Sewage Works

Summerhouse Farm

Church Farm

Long Spinney

Litchborough Farm

Litchborough House

Industrial Estate

Needles

Spring Farm

Manor Farm

KILN LA.

VENS LA.

CHAPEL CL.

ROAD NORTHAMPTON

ROAD TOWCESTER

BANBURY

Wrighton's Farm

Tivy Farm

MAIDFORD ROAD

GRIMSCOTE ROAD LITCHBOROUGH RD.

Barnstones Farm

BARNSTONES BUSINESS PARK

Cherry Bungalow

MAIDFORD RD.

Briar Hill Farm

Cemy.

Cemy.

STREET

Church Farm

Windmill (disused)

COLLSWELL LA.

KINGSTON CL.

COBBLERS CL.

THE GREEN

CHURCH

SYCAMORE YD.

Sch.

BARTON

HOLME

OLD SCHOOL LA.

HIGH ST.

Hall

HILLCROW

ST.

POTE

BARTHOLOMEW GDS.

Rec. Grd.

Sewage Works

Southbourne House

Blakesley Hall Lodge

Exchange

Brookside

Hootens Farm

COLLEGE LA.

Hicks Farm

BLAKESLEY RD.

College Farm

MAIN ST. RD.

Allwood Farm

TOP GREEN

PLUMPTON

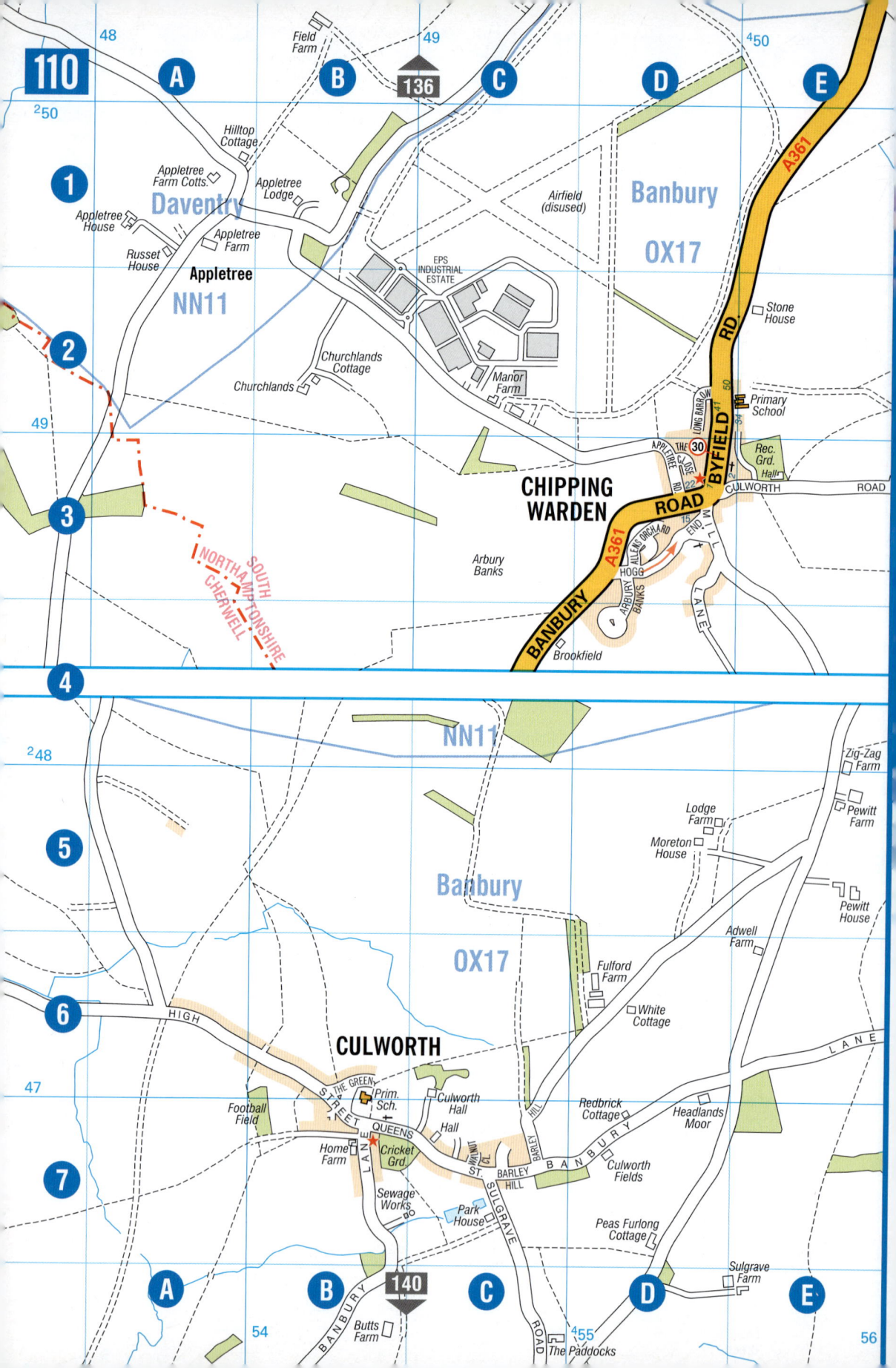

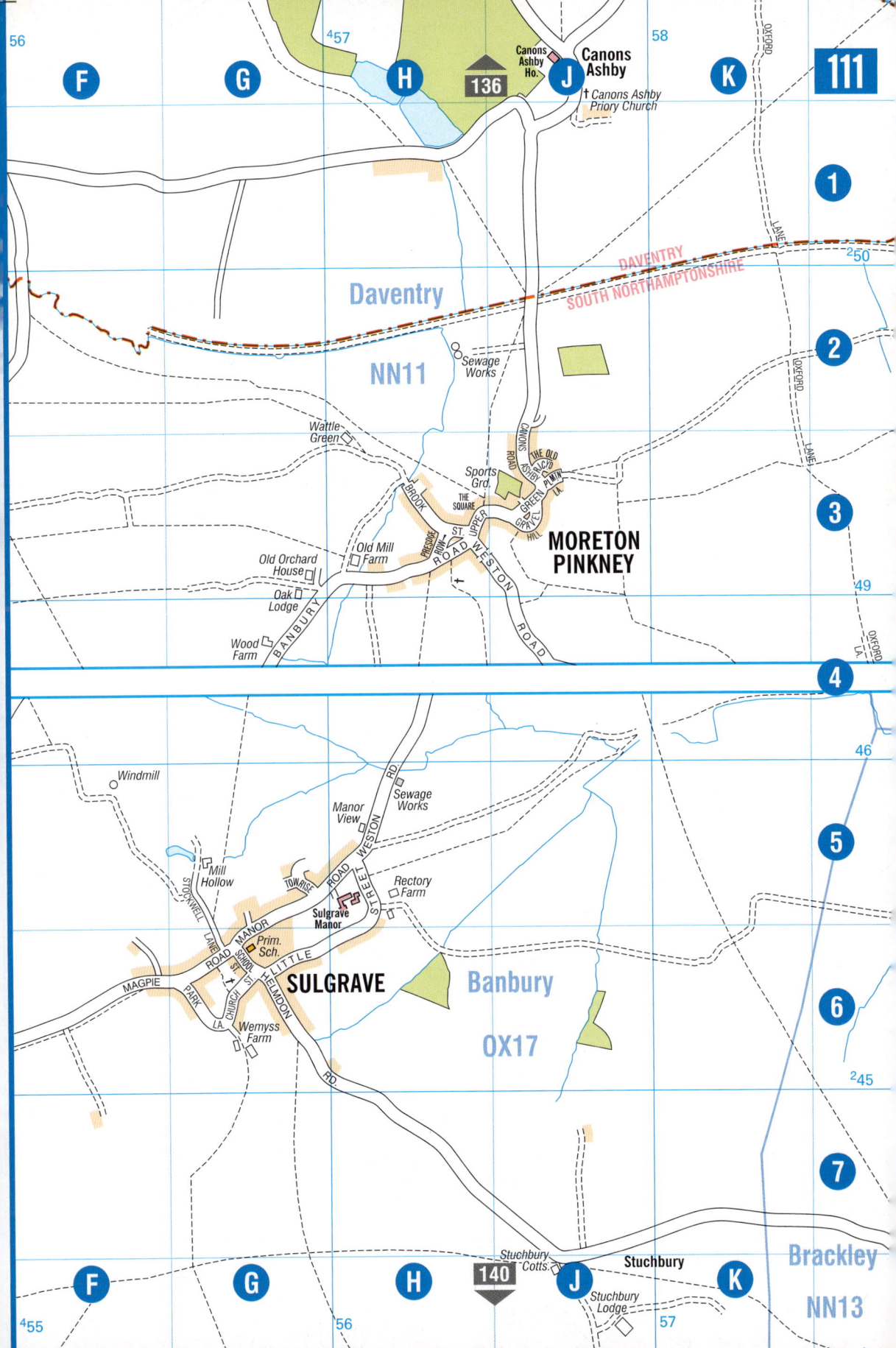

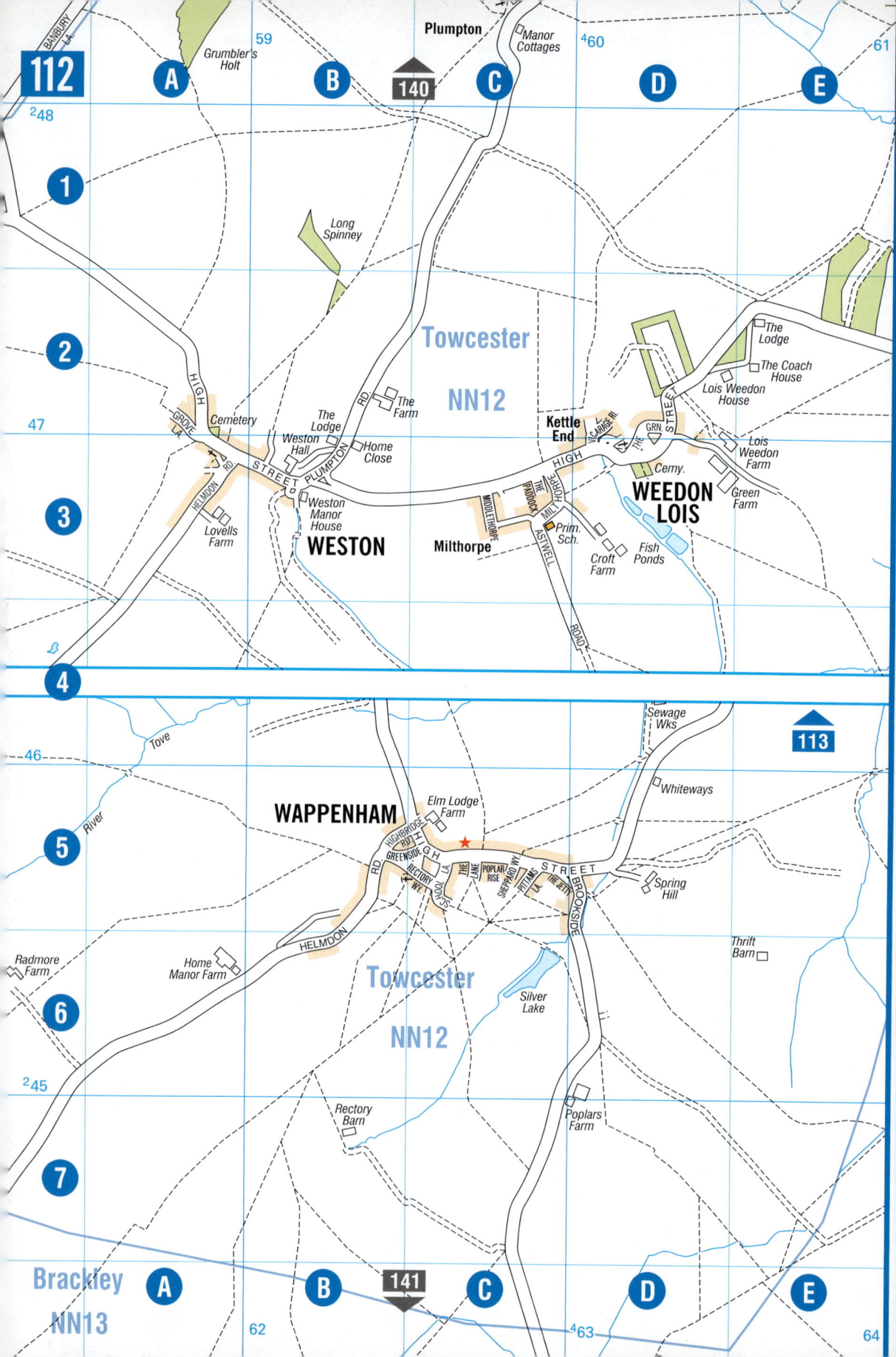

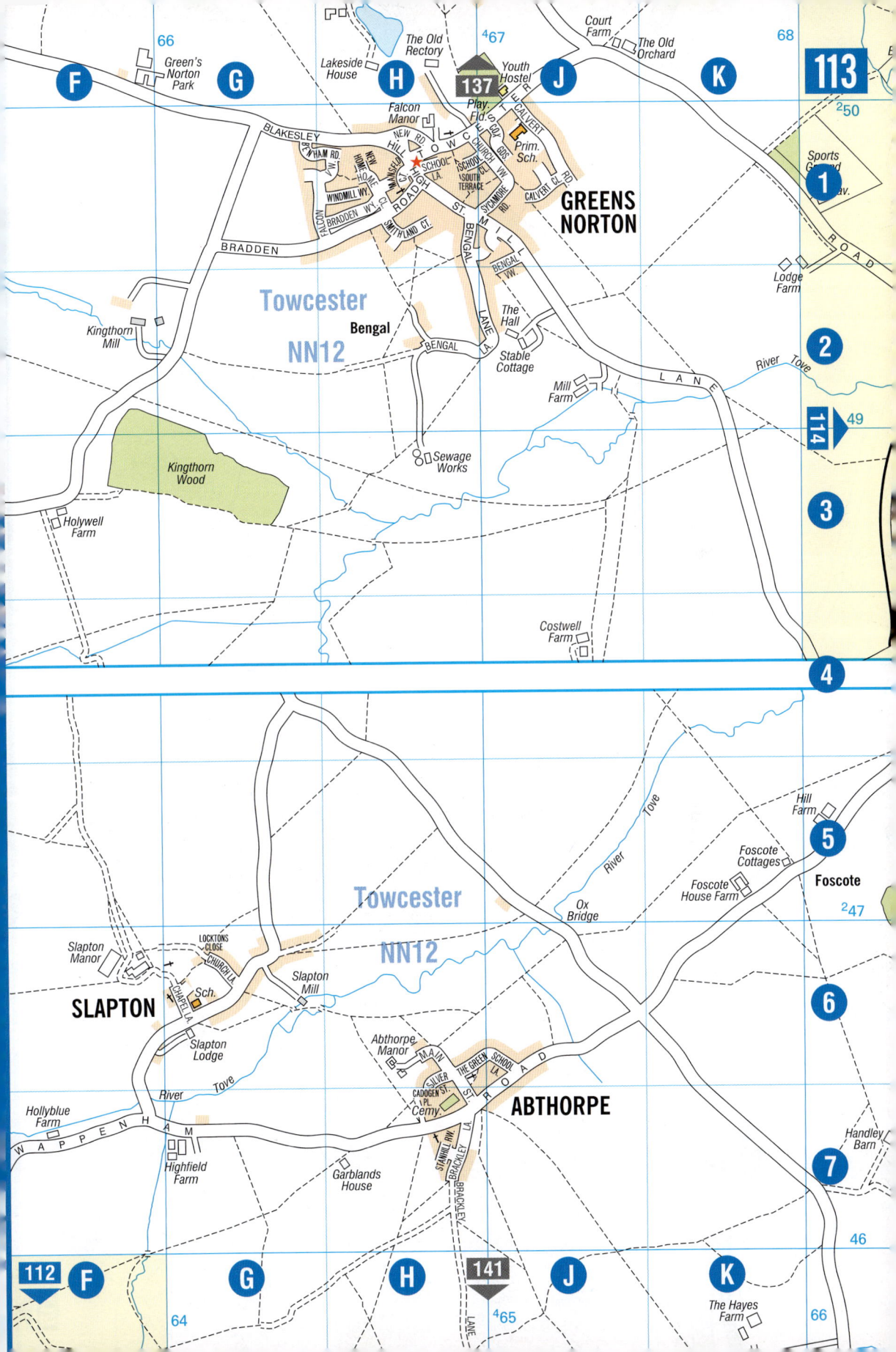

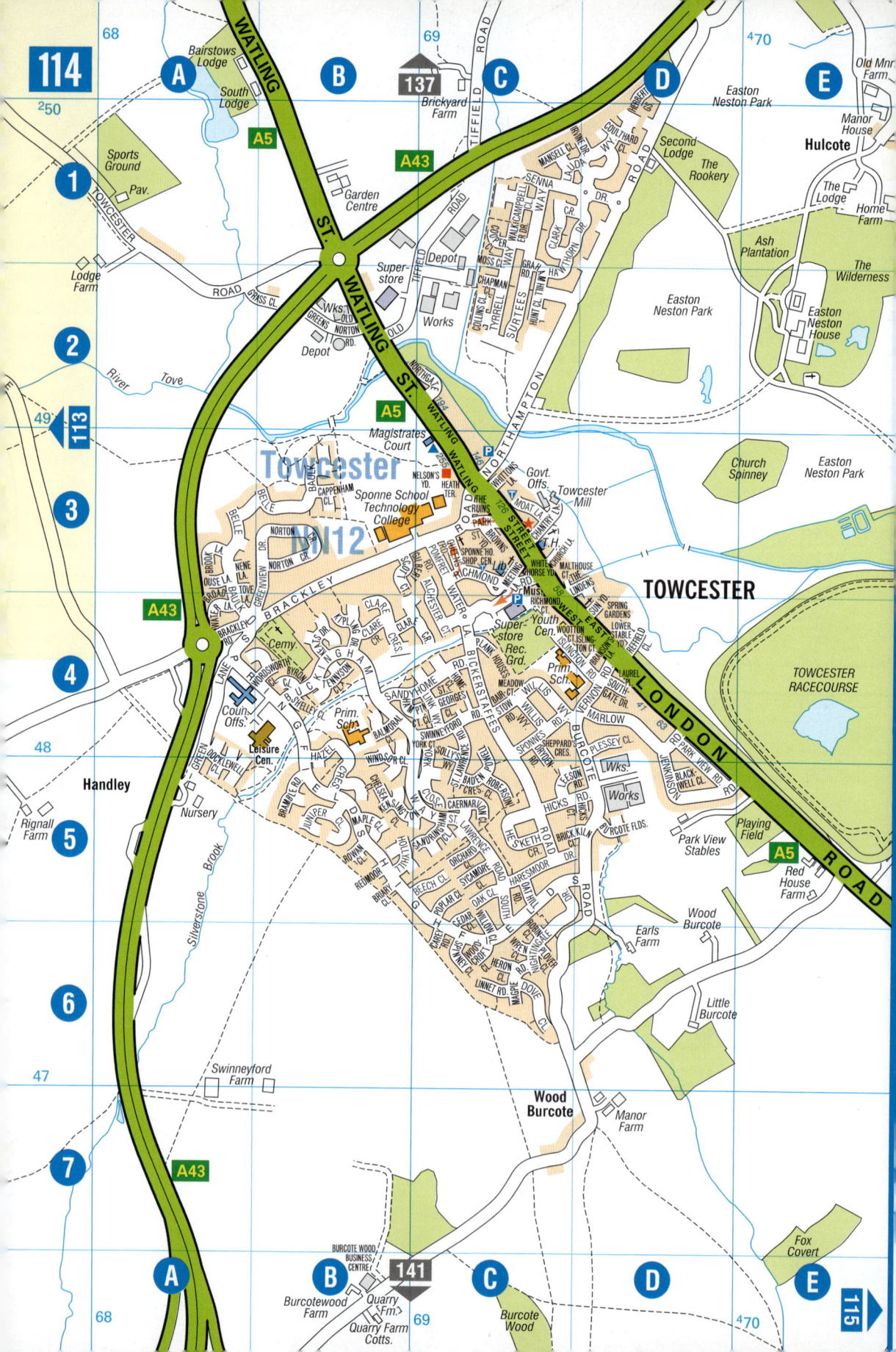

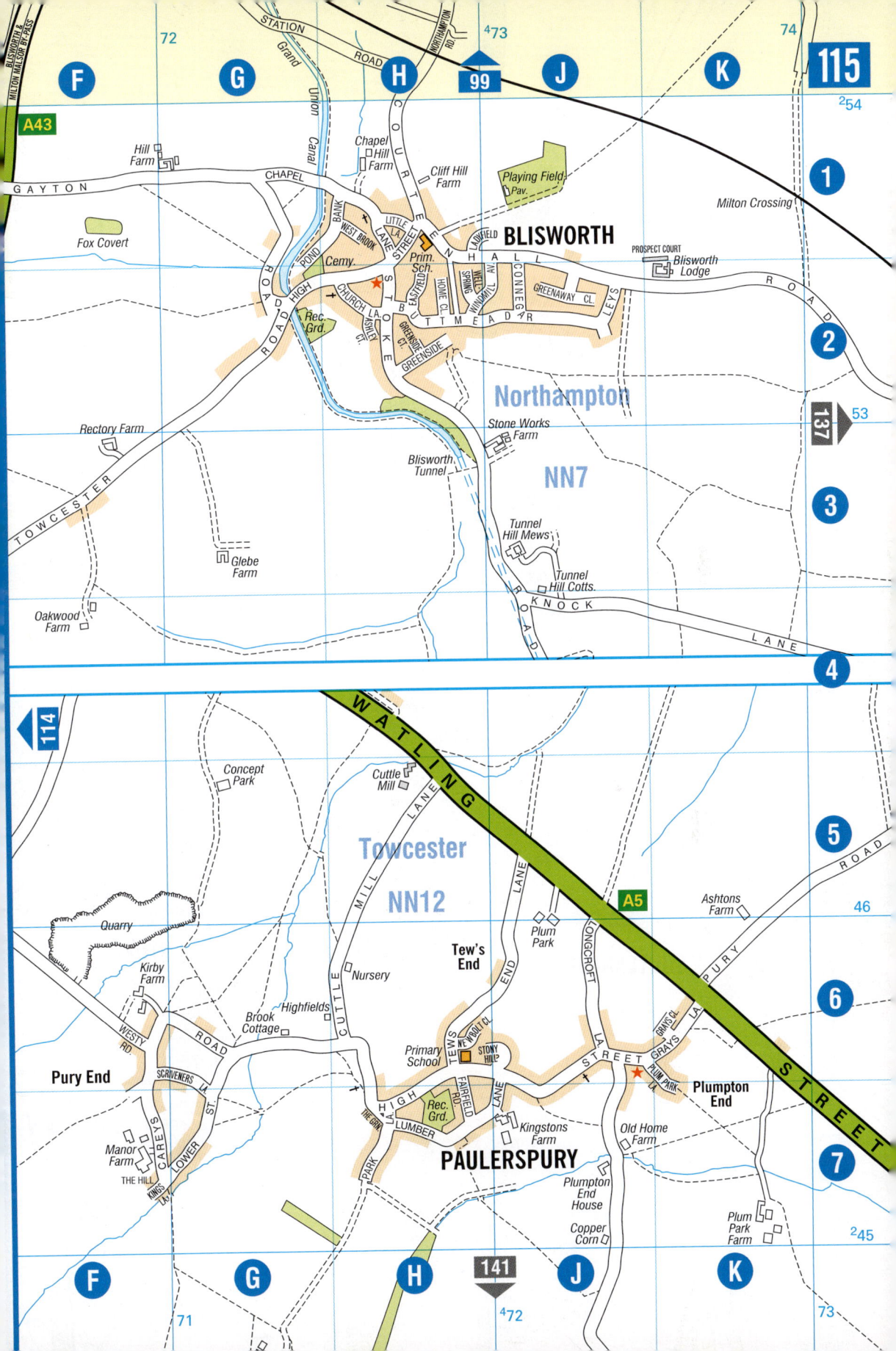

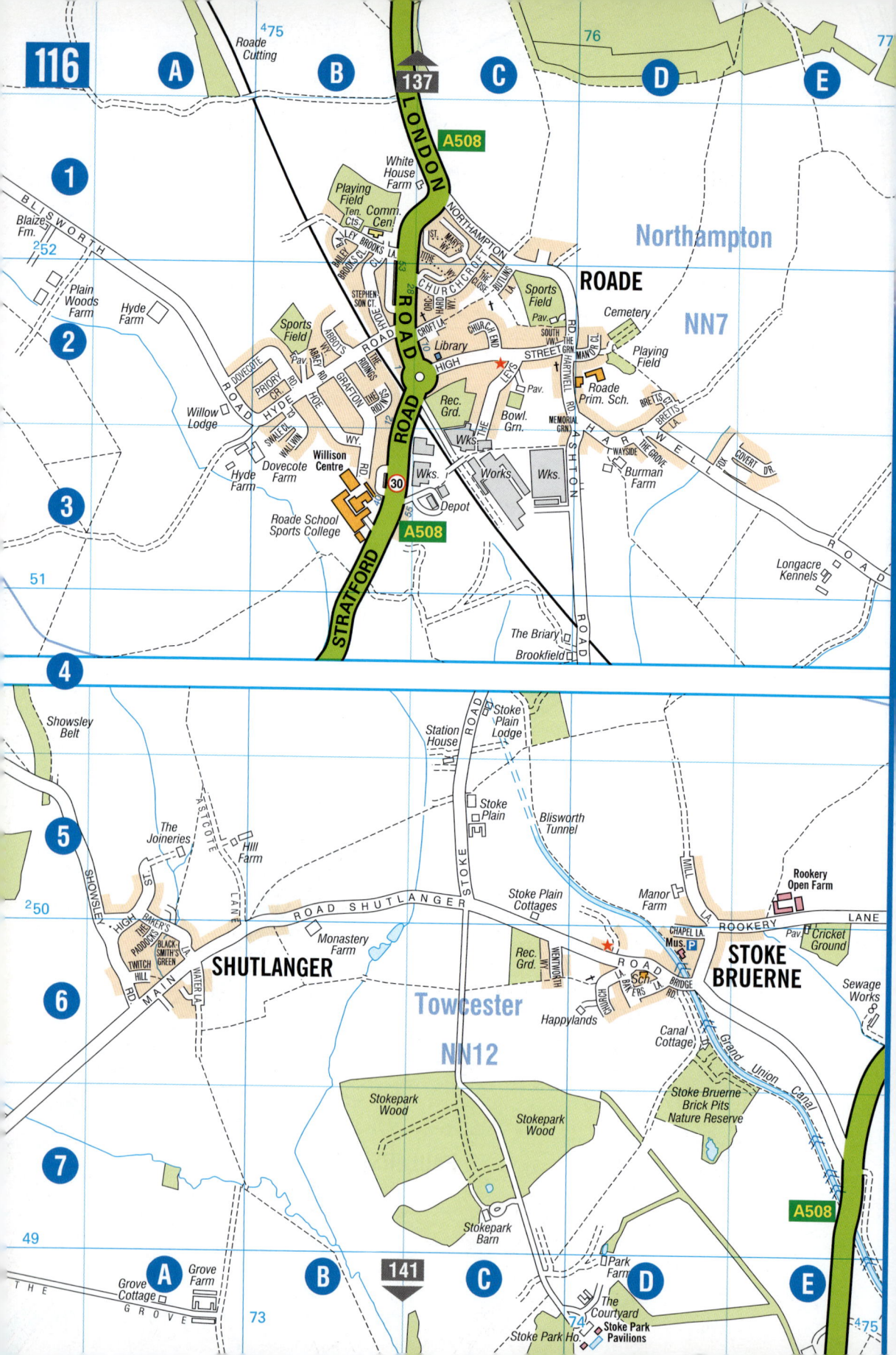

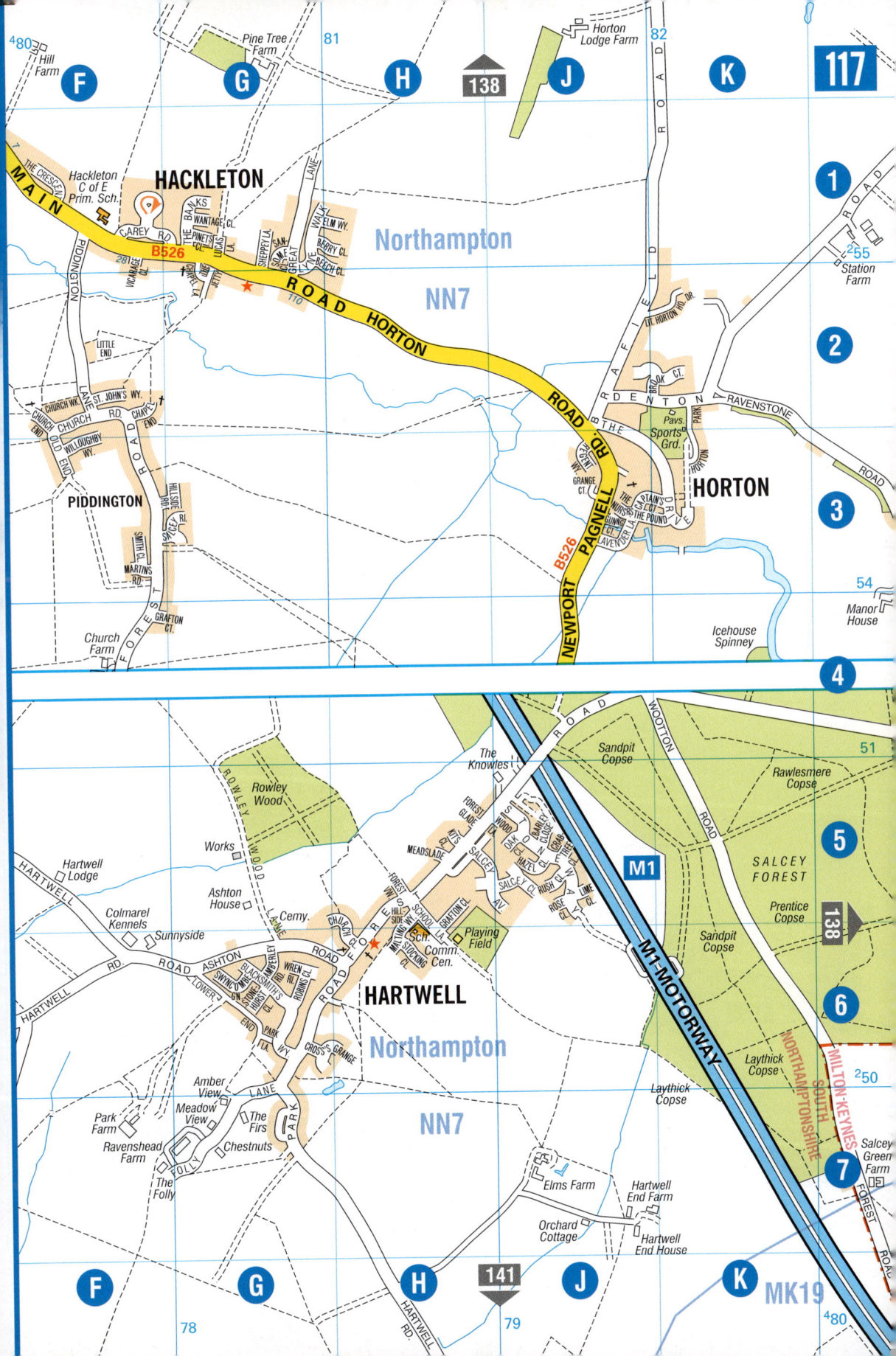

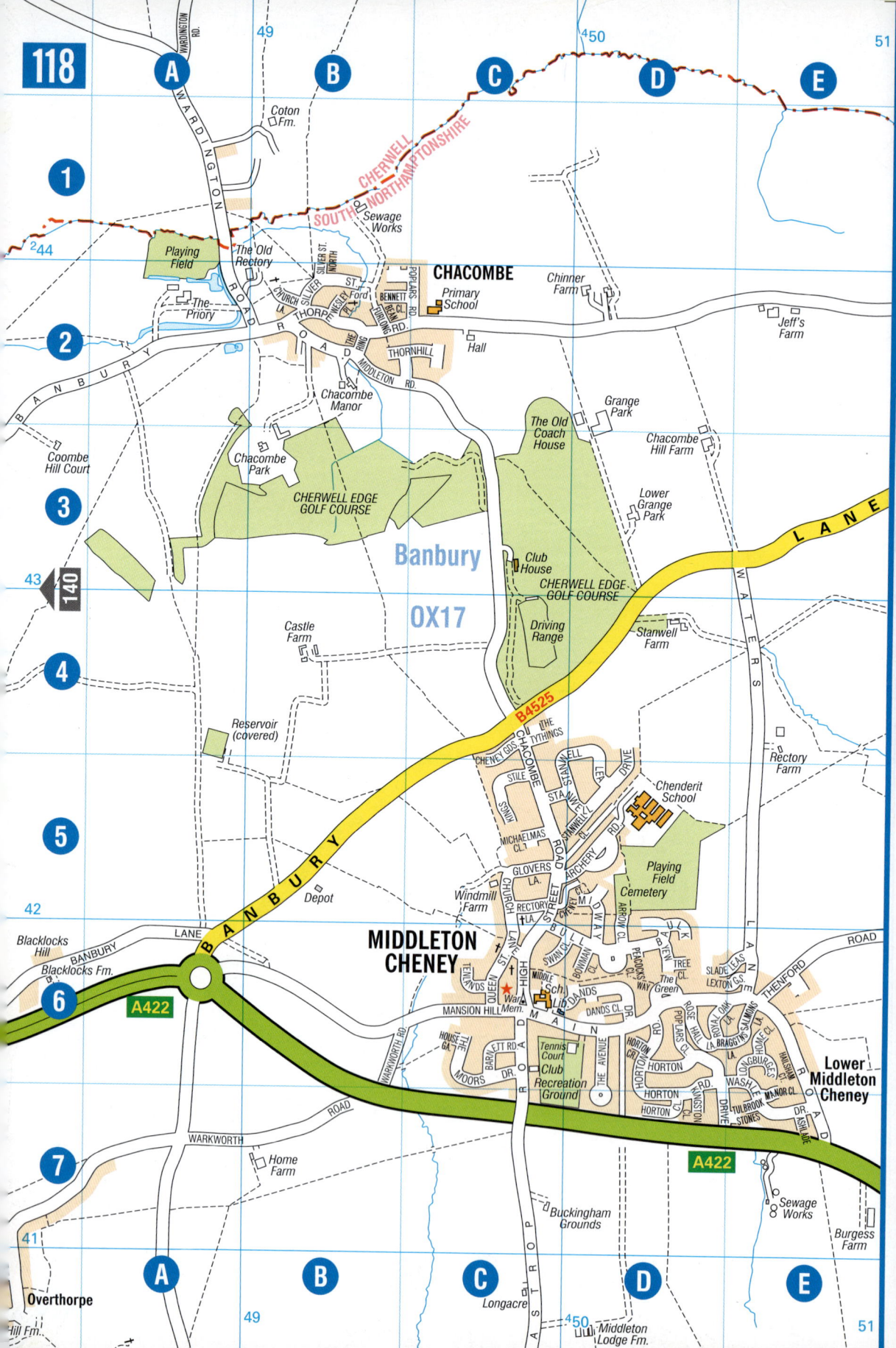

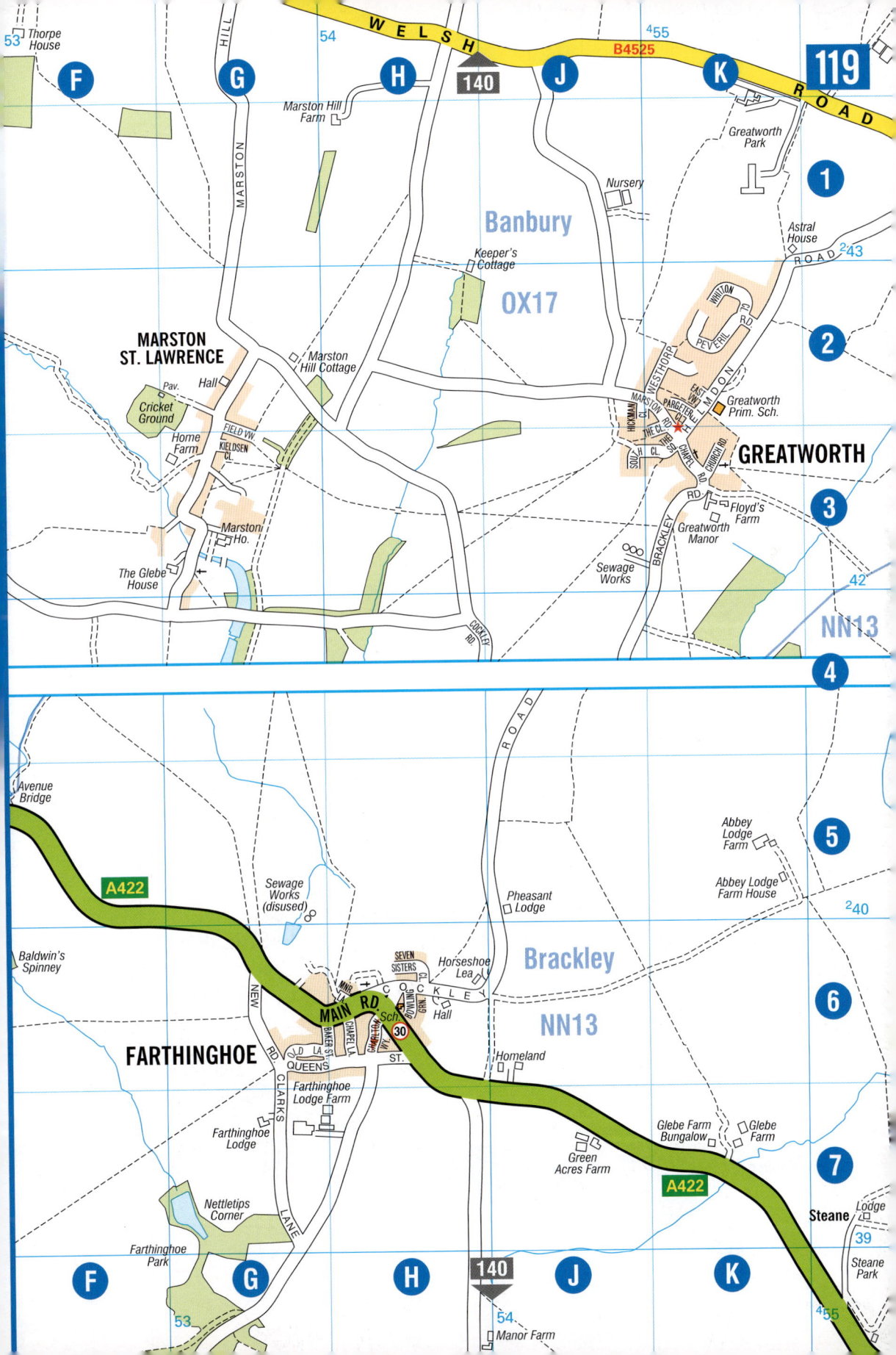

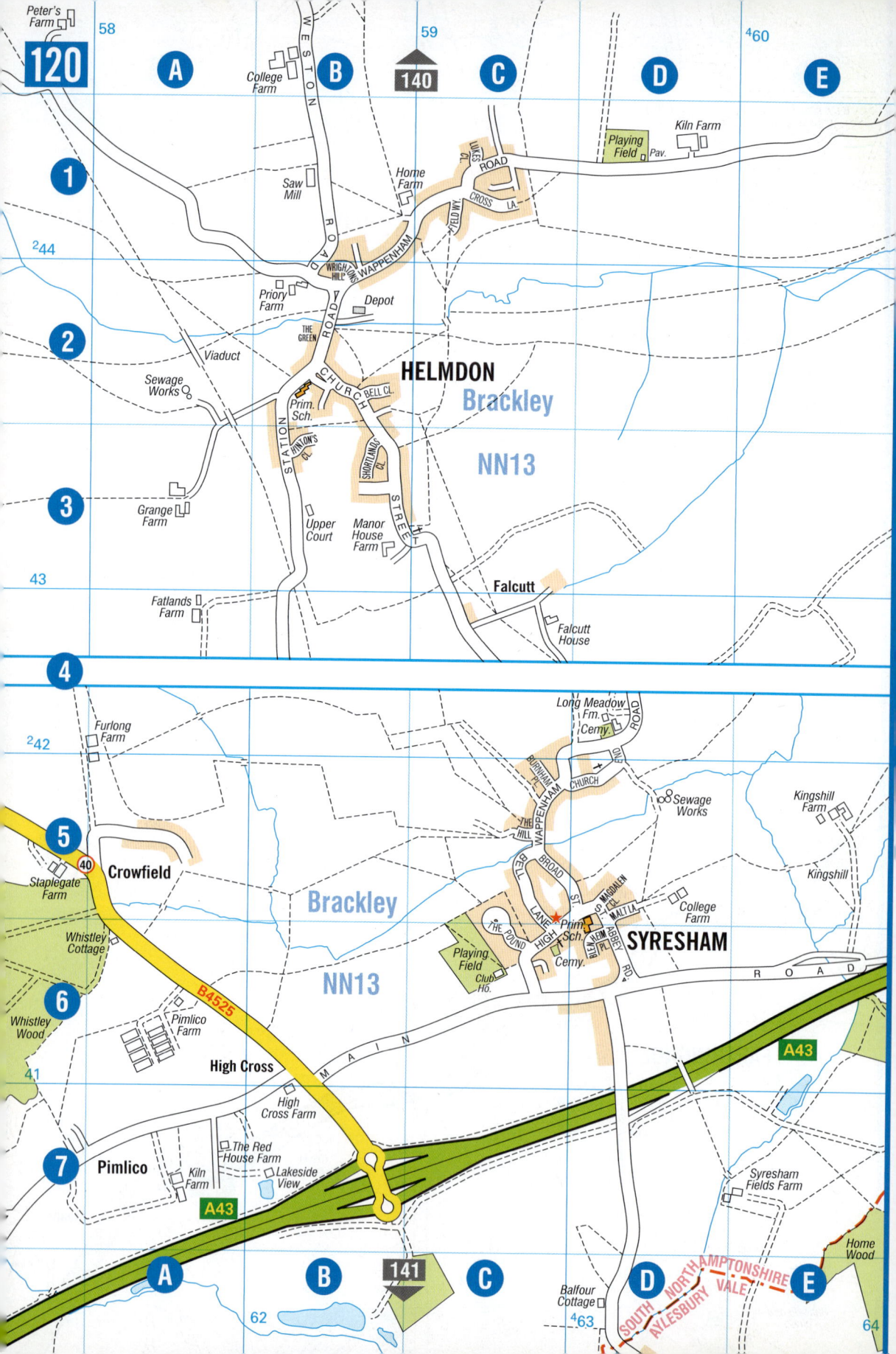

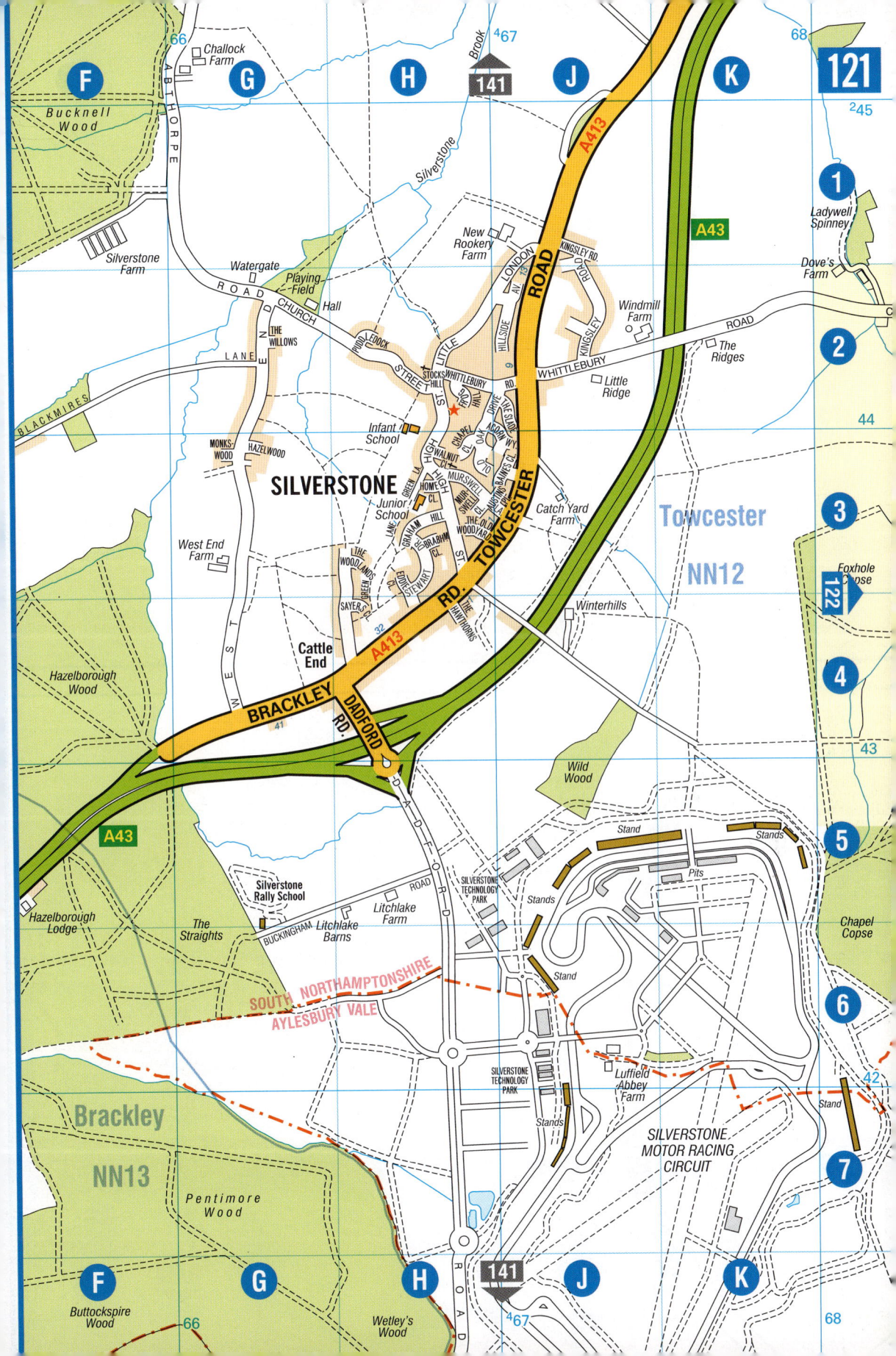

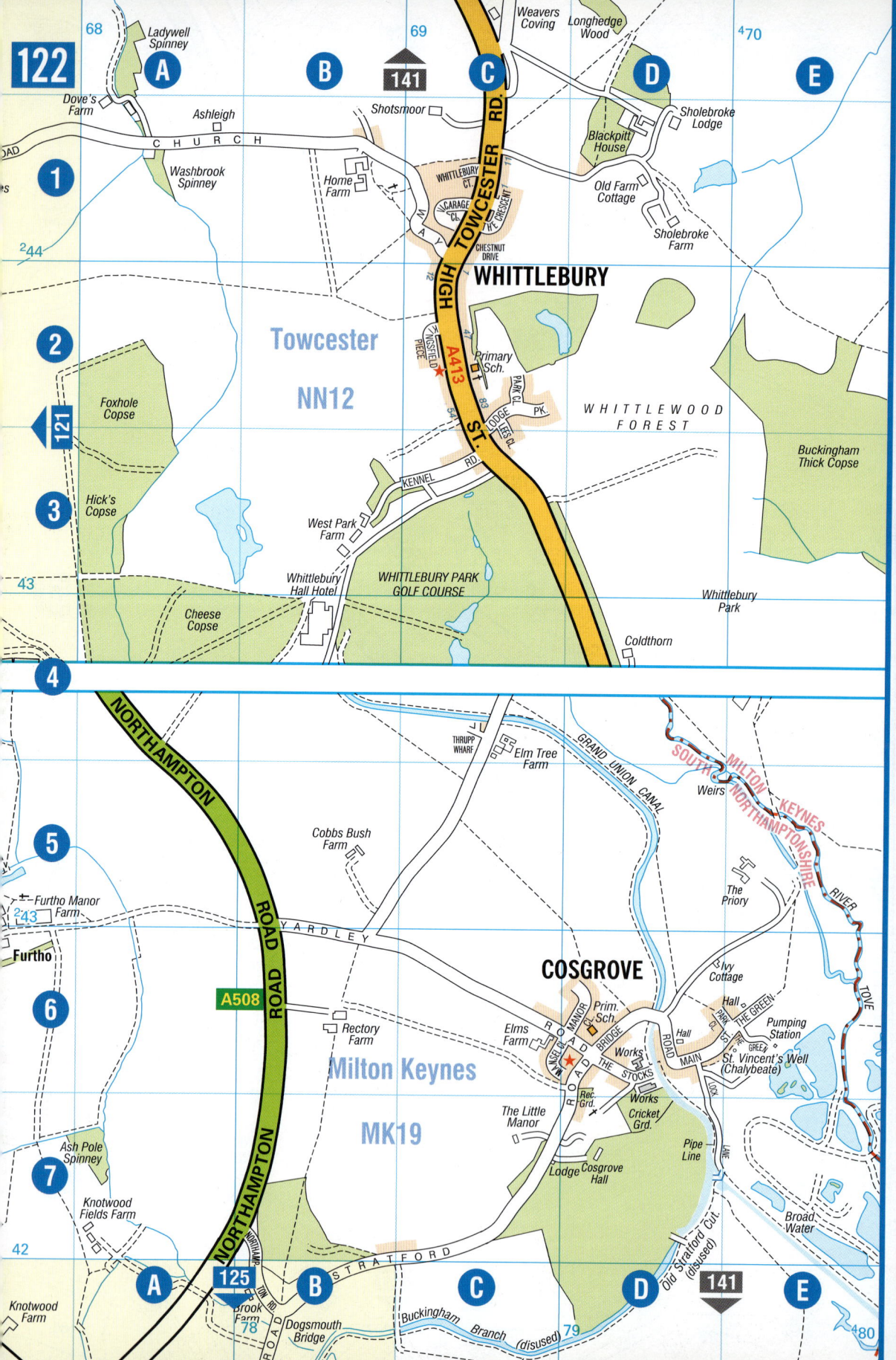

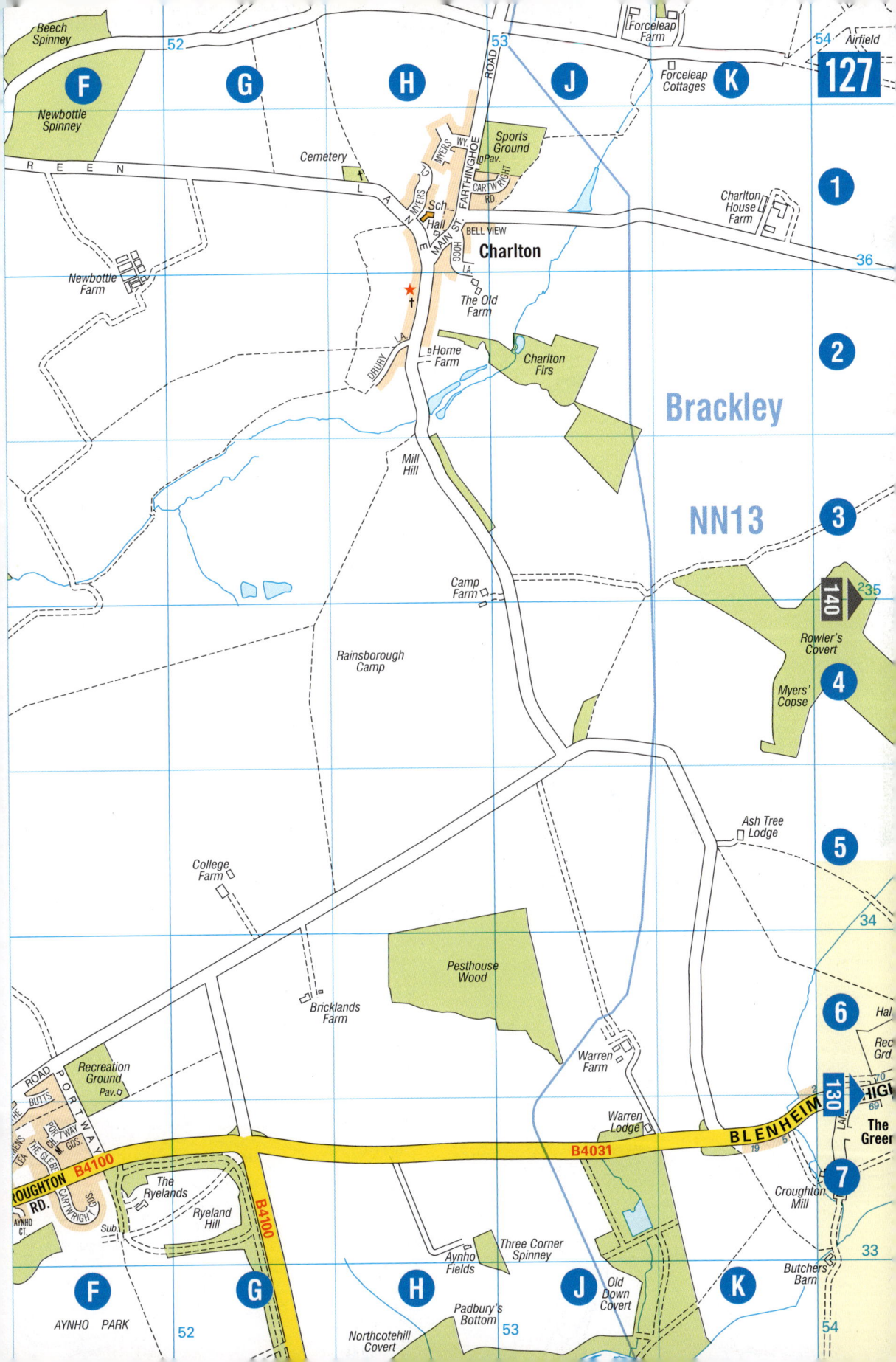

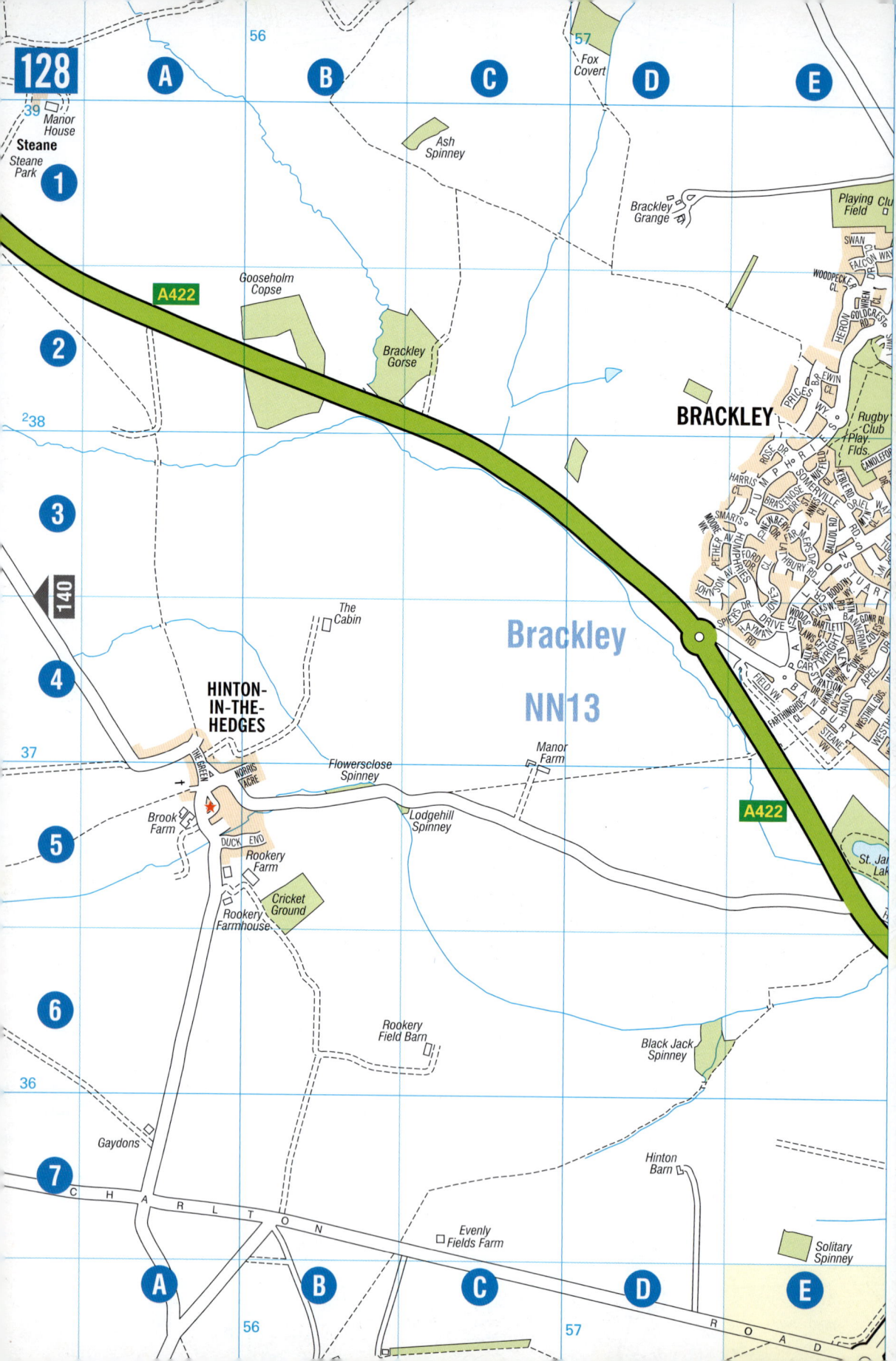

128

39

A B C D E

57

Fox
Covert

Manor
House

Steane
Steane
Park

1

Ash
Spinney

Brackley
Grange

Playing Club
Field

SWAN

FALCON WAY

WOODPECKER CL.

A422

Gooseholm
Copse

Brackley
Gorse

HERON

GOLDCREST RD

WREN

PRICES

SWIFT

EWIN CL.

WS

Rugby
Club
Play.
Flds.

BRACKLEY

2

38

CANDLEFORD

ROSE DR

HARRIS

M P

He

SOMERVILLE

PETHER AV

HUMPHRIES

BRASENOSE

JOHNSON AV

SMARTS

WK

CHUBB

CL

ATWELL RD

OBRIEN

BALLIOL RD

WAY

HAWKE

3

140

The
Cabin

FORD CL

HBURY RD

STONES

STUART

Brackley

Manor
Farm

4

NN13

SPIERS DR

WOODS

CL

BARTLETT

GDNR RD

BRATTON

HINTON-
IN-THE-
HEDGES

37

THE GREEN

NORRIS
ACRE

Flowersclose
Spinney

BaP

CAR

FARTHINGHOEDGE

STRATTON

APEL

WESTHALL GDS

FIELD VW.

AYMAN

STEANE

5

Brook
Farm

DUCK END

Lodgehill
Spinney

A422

Rookery
Farm

Cricket
Ground

St. Ja
Lak

Rookery
Farmhouse

6

36

Rookery
Field Barn

Black Jack
Spinney

Gaydons

Hinton
Barn

7

C H A R L T O N

Evenly
Fields Farm

Solitary
Spinney

A B C D E

56

57

R O A D

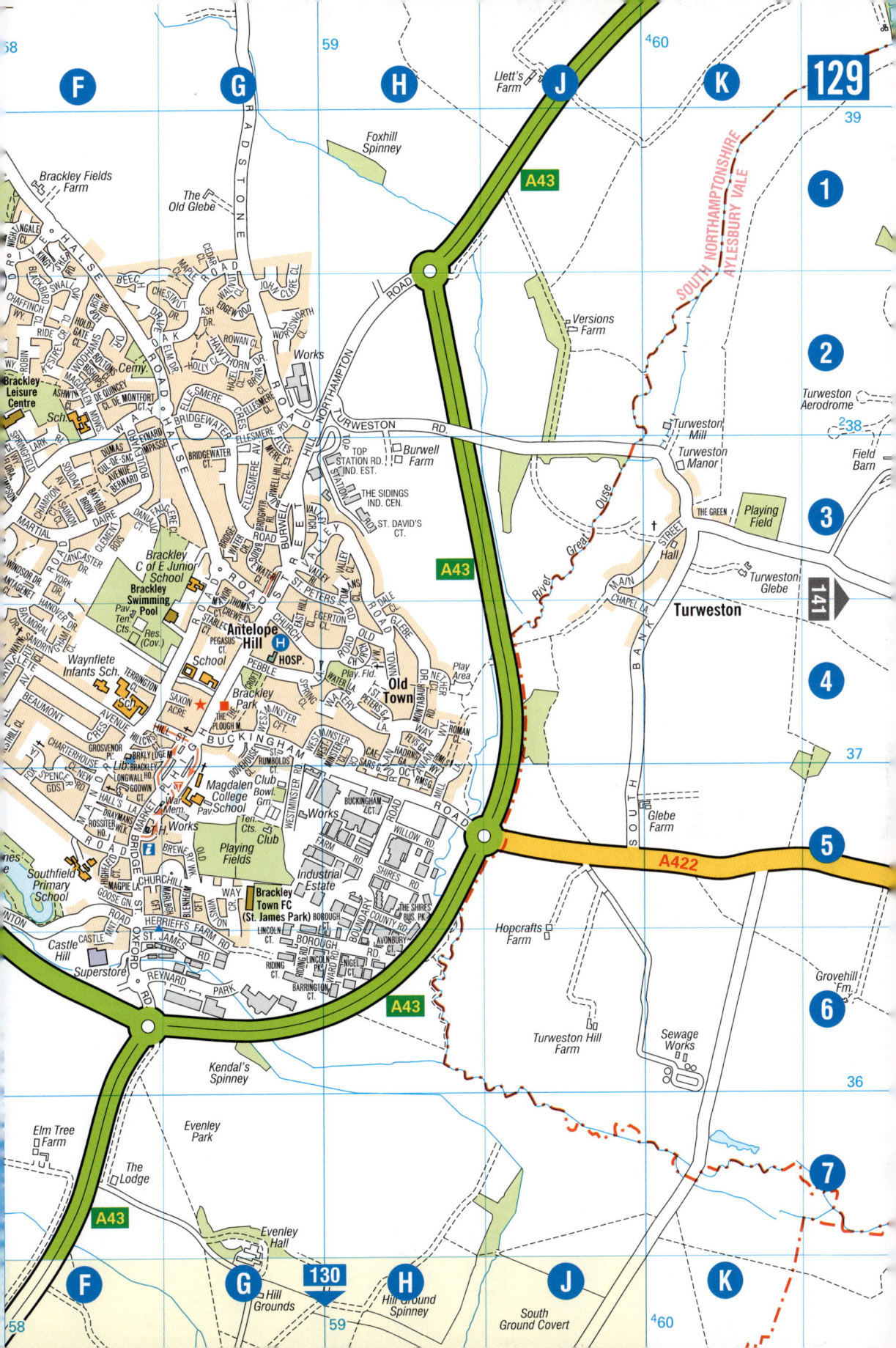

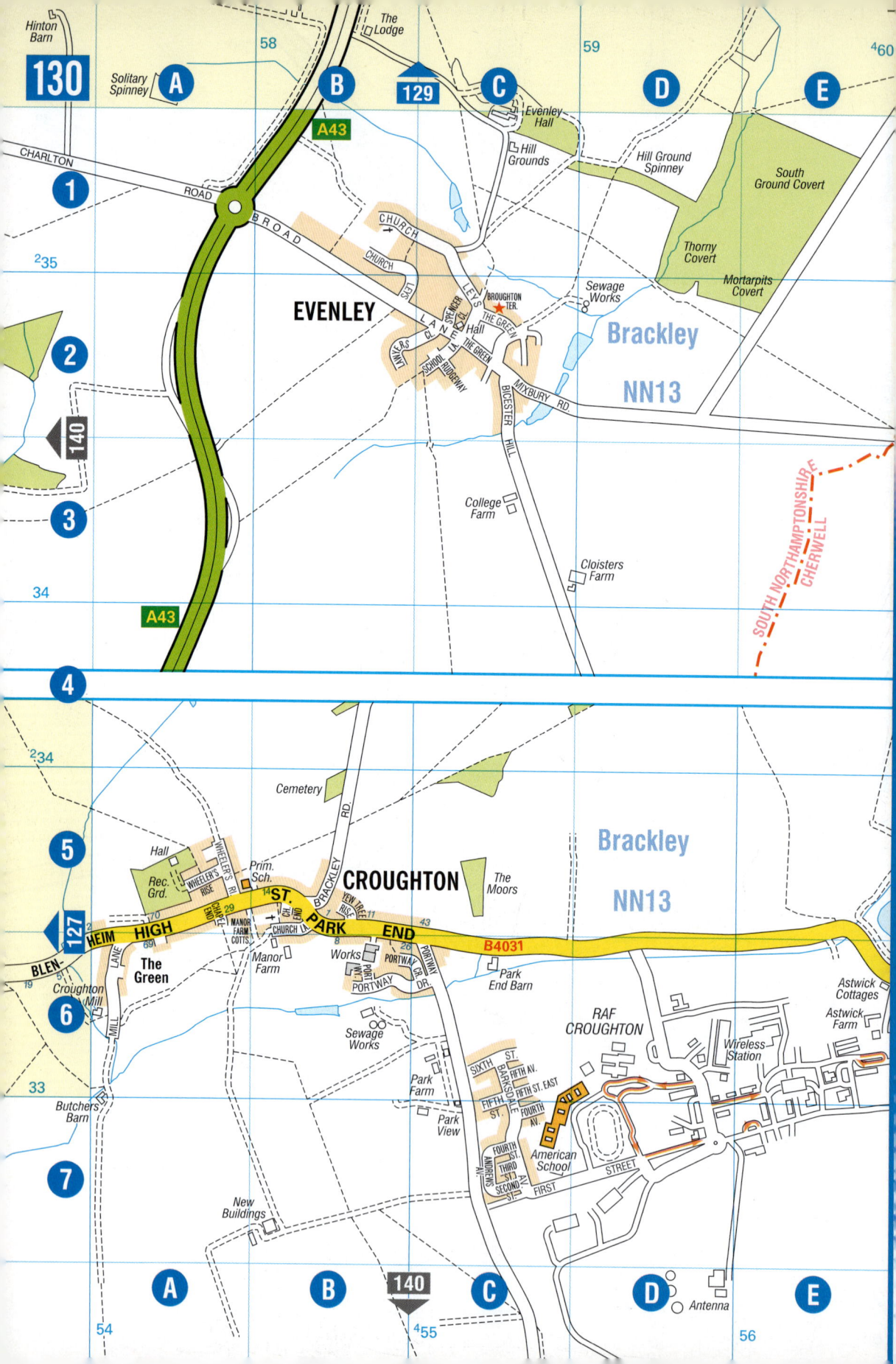

130

Hinton Barn

Solitary Spinney **A**

The Lodge

B **C** 129 **D** **E**

58 59 460

A43

CHARLTON ROAD **1**

35

BROAD

CHURCH LA.

CHURCH ST.

EVENLEY

2

140

3

34

SPENCER CL.

TWINNERS RD.

SCHOOL LA.

RIDGEWAY

Hall

BROUGHTON TER.

THE GREEN

MIXBURY RD.

BICESTER HILL

Evenley Hall

Hill Grounds

Hill Ground Spinney

South Ground Covert

Thorny Covert

Mortarpits Covert

Sewage Works

Brackley

NN13

College Farm

Cloisters Farm

SOUTH NORTHAMPTONSHIRE

CHERWELL

A43

4

234

Cemetery

Hall

Rec. Grd.

WHEELER'S RISE

Prim. Sch.

CHAPEL END

MANOR FARM COTTS.

CROUGHTON

BRACKLEY RD.

The Moors

Brackley

NN13

5

127

BLEN.

HEIM

HIGH

LANE

MILL

CH. END

ST.

YEW TREE RISE

CHURCH LA.

PARK

END

B4031

The Green

Croughton Mill

Manor Farm

Works

PORTWAY DR.

PORTWAY

Park End Barn

Astwick Cottages

Astwick Farm

Wireless Station

RAF CROUGHTON

6

33

Butchers Barn

Sewage Works

Park Farm

Park View

SIXTH ST.

BARKSDALE

FIFTH ST.

FIFTH AV.

FIFTH ST. EAST

FOURTH AV.

FOURTH ST.

ANDREWS

THIRD ST.

SECOND ST.

FIRST

STREET

American School

7

New Buildings

A **B** 140 **C** **D** Antenna **E**

54 455 56

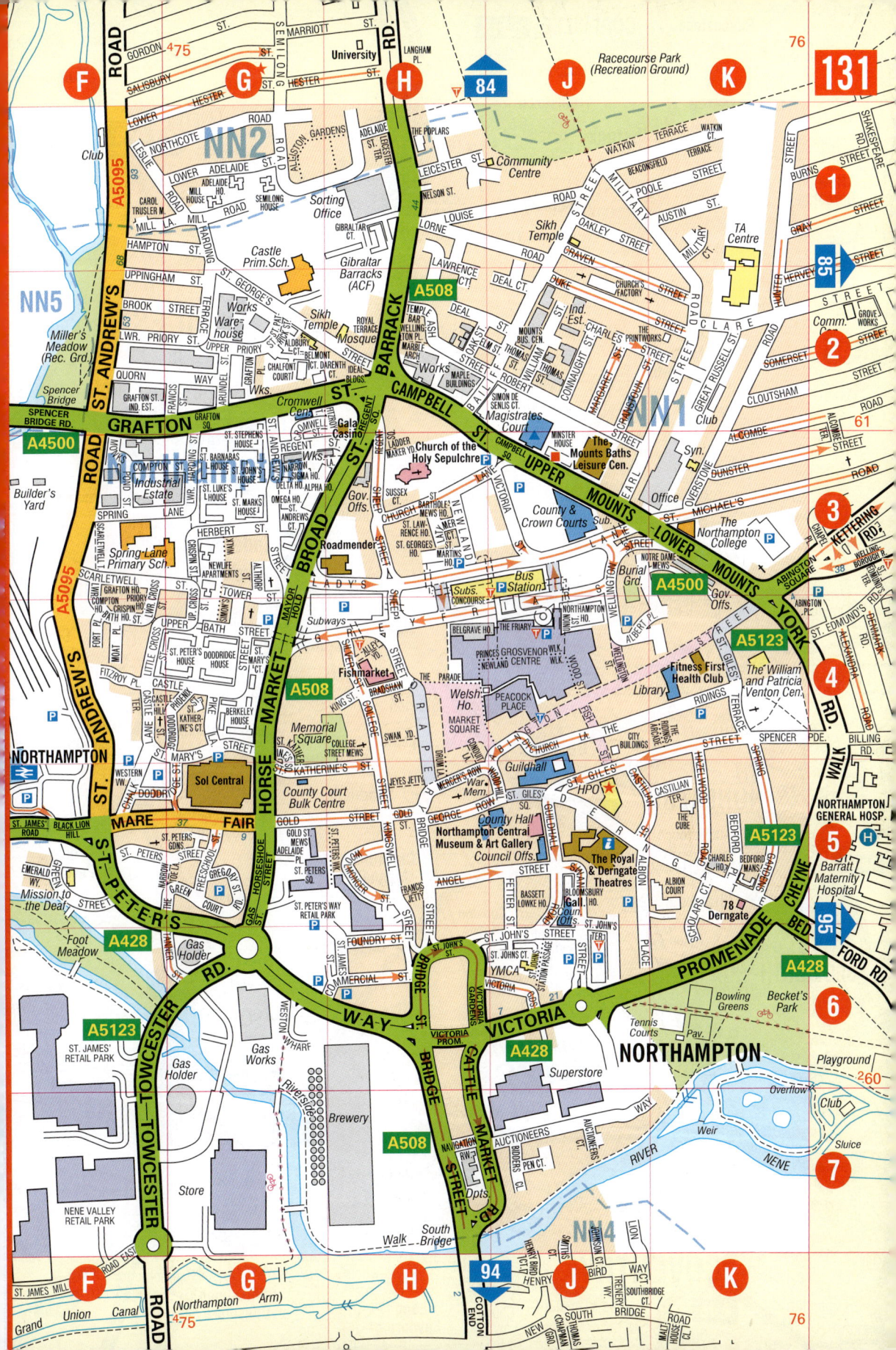

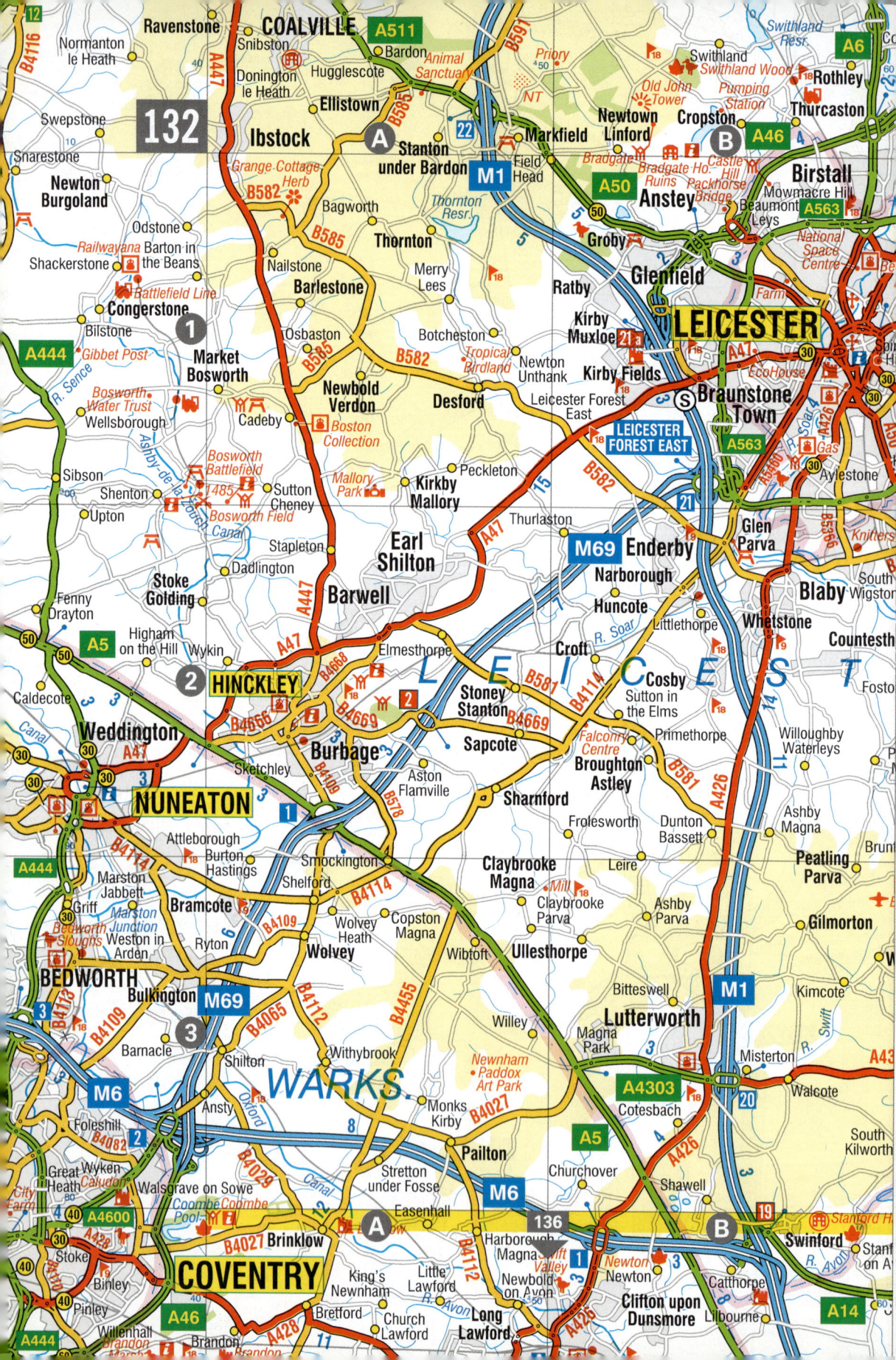

INDEX

Including Streets, Places & Areas, Industrial Estates,
Selected Flats & Walkways, Service Areas, Stations and Selected Places of Interest.

HOW TO USE THIS INDEX

1. Each street name is followed by its Postcode District, then by its Locality abbreviation(s) and then by its map reference; e.g. **Abington Pk. Cres.** NN3: Abing . . . .7J **85** is in the NN3 Postcode District and the Abington Locality and is to be found in square 7J on page **85**. The page number is shown in bold type.

2. A strict alphabetical order is followed in which Av., Rd., St., etc. (though abbreviated) are read in full and as part of the street name; e.g. **Ash La.** appears after **Ashlade** but before **Ashlar.**

3. Streets and a selection of flats and walkways that cannot be shown on street map pages **6-131**, appear in the index with the thoroughfare to which they are connected shown in brackets; e.g. **Abbey Ho.** NN5: N'ton . . . . 1B **94** (off Abbey St.)

4. Addresses that are in more than one part are referred to as not continuous.

5. Places and areas are shown in the index in BLUE TYPE and the map reference is to the actual map square in which the town centre or area is located and not to the place name shown on the map. Map references for entries that appear on street map pages **6-131** are shown first, with references to road map pages **132-141** shown in brackets; e.g. **ABTHORPE** 6H **113** (1C **141**)

6. An example of a selected place of interest is **Abington Pk. Mus.** 6H **85**

7. An example of a station is **Corby Station (Rail)** 7B **14**

8. Service Areas are shown in the index in **BOLD CAPITAL TYPE**; e.g. **NORTHAMPTON SERVICE AREA** 1H **99**

9. Map references for entries that appear on the large scale page **131** are shown first, with small scale map references shown in brackets; e.g. **Abington Pl.** NN1: N'ton 4K **131** (1F **95**)

GENERAL ABBREVIATIONS

All. : Alley	**Dr.** : Drive	**La.** : Lane	**Ri.** : Rise
App. : Approach	**E.** : East	**Lit.** : Little	**Rd.** : Road
Arc. : Arcade	**Ent.** : Enterprise	**Lwr.** : Lower	**Shop.** : Shopping
Av. : Avenue	**Est.** : Estate	**Mnr.** : Manor	**Sth.** : South
Blvd. : Boulevard	**Fld.** : Field	**Mans.** : Mansions	**Sq.** : Square
Bri. : Bridge	**Flds.** : Fields	**Mkt.** : Market	**Sta.** : Station
Bldgs. : Buildings	**Gdn.** : Garden	**Mdw.** : Meadow	**St.** : Street
Bus. : Business	**Gdns.** : Gardens	**Mdws.** : Meadows	**Ter.** : Terrace
Cvn. : Caravan	**Ga.** : Gate	**M.** : Mews	**Trad.** : Trading
Cen. : Centre	**Gt.** : Great	**Mt.** : Mount	**Up.** : Upper
Chu. : Church	**Grn.** : Green	**Mus.** : Museum	**Va.** : Vale
Circ. : Circle	**Gro.** : Grove	**Nth.** : North	**Vw.** : View
Cl. : Close	**Hgts.** : Heights	**Pde.** : Parade	**Vs.** : Villas
Cnr. : Corner	**Ho.** : House	**Pk.** : Park	**Vis.** : Visitors
Cotts. : Cottages	**Ho's.** : Houses	**Pas.** : Passage	**Wlk.** : Walk
Ct. : Court	**Ind.** : Industrial	**Pl.** : Place	**W.** : West
Cres. : Crescent	**Info.** : Information	**Prom.** : Promenade	**Yd.** : Yard
Cft. : Croft	**Intl.** : International	**Res.** : Residential	

LOCALITY ABBREVIATIONS

Abing : **Abington**	Cotte : **Cotterstock**	Gt Oxe : **Great Oxendon**	Lut : **Lutton**
Abt : **Abthorpe**	Cotti : **Cottingham**	Greatw : **Greatworth**	Maid : **Maidwell**
Add : **Adderbury**	Court : **Courteenhall**	Greens N : **Greens Norton**	Mkt H : **Market Harborough**
Ald : **Aldwincle**	C'ord : **Cranford**	Gren : **Grendon**	Mar L : **Marston St Lawrence**
A'ley : **Ashley**	C'ley : **Cransley**	Gret : **Gretton**	Mar T : **Marston Trussell**
A'ton : **Ashton**	Crea : **Creaton**	Grim : **Grimscote**	Maw : **Mawsley**
Ast : **Astcote**	Crick : **Crick**	Guil : **Guilsborough**	Mears A : **Mears Ashby**
Ast W : **Aston le Walls**	Crou : **Croughton**	Hack : **Hackleton**	Med : **Medbourne**
Ayn : **Aynho**	Cul : **Culworth**	Hann : **Hannington**	Mid : **Middleton**
Badby : **Badby**	Dall : **Dallington**	H'stone : **Hardingstone**	Mid C : **Middleton Cheney**
Ban : **Banbury**	Dals : **Dalscote**	H'wick : **Hardwick**	Mil M : **Milton Malsor**
Bar : **Barby**	Dav : **Daventry**	Harg : **Hargrave**	Mor P : **Moreton Pinkney**
Barn : **Barnwell**	Dean : **Deanshanger**	Harp : **Harpole**	Moul : **Moulton**
Bar S : **Barton Seagrave**	Dee : **Deene**	Harr : **Harringworth**	Moul P : **Moulton Park**
Blak : **Blakesley**	Del : **Delapre**	Hart : **Hartwell**	Nas : **Naseby**
Blis : **Blisworth**	Den : **Denford**	Hell : **Hellidon**	Nass : **Nassington**
Bou : **Boughton**	D'ton : **Denton**	Helm : **Helmdon**	Neth H : **Nether Heyford**
Boz : **Bozeat**	Des : **Desborough**	High F : **Higham Ferrers**	Newb : **Newbottle**
B'ley : **Brackley**	Dod : **Dodford**	Hill : **Hillmorton**	New D : **New Duston**
Brack : **Brackmills**	Drau : **Draughton**	Hin H : **Hinton-in-the-Hedges**	Newn : **Newnham**
Braf G : **Brafield on the Green**	Dray : **Drayton**	Holc : **Holcot**	New : **Newton**
Bram A : **Brampton Ash**	Dus : **Duston**	Hold : **Holdenby**	N'ton : **Northampton**
Braun : **Braunston**	E Bart : **Earls Barton**	Holl : **Hollowell**	Nor : **Norton**
Bray : **Braybrooke**	E Car : **East Carlton**	Hort : **Horton**	Old : **Old**
Brig : **Brigstock**	E Far : **East Farndon**	Irch : **Irchester**	Old S : **Old Stratford**
Brin : **Bringhurst**	E Had : **East Haddon**	Irth : **Irthlingborough**	Orl : **Orlingbury**
Brix : **Brixworth**	East : **Eastcote**	Ish : **Isham**	Oun : **Oundle**
Broc : **Brockhall**	Eas H : **Easton on the Hill**	Isl : **Islip**	Over : **Overstone**
Brou : **Broughton**	Ect : **Ecton**	K'ing : **Kettering**	Pat : **Pattishall**
Bug : **Bugbrooke**	Even : **Evenley**	K'ton : **Ketton**	Paul : **Paulerspury**
Bur L : **Burton Latimer**	Eyd : **Eydon**	Kil : **Kilsby**	Pid : **Piddington**
Byf : **Byfield**	Far C : **Far Cotton**	King C : **King's Cliffe**	Pipe : **Pipewell**
Cald : **Caldecott**	Farn : **Farndish**	King S : **Kings Sutton**	Pits : **Pitsford**
Can A : **Canons Ashby**	F'hoe : **Farthinghoe**	K'thpe : **Kingsthorpe**	Pole : **Polebrook**
Catt : **Catthorpe**	F'one : **Farthingstone**	Kisl : **Kislingbury**	Pot : **Potterspury**
Chac : **Chacombe**	Fine : **Finedon**	Knus : **Knuston**	Pres D : **Preston Deanery**
Chap B : **Chapel Brampton**	Flore : **Flore**	Leck : **Leckhampstead**	P Mar : **Priors Marston**
Char : **Charlton**	Fos B : **Foster's Booth**	Lil : **Lilbourne**	Pur E : **Pury End**
Chel : **Chelveston**	Foth : **Fotheringhay**	Lit : **Litchborough**	Pux : **Puxley**
Chip W : **Chipping Warden**	G'ton : **Gayton**	L Add : **Little Addington**	Pyt : **Pytchley**
Chu B : **Church Brampton**	Ged : **Geddington**	L Bill : **Little Billington**	Quin : **Quinton**
Chu S : **Church Stowe**	Glap : **Glapthorn**	L Brin : **Little Brington**	Raun : **Rauns**
Clif D : **Clifton upon Dunsmore**	Graf R : **Grafton Regis**	L Harr : **Little Harrowden**	Rav : **Ravensthorpe**
Clip : **Clipston**	Gra P : **Grange Park**	L Hou : **Little Houghton**	Rin : **Ringstead**
Cog : **Cogenhoe**	Gt Ad : **Great Addington**	L Irch : **Little Irchester**	Roa : **Roade**
Col A : **Cold Ashby**	Gt Bil : **Great Billing**	L Oak : **Little Oakley**	Rock : **Rockingham**
Col H : **Cold Higham**	Gt Bri : **Great Brington**	Lod : **Loddington**	Roth : **Rothersthorpe**
Col : **Collingtree**	Gt Dod : **Great Doddington**	Long B : **Long Buckby**	R'ell : **Rothwell**
Colly : **Collyweston**	Gt Har : **Great Harrowden**	Lwr B : **Lower Boddington**	R'den : **Rushden**
Corby : **Corby**	Gt Hou : **Great Houghton**	Lwr H : **Lower Harlestone**	R'ton : **Rushton**
Cos : **Cosgrove**	Gt Oak : **Great Oakley**	Low : **Lowick**	Scal : **Scaldwell**

78 Derngate—Arthingworth

Sea : **Seaton**
Sem : **Semilong**
Shut : **Shutlanger**
Sibb : **Sibbertoft**
Silv : **Silverstone**
Slapt : **Slapton**
Spin H : **Spinney Hill**
Spra : **Spratton**
Stan : **Stanion**
Stanw : **Stanwick**
Stav : **Staverton**
Stoke A : **Stoke Albany**
Stoke B : **Stoke Bruerne**
Stony S : **Stony Stratford**
Strix : **Strixton**
Sud : **Sudborough**
Sulb : **Sulby**
Sulg : **Sulgrave**
Sutt B : **Sutton Bassett**
Swan H : **Swan Valley**
Syre : **Syresham**
Syw : **Sywell**
Thorn : **Thornby**
Thor M : **Thorpe Malsor**
Thor U : **Thorpe Underwood**
Thor W : **Thorpe Waterville**
Thra : **Thrapston**
Titch : **Titchmarsh**
Tow : **Towcester**
Turw : **Turweston**
Twy : **Twywell**
Up Bod : **Upper Boddington**
Up Harl : **Upper Harlestone**
Up Hey : **Upper Heyford**
Up St : **Upper Stowe**
Upton : **Upton**
Wal : **Walgrave**
Wans : **Wansford**
Wap : **Wappenham**
Warkt : **Warkton**
Warkw : **Warkworth**
Warm : **Warmington**
Wash : **Washingley**
Wat : **Watford**
Weed : **Weedon**
Weed L : **Weedon Lois**
Week : **Weekley**
Weld : **Weldon**
Welf : **Welford**
Well : **Wellingborough**
Welt : **Welton**
W Had : **West Haddon**
West : **Weston**
West W : **Weston by Welland**
West F : **Weston Favell**
Whil : **Whilton**
Whit : **Whittlebury**
Wick : **Wicken**
Wilb : **Wilbarston**
Wilby : **Wilby**
Woll : **Wollaston**
Wood B : **Wood Burcote**
Woode : **Woodend**
Woodf : **Woodford**
Woodf H : **Woodford Halse**
Wood : **Woodnewton**
Woot : **Wootton**
Wym : **Wymington**
Yar G : **Yardley Gobion**
Yar H : **Yardley Hastings**
Yar : **Yarwell**
Yel : **Yelvertoft**

78 Derngate **5K 131**
384th Bombardment Group Memorial **3B 134**

A

A1/M1 Bus. Cen. NN16: K'ing 6B **38**
A6 Bus. Cen. NN16: K'ing 5A **38**
Abbey Cl. NN29: Boz 3G **103**
Abbey Ho. *NN5: N'ton 1B* ***94***
(off Abbey St.)
Abbey Lodge NN3: N'ton 7K **85**
Abbey Ri. NN29: Woll 3E **90**
Abbey Rd. NN4: Far C 4C **94**
NN7: Roa 2B **116**
NN8: Well 2A **78**
NN13: Syre 6D **120**
Abbey St. NN5: N'ton 1B **94**
NN11: Dav 1H **61**
Abbey Way NN10: R'den 5D **80**
Abbot Cl. NN11: Dav 3J **61**
Abbots Cl. NN15: K'ing 3D **42**
ABBOTSLEY **3D 139**
ABBOTS RIPTON **1D 139**
Abbots Way NN5: N'ton 1A **94**
NN7: Roa 2B **116**
NN8: Well 1A **78**
NN15: K'ing 4C **42**
Abbotts Cl. NN14: Titch 2J **49**
Abbotts Way NN10: R'den 4C **80**
Aberdare Rd. NN5: N'ton 6B **84**
Aberdeen Ter. *NN5: N'ton 1B* ***94***
(off Harlestone Rd.)
ABINGTON **7H 85**
Abington Av. NN1: N'ton 6G **85**
NN3: N'ton 6G **85**
Abington Cotts. NN1: N'ton 6H **85**
Abington Ct. NN3: N'ton 5J **85**
NN5: Upton 3J ***93***
(off Black Cat Dr.)
Abington Gro. NN1: N'ton 6G **85**
Abington Pk. Cres. NN3: Abing 7J **85**
Abington Pk. Mus. **6H 85**
Abington Pl. NN1: N'ton ...4K **131** (1F **95**)
Abington Rd. NN17: Corby 6G **13**
NN18: Corby 6G **13**
Abington Sq. NN1: N'ton ...3K **131** (1E **94**)
Abington St. NN1: N'ton ...4J **131** (1E **94**)
(not continuous)
ABINGTON VALE **7K 85**
Ablett Cl. NN14: Thra 3H **51**
ABTHORPE .... **6H 113 (1C 141)**
Abthorpe Av. NN2: K'thpe 1E **84**
Abthorpe Rd. NN12: Silv 1G **121**
Accurate Boot, The *NN1: N'ton 7F* ***85***
(off Hood St.)
Ace La. NN7: Bug 2J **105**
ACHURCH **3C 135**
Acorn Cl. NN5: Dus 7F **83**
NN14: Isl 2F **51**
NN15: Bar S 5K **43**
Acorn Ind. Est. NN14: Isl 2F **51**
Acorn Pk. NN15: Bur L 1K **45**
Acorn Rd. NN5: Dus 7F **83**
Acorn Way NN12: Silv 2J **121**
Acre Cl. NN11: Dav 3H **59**
Acre Ct. *NN16: K'ing 6F* ***39***
(off Acre St.)
Acre La. NN2: K'thpe 1B **84**
Acremead PE8: Warm 2H **23**
Acre St. NN16: K'ing 6F **39**
Adam Bus. Cen. NN16: K'ing 5B **38**
Adams Av. NN1: N'ton 7G **85**
Adams Cl. NN8: Well 7C **66**
NN9: Stanw 7F **53**
Adams Dr. NN14: R'ell 6E **26**
Adams Rd. NN11: Woodf H 2C **108**
ADDERBURY **2A 140**
ADDINGTON **3D 141**
Addington Pk. Ind. Est.
NN14: L Add 5B **52**
Addington Rd. NN9: Irth ...2C **68** & 7A **52**
(not continuous)
NN14: Woodf 7B **50**
Addis Cl. NN15: Bur L 3K **45**
Addison Rd. NN3: N'ton 4H **85**
NN14: Des 2C **26**
Addlecroft Cl. NN2: K'thpe 3C **84**
Adelaide Ho. NN2: Sem 1G **131**
Adelaide Pl. NN1: N'ton ...5G **131** (2D **94**)
Adelaide St. NN2: Sem ...1H **131** (7D **84**)
Adelaide Ter. *NN2: N'ton 6D* ***84***
(off Barrack Rd.)
Adit Vw. NN9: Irth 4B **68**
Admiral Ct. *NN16: K'ing 6E* ***38***
(off Club St.)
Admirals Way NN11: Dav 7K **59**
Adnitt Rd. NN1: N'ton 7G **85**
NN10: R'den 3D **80**
ADSTOCK **2D 141**
ADSTONE **3B 136**
Afan Cl. NN16: K'ing 4C **38**
Affleck Bri. NN9: Fine 7H **47**
Aggate Way NN6: E Bart 4C **88**
Agnes Rd. NN2: Sem 6D **84**
AILSWORTH **2D 135**
Ainsdale Cl. NN2: N'ton 3G **85**
Aintree Dr. NN10: R'den 5G **81**
Aintree Rd. NN3: N'ton 2G **85**
NN18: L Oak 5K **17**
Akela Cl. NN15: K'ing 2E **42**
AKELEY **2D 141**
Alanbrooke Cl.
NN15: K'ing 1G **43**
Alastor NN8: Well 7G **65**
Albany, The *NN11: Dav 1H* ***61***
(off Primrose Hill)
Albany Gdns. NN18: Corby 4G **17**
Albany Rd. NN1: N'ton 7H **85**
Alberta Cl. NN18: Corby 3G **17**
Albert Pl. NN1: N'ton 4J **131** (1E **94**)
Albert Rd. NN8: Well 6C **66**
NN10: R'den 3E **80**
Albert St. NN16: K'ing 7E **38**
(not continuous)
Albion Ct. NN1: N'ton 5K **131**
NN9: L Harr 1H **65**
Albion Pl. NN1: N'ton 5J **131** (2E **94**)
NN10: R'den 4E **80**
Albion Rd. NN16: K'ing 6D **38**
Alchester Ct. NN12: Tow 3C **114**
Alcombe Rd. NN1: N'ton ...3K **131** (7E **84**)
Alcombe Ter. NN1: N'ton ...2K **131** (7F **85**)
ALCONBURY **1D 139**
ALCONBURY WESTON **1D 139**
Aldbury Ct. NN1: N'ton 2G **131**
Alder Cl. NN14: Des 2F **27**
Alder Ct. NN3: N'ton 1C **86**
Alderley Cl. NN5: Dus 6G **83**
ALDERTON **1D 141**
ALDGATE **1B 134**
Aldsworth Cl. NN8: Well 5K **77**
Aldwell Cl. NN4: Woot 1G **101**
ALDWINCLE .... **6B 20 (3C 135)**
Aldwincle Rd. NN14: Low 6D **48**
Alexander Ct. NN3: N'ton 3B **86**
NN17: Corby 3B **14**
NN29: Irch 5J **79**
Alexander Pl. NN9: Irth 7A **52**
Alexander Rd. NN9: Irth 7A **52**
Alexandra Rd.
NN1: N'ton 4K **131** (1F **95**)
NN8: Well 6C **66**
NN10: R'den 2G **81**
NN14: Des 2C **26**
NN17: Corby 7K **13**
Alexandra St. NN15: Bur L 3J **45**
NN16: K'ing 7E **38**
Alexandra Ter. NN2: K'thpe 3D **84**
Alfoxden NN8: Well 2G **77**
Alfred East Art Gallery, The **1D 42**
Alfred Knight Cl. NN5: Dus 7H **83**
Alfred St. NN1: N'ton 1G **95**
NN9: Stanw 1J **69**
NN10: R'den 3E **80**
NN16: K'ing 7E **38**
NN29: Irch 5H **79**
Alibone Cl. NN3: Moul 4A **74**
Alice Cl. NN6: Crick 3H **31**
Alice Dr. NN15: Bur L 3J **45**
Alice Gdns. NN16: K'ing 6F **39**
Alington Cl. NN9: Fine 6J **47**
Alken Cl. NN8: Well 4A **66**
ALKERTON **1A 140**
Allan Bank NN8: Well 2G **77**
Allard Cl. NN3: N'ton 1G **87**
Allebone Rd. NN6: E Bart 3D **88**
Alledge Dr. NN14: Woodf 6B **50**
Allen Ct. NN9: Fine 6J **47**
Allen Rd. NN1: N'ton 7G **85**
NN9: Fine 6J **47**
NN9: Irth 3B **68**
NN10: R'den 2F **81**
Allens Ga. NN13: B'ley 4E **128**
Allens Hill NN29: Boz 2H **103**
Allens Orchard OX17: Chip W 3D **110**
ALLEXTON **1A 134**
Alley Yd. NN1: N'ton 4H **131** (1D **94**)
Alliance Ter. NN8: Well 7B **66**
Alliston Gdns.
NN2: Sem 1G **131** (7D **84**)
All Saints Ter. *LE16: Wilb 5H* ***11***
(off Carlton Rd.)
Alma St. NN5: N'ton 1B **94**
NN8: Well 7B **66**
Almond Cl. CV23: Bar 2C **54**
NN7: Bug 2K **105**
Almond Gro. NN3: N'ton 5K **85**
Almond Rd. NN16: K'ing 5F **39**
Alness Cl. NN15: K'ing 2G **43**
Alpha Ct. NN17: Corby 3C **14**
Alpha Ho. NN1: N'ton 3G **131**
Alpine Rd. NN10: R'den 3C **80**
Alpine Way NN5: Dus 3F **83**
Alsace Cl. NN5: Dus 5E **82**
Altendiez Way NN15: Bur L 6J **43**
Althorp Cl. NN8: Well 5H **65**
Althorpe Pl. NN16: K'ing 6F **39**
Althorp **6A 70**
Althorp Pk. **6B 70**
Althorp Pl. NN18: Corby 3G **17**
Althorp Rd. NN5: N'ton 1B **94**
Althorp St. NN1: N'ton ...3G **131** (1D **94**)
Alton St. NN4: Far C 4C **94**
Alvert Rd. NN9: Fine 6H **47**
Alvis Ct. NN3: N'ton 2F **87**
Alvis Way NN11: Dav 7E **58**
ALWALTON **2D 135**
Alwyn Wlk. NN3: N'ton 7F **75**
Amber Dr. NN6: Wal 1H **37**
Amberley Rd. NN7: Hart 6G **117**
Ambidge Ct. *NN1: N'ton 1G* ***95***
(off South St.)
Ambleside Cl. NN3: N'ton 2K **85**
NN8: Well 7H **65**
Ambridge Cl. NN4: N'ton 7A **94**
AMBROSDEN **3C 141**
Ambush St. NN5: N'ton 1C **94**
Amen Cnr. NN14: L Add 4B **52**
Amen Pl. NN14: L Add 4B **52**
AMF Bowling
Northampton **3C 78**
Amundsen Cl. NN11: Dav 5G **59**
Anchor Dr. NN2: K'thpe 7C **72**
Anderson Dr. NN15: K'ing 1H **43**
Anderson Grn. NN8: Well 1H **77**
Andrew Cl. NN10: High F 5F **69**
Andrews Av. NN13: Crou 7C **130**
Andrews Ct. NN6: Brix 3H **35**
Andrews Way NN9: Raun 7G **53**
Angel La. NN8: Well 1B **78**
Angel St. NN1: N'ton 5H **131** (2D **94**)
Angel Yd. NN16: K'ing 7D **38**
Anglian Rd. NN11: Dav 2G **61**
Anglia Way NN3: Moul P 1G **85**
Angus Ho. *NN17: Corby 7A* ***14***
(off Argyll St.)
Anjou Ct. NN5: New D 4E **82**
Annandale Rd. NN17: Corby 6K **13**
Anna's La. NN12: Dals 5K **105**
Anne Cl. NN10: High F 5F **69**
Anne Rd. NN8: Well 3K **77**
Annesley Cl. NN3: N'ton 1A **96**
Anne St. NN17: Corby 1K **17**
Ann Sq. NN16: K'ing 6G **39**
(not continuous)
Anscomb Way NN11: Woodf H ...2C **108**
Ansell Way NN4: H'stone 7F **95**
Anson Cl. NN11: Dav 2J **61**
NN17: Corby 6G **13**
ANSTEY **1B 132**
ANSTY **3A 132**
ANTELOPE HILL **4G 129**
Antona Cl. NN9: Raun 7G **53**
Antona Dr. NN9: Raun 7G **53**
Antona Gdns. NN9: Raun 7G **53**
Anvil, The NN7: Bug 2J **105**
APETHORPE **2C 135**
Apethorpe Rd. PE8: Nass 4F **7**
Apollo Cl. NN11: Dav 7G **59**
Applebarn Cl. NN4: Col 4D **100**
Appleby Cl. NN9: Well 3A **66**
Appleby Wlk. NN3: N'ton 2K **85**
Appledore Cl. NN2: K'thpe 1D **84**
Applegarth, The NN6: Long B 1J **55**
Applegarth Cl. NN18: Corby 4J **17**
Appleton Gdns. NN17: Gret 7D **8**
APPLETREE .... **1A 110 (1A 140)**
Appletree Ct. NN9: Fine 6H **47**
Appletree La. NN11: Ast W 7D **106**
Appletree Rd. OX17: Chip W 3D **110**
Approach, The NN5: N'ton 1A **94**
Aquitaine Cl. NN5: Dus 5E **82**
Arbour Ct. NN3: N'ton 2B **86**
ARBOURS, THE **3J 85**
Arbour Vw. Ct. NN3: N'ton 1B **86**
Arbour Wlk. NN3: N'ton 1B **86**
Arbury Banks OX17: Chip W 3D **110**
Archangel Rd. NN4: N'ton 5K **93**
Archangel Sq. NN4: N'ton 5A **94**
Archer Av. NN11: Braun 1B **58**
Archers Cl. NN2: K'thpe 1B **84**
Archery Rd. OX17: Mid C 5D **118**
Archfield NN8: Well 1A **78**
Archfield Ter. *NN9: Irth 2C* ***68***
(off Lilley Ter.)
Arden Cl. NN11: Dav 6G **59**
NN15: Bar S 5H **43**
NN18: Corby 3D **18**
Ardens Gro. NN7: Roth 1F **99**
Ardington Rd. NN1: N'ton 7H **85**
ARDLEY **3B 140**
Argyle St. NN5: N'ton 1B **94**
Argyll Ho. *NN17: Corby 7K* ***13***
(off Argyll St.)
Argyll St. NN15: K'ing 2D **42**
NN17: Corby 7K **13**
Ariel Cl. NN5: Dus 5F **83**
Ark Farm Sheep Dairy **3D 137**
Arkwright Rd. NN17: Corby 4D **14**
NN29: Irch 5J **79**
Arlbury Rd. NN3: N'ton 2D **86**
ARLESCOTE **1A 140**
Armley Cl. NN6: Long B 1J **55**
ARMSTON **3C 135**
Armston Rd. PE8: Barn 4B **22**
Arndale NN2: K'thpe 1A **84**
ARNESBY **2C 133**
Arnhill Rd. NN17: Gret 7B **8**
Arnills Way CV23: Kil 7C **30**
Arnold Rd. NN2: Sem 6D **84**
Arnsby Cres. NN3: Moul 4J **73**
Arnsley Rd. NN17: Corby 4G **15**
Arnull Cres. NN11: Dav 6G **59**
Arran Way NN17: Corby 5H **13**
Arrow Cl. OX17: Mid C 5D **118**
Arrow Head Rd. NN4: N'ton 4A **94**
ARTHINGWORTH **3D 133**

Arthingworth Rd. NN14: Des 2A 26
Arthur St. NN2: N'ton 5D 84
  NN8: Well 1K 77
Arthur's Way NN16: K'ing 7E 38
Arthur Ter. NN2: N'ton 5D 84
Artizan Rd. NN1: N'ton 7G 85
Arum Cl. NN10: R'den 6F 81
Arundel Cl. NN14: Thra 3K 51
  OX17: King S 1B 126
Arundel Ct. NN10: R'den 5D 80
  NN15: K'ing 2H 43
Arundel St. NN1: N'ton 2G 131 (7D 84)
Arundel Wlk. NN18: Corby 1G 17
Ascot Cl. NN8: Gt Oak 5K 17
Ascot Rd. NN10: R'den 5G 81
Ashbourne Dr. NN14: Des 1B 26
Ashbrook Cl. NN1: Brou 6G 41
Ashbrow Rd. NN4: N'ton 4A 94
Ashburnham Rd. NN1: N'ton 6G 85
Ashby Cl. NN8: Well 5J 65
  NN15: Bur L 3K 45
Ashby Ct. NN3: Moul 4K 73
  NN5: Upton 3J 93
    (off Clickers M.)
  NN6: Guil .6D 32
  NN7: Kisl .4C 92
Ashby Dr. NN6: Crick 5H 31
  NN10: R'den 5D 80
Ashby Folville **1D 133**
Ashby Gdns. *NN3: Moul* 4K 73
    (off Ashby Ct.)
Ashby Magna **2B 132**
Ashby Pk. NN11: Dav 6H 59
Ashby Parva **3B 132**
Ashby Rd. CV23: Kil 7C 30
  NN11: Braun 1B 58
  NN11: Dav 2G 59
    (not continuous)
  NN11: Welt 1J 59
Ashby St Ledgars **2B 136**
Ashby Wood Dr. NN5: Upton 3H 93
Ashby Wood M. NN5: Upton 3H 93
Ash Cl. NN11: Dav 6H 59
  NN29: Irch 6H 79
Ash Ct. NN14: Thra 4H 51
Ashcroft Cl. NN5: Dus 5G 83
Ashcroft Gdns. NN3: N'ton 4H 85
Ashdale Cl. NN6: Syw 4G 75
Ashdown Cl. NN15: Bar S 5J 43
Ashdown Pl. NN17: Corby 6K 13
Ashdown Rd. NN11: Dav 4G 59
Ash Dr. NN6: Syw 6G 75
  NN13: B'ley 2G 129
Ashes, The NN4: Woot 2J 101
  NN7: Bug .2J 105
  NN17: Weld 5K 15
Ashfield Av. NN9: Raun 6H 53
Ashfield Ri. NN9: Raun 6H 53
Ashfield Rd. NN8: Well 1K 77
Ashford Cl. NN3: N'ton 1K 95
Ashford Lea NN14: Des 1B 26
Ash Gro. NN2: K'thpe 7C 72
  NN7: Bug .2J 105
  NN14: Des 1B 26
Ashlade OX17: Mid C 7E 118
Ash La. NN4: Col 4C 100
Ashlar NN5: Upton 7F 83
Ashleigh Cl. CV23: Bar 1C 54
Ashley . . . .**3G 11 (2D 133)**
Ashley Av. NN17: Corby 6G 13
Ashley Cl. NN3: Moul 4B 74
Ashley Ct. NN7: Blis 2H 115
  NN16: K'ing 6C 38
Ashley La. NN3: Moul 4A 74
Ashley Rd. LE16: Med 1G 11
  LE16: Mid 3A 12
  LE16: Stoke A 4F 11
  LE16: West W 2D 10
Ashley Way NN3: N'ton 4A 86
Ashmead NN3: N'ton 4D 86
Ashmore NN6: Long B 1J 55
Ashpole Spinney NN4: N'ton 5H 93
Ashridge Cl. NN10: R'den 5D 80
Ash Ri. NN2: K'thpe 6D 72
Ash Rd. NN15: K'ing 1F 43
Ash St. NN1: N'ton 2H 131 (7D 84)
Ashton
  Barnack **1D 135**
  Oundle . . . .**1B 22 (3C 135)**
  Roade **1D 141**
Ashton Cl. NN11: Dav 7F 59
Ashton Gro. NN8: Well 4J 65
Ashton Rd. NN7: Hart 6G 117
  NN7: Roa 3C 116
  PE8: Oun .5J 21
Ashtree Gdns. PE9: Colly 6C 6
Ashtree Way NN5: Dus 7H 83
Ashurst Cres. NN18: Corby 1G 17
Ash Way NN11: Braun 1A 58
Ashway, The NN6: Brix 3J 35
Ashwell Rd. NN10: R'den 3G 81
Ashwells La. NN6: Yel 5C 28
Ashwin Cl. NN13: B'ley 2F 129

Ashwood Rd. NN5: Dus 7H 83
Ashworth Cl. NN6: Crick 3J 31
Ashworth St. NN11: Dav 2H 61
Askham Av. NN8: Well 4K 77
Aspen Cl. NN3: N'ton 1F 87
  NN10: R'den 2E 80
Aspen Ho. *NN15: K'ing* *1C 42*
    (off Station Rd.)
Astbury Cl. NN11: Dav 3H 61
Astbury Ter. NN11: Dav 3J 61
Astcote . . . .**7J 105 (3C 137)**
Astcote La. NN12: Shut 5A 116
Aster Cl. NN3: N'ton 1K 95
Aster Rd. NN16: K'ing 5F 39
Aston Abbotts **3D 141**
Aston Flamville **2A 132**
Aston Le Walls . . . .**7E 106 (3A 136)**
Aston Ri. NN5: Dus 6G 83
Astrop . . . .**1C 126 (2B 140)**
Astrop Gdns. OX17: King S 1C 126
Astrop Grange OX17: King S 1C 126
Astrop Rd. OX17: King S 1B 126
  OX17: Mid C 7C 118
Astwell Rd. NN12: Weed L 3C 112
Astwood **3B 138**
Athelstan Rd. NN16: K'ing 6F 39
Atterbury Cl. NN6: W Had 5H 29
Atterbury Way NN4: Gt Hou 5C 96
Attleborough **2A 132**
Attlee Cl. NN3: N'ton 2J 85
Attley Cl. NN8: Well 7H 65
Attley Way NN9: Irth 1D 68
Auckland Cl. NN2: K'thpe 4E 84
Auctioneers Ct.
  NN1: N'ton 7J 131 (3E 94)
Auctioneers Way
  NN1: N'ton 7J 131 (3E 94)
Auden Way NN17: Corby 5H 13
Augusta Av. NN4: N'ton 2C 100
Austin Cl. NN29: Irch 5K 79
Austins Pl. NN12: Silv 3J 121
Austin St. NN1: N'ton 1K 131 (7E 84)
Austins Yd. NN6: E Bart 2D 88
Austin Way NN11: Dav 7E 58
Avalon Ct. NN14: R'ell 6H 27
Avebury Way NN4: N'ton 7C 94
Avenue, The NN1: N'ton 2G 95
  NN2: K'thpe 7A 72
  NN3: Moul 5B 74
  NN3: Spin H 3H 85
  NN5: Dall .7A 84
  NN6: Over .5B 74
  NN7: Flore 2F 63
  NN8: Well .6B 66
  NN9: Stanw 1K 69
  NN14: R'ell 6G 27
  OX17: Mid C 6D 118
Avenue Bernard
  NN13: B'ley 3F 129
Avenue Cl. NN9: Fine 6G 47
Avenue Rd. NN8: Well 7B 66
  NN9: Fine .6G 47
  NN10: R'den 7J 81
Avenue Ter. NN16: K'ing 6G 39
Aviemore Gdns. NN4: N'ton 6K 93
Avignon Cl. NN5: New D 4F 83
Avonbury Ct. NN13: B'ley 6H 129
Avon Cl. NN8: Well 6H 65
  NN11: Dav 3F 61
  NN16: K'ing 4C 38
Avondale Cl. NN14: Thra 4H 51
Avondale M. NN16: K'ing 6F 39
Avondale Rd. NN16: K'ing 5C 80
Avon Dassett **3A 136**
Avon Dr. NN5: N'ton 5K 83
Avon Flds. NN6: Welf 2H 29
Axe Head Rd. NN4: N'ton 3A 94
Aylestone **1B 132**
Aynho . . . .**7E 126 (2B 140)**
Aynho Cl. OX17: Ayn 7F 127
Aynho Cres. NN2: K'thpe 1D 84
Aynhoe Pk. OX17: Ayn 7E 126
Aynho Rd. OX17: Add 4A 126
Aynho Wlk. NN2: K'thpe 1E 84
Aynsley Cl. NN14: Des 2C 26
Ayr Cl. NN18: Gt Oak 5J 17
Ayston **1A 134**
Azalea Cl. NN3: N'ton 1A 96

B

Babbage Cres. NN17: Corby 4A 14
Back La. LE16: E Far 2J 25
  NN4: H'stone 7G 95
  NN6: Chap B 4J 71
  NN6: Holc .6H 37
  NN6: Scal .7A 36
    (not continuous)
  NN7: Gt Bri 2H 57
  NN7: G'ton 6D 98
  NN14: Brig 1D 20
  NN14: L Add 4A 52

Back La. NN14: Rin 1F 53
  PE9: Colly .6B 6
Backley La. NN15: K'ing 2A 42
Backway NN29: Woll 4E 90
Bacon Rd. NN8: Well 4A 66
Badby . . . .**5C 104 (3B 136)**
Badby Cl. NN2: K'thpe 2F 85
Badby La. NN11: Stav 5B 60
Badby Pk. NN11: Dav 5F 59
Badby Rd. NN11: Dav 3G 61
  NN11: Newn 7J 61
Badby Rd. W. NN11: Dav 4F 61
    (not continuous)
Baden Powell Cres. NN12: Tow 5C 114
Badger La. NN4: Gra P 5G 101
Badgers Cl. NN7: Bug 2J 105
Badgers La. NN14: Maw 5C 40
Badgers Wlk. NN2: K'thpe 1C 84
Baffin Cl. NN14: R'ell 4F 51
Baggrave **1C 133**
Baginton **1A 136**
Bag La. NN29: Boz 2H 103
Bagworth **1A 132**
Bailey Brooks Cl. NN7: Roa 2B 116
Bailey Brooks La. NN7: Roa 1B 116
Bailey Ct. NN10: High F 7E 68
Bailey Wills Bldg., The
  NN1: N'ton *7F 85*
    (off Market St.)
Bailiff St. NN1: N'ton 2H 131 (7D 84)
Baines Cl. NN12: Silv 3J 121
Baines Way NN4: Gra P 5F 101
Bainton
  Oxfordshire **3B 140**
  Peterborough **1C 135**
Baird Av. NN5: Upton 3J 93
Baird Cl. NN11: Dav 5G 59
Baird Ct. NN8: Well 6G 65
Baird Rd. NN17: Corby 4E 14
Bairstow Rd. NN12: Tow 4C 114
Bakehouse Hill NN14: Ged 5C 46
  NN14: L Add 4A 52
Bakehouse La. NN6: Mears A 3A 76
  NN15: Bur L 1K 45
Bakehouse M. NN14: Brou 5H 41
Bakehouse Ri. NN6: Nas 3H 33
Baker Av. NN6: Brou 7G 41
Baker Cl. NN14: Thra 4H 51
Baker Cres. NN29: Irch 5H 79
Bakers Ct. NN9: Raun 6J 53
  NN14: Isl 3F 51
Bakers La. NN6: Spra 5C 34
  NN6: Wal .2H 37
  NN11: Nor .7G 55
  NN12: Stoke B 6D 116
  NN12: Shut 6A 116
  NN14: Woodf 7B 50
  NN17: Weld 7A 16
Baker St. NN2: Sem 6D 84
  NN7: G'ton 6D 98
  NN8: Well .7B 66
  NN9: Irth 3B 68
  NN13: F'hoe 6G 119
Bakewell Cl. NN4: N'ton 7A 94
Balcombe Pl. NN18: Corby 1F 17
Balding Cl. CV23: Bar 2C 54
Baldwin Cl. NN3: N'ton 2J 85
Baler Cl. NN11: Dav 4H 59
Balfour Cl. NN2: N'ton 5D 84
Balfour Dr. NN14: R'ell 6H 27
Balfour Rd. NN2: N'ton 5D 84
Balfour St. NN16: K'ing 5E 38
Balham Cl. NN10: R'den 5C 80
Balland Way NN4: Woot 1G 101
Ballantyne Rd. NN10: R'den 4D 80
Balliol Rd. NN11: Dav 3G 61
  NN13: B'ley 3E 128
Balmoral Av. NN10: R'den 2F 81
Balmoral Cl. NN6: E Bart 3E 88
  NN8: Well .4K 77
  NN12: Tow 4B 114
Balmoral Ct. NN15: K'ing 5E 42
Balmoral Dr. NN13: B'ley 4F 129
Balmoral Ho. *NN2: K'thpe* *5D 84*
    (off Queen's Pk. Pde.)
Balmoral Rd. NN2: K'thpe 5D 84
Balmoral Way OX17: King S 1B 126
Balscote **1A 140**
Baltic Cl. NN18: Corby 3F 17
Bamburg Cl. NN18: Corby 5F 17
Bampton Ct. NN18: Corby 5H 17
Banbury **1A 140**
Banbury Bus. Pk. OX17: Add 3A 126
Banbury Cl. NN4: N'ton 5J 93
  NN8: Well .4K 77
Banbury La. NN4: N'ton 5J 93
  NN7: Roth .2E 98
  NN11: Byf .7H 57
  NN11: Mor P 1A 112
  NN12: Col H, Fos B 7F 105
  NN12: Pat, Roth 5A 105
  OX17: Ban, Mid C 6A 118

Banbury La. OX17: Cul 7B 110
    (not continuous)
  OX17: King S 1B 126
Banbury Rd. NN7: Kisl 3C 92
  NN11: Lwr B 4B 106
  NN11: Mor P 4G 111
  NN12: Lit 3G 109
  NN13: B'ley 4E 128
  OX17: Ayn 7D 126
  OX17: Chac 2A 118
  OX17: Chip W 4C 110
Bancroft Cl. NN4: Woot 2G 101
Bancroft Rd. LE16: Cotti 4C 12
Bancroft Way NN4: Woot 2H 101
Bangrave Rd. NN17: Corby, Weld 5G 15
Bangrave Rd. Sth. NN17: Weld 1F 19
Bank, The *NN1: N'ton* *1F 95*
    (off Pytchley St.)
Bankhill Vw. NN9: L Harr 1H 65
Banks, The CV23: Kil 7C 30
  NN6: Long B 1H 55
  NN7: Hack 1G 117
  NN9: Well .3A 66
  NN14: Brou 5H 41
Bankside NN2: N'ton 3G 85
  NN10: High F 5E 68
  NN11: Woodf H 2D 108
  NN18: Corby 3J 17
Banks La. NN5: Dus 1C 100
Banner Cl. NN10: R'den 4D 80
Banner St. NN13: B'ley 4E 128
Bants La. NN5: Dus 7J 83
    (not continuous)
Baptists Cl. NN7: Bug 1J 105
Barby . . . .**2C 54 (1B 136)**
Barby La. CV23: Bar 1C 54
Barby Nortoft . . . .**3B 30 (1B 136)**
Barby Rd. CV23: Bar, Kil 6A 30
  NN11: Braun 1B 58
Bardon **1A 132**
Bardsley Rd. NN17: Corby 2K 13
Barford St John **2A 140**
Barford St Michael **2A 140**
Barham **1D 139**
Barholm **1C 135**
Baring Rd. NN5: N'ton 7B 84
Barkby **1C 133**
Barker Cl. NN10: R'den 3E 80
Barker Rd. NN6: E Bart 3D 88
Barksdale Av. NN13: Crou 6C 130
Barlestone **1A 132**
Barley Cl. NN7: Hart 5J 117
  NN11: Dav 4H 59
Barley Ct. NN10: R'den 4F 81
Barley Cft. NN6: Crick 3H 31
Barley Dr. NN15: Bur L 2K 45
Barley La. NN2: K'thpe 1C 84
Barleythorpe **1A 134**
Barlow Cl. NN14: R'ell 6E 26
Barlow Ct. NN15: Bur L 3J 45
Barlow La. NN3: Moul 4K 73
Barlows La. LE16: Wilb 5H 11
Barnack **1C 135**
Barnacle **3A 132**
Barn Acre NN6: E Had 2C 56
Barnard NN18: Corby 3H 17
Barnard Cl. NN5: Dus 6G 83
Barnard Gdns. LE16: Mkt H 1K 95
Barnard's Way NN14: Brig 3E 20
Barn Cl. NN4: Gra P 5G 101
  NN18: Gt Oak 5A 18
Barn Cnr. NN4: Col 4D 100
Barn Ct. NN9: L Harr . . . . . .7D 44 & 1H 65
Barnes Cl. NN6: Old 5D 36
  NN11: Dav 3D 42
  NN15: K'ing 3D 42
Barneswell Cl. NN6: Brix 3H 35
Barnet Cl. NN4: N'ton 5B 94
Barnet's Stile NN2: K'thpe 3D 84
Barnett Cres. NN11: Woodf H 2C 108
Barnett Rd. OX17: Mid C 6C 118
Barnfield Cl. NN2: K'thpe 2C 84
Barnhill Sq. NN3: N'ton 7D 74
Barn La. NN7: Mil M 5A 100
Barn M. NN4: Col 4D 100
Barn Owl Cl. NN4: N'ton 7B 94
Barnsley Sq. NN18: Corby 1H 17
Barnstaple Cl. NN3: N'ton 7B 86
Barnstones Bus. Pk.
  NN12: Grim 4K 109
Barn Way NN5: Dus 3G 83
Barnwell . . . .**6C 22 (3C 135)**
Barnwell All Saints **7C 22**
Barnwell Cl. NN14: Thra 3J 51
Barnwell Country Pk. **7H 21**
Barnwell Country Pk. Vis. Cen. . . .**7H 21**
Barnwell Ct. NN14: Maw 6C 40
Barnwell Dr. NN10: R'den 5D 80
Barnwell Gdns. NN8: Well 5J 65

Barnwell Rd. NN2: K'thpe 2E 84
  NN8: Well 5J 65
  PE8: Oun 6H 21
BARNWELL ST ANDREW 6B 22
Barnwell St. NN16: K'ing 6F 39
Baron Av. NN6: E Bart 1E 88
  NN16: K'ing 6A 38
Baron Ct. NN17: Corby 4F 15
Baronson Gdns. NN1: N'ton 6G 85
Barons Way NN2: K'thpe 2B 84
Barrack Rd. NN1: N'ton 2H 131 (7D 84)
  NN2: N'ton 2H 131 (7D 84)
Barracks, The NN7: Braf G 5H 97
Barret Cl. NN8: Well 1H 77
Barrett Cl. NN10: High F 7E 68
Barringers Ct. NN29: Irch 4J 79
Barringers Gdns. NN29: Irch 4J 79
Barring M. NN5: Upton 2H 93
Barring St. NN5: Upton 2H 93
Barrington Ct. NN13: B'ley 6G 129
Barrington Rd. NN10: R'den 5F 81
Barron Cl. NN15: K'ing 4E 42
BARROWDEN 1B 134
Barry Rd. NN1: N'ton 7H 85
BARSBY 1C 133
Barth Cl. NN18: Gt Oak 4G 17
Bartholomew Gdns. NN12: Blak 5J 109
Bartlett Cl. NN13: B'ley 4E 128
Bartley Dr. NN16: K'ing 5B 38
Barton Cl. OX17: King S 1B 126
Barton Flds. NN6: Ect 3J 87
BARTON HARTSHORN 2C 141
Barton Holme NN12: Blak 5H 109
BARTON IN THE BEANS 1A 132
Barton Rd. NN15: Bar S, K'ing 3F 43
Bartons Cl., The NN5: Dall 5A 84
BARTON SEAGRAVE 1J 43 (1A 138)
Barton Sq. NN18: Corby 7G 13
BARWELL 2A 132
Barwick Ho. NN10: R'den 3D 80
BASCOTE 2A 136
Basil La. NN4: N'ton 2E 100
Basset Lowe Dr. NN5: Upton 3H 93
Bassett Ct. NN4: Gra P 6E 100
Bassett Ford Rd. PE8: Oun 6J 21
Bassett Lowe Hall NN2: N'ton 6E 84
Bassett Lowe Ho. NN1: N'ton 5J 131
Bassett Pl. PE8: Oun 6J 21
Bassett's Ct. NN8: Well 1A 78
Bassett Way LE16: Clip 6D 24
Bates Av. NN14: Rin 1G 53
Bates Ct. NN10: High F 7E 68
Bath La. NN16: K'ing 6E 38
Bath Rd. NN16: K'ing 6E 38
Batsmans Dr. NN10: R'den 1D 80
Battalion Dr. NN4: Woot 1F 101
Battle Cl. NN4: Woot 1E 100
  NN14: C'ord 3G 47
Baukewell Ct. NN3: N'ton 3B 86
Baulks La. NN14: Ald 6B 20
Baulmsholme Cl. NN4: N'ton 3D 94
Baunhill Cl. NN3: N'ton 7A 86
Baxter Ct. NN4: H'stone 7G 95
Baxters La. PE9: Eas H 2C 6
Bayard Brow NN13: B'ley 3F 129
Bayes St. NN16: K'ing 6C 38
BAYNARD'S GREEN 3B 140
Baysdale Av. NN17: Corby 7K 13
BEACHAMPTON 2D 141
Beacon Bingo
  Northampton 1A 94
Beacon Ct. NN4: N'ton 4K 93
Beaconsfield Pl. NN10: R'den 2E 80
Beaconsfield Ter.
  NN1: N'ton 1J 131 (7E 84)
  NN10: R'den 2E 80
Beanfield Av. NN18: Corby 7G 13
Bean Furlong OX17: Chac 2B 118
Beardsley Ct. NN18: Corby 2J 17
Beardsley Gdns. NN15: Bar S 3J 43
Bear Way NN14: Des 1C 26
Beatrice Rd. NN16: K'ing 4D 38
Beatty Cl. NN11: Dav 2K 61
Beatty Gdns. NN17: Corby 6G 13
Beaufort Dr. NN5: Dus 5H 83
  NN15: Bar S 4J 43
Beauly Ct. NN15: K'ing 2G 43
Beaumaris Cl. NN10: R'den 4F 81
Beaumont Cl. NN16: K'ing 3D 38
Beaumont Cres. NN13: B'ley 4F 129
Beaumont Dr. NN3: N'ton 3E 86
BEAUMONT LEYS 1B 132
Beaune Cl. NN5: Dus 5E 82
Beauvais Ct. NN5: Dus 4E 82
Beaver Cen., The
  NN11: Woodf H 1D 108
Beck Ct. NN8: Well 6J 65
Becket's Vw. NN1: N'ton 2F 95
Beckett Ho. NN1: N'ton 1F 95
Becketts Cl. NN11: Byf 2J 107
Becket Way NN3: N'ton 1J 85
Bective Rd. NN2: K'thpe 2D 84
Bective Vw. NN2: K'thpe 2E 84

Bedale Rd. NN8: Well 6B 66
Beddoes Cl. NN4: Woot 2H 101
Bede Cl. NN10: High F 7F 69
  NN18: Corby 5F 17
BEDFORD 3C 139
Bedford Cl. NN15: Bar S 5H 43
Bedford Mans. NN1: N'ton 5K 131
Bedford Pl. NN1: N'ton 5K 131 (2E 94)
Bedford Rd. NN1: N'ton 6K 131 (2F 95)
  NN4: N'ton 3H 95
  NN7: D'ton 6B 102
  NN7: L Hou, Braf G 4C 96
  NN10: R'den 4F 81
Bedford Rd. E. NN7: Yar H 6H 103
Bedford Rd. W. NN7: Yar H 6G 103
BEDWORTH 3A 132
BEEBY 1C 133
Beech Av. NN3: Spin H, N'ton 4H 85
  NN6: Ect 2J 87
Beech Cl. NN7: Bug 2J 105
  NN7: Hack 1H 117
  NN12: Tow 5C 114
  NN14: Des 2D 26
  NN17: Corby 4K 13
Beech Ct. NN14: Thra 3H 51
Beech Cres. NN15: K'ing 1F 43
  NN29: Irch 6H 79
Beechcroft Gdns. NN3: N'ton 4H 85
Beech Dr. NN8: Well 7K 65
  NN11: Woodf H 2B 108
  NN13: B'ley 2F 129
Beeches, The MK19: Dean 6F 125
  NN12: Pat 5H 105
Beeches Ct. LE16: Sibb 2C 24
Beech Gro. NN3: N'ton 1A 86
  NN10: R'den 2C 80
Beech Hill NN11: Hell 2C 104
Beech Ho. Dr. NN12: Pot 6J 123
Beech La. NN7: Kisl 3D 92
Beech Rd. NN10: R'den 1E 80
Beechwood Dr. NN3: N'ton 5B 86
Beechwood Rd. NN5: Dus 7H 83
BEESTON 3D 139
Beeston Av. NN3: N'ton 6C 86
Beeston Pl. NN18: Corby 1H 17
Belfield Cl. NN3: N'ton 3J 85
Belfry La. NN4: Col 3C 100
Belfry Way NN11: Dav 1K 61
Belgrade Cen. NN8: Well 3B 78
Belgrave Cl. NN15: Bar S 5J 43
Belgrave Ho. NN1: N'ton 4H 131 (1D 94)
Bellamy Rd. PE8: Oun 3H 21
Bell Cl. NN13: Helm 2B 120
Bell Ct. NN8: Well 7B 66
  NN18: Corby 2J 17
Belle Baulk NN12: Tow 3A 114
Bell End NN29: Woll 4E 90
Bellfoundry La. NN16: K'ing 7D 38
    (off Wadcroft)
Bell Hill NN9: Fine 7G 47
  NN14: R'ell 6G 27
BELLINGE 4E 86
Bell La. NN11: Byf 2H 107
  NN13: Syre 5C 120
Bellman Ga. NN6: Syw 1G 75
Bellropes Sq. NN3: N'ton 4G 87
Bells Cl. NN14: Brig 1C 20
Bell St. NN8: Well 7B 66
Bell Vw. OX17: Char 1H 127
Bellway Cl. NN16: K'ing 6C 38
Bell Yd. PE9: Colly 6C 6
BELMESTHORPE 1C 135
Belmont Cl. NN1: N'ton 2G 131
Belmont Gdns. NN9: Raun 6H 53
Belmont Rd. NN11: Dav 2G 61
Belstead Rd. NN16: K'ing 1A 96
Belton Cl. NN4: N'ton 7D 94
BELTON-IN-RUTLAND 1A 134
Belvedere Cl. NN5: Dall 7A 84
Belvedere Rd. NN15: K'ing 1E 42
Belvoir Cl. NN5: Dus 5G 83
  NN10: R'den 5F 81
  NN17: Corby 4K 17
Belvoir Dr. NN15: Bar S 5J 43
Bembridge Dr. NN2: K'thpe 5C 84
Benbow Cl. NN11: Dav 1K 61
Benedict Cl. NN10: R'den 5C 80
Benefield Rd. NN14: Brig 2D 20
  PE8: Oun 5F 21
BENGAL 2H 113
Bengal La. NN12: Greens N 1H 113
Bengal Vw. NN12: Greens N 1J 113
Bengeworth Ct. NN8: Well 7B 66
Benham Ct. NN3: N'ton 3C 86
Benham Sports Arena 7G 73
Benjamin Sq. NN4: N'ton 5A 94
Bennett Cl. NN11: Dav 6F 59
  OX17: Chac 2B 118
Bennett Rd. NN18: Gt Oak 5J 17
Bentley Cl. NN3: N'ton 2G 87
Bentley St. NN8: Well 3C 66
Bentley Wlk. NN18: Corby 2H 17

Bentley Way NN11: Dav 7E 58
Bergen Wlk. NN18: Corby 4F 17
Bergerac Cl. NN5: New D 4E 82
Berkeley Cl. NN1: N'ton 1G 95
Berkeley Ho. NN1: N'ton 4G 131
Berkeley St. LE16: Sibb 2C 24
Berneshaw Cl. NN18: Corby 3J 17
Bern Links NN4: N'ton 4B 94
Bern Side NN4: N'ton 4B 94
Berrill St. NN29: Irch 6H 79
Berrister Pl. NN9: Raun 5K 53
Berry Cl. NN6: E Bart 1D 88
  NN7: Hack 1H 117
  NN7: Roth 2G 99
Berrydale NN3: N'ton 2G 87
Berryfield NN6: Long B 1J 55
Berryfield Rd. LE16: Cotti 4B 12
Berry Grn. Rd. NN9: Fine 6G 47
Berry La. NN4: Woot 3E 100
  NN11: Hell 2B 104
Berrymoor Cl. NN8: Well 3K 77
Berrymoor Rd. NN8: Well 4K 77
Berry Rd. LE16: Cotti 4B 12
Berrystead PE8: Oun 5J 21
Berrywood Dr. NN5: Dus 7F 83
Berrywood Dr. NN5: Dus 7E 82
Berrywood Rd. NN5: Dus 6E 82
Bertha Way NN16: K'ing 5G 39
Berwick Ho. NN2: K'thpe 1E 84
Berwick Rd. NN14: Stan 3F 19
Berwick Way NN15: K'ing 2J 43
Bessemer Gro. NN18: Corby 7C 14
Bestwell Cl. NN3: N'ton 6D 86
Bestwood Cl. NN14: Des 1C 26
Bestwood Grn. NN18: Corby 1H 17
Beswick Cl. NN14: Stan 1B 46
Bethany Homestead NN2: N'ton 5F 85
Betjeman Cl. NN10: High F 7D 68
  NN11: Dav 7F 59
Betony Wlk. NN10: R'den 5E 80
Bettycroft Cl. NN6: Rav 2C 34
Bevan Cl. NN8: Well 5D 66
  PE8: Warm 2H 23
Bevan Ct. NN8: Well 4D 66
Beverley Cl. NN14: R'ell 6E 26
Beverley Cres. NN3: N'ton 4J 85
Beverley Rd. NN15: K'ing 2F 43
Beverley Wlk. NN18: Corby 1H 17
Bewick Cl. NN18: Corby 2K 17
Bewick Rd. NN3: West F 7B 86
Bexhill Wlk. NN18: Corby 2H 17
Bibury Cl. NN8: Well 4J 77
Bibury Cres. NN3: N'ton 1A 86
BICESTER 3B 140
Bicester Hill NN13: Even 2C 130
Bickerstaffes Rd. NN12: Tow 4C 114
BIDDENHAM 3C 139
Bidders Cl. NN1: N'ton 7J 131 (3E 94)
Bideford Cl. NN3: N'ton 1A 86
Bideford Sq. NN18: Corby 1A 18
Bies Cl. NN18: Gt Oak 4H 17
Big Green PE8: Warm 2J 23
Bignal Ct. NN15: K'ing 2A 42
BILLESDON 1D 133
Billing Aquadrome 7E 86
Billing Arbours Ho. NN3: N'ton 2B 86
Billing Brook Rd. NN3: N'ton 1A 86
Billing Gdn. Village NN3: L Bill 7G 87
Billing La. NN3: N'ton 7D 74
  NN6: Over 5C 74
Billingmead Wlk. NN3: N'ton 4E 86
    (Camberley Cl.)
  NN3: N'ton 5F 87
    (Gibbsacre Ct.)
Billing Rd. NN1: N'ton 4K 131 (1F 95)
  NN7: Braf G 1G 97
Billing Rd. E. NN3: N'ton 1J 95
Billing School Pl. NN7: Weed 4D 62
Billington St. NN1: N'ton 7G 85
Bilsdon Pl. NN10: R'den 5C 80
BILSTONE 1A 132
BILTON 1A 136
Bilton Cl. NN8: Well 7J 65
Binbrook Wlk. NN18: Corby 2H 17
    (off Boston Cl.)
Binder Cl. NN10: High F 5D 68
Binders Cl. NN14: Stan 4G 19
Bingham Wlk. NN18: Corby 1H 17
BINLEY 1A 136
Birchall Rd. NN10: R'den 3C 80
Birch Av. NN10: R'den 3C 80
Birch Barn La. NN2: K'thpe 1B 84
Birch Barn Way NN2: K'thpe 1C 84
Birch Cl. NN4: Gra P 6F 101
  NN11: Woodf H 2C 108
Birchfield Cl. NN3: N'ton 4K 85
Birchfield Cres. NN3: N'ton 4K 85
Birchfield Rd. NN1: N'ton 6G 85
  NN8: Well 1J 77

Birchfield Rd. E. NN3: N'ton 5H 85
Birchington Rd. NN17: Corby 3G 15
Birch Rd. NN10: R'den 3F 81
  NN16: K'ing 6F 39
Birch Spinney NN14: Maw 6A 40
Birchvale Ct. NN14: Des 1B 26
BIRDINGBURY 2A 136
Birds Hill Rd. NN3: N'ton 3C 86
  NN12: East 6J 105
Birds Hill Wlk. NN3: N'ton 4C 86
    (not continuous)
Birkdale Cl. NN2: N'ton 3G 85
  NN11: Dav 1K 61
Birkdale Dr. NN10: R'den 4G 81
Birling Pl. NN18: Corby 1F 17
BIRSTALL 1B 132
BISBROOKE 2A 134
Biscay Cl. NN29: Irch 5J 79
Bishops Cl. NN13: B'ley 2F 129
Bishops Ct. NN10: High F 6F 69
  NN11: Dav 1H 61
Bishops Dr. NN2: K'thpe 3C 84
  NN15: K'ing 3D 42
BISHOP'S ITCHINGTON 3A 136
Bishop Stopford Community Sports Cen. 3D 42
Bishops Way NN18: Corby 2F 17
Bitten Cl. NN3: N'ton 3B 86
Bitten St. NN4: N'ton 7K 93
Bittern Cl. NN14: Des 1E 26
BITTESWELL 3B 132
BLABY 2B 132
Blackberry Cl. NN16: K'ing 3D 38
Blackberry La. NN4: N'ton 4A 94
Blackbird Cl. NN13: B'ley 2F 129
Blackbird Ct. NN8: Well 6C 66
Blackbird Rd. NN18: Corby 3K 17
Blackbridge Ct. NN14: Thra 3G 51
Black Cat Dr. NN5: Upton 3J 93
Black Cat St. NN5: Upton 3J 93
Blackfriars NN1: N'ton 4C 80
Black Horse Ct. PE8: Oun 5G 21
Black Lion Hill
  NN1: N'ton 5F 131 (2C 94)
Blackmile La. NN7: Gren 7K 89
Blackmires La. NN12: Silv 2F 121
Blackmoor Cl. NN18: Corby 2A 18
Black Pot La. PE8: Oun 5J 21
Blacksmith's Cl. NN12: Pat 5G 105
Blacksmith's Grn. NN12: Shut 6A 116
Blacksmiths Hill OX17: Ayn 7E 126
Blacksmiths La. NN7: L Brin 5F 57
  NN11: Ast W 7E 106
  NN11: Eyd 7D 108
  NN14: Pyt 2A 44
Blacksmith's Way NN7: Hart 6G 117
Blacksmith's Yd. NN6: Ect 2J 87
    (off High St.)
BLACKTHORN
  Northamptonshire 2E 86
  Oxfordshire 3C 141
Blackthorn Bri. Ct. NN3: N'ton 2E 86
Blackthorn Cl. NN6: Spra 5B 34
    (off Gorse Rd.)
  NN16: K'ing 3E 38
Blackthorn Local Cen. NN3: N'ton 2E 86
    (off Blackthorn Bri. Ct.)
Blackthorn Rd. NN3: N'ton 2E 86
Blackthorn Wlk. NN3: N'ton 3E 86
    (not continuous)
Blackwall Cl. NN4: N'ton 5B 94
Blackwell Cl. NN6: E Bart 2D 88
  NN10: High F 4E 68
  NN12: Tow 5D 114
Blackwell End NN12: Pot 6G 123
Blackwell Hill NN4: N'ton 7A 94
Blackwell Rd. NN15: Bar S 6H 43
Blackwells Yd. NN7: Yar H 6H 103
BLACKY MORE 2E 100
Blackymore La. NN4: N'ton 3E 100
Bladon Cl. NN3: N'ton 1K 85
Blake Cl. NN11: Dav 3K 61
Blake Ct. NN15: Bar S 2J 43
Blake Rd. NN18: Corby 2J 17
BLAKESLEY 5J 109 (3C 137)
Blakesley Hill NN12: Greens N 1G 113
Blakesley Rd. NN12: Woode 7G 109
Blake Wlk. NN10: High F 7D 68
Blanchard Cl. NN4: Woot 1F 101
Blandford Av. NN16: K'ing 4D 38
Blandford Ct. NN18: Corby 7F 13
    (off Glastonbury Rd.)
BLASTON 2A 134
BLATHERWYCKE 2B 134
Blatherwyke Rd. PE8: King C 3F 9
Blaydon Wlk. NN8: Well 5K 65
Bleaklow Cl. NN14: Des 2A 26
Bledlow Ri. NN4: N'ton 7A 94
Blencowe Dr. NN13: B'ley 4E 128
Blenheim NN13: Crou 7K 127
Blenheim Cl. NN10: R'den 4D 80
Blenheim Cft. NN13: B'ley 5G 129

Blenheim Pl.—Broadhurst Dr.

Blenheim Pl. NN13: Syre 6D 120
Blenheim Ri. OX17: King S 1B 126
Blenheim Rd. NN4: Far C 5C 94
NN8: Well 5J 65
Blenheim Wlk. NN18: Corby 3H 17
Blenheim Way NN15: K'ing 5E 42
BLETCHINGDON 3B 140
BLETCHLEY 2D 141
BLETSOE 3C 139
Blinco Rd. NN10: R'den 3F 81
Blind La. LE16: Cotti 4C 12
Bliss La. NN7: Flore 2G 63
BLISWORTH 2H 115 (3D 137)
Blisworth & Milton Malsor By-Pass
NN7: Blis, G'ton, Roth 7G 99
NN4: N'ton 5J 93
Blisworth Cl. NN4: N'ton 5B 94
Blisworth Pk. NN7: Blis 7G 99
Blisworth Rd. NN7: G'ton 6E 98
NN7: Roa 1A 116
Blisworth Tunnel 3D 137
Bloomfield Cl. NN10: R'den 3D 80
Bloomsbury Gallery 5J 131
Bloomsbury Ho. NN1: N'ton 5J 131
Blossac Ct. NN5: Dus 5E 82
Blossom Ct. NN16: K'ing 5E 38
Blossom Way NN3: N'ton 5D 86
Blott's Gdns. NN9: Raun 5J 53
BLOXHAM 2A 140
Bluebell Cl. NN8: Well 6C 66
NN11: Woodf H 1C 108
NN16: K'ing 5F 39
NN18: Corby 4J 17
Bluebell Ct. NN3: N'ton 1K 95
Bluebell Pk. NN3: Moul 4K 73
Bluebell Ri. NN4: Gra P 7G 101
NN10: R'den 5F 81
Blueberry Cl. NN6: Maid 2B 36
Blueberry Ri. NN3: N'ton 4F 87
BLUNHAM 3D 139
Bly La. NN4: Upton 5G 93
NN5: Upton 2G 93
Blyth Cl. NN14: R'ell 7H 27
Blyton Ct. NN18: Corby 2H 17
Boarden Cl. NN3: Moul P 6H 73
Boardman Rd. NN15: K'ing 2B 42
Board St. NN9: Irth 2C 68
Boat Horse La. NN6: Crick 4J 31
Bobtail Ct. NN5: Dus 5H 83
Boddington Meadow Nature Reserve
. . . . .2D 106
Boddington M. NN15: K'ing 2E 42
(off Boddington Rd.)
Boddington Rd. NN11: Byf 2G 107
NN15: K'ing 2E 42
Boddington Way NN13: B'ley 3E 128
Boden Cl. NN18: Corby 4F 17
Bodiam Cl. NN14: Thra 3J 51
Bodiam Pl. NN18: Corby 1F 17
BODICOTE 2A 140
Bodleian Cl. NN11: Dav 3G 61
Bodyshapers 7D 38
(off School La.)
Bodytalk Fitness Studio 1D 42
(within Kettering Swimming Pool)
Bognor Rd. NN18: Corby 2G 17
Bolingbroke Pl. NN10: High F 4F 69
Bollinger Cl. NN5: Dus 5E 82
BOLNHURST 3C 139
Boltons Cl. NN13: B'ley 2F 129
Bondfield Av. NN2: K'thpe 3E 84
Bonham Ct. NN16: K'ing 6E 38
Bonners Fitness Cen. 2K 45
(off High St.)
Bonnington Wlk. NN18: Corby 1J 17
Bonsor Gdns. NN14: Rin 1F 53
Boon Wlk. NN17: Corby 6C 14
(off Stock's La.)
Booth Cl. NN12: Pat 5G 105
Booth Dr. NN8: Well 7F 65
Booth La. Nth. NN3: N'ton 1K 85
Booth La. Sth. NN3: N'ton 3A 86
Booth Mdw. Ct. NN3: N'ton 1B 86
Booth Mdw. Wlk. NN3: N'ton 1A 86
Booth Ri. NN3: N'ton 7K 73
BOOTHVILLE 1K 85 (2D 137)
Boothville Grn. NN3: N'ton 1A 86
Bordeaux Cl. NN5: Dus 5E 82
Borough Ct. NN10: High F 7E 68
NN13: B'ley 5H 129
BOROUGH HILL 2K 61
Borough Hill Country Pk. 1K 61
Borough Rd. NN13: B'ley 6G 129
Borrowdale Rd. NN17: Corby 5J 13
Borrowdale Wlk. NN3: N'ton 2K 85
Bostock Av. NN1: N'ton 7G 85
Bostock M. NN1: N'ton 7G 85
Boston Cl. NN18: Corby 2H 17
Boswell La. MK19: Dean 5F 125
Bosworth Cl. NN4: N'ton 6B 94
PE8: Warm 2H 23
BOTCHESTON 1A 132
Botmead Rd. NN3: N'ton 2F 87
BOTOLPH CLAYDON 3D 141
Bottom La. LE16: Stoke A 6G 11
Bougainvillea Dr. NN3: N'ton 1K 95
BOUGHTON 5D 72 (2D 137)
Boughton NN15: K'ing 6F 43
Boughton Cl. NN18: Corby 2F 17
Boughton Dr. NN10: R'den 5C 80
Boughton Fair La. NN3: Moul 2J 73
BOUGHTON GREEN 7D 72
Boughton Grn. NN2: Moul P 6F 73
Boughton Grn. Rd.
NN2: K'thpe, Moul P 2D 84
Boughton House 1K 39
Boughton La. NN3: Moul 6G 73
Boughton Pk. 2K 39
Boughton Rd. NN2: Moul 5G 73
NN3: Moul 5G 73
NN18: Corby 4J 17
Boundary Av. NN10: R'den 3B 80
Boundary Rd. NN13: B'ley 5H 129
Bourne Cl. NN8: Well 6H 65
NN18: Corby 4J 17
Bourne Cres. NN5: N'ton 5K 83
BOURNE END 2C 139
Bourton Cl. NN4: N'ton 7A 94
BOURTON ON DUNSMORE 1A 136
Bourton Way NN8: Well 5K 77
Bouverie Rd. NN4: H'stone 7G 95
Bouverie St. NN1: N'ton 1G 95
Bouverie Wlk. NN1: N'ton 1G 95
Bow Ct. NN4: N'ton 4K 93
Bowden La. LE16: Mkt H 1A 10
Bowden Rd. NN5: N'ton 1B 94
Bowen Sq. NN11: Dav 2H 61
Bower Wlk. NN3: N'ton 7B 74
(East Bank)
NN3: N'ton 1B 86
(Farm Fld. Ct.)
Bowhill NN16: K'ing 1B 42
Bowland Dr. NN15: Bar S 5J 43
Bowlers Yd. NN6: E Bart 2D 88
Bowling Grn. NN13: F'hoe 6H 119
Bowling Grn. Av. NN15: K'ing 1D 42
Bowling Grn. La. NN5: Upton 1F 93
Bowling Grn. Rd. NN16: K'ing 1D 42
Bowman Cl. OX17: Mid C 6D 118
Bowmans Cl. NN4: N'ton 6J 93
Bowmens Lea OX17: Ayn 7E 126
Bowness NN8: Well 7H 65
Bowthorpe Cl. NN3: N'ton 1A 96
BOX END 3C 139
Box Gdns. NN8: Well 7B 66
Boxwood Dr. CV23: Kil 6C 30
Boyle Rd. NN17: Corby 4D 14
BOZEAT 3H 103 (3B 138)
Brabham Cl. NN12: Silv 3H 121
Bracadale Wlk. NN17: Corby 4H 13
BRACEBOROUGH 1C 135
Brackenborough
NN6: Brix 4J 35
Bracken Cl. NN16: K'ing 4D 38
Brackendale Dr. CV23: Bar 2C 54
Brackenfield Sq. NN3: N'ton 6C 74
Brackenhill Cl. NN2: N'ton 3F 85
BRACKLEY . . . . .2B 140 & 4G 129
Brackley Cl. NN2: K'thpe 7E 72
BRACKLEY HATCH 1C 141
Brackley Ho. NN13: B'ley 4F 129
Brackley La. NN12: Abt 7H 113
Brackley Leisure Cen. 2E 128
Brackley Lodge M.
NN13: B'ley 4F 129
Brackley Rd. NN12: Silv 4G 121
NN12: Tow 4A 114
NN13: Crou 5B 130
OX17: Greatw 3K 119
Brackley Swimming Pool 3F 129
Brackley Town FC 5G 129
BRACKMILLS 5H 95
Brackmills Bus. Pk.
NN4: Brack 5H 95
Bracknell NN8: Well 7H 65
Bradbury Rd. NN11: Newn 7J 61
BRADDEN 1C 141
Bradden Cl. NN2: K'thpe 1E 84
Bradden Rd. NN12: Greens N 1G 113
Bradden Way NN12: Greens N 1H 113
Bradfield Cl. NN8: Well 3B 66
NN10: R'den 2G 81
Bradfield Rd. NN8: Well 3B 66
Bradford Wlk. NN18: Corby 1H 17
Bradgate Ho. NN1: N'ton 1F 95
(off Billing Rd.)
Bradlaugh Cres. NN3: N'ton 7F 75
Bradmoor Ct. NN3: N'ton 1E 86
Bradmore Gdns. NN18: Corby 7H 13
Bradshaw St.
NN1: N'ton 4H 131 (1D 94)
Bradshaw Way NN29: Irch 5G 79
Brad St. NN3: N'ton 1J 85
BRADWELL 2D 141
Braemar Cl. NN15: K'ing 2G 43
Braemar Cres. NN4: N'ton 7C 94
BRAFIELD-ON-THE-GREEN
. . . . .5H 97 (3A 138)
Brafield Rd. NN7: Cog 3G 97
Braggintons La. OX17: Mid C 6E 118
Braid Ct. NN8: Well 5J 65
Braithwaite Cl. NN15: K'ing 2B 42
Brakey Rd. NN17: Corby 4G 15
Bramber Ct. NN18: Corby 1F 17
Bramble Cl. NN14: Rin 1F 53
NN16: K'ing 3D 38
Bramble End NN4: N'ton 7A 94
Bramble Rd. NN12: Tow 5B 114
Brambles, The NN10: Wym 7E 80
(off High St.)
Brambleside NN14: Thra 4H 51
NN16: K'ing 3D 38
Brambleside Ct. NN16: K'ing 3D 38
Bramblewood Rd. NN17: Weld 5H 15
BRAMCOTE 3A 132
Bramcote Dr. NN3: N'ton 6C 86
Bramhall Ri. NN5: Dus 6G 83
Bramley Cl. NN7: Cog 1H 97
NN10: R'den 2C 80
Bramley Ct. NN29: Woll 3E 90
Bramley Gro. NN3: N'ton 4E 86
Bramley Ho. NN11: Dav 1H 61
(off Brook St.)
Brammar Ho. NN5: N'ton 7A 84
BRAMPTON 1D 139
BRAMPTON ASH 3D 133
Brampton Cl. NN8: Well 5J 65
NN15: Bar S 5J 43
Brampton La. NN2: Chap B 6A 72
NN6: Chap B 3A 72
(Pitsford Rd.)
NN6: Chap B 6A 72
(Welford Rd.)
Brampton Valley Way Linear Pk. . . .4C 36
Brampton Wlk. NN3: N'ton 1G 85
Brampton Way NN6: Brix 4H 35
Bramshill Av. NN16: K'ing 4C 38
Bramston PE8: Oun 5J 21
(off Market Pl.)
Bramston Cl. PE8: Oun 6J 21
Brancey Cl. NN14: Thra 3G 51
Brandenburg Rd. NN18: Corby 4E 16
BRANDON 1A 136
Brangwyn Wlk. NN18: Corby 1K 17
Branksome Av. NN2: K'thpe 5C 84
Branksome Ct. NN18: Corby 7F 13
Branson Ct. NN16: K'ing 6C 38
(off Cobden St.)
Branson's La. NN12: Tow 4D 114
Brasenose Dr. NN13: B'ley 3E 128
Brashland Dr. NN4: N'ton 2E 100
BRAUNSTON 1B 58 (2B 136)
Braunston Cl. NN4: N'ton 5B 94
BRAUNSTONE TOWN 1B 132
BRAUNSTON-IN-RUTLAND 1A 134
Braunston La. NN11: Stav 4B 60
Braunston Rd. NN11: Dav 4C 58
Braunton Pl. NN18: Corby 2A 18
Brawn Cl. NN9: Irth 4B 68
BRAYBROOKE 7C 10 (3D 133)
Braybrooke Cl. NN14: Rin 1H 53
Braybrooke Rd. LE16: Gt Oxe 7J 25
NN14: Des 1A 26
Brayford Av. NN18: Corby 1A 18
Brayford Cl. NN3: N'ton 7K 85
Breach Cl. NN6: Brix 3J 35
Breakleys Rd. NN14: Des 2E 26
Breck Cl. NN18: Gt Oak 6G 17
Brecon Cl. NN16: K'ing 2D 38
Brecon St. NN5: N'ton 6B 84
Breedon Cl. NN18: Corby 5F 17
Breezehill NN4: Woot 2G 101
Breezehill Way NN8: Well 5B 66
Brembridge Cl. NN6: Syw 3G 75
Brendon Cl. NN3: West F 7K 85
Brent Cl. NN15: Bur L 2H 45
Brentford NN8: Well 7G 65
Brer Ct. NN4: N'ton 2G 95
Bressingham Gdns. NN4: N'ton . . .1D 100
BRETFORD 1A 136
BRETTON 1D 135
Bretton Cl. NN5: Dus 5F 83
Bretts La. NN7: Roa 2D 116
Brewery Ct. PE8: Oun 6H 21
Brewery Yd. NN14: Sud 3C 48
Brewin Cl. NN13: B'ley 2E 128
Briar Cl. NN13: B'ley 2G 129
BRIAR HILL 4A 94
Briar Hill Rd. NN4: N'ton 5C 94
Briar Hill Wlk. NN4: N'ton 5C 94
Briar Rd. NN16: K'ing 4G 39
Briars, The NN4: N'ton 4B 94
Briarwood Way NN29: Woll 5E 90
Briary Cl. NN12: Tow 5B 114
Brickett's La. NN7: Flore 2F 63
Brickhill Ct. NN8: Well 1K 77
Brickhill M. NN8: Well 1K 77
Brickhill Rd. NN8: Well 1H 77
Brick Kiln Cl. NN12: Tow 5C 114
Brick Kiln La. NN2: N'ton 6D 84
Brick Kiln Rd. NN9: Raun 4H 53
Brickwell Ct. NN3: N'ton 5D 86
Brickyard NN3: Moul P 7J 73
Bridewell La. NN16: K'ing 7D 38
Bridge Alexander Cl. NN9: Fine 7H 47
Bridge Ct. NN14: Thra 3G 51
NN17: Corby 6B 14
BRIDGE END 3C 139
Bridge End NN6: Yel 5C 28
Bridge Ho. NN14: R'ell 6G 27
(off Bridge St.)
Bridge Mdw. NN7: D'ton 6B 102
Bridge Mdw. Way
NN4: Gra P 4F 101
Bridge Rd. MK19: Cos 6D 122
NN12: Stoke B 6D 116
NN14: Des 1C 26
Bridge St. NN1: N'ton 5H 131 (2D 94)
NN7: Weed 3C 62
NN9: Raun 5J 53
NN13: B'ley 5F 129
NN14: Brig 2C 20
NN14: Ged 6C 46
NN14: R'ell 6G 27
NN14: Thra 3G 51
NN16: K'ing 6E 38
NN17: Weld 5J 15
PE8: King C 2H 9
Bridge Vw. PE8: Oun 4J 21
Bridge Wlk. MK19: Dean 5F 125
Bridgewater Cl. NN13: B'ley 3G 129
Bridgewater Ct. NN13: B'ley 3G 129
Bridgewater Cres. NN13: B'ley 3G 129
Bridgewater Dr.
NN3: West F, N'ton 7K 85
Bridgewater Ho. NN13: B'ley 3G 129
(off Halse Rd.)
Bridgewater Ri. NN13: B'ley 3G 129
Bridgewater Rd. NN13: B'ley 2G 129
Bridgford Pl. NN18: Corby 7H 13
Bridgwater Ct. NN18: Corby 7F 13
Bridle Cl. NN7: Braf G 5G 97
NN8: Well 3B 66
Bridle La. NN6: Col A 2B 32
Bridle Path NN7: Braf G 5G 97
Bridle Rd. NN6: Hann 3K 37
NN6: Old .5E 36
NN15: Bur L 2H 45
Bridle Way NN14: C'ley 4G 41
Briery Cl. NN18: Gt Oak 5G 17
Brigadier Cl. NN4: Woot 1E 100
Brigg Ct. NN18: Corby 2H 17
Brighouse Cl. NN18: Corby 2H 17
Brighton Rd. NN18: Corby 2G 17
Bright Trees Rd. NN14: Ged 5D 46
Brightwell Wlk. NN9: Irth 4A 68
Brig La. LE16: Wilb 4H 11
BRIGSTOCK 2D 20 (3B 134)
Brigstock Rd. NN14: Stan 3F 19
Brindlestone Cl. NN4: N'ton 5J 93
Brindley Cl. NN10: R'den 1C 80
NN11: Dav 5E 58
Brindley Ct. NN11: Braun 2A 58
Brindley Quays NN11: Braun 2A 58
BRINGHURST 1B 12 (2A 134)
BRINGTON 1C 139
Brington Dr. NN15: Bar S 5H 43
Brington La. NN11: Whil 6D 56
Brington Rd. NN6: Long B 2H 55
NN7: Flore, L Brin . . . . .2G 63 & 6F 57
Brinkhill Wlk. NN18: Corby 2H 17
BRINKLOW 1A 136
Brinsley Grn. NN18: Corby 7H 13
Brisbane Gdns. NN18: Corby 4G 17
Briscoe Cl. NN2: K'thpe 7F 73
Bristle St. NN5: Upton 3H 93
Britannia Gdns. NN8: Well 1D 78
Britannia Rd. NN16: K'ing 5D 38
Britannia Trade Cen. NN5: Dus 4J 83
British La. NN16: K'ing 7D 38
Briton Gdns. NN3: N'ton 5J 85
Briton Rd. NN3: N'ton 6J 85
Briton Ter. NN3: N'ton 5J 85
Britten Cl. NN9: Chel 6K 69
Brittens Vw. NN6: Holc 6H 37
Brittons Dr. NN3: N'ton 6C 74
Brixham Wlk. NN18: Corby 1A 18
BRIXWORTH 3H 35 (1D 137)
Brixworth All Saints Saxon Church
. . . . .2H 35
Brixworth Country Pk. 5J 35
Brixworth Country Pk. Vis. Cen. . . .5J 35
Brixworth Ct. NN5: Upton 3J 93
(off Clickers Dr.)
Brixworth Hall Pk. NN6: Brix 3H 35
Brixworth Ind. Est. NN6: Brix 3J 35
Brixworth Rd. NN6: Crea 5K 33
NN6: Holc 5F 37
NN6: Spra . . . . .5B 34 & 3F 35
Broadgate Way PE8: Warm 2H 23
Broad Grn. NN8: Well 7A 66
Broadhurst Dr. NN3: N'ton 6C 86

Broadlands—Cardigan Cl.

Broadlands NN6: Brix .4G 35
NN6: Pits .1E 72
NN9: Raun .6K 53
NN10: R'den .2E 80
NN14: Des .3F 27
Broad La. NN13: Even .1B 130
Broad March NN11: Dav .3J 61
Broadmead Av. NN3: N'ton .4H 85
Broadstone Ct. NN18: Corby .7F 13
Broad St. NN1: N'ton .3G 131 (1D 94)
NN6: Brix .4H 35
NN6: E Bart .2D 88
NN13: Syre .5C 120
Broadwater La. NN12: Tow .4A 114
Broadway NN1: N'ton .5G 85
NN8: Well .2B 78
NN15: K'ing .2D 42
Broadway, The NN11: Nor .7G 55
Broadway E. NN3: N'ton .5H 85
BROADWELL .2A 136
Brocade Cl. NN4: N'ton .5A 94
BROCKHALL .2C 137
Brockhall Cl. NN2: K'thpe .2F 85
Brockhall Rd. NN2: K'thpe .2F 85
NN7: Dod .1A 62
NN7: Flore .1F 63
Brockhill Cl. NN15: K'ing .1G 43
Brockton St. NN2: N'ton .5E 84
Brockwood Cl. NN5: Dus .5F 83
Bromford Cl. NN3: N'ton .6D 86
BROMHAM .3C 139
Bromley Farm Ct.
NN11: Woodf H .3C 108
Bronte Cl. NN16: K'ing .3E 38
Brontes, The NN17: Corby .5J 13
Brook Ct. NN7: Hort .2K 117
BROOKE .1A 134
Brooke Cl. NN8: Well .7G 65
NN10: R'den .4E 80
NN14: Des .3D 26
Brooke Grn. NN8: Well .7G 65
Brooke M. NN8: Well .7G 65
Brookend NN4: Woot .3F 101
Brooke Rd. NN18: Gt Oak .5G 17
Brookes Gro. NN17: Corby .4K 13
Brookes M. NN6: E Bart .1D 88
Brook Farm Cl. NN10: Wym .7E 80
Brookfield Rd. NN2: N'ton .4F 85
NN10: R'den .3D 80
Brookhaven NN14: Brou .6H 41
Brookland Cres. NN1: N'ton .5H 85
Brookland Rd. NN1: N'ton .5G 85
Brooklands Cl. NN11: Dav .2H 61
Brooklands Ct. NN15: K'ing .5F 43
Brook La. NN5: Dall .6A 84
NN12: Tow .3A 114
PE8: Barn .7B 22
Brooks Cl. NN4: Woot .2G 101
NN15: Bur L .3K 45
Brooksdale Cl. NN16: K'ing .3D 38
Brookside NN7: Weed .4C 62
NN9: Stanw .1K 69
NN11: Woodf H .2B 108
NN12: Wap .5D 112
NN14: Des .3E 26
NN29: Boz .3H 103
Brookside Cl. MK19: Old S .3J 125
NN6: Yel .5C 28
Brookside La. NN11: Badby .6D 104
Brookside Mdws. NN5: N'ton .5K 83
Brookside M. NN6: Yel .5C 28
Brookside Pl. NN7: Neth H .5K 63
Brooks Rd. NN9: Raun .5K 53
Brook St. NN1: N'ton .2F 131 (7C 84)
NN9: Harg .5H 49
NN9: Raun .6J 53
NN11: Dav .1H 61
(not continuous)
NN11: Mor P .3H 111
Brook St. E. NN8: Well .1C 78
Brook St. W. NN8: Well .1A 78
Brook Ter. NN9: Irth .2C 68
Brook Va. NN8: Wilby .4H 77
Brook Vw. NN3: N'ton .3C 86
NN4: Gra P .5F 101
Brook Wlk. NN14: Rin .1F 53
Brook Way MK19: Dean .5E 124
Broom Ct. NN4: N'ton .4A 94
Broomecroft NN6: Wal .1G 37
Broomhill Cres. NN3: N'ton .7D 74
Broom Way NN15: K'ing .2B 42
Brough Cl. NN5: Dus .5E 82
BROUGHTON
Northamptonshire .6G 41 (1A 138)
Oxfordshire .2A 140
BROUGHTON ASTLEY .2B 132
Broughton Grange Bus. Cen.
NN15: Brou .5B 42
Broughton Hill NN14: C'ley .4G 41
Broughton Pl. NN3: Spin H .3J 85
Broughton Rd. NN6: Old .5E 36
NN14: Maw .7B 40
NN14: Pyt .2A 44
Broughton Ter. NN13: Even .2C 130
Brown Cl. NN5: Upton .1G 93
Browning Av. NN16: K'ing .3E 38
Browning Cl. NN10: R'den .5G 81
NN11: Dav .6G 59
Browning Rd. NN8: Well .1H 77
Browning Wlk. NN17: Corby .5J 13
Brownlow Ct. NN3: N'ton .2B 86
Browns Cl. NN3: Moul .3K 73
NN14: Maw .6B 40
Brownsfield Rd. NN12: Yar G .3J 123
Brown's La. NN14: Den .7G 51
Browns Rd. NN11: Dav .2E 60
Browns Way NN1: N'ton .2F 95
Brownswood Dr. NN12: Pot .6H 123
Browns Yd. NN12: Tow .3C 114
Bruce St. NN5: N'ton .1A 94
Brundall Cl. NN3: N'ton .7A 86
Brunel Cl. NN8: Well .6G 65
NN11: Dav .6E 58
NN16: K'ing .5C 38
Brunel Ct. NN17: Corby .3B 14
Brunel Dr. NN5: Upton .2H 93
Brunel Rd. NN17: Corby .3A 14
Brunswick Gdns. NN18: Corby .4E 16
Brunswick Pl. NN1: N'ton .7F 85
Brunswick Wlk. *NN1: N'ton .7F 85*
(off Brunswick Pl.)
Brunting Rd. NN3: Moul .5K 73
BRUNTINGTHORPE .2C 133
Bryant Rd. NN15: K'ing .4E 42
Bryant Way NN10: High F .6E 68
Bryerhill Furlongs NN7: Cog .1H 97
BUBBENHALL .1A 136
Buccleuch St. NN16: K'ing .6C 38
Buchanan Cl. NN4: N'ton .4B 94
Buckby La. NN11: Whil .6C 56
BUCKDEN .2D 139
Buckfast Sq. NN18: Corby .2A 18
Buckhills La. NN6: Crick .4H 31
BUCKINGHAM .2C 141
Buckingham Cl. NN4: N'ton .1C 100
NN8: Well .4K 77
Buckingham Ct. NN13: B'ley .5H 129
NN15: Bar S .3H 43
Buckingham Rd. MK19: Dean .6G 125
NN12: Silv .6G 121
NN13: B'ley .4G 129
Buckingham Stardust Bingo Club .*7K 13*
(off George St.)
Buckingham Way NN12: Tow .4B 114
Buckle Ho. *NN5: N'ton .2C 94*
(off Byfield Rd.)
BUCKNELL .3B 140
Buckwell Cl. NN8: Well .7A 66
NN14: Des .2D 26
Buckwell End NN8: Well .7A 66
Buckwell Pl. NN8: Well .1A 78
BUCKWORTH .1D 139
Budge Rd. NN12: Yar G .4K 123
BUFFLER'S HOLT .2C 141
BUGBROOKE .2J 105 (3C 137)
Bugbrooke Rd. NN7: G'ton .5B 98
NN7: Kisl .6A 92
NN7: Neth H .6K 63
Bugby Dr. NN9: Irth .7A 52
Bugby Way NN9: Raun .5J 53
BULKINGTON .3A 132
Bull Baulk OX17: Mid C .6C 118
Bull Cl. NN29: Boz .2H 103
Bullfinch Way NN8: Well .6C 66
Bullock Rd. PE7: Wash .4K 23
Bullrush Wlk. *NN4: N'ton .7K 93*
(off Bitten St.)
Bulls La. OX17: King S .1B 126
Bulwell Grn. NN18: Corby .7H 13
BULWICK .2B 134
Bungalows, The NN16: Week .3H 39
NN17: Harr .1D 8
Bunkers Hill NN11: Badby .6C 104
Bunting Cl. NN15: Bur L .2H 45
Bunting Rd. NN2: N'ton .5D 84
NN18: Corby .3K 17
Bunting Rd. Ind. Est. NN2: N'ton .5D 84
Bunting's La. PE8: Warm .2H 23
BURBAGE .2A 132
Burcote Flds. NN12: Tow .5D 114
Burcote Rd. NN12: Tow .4D 114
Burcote Wood Bus. Cen.
NN12: Wood B .7B 114
Burditt Cl. NN14: R'ell .7J 27
Burdock Way NN14: Des .1D 26
BURDROP .2A 140
Burford Av. NN3: N'ton .1A 86
Burford Way NN8: Well .3J 77
Burgess Ct. NN18: Corby .2G 17
Burghley Cl. NN14: Des .1D 26
NN18: Corby .2A 18
Burghley Dr. NN18: Corby .1A 18
Burghley St. NN16: K'ing .5E 38
Burham Cl. NN4: Woot .3F 101
Burkitt Rd. NN17: Corby .2K 13
Burleigh Rd. NN2: K'thpe .5D 84
Burleigh Ter. NN29: Boz .2H 103
BURLEY .1A 134
Burling Ho. NN1: N'ton .7H 85
Burlington Apartments
NN1: N'ton .7H 85
(off Roseholme Rd.)
Burmans Way NN7: Cog .1H 97
Burnell Cl. NN14: Rin .1G 53
Burnham Pl. NN13: Syre .5C 120
Burns Cl. NN6: E Bart .2E 88
Burns Dr. NN17: Corby .5J 13
Burns Rd. NN8: Well .1G 77
NN11: Dav .6G 59
NN16: K'ing .4E 38
Burns St. NN1: N'ton .1K 131 (7F 85)
BURROUGH ON THE HILL .1D 133
BURROWS BUSH .5B 66
Burrows Bush *NN8: Well .6C 66*
(off Pym Cl.)
Burrows Cl. NN11: Welt .1K 59
Burrows Ct. NN3: N'ton .2B 86
Burrows Farm La. NN14: L Add .4A 52
Burrows Va. NN6: Brix .3J 35
Burryport Rd. NN4: Brack .5J 95
Burton Cl. NN11: Dav .5G 59
Burtone Cl. NN14: Brou .6G 41
BURTON HASTINGS .3A 132
Burton Ho. NN15: Bur L .2K 45
BURTON LATIMER .3J 45 (1B 138)
BURTON OVERY .2C 133
Burton Rd. NN9: Fine .4G 47
Burton Ter. *NN29: Boz .2H 103*
(off Pudding Bag La.)
Burtram Cl. NN3: West F .5B 86
Burwell Hill NN13: B'ley .3G 129
Burwell Hill Cl. NN13: B'ley .3G 129
Burwell Wlk. *NN18: Corby .2H 17*
(off Boston Cl.)
Burwood Rd. NN3: N'ton .4J 85
BURY CLOSE .7E 68
Bury Cl. LE16: Cotti .4B 12
NN10: High F .6F 69
Bury Dyke NN6: Crick .3J 31
Burystead Pl. NN8: Well .1B 78
Burystead Ri. NN9: Raun .5K 53
Burywell Rd. NN8: Well .6C 66
Buscot Pk. Way NN11: Dav .3G 59
Bushacre Ct. NN16: K'ing .6B 38
BUSHBY .1C 133
Bush Cl. NN8: Well .7K 65
Bushey Balk Cl. NN18: Gt Oak .5G 17
Bush Hill NN3: N'ton .5K 85
Bushland Rd. NN3: N'ton .4K 85
BUSHMEAD .2D 139
Business Cen., The NN5: N'ton .1A 94
Buswell Cl. NN7: Weed .4C 62
Buswell Ri. NN14: R'ell .6H 27
Butchers Ct. NN8: Well .6C 66
Butcher's La. NN2: Bou .5D 72
NN12: Pat .6G 105
NN14: Pyt .2A 44
Butchers Paddock
NN14: C'ord .1G 47
Bute Cl. *NN17: Corby .5G 13*
(off Grafton Dr.)
Butland Rd. NN18: Corby .4H 17
Butler Gdns. LE16: Mkt H .1K 25
Butlers Cl. NN11: Ast W .6E 106
Butlin Cl. NN11: Dav .7G 59
NN14: R'ell .6E 26
Butlin Ct. NN8: L Irch .4D 78
Butlins La. NN7: Roa .2C 116
Buttercup Cl. NN18: Corby .4H 17
Buttercup Rd. NN14: Des .1D 26
Butterfields NN8: Well .3A 78
Buttermere NN8: Well .7H 65
Buttermere Cl. NN3: N'ton .3K 85
NN16: K'ing .6A 38
Butterwick Wlk.
NN18: Corby .2H 17
Buttmead NN7: Blis .2H 115
Butts, The OX17: Ayn .7F 127
Butts Cl. OX17: Ayn .7E 126
Butts Cft. Cl. NN4: N'ton .2D 100
Butts Hill Cres. NN7: Bug .1K 105
Butts Rd. NN4: N'ton .2D 100
NN8: Well .4K 77
NN9: Raun .6K 53
Buxton Dr. NN14: Des .2B 26
BYFIELD .2J 107 (3B 136)
Byfield Reservoir Nature Reserve
.3E 106
Byfield Rd. NN5: N'ton .1B 94
NN11: Eyd .6D 108
NN11: Woodf H .1A 108
OX17: Chip W .3D 110
By Pass Way NN7: D'ton .6B 102
Byron Cl. NN12: Tow .4B 114
Byron Cres. NN10: High F .7D 68
NN10: R'den .3B 80
Byron Rd. NN8: Well .1J 77
NN16: K'ing .4E 38
NN17: Corby .5J 13
Byron St. NN2: N'ton .5G 85
Byron Wlk. NN11: Dav .7G 59
BYTHORN .1C 139

C

Cabot Cl. NN11: Dav .5H 59
NN14: R'ell .6H 27
CADEBY .1A 132
Cadogen Pl. NN12: Abt .7H 113
Caernarvon Cl. NN12: Tow .5C 114
Caesars Ga. NN13: B'ley .4H 129
Caistor Rd. NN17: Gret .6D 8
Caldbeck Wlk. NN3: N'ton .2K 85
CALDECOTE
Cambridgeshire .3D 135
Warwickshire .2A 132
CALDECOTT
Northamptonshire .7J 69 (2B 138)
Rutland .2A 134
Caldecott Rd. LE16: Rock .1G 13
NN9: Cald, Chel .7J 69
Calder Cl. NN17: Corby .4J 13
Calder Grn. NN5: N'ton .5K 83
(not continuous)
CALDESCOTE .3C 137
Caledonian Ho. *NN5: N'ton .1B 94*
(off Argyle St.)
Callcott Dr. NN15: K'ing .2J 43
Calstock Cl. NN3: N'ton .7A 86
CALVERT .3C 141
Calvert Cl. NN8: Well .4A 66
NN12: Greens N .1J 113
CALVERTON .6K 125 (2D 141)
Calvert Rd. NN12: Greens N .1J 113
Camberley Cl. NN3: N'ton .4E 86
Cambium Cl. NN16: K'ing .3E 38
Camborne Cl. NN4: Del .6C 94
Cambria Cres. NN3: N'ton .5K 85
Cambridge Av. NN17: Corby .6G 13
Cambridge St. NN2: Sem .6D 84
NN8: Well .7B 66
NN10: Wym .6D 80
NN14: R'ell .5G 27
NN16: K'ing .6E 38
Cam Cl. NN17: Corby .4H 13
Camden Sq. NN29: Boz .3H 103
Camelot Way NN5: Dus .6F 83
Cameron Cl. NN5: N'ton .7K 83
NN11: Dav .2G 61
Cameron Ct. NN17: Corby .1A 18
Cameron Cres. NN5: N'ton .7K 83
Cameron Dr. NN5: N'ton .7K 83
Campaign Cl. NN4: Woot .1F 101
Campanula Cl. NN3: N'ton .1K 95
Campbell Cl. NN7: Weed .3B 62
NN10: R'den .5G 81
NN12: Tow .1C 114
Campbell Rd. NN8: Well .3B 78
NN17: Corby .1A 18
Campbell Sq.
NN1: N'ton .3J 131 (1D 94)
Campbell St.
NN1: N'ton .2H 131 (7D 84)
Camp Cl. NN7: Bug .3K 105
CAMP HILL .5K 93
Camp Hill NN7: Bug .3J 105
Campion Cl. NN10: R'den .5E 80
Campion Ct. NN3: N'ton .5E 86
Campion Wlk. NN3: N'ton .5E 86
Camp La. NN4: Kisl .4C 92
NN7: Kisl .4C 92
Camrose Rd. NN5: N'ton .6B 84
Camsdale Wlk. LE16: Mid .5B 12
Canada Sq. NN18: Corby .3H 17
Canal La. MK19: Dean .5F 125
Canalside MK19: Old S .2K 125
Canberra Ho. *NN17: Corby .4G 15*
(off Corby Ga.)
Candace Ct. NN5: N'ton .6K 83
Candleford NN3: N'ton .2E 86
Candleford Cl. NN13: B'ley .3E 128
Canford Grn. NN18: Corby .7F 13
Cannam Cl. LE16: Mid .4A 12
Cannock Rd. NN17: Corby .5A 14
Cannon St. NN8: Well .7B 66
Canonbury NN8: Well .1H 77
CANONS ASHBY .1J 111 (3B 136)
Canons Ashby House .1J 111
Canons Ashby Rd.
NN11: Mor P .3J 111
Canon St. NN16: K'ing .6D 38
(not continuous)
Canons Wlk. NN2: K'thpe .3B 84
Canterbury Ct. *NN1: N'ton .2F 95*
(off Becket's Vw.)
Cantle Cl. NN18: Corby .3J 17
Capell Gdns. NN18: Corby .2K 17
Capell Ri. NN7: Flore .2F 63
Cappenham Cl. NN12: Tow .3B 114
Captain's Ct. NN7: Hort .3J 117
Cardigan Cl. NN5: Dall .6A 84

A-Z Northamptonshire Atlas 147

Cardigan Ho.—Chestnut Cl.

Cardigan Ho. *NN17: Corby* .7K **13**
(off Corporation St.)
Cardigan Pl. NN16: K'ing .6F **39**
NN17: Corby .1K **17**
Cardigan Rd. NN14: Stan .4F **19**
Cardinal Cl. NN4: N'ton .1C **100**
CARDINGTON .3C **139**
Cares Orchard NN7: Braf G .4G **97**
Carey Cl. NN3: Moul .4J **73**
Carey Ct. NN3: Moul .4J **73**
Carey Dr. NN17: Corby .5H **13**
Carey Rd. NN7: Hack .1F **117**
NN12: Tow .6C **114**
Careys Rd. NN12: Pur E .7F **115**
Carey St. NN1: N'ton .7F **85**
NN16: K'ing .6E **38**
Carey Way NN10: R'den .2G **81**
Carina Rd. NN15: K'ing .5E **42**
Carisbrooke Cl. NN15: K'ing .2H **43**
Carline Ct. NN3: N'ton .2A **86**
Carlisle Cl. NN18: Gt Oak .5J **17**
Carlow Rd. NN14: Rin .1F **53**
Carlow St. NN14: Rin .1F **53**
CARLTON
Bedford .3B **138**
Leicestershire .1A **132**
Carlton Cl. NN10: R'den .6D **80**
CARLTON CURLIEU .2C **133**
Carlton Gdns. NN2: N'ton .5F **85**
Carlton M. NN10: High F .7F **69**
Carlton Pl. NN18: Corby .7G **13**
CARLTON PURLIEUS .3B **16**
Carlton Rd. LE16: Wilb .5H **11**
NN2: N'ton .4F **85**
Carlton St. NN16: K'ing .6C **38**
Carlyle Av. NN5: N'ton .7K **83**
Carmarthen Way NN10: R'den .5F **81**
Carnegie St. NN10: R'den .3D **80**
Carol Trusler M. NN2: Sem .1F **131**
Carousel Way NN3: N'ton .7C **86**
Carpenters Yd. NN14: Orl .7B **44**
Carradale Cl. NN16: K'ing .3C **38**
Carriage Dr. NN16: K'ing .3D **38**
Carrington Gdns. NN3: N'ton .6C **86**
Carrington St. NN16: K'ing .7D **38**
Carron Cl. NN17: Corby .4H **13**
Carr's Way NN7: Harp .1B **92**
Carsington Cl. NN16: K'ing .6A **38**
Carter Av. NN14: Brou .7G **41**
Carter Cl. NN8: Well .1C **78**
Cartmel Pl. NN3: N'ton .3J **85**
Cartmel Way NN10: R'den .2G **81**
Cartrill St. NN9: Raun .6H **53**
Cartwright Cres. NN13: B'ley .4E **128**
Cartwright Gdns. OX17: Ayn .7F **127**
Cartwright Rd. NN2: K'thpe .5D **84**
OX17: Char .1H **127**
Carvells La. NN6: Nas .2F **33**
Casterbridge Ct. NN4: H'stone .1F **101**
Casterton Cl. NN9: Stanw .7F **53**
Casterton Wlk. NN3: N'ton .1F **87**
Castilian St. NN1: N'ton .5J **131** (2E **94**)
Castilian Ter. NN1: N'ton .5K **131** (2E **94**)
Castle, The
Wellingborough .1C **78**
CASTLE ASHBY .3A **138**
Castle Ashby Gdns. .3A **138**
Castle Ashby Rd. NN7: Yar H .5G **103**
Castle Av. NN5: Dus .6H **83**
Castle Bush NN5: Dus .6H **83**
Castle Cl. NN5: Dus .6H **83**
NN18: Corby .2F **17**
Castle Ct. NN8: Well .1C **78**
NN10: R'den .5D **80**
Castlefields Cl. NN10: High F .6F **69**
Castle Gdns. NN14: Ged .5C **46**
Castle Hill NN1: N'ton .4F **131** (1C **94**)
NN11: Dav .2G **61**
NN14: R'ell .6G **27**
Castle La. NN8: Well .1B **78**
Castle M. NN8: Well .1C **78**
Castle Mound CV23: Bar .1C **54**
Castle Mt. NN13: B'ley .6F **129**
Castle Rd. NN8: Well .1C **78**
NN11: Woodf H .2D **108**
Castle St. NN1: N'ton .4F **131** (1D **94**)
NN8: Well .1C **78**
Castle Ter. NN1: N'ton .4F **131** (1C **94**)
CASTLETHORPE .1D **141**
Castleton Rd. NN14: Des .1B **26**
Castle Vw. NN8: Well .1C **78**
PE8: Barn .5B **22**
Castle Way NN8: Well .1B **78**
NN15: Bar S .4H **43**
CASTOR .2D **135**
Caswell Cl. NN15: K'ing .1E **42**
Caswell Rd. NN4: Brack .6H **95**
Catchland Cl. NN18: Gt Oak .5H **17**
Catchpole Cl. NN18: Corby .3J **17**
Catesby Cl. NN2: K'thpe .2F **85**
Catesby End NN11: Hell .2C **104**
Catesby Rd. NN11: Stav .7A **60**
Catesby Rd. NN14: R'ell .6H **27**
Catesby St. NN16: K'ing .6E **38**
Cathedral of Our Lady & St Thomas .6D **84**
Catlow Cl. NN9: Raun .4H **53**
Catterick Cl. NN18: L Oak .5K **17**
CATTHORPE .1A **28** (1B **136**)
Catthorpe Mnr. LE17: Catt .1B **28**
Catthorpe Rd. LE17: Catt .1A **28**
CATTLE END .4H **121**
Cattle Hill NN3: Gt Bil .4F **87**
Cattle Mkt. Rd.
NN1: N'ton .6H **131** (2D **94**)
Catton Cl. NN6: Nas .3H **33**
Catton Cres. NN2: K'thpe .1A **84**
CATWORTH .1C **139**
CAULCOTT .3B **140**
Cauldecott Cl. NN4: N'ton .6H **93**
Causeway, The NN3: L Bill .7F **87**
NN4: N'ton .4A **94**
NN11: Byf .1K **107**
Causeway Rd. NN17: Corby .3K **13**
Causin Cl. NN14: Brig .1D **20**
Cavalry Dr. NN11: Dav .2G **61**
Cavalry Flds. NN7: Weed .3B **62**
Cavalry Hill NN7: Weed .3B **62**
Cavalry Hill Ind. Pk. NN7: Weed .3B **62**
Cavendish Cl. NN15: Bar S .5H **43**
Cavendish Courtyard
NN17: Corby .4F **15**
Cavendish Dr. NN3: N'ton .1A **96**
CAVERSFIELD .3B **140**
CAWSTON .1A **136**
Caxton Cl. NN11: Dav .6F **59**
Caythorpe Sq. NN18: Corby .7G **13**
Cecil Cl. NN18: Corby .2K **17**
Cecil Dr. NN18: Corby .2K **17**
Cecil Rd. NN2: K'thpe .5D **84**
Cecil St. NN14: R'ell .6G **27**
NN16: K'ing .5E **38**
Cedar Cl. MK19: Old S .2J **125**
NN6: Syw .6G **75**
NN10: R'den .5D **80**
NN11: Dav .5H **59**
NN12: Tow .5C **114**
NN13: B'ley .1G **129**
NN14: Des .3F **27**
NN29: Irch .6H **79**
Cedar Ct. NN3: Moul .6K **73**
NN5: N'ton .6K **83**
NN16: K'ing .5E **38**
NN17: Corby .4K **13**
Cedar Dr. NN14: Thra .4G **51**
Cedar Hythe NN6: Chap B .4J **71**
Cedar Rd. NN1: N'ton .5G **85**
NN16: K'ing .5E **38**
Cedar Rd. E. NN3: N'ton .5H **85**
Cedar Way NN8: Well .5A **66**
NN10: High F .6E **68**
Cedrus Ct. NN2: K'thpe .7A **72**
Celandine Cl. NN10: R'den .6F **81**
Celeborn Pl. NN3: N'ton .1E **86**
Celtic Cl. NN10: High F .5E **68**
Celtic Way NN6: Crick .3D **30**
Cemetery La. NN10: High F .6E **68**
Centaine Rd. NN10: R'den .4D **80**
Central Av. NN2: K'thpe .7C **72**
NN8: Well .3K **77**
NN11: Woodf H .1B **108**
NN16: K'ing .6F **39**
Centre 2000 NN16: K'ing .5B **38**
Centre Pde. NN16: K'ing .5F **39**
Centurion Way NN4: Woot .3G **101**
Chace Rd. NN8: Well .1D **78**
CHACKMORE .2C **141**
CHACOMBE .2B **118** (1A **140**)
Chacombe Rd. OX17: Mid C .4C **118**
Chadleigh Ct. *NN13: B'ley* .5F **129**
(off Bridge St.)
CHADSHUNT .3A **136**
CHADSTONE .4E **102** (3A **138**)
Chadstone Av. NN2: K'thpe .7E **72**
Chadwick Gdns. NN5: Dus .5J **83**
Chaffinch Cl. NN4: N'ton .1A **100**
Chaffinch Way NN13: B'ley .2F **129**
Chainbridge Ct. NN14: Thra .3G **51**
Chalcombe Av. NN2: K'thpe .1D **84**
Chalcombe Rd. NN2: K'thpe .2D **84**
Chalfont Ct. NN1: N'ton .2G **131**
Chalk La. NN1: N'ton .5F **131** (2C **94**)
Chalon Cl. NN8: Well .4A **66**
CHALTON .3D **139**
Chamberlain Av. NN8: Well .4K **77**
Chamberlain Way NN9: Raun .7H **53**
NN10: High F .7F **69**
Chambers, The *NN1: N'ton* .1F **95**
(off St Edmund's Rd.)
Chambers Hill NN14: Maw .6B **40**
Chambers Row *NN6: Welf* .2H **29**
(off Salford Cl.)
Champion Ct. NN13: B'ley .3F **129**
Chancel Ter. PE8: Barn .7C **22**
Chancery La. NN14: Thra .3H **51**
Chandler Gdns. NN14: Thra .4J **51**
Chandlers Way NN17: Corby .1K **17**
Chandos Ho. *NN17: Corby* .1K **17**
(off Chandlers Way)
CHANNEL'S END .3D **139**
Channing St. NN16: K'ing .7E **38**
Chantelle Ct. NN11: Dav .7G **59**
Chantry Cl. NN3: Gt Bil .3E **86**
Chantry La. NN12: Tow .3C **114**
CHAPEL BRAMPTON .4J **71** (2D **137**)
Chapel Cl. NN10: R'den .2F **81**
NN12: Silv .3H **121**
NN14: Gt Ad .2B **52**
CHAPEL END .7H **23**
Chapel End NN7: Pid .2F **117**
NN13: Crou .5A **130**
CHAPEL GREEN .2A **136**
Chapel Grn. NN5: N'ton .4B **84**
Chapel Hill NN10: High F .5E **68**
NN14: Isl .3F **51**
NN14: L Add .5A **52**
NN29: Irch .5J **79**
Chapel La. CV23: Lil .3C **28**
LE16: Clip .5C **24**
LE16: Stoke A .6G **11**
LE16: Wilb .5H **11**
NN6: Crick .4J **31**
NN6: Old .5D **36**
NN7: Blis .1G **115**
NN7: Braf G .5H **97**
NN7: Flore .2G **63**
NN7: Hack .2G **117**
NN7: Kisl .4C **92**
NN9: L Harr .1H **65**
NN9: Stanw .1J **69**
NN11: Badby .5D **104**
NN11: Dav .1H **61**
NN12: Lit .2H **109**
NN12: Stoke B .6D **116**
NN12: Slapt .6G **113**
NN13: F'hoe .6H **119**
NN13: Turw .4J **129**
NN14: Den .7G **51**
NN14: Ged .6C **46**
NN14: R'ton .2B **46**
NN14: Stan .4F **19**
NN17: Corby .7C **14**
NN29: Gt Dod .7K **77**
Chapel Pl. NN1: N'ton .3K **131** (1F **95**)
Chapel Rd. NN17: Weld .5H **15**
OX17: Greatw .3K **119**
Chapel Row *NN3: Gt Bil* .4F **87**
(off High St.)
Chapel St. CV23: Kil .7C **30**
NN14: Rin .1F **53**
NN14: Titch .1H **49**
PE8: Warm .2H **23**
Chapel Vw. NN14: Brou .5G **41**
Chaplins La. NN14: Des .2D **26**
Chapman Cl. NN12: Tow .2C **114**
Chapman Gro. NN17: Corby .5K **13**
Chapman Rd. NN8: Well .2D **78**
Chapmans Cl. LE16: Stoke A .6G **11**
Chapmans Dr. MK19: Old S .2J **125**
Chapmans La. NN29: Irch .5J **79**
Chappell Ho. NN3: Moul .5K **73**
Chardonnay Cl. NN5: New D .4F **83**
Chariot Rd. NN4: Woot .3G **101**
CHARLBURY .3A **140**
Charlbury Cl. NN8: Well .5K **77**
Charlecote Cl. NN11: Dav .4G **59**
Charles Bradlaugh Hall
NN2: K'thpe .1F **85**
Charles Cl. NN6: Long B .2H **55**
NN6: Old .5D **36**
NN10: High F .5F **69**
Charles Ct. NN15: Bur L .2J **45**
Charles Ho. NN1: N'ton .5K **131**
Charles Parker Bldg., The
NN10: High F .6F **69**
(off Midland Rd.)
Charles Partridge Ct. NN8: Wilby .4H **77**
Charles Robinson Ct. NN8: Well .2K **77**
Charles St. NN1: N'ton .2J **131** (7E **84**)
NN8: Well .3K **77**
NN14: R'ell .6F **27**
NN14: Thra .3J **51**
NN16: K'ing .5D **38**
NN17: Corby .1A **18**
Charles Studd Rd. NN3: N'ton .7F **75**
Charles Ter. *NN11: Dav* .2H **61**
(off Oxford St.)
Charlotte Pl. NN16: K'ing .5G **39**
CHARLTON .1H **127** (2B **140**)
Charlton Cl. NN2: K'thpe .1D **84**
CHARLTON-ON-OTMOOR .3B **140**
Charlton Rd. NN13: Even, Hin H .7A **128**
OX17: Ayn .7E **126**
Charlton Way NN13: F'hoe .6H **119**
CHARNDON .3C **141**
Charnwood Av. NN3: N'ton .4A **86**
Charnwood Cl. NN11: Dav .6G **59**
Charnwood Dr. NN15: Bar S .5J **43**
Charnwood Rd. NN17: Corby .6K **13**
Charter Ct. NN18: Corby .4K **17**
Charter Ga. NN3: Moul P .7J **73**
Charterhouse Cl. NN13: B'ley .4F **129**
Chartwell Av. NN3: N'ton .1K **85**
Chartwell Cl. NN11: Dav .3G **59**
CHARWELTON .3B **136**
Charwelton La. NN11: Hell .4C **104**
Charwelton Packhorse Bridge .3B **136**
Charwelton Rd. NN11: Byf .1J **107**
Chase, The NN6: Long B .1H **55**
NN6: Pits .1E **72**
Chase Cl. NN14: Stan .3F **19**
Chase Farm NN14: Ged .6D **46**
Chase Hill NN14: Ged .5C **46**
Chase Pk. Rd. NN7: Yar H .7F **103**
Chase Vw. Rd. NN14: Ged .5C **46**
Chaston Pl. NN16: K'ing .5G **39**
Chatelleraut Ct. NN17: Corby .5J **13**
Chater St. NN3: Moul .4A **74**
Chatsworth Av. NN3: N'ton .1C **86**
NN15: K'ing .5E **42**
Chatsworth Dr. NN8: Well .5H **65**
Chatsworth Rd. NN18: Corby .4J **17**
Chaucer Ct. NN2: N'ton .4G **85**
Chaucer Rd. NN8: Well .1H **77**
Chaucer St. NN2: N'ton .4G **85**
Chaucer Way NN11: Dav .1G **61**
CHAWSTON .3D **139**
Cheaney Dr. NN4: Gra P .6E **100**
Cheddar Cl. NN5: Dus .7J **83**
Cheddar Wlk. NN18: Corby .7F **13**
Chedington Cl. NN15: Bar S .5J **43**
Chedworth Cl. NN3: N'ton .4G **87**
Cheese La. *NN8: Well* .1B **78**
(off Market St.)
Chelfham Cl. NN3: West F .7A **86**
CHELLINGTON .3B **138**
Chelmorton Va. NN14: Des .1B **26**
Chelmsford Cl. NN4: N'ton .5B **94**
Cheltenham Cl. NN10: R'den .5F **81**
Cheltenham Rd.
NN18: Gt Oak, L Oak .5K **17**
CHELVESTON .6K **69** (2B **138**)
Chelveston Dr. NN17: Corby .6G **13**
Chelveston Rd. NN9: Raun .7H **53**
NN9: Stanw .1K **69**
NN10: High F .6G **69**
Cheney Ct. OX17: Mid C .5D **118**
Cheney Gdns. OX17: Mid C .5C **118**
Chepstow Cl. NN5: N'ton .7B **84**
NN15: K'ing .2H **43**
Chepstow Dr. NN8: Well .5H **65**
Chepstow Rd.
NN18: Gt Oak, L Oak .5J **17**
Chequers Cl. NN18: Corby .4K **17**
Chequers La. NN6: Rav .2B **34**
NN7: Gren .2C **102**
NN8: Well .7B **66**
Cheriton Cl. NN11: Dav .4H **59**
Cheriton Rd. NN18: Corby .2A **18**
Cheriton Way NN1: N'ton .1K **95**
Cherry Av. NN8: Well .5B **66**
Cherry Blossom Cl. NN3: N'ton .4E **86**
Cherry Cl. NN3: N'ton .4K **85**
Cherry Ct. NN9: Irth .3B **68**
Cherry Hall Rd. NN14: Week .1D **38**
Cherry Hill NN6: Old .6E **36**
Cherry Lodge Rd. NN3: N'ton .2E **86**
Cherry Orchard NN10: R'den .4F **81**
Cherry Rd. NN16: K'ing .5F **39**
Cherry St. NN9: Irth .3B **68**
NN14: Rin .1G **53**
Cherry Tree Cl. NN14: Des .3E **26**
Cherry Tree La. NN4: Gt Hou .4B **96**
Cherrytree Wlk. NN6: Syw .5G **75**
Cherry Wlk. NN9: Raun .7G **53**
Cherwell, The NN11: Dav .2E **60**
Cherwell Banks OX17: King S .1C **126**
Cherwell Grn. NN5: N'ton .5A **84**
Cherwell Ter. NN11: Woodf H .2D **108**
Cherwell Wlk. NN17: Corby .4J **13**
Chesham Ri. NN3: N'ton .2E **86**
Chesil Wlk. NN18: Corby .7F **13**
Chester Av. NN7: Harp .1A **92**
Chester Ct. NN15: K'ing .4D **42**
Chester Rd. NN8: Well .1D **78**
NN10: R'den .3C **80**
NN29: Irch .3H **79**
Chester Ter. NN7: Weed .3D **62**
CHESTERTON
Cambridgeshire .2D **135**
Oxfordshire .3B **140**
CHESTERTON GREEN .3A **136**
Chestnut Av. NN4: Woot .3E **100**
NN15: K'ing .1E **42**
NN17: Corby .4J **13**
Chestnut Cl. MK11: Stony S .4K **125**
NN6: Long B .2H **55**
NN7: Mil M .4K **99**
NN10: R'den .2C **80**
NN10: Wym .7E **80**
(off South Gro.)
NN11: Woodf H .2B **108**

148 A-Z Northamptonshire Atlas

Chestnut Ct. NN3: N'ton 4H 85
Chestnut Dr. NN12: Whit ...1C 122
NN13: B'ley ...2G 129
NN14: Des ...3F 27
NN14: Thra ...4H 51
Chestnut Gro. LE16: Clip ...6D 24
Chestnut Rd. NN3: N'ton ...5H 85
NN12: Yar G ...3K 123
Chestnut Ter. NN3: N'ton ...4H 85
Chettle Pl. NN12: Pot ...7J 123
CHETWODE ...3C 141
Cheviot Cl. NN16: K'ing ...2D 38
Cheviot Cl. NN4: N'ton ...4K 93
Chewton Cl. NN5: Dus ...7J 83
Cheyne Wlk. NN1: N'ton ...5K 131 (2E 94)
NN15: K'ing ...2G 43
Chichele Cl. NN10: High F ...7E 68
(off Hind Stile)
Chichele College ...6E 68
Chichele Ct. NN10: R'den ...2E 80
(off North St.)
Chichele St. NN10: High F ...6F 69
Chicheley Cotts. NN14: Thra ...3H 51
Chichester Cl. NN11: Dav ...2J 61
NN14: R'ell ...7H 27
Chieftan Bus. Pk. NN8: Well ...6F 65
Child's St. NN14: Den ...7G 51
Chiltern Av. NN5: Dus ...6J 83
Chiltern Cl. NN5: Dus ...6J 83
Chiltern Rd. NN11: Dav ...5G 59
NN16: K'ing ...3D 38
Chiltern Way NN5: Dus ...6J 83
Chilwell Cl. NN3: N'ton ...6C 86
CHIPPING WARDEN ...3D 110 (1A 140)
Chipsey Av. NN1: N'ton ...1J 95
NN7: Bug ...1J 105
Chisholm Cl. NN4: Woot ...3F 101
Choakles, The NN4: Woot ...2J 101
Chowns Mill Bus. Pk. NN9: Irth ...4E 68
Christchurch Dr. NN11: Dav ...3G 61
Christchurch Rd. NN1: N'ton ...7H 85
Christie Way NN15: K'ing ...2B 42
Christine Ct. NN9: Raun ...6J 53
Christopher Ct. NN6: Welf ...3G 29
Chulmleigh Wlk. NN3: N'ton ...7K 85
(not continuous)
Church Av. OX17: King S ...1B 126
CHURCH BRAMPTON ...5H 71 (2D 137)
Church Cl. LE16: Bray ...6B 10
LE16: Clip ...6D 24
MK19: Wick ...6C 124
NN6: W Had ...5H 29
NN7: Hart ...5H 117
NN7: Mil M ...4A 100
Churchcroft NN7: Roa ...2C 116
Church Dr. NN18: Gt Oak ...6G 17
CHURCH END
Cambridgeshire ...3D 135
Northamptonshire ...2J 107
Church End NN7: Pid ...2F 117
NN7: Roa ...2C 116
NN12: Pot ...6J 123
NN13: Crou ...5B 130
NN13: Syre ...5D 120
CHURCH ENSTONE ...3A 140
Church Farm NN6: Chu B ...4G 71
Church Farm Cl. NN29: Boz ...2H 103
Churchfield Cl. NN2: K'thpe ...2F 85
Church Flds. NN11: Stav ...4B 60
Church Gdns. NN6: Rav ...2C 34
Church Grn. NN5: N'ton ...4A 84
(not continuous)
NN11: Badby ...6D 104
NN14: Woodf ...7B 50
PE8: Barn ...6B 22
Church Hall Rd. NN10: R'den ...4C 80
Church Hill NN3: Moul ...4K 73
NN4: Woot ...3F 101
NN6: Holl ...6F 33
NN6: Rav ...2B 34
NN9: Fine ...6G 47
NN11: Badby ...6C 104
NN14: Ged ...5D 46
Churchill Av. NN3: N'ton ...2J 85
NN8: Well ...5K 65
NN9: Irth ...7A 52
Churchill Cl. NN14: R'ell ...6H 27
Churchill Rd. NN6: E Bart ...2D 88
NN11: Welt ...4C 59
Churchill Way NN13: B'ley ...5F 129
NN15: Bur L ...3J 45
NN15: K'ing ...1H 43
Church La. LE16: Clip ...6D 24
MK19: Dean ...5F 125
MK19: Wick ...6C 124
NN1: N'ton ...3H 131 (1D 94)
NN3: N'ton ...5D 86
NN6: Chu B ...5G 71
NN6: Col A ...2A 32
NN6: E Had ...3C 56
NN6: Holl ...6F 33
NN6: Old ...5D 36
NN6: Pits ...1E 72

Church La. NN6: Spra ...5C 34
NN6: Syw ...2G 75
NN6: Thorn ...3D 32
NN6: Wal ...1H 37
NN6: Welf ...3H 29
NN7: Blis ...2H 115
NN7: Braf G ...5H 97
NN7: Bug ...2H 105
NN7: Dod ...1A 62
NN7: Kisl ...3C 92
NN7: Lwr H ...7D 70
NN7: Neth H ...5J 63
NN7: Yar H ...5H 103
NN8: Wilby ...4G 77
NN10: Wym ...7E 80
NN11: Hell ...2B 104
NN12: Col H ...6F 105
NN12: Pot ...6J 123
NN12: Stoke B ...6D 116
NN12: Slapt ...6G 113
NN12: Tow ...3C 114
NN13: Crou ...5B 130
NN14: C'ley ...4F 41
NN14: C'ord ...3G 47
NN14: Den ...7G 51
NN15: Bur L ...2K 45
NN29: Gt Dod ...7K 77
NN29: Woll ...3E 90
OX17: Chac ...2B 118
OX17: Mid C ...5C 118
PE8: Barn ...6B 22
PE8: Warm ...2H 23
CHURCH LANGTON ...2D 133
CHURCH LAWFORD ...1A 136
Church Leys NN13: Even ...1B 130
(not continuous)
Church M. MK11: S Stra ...4K 125
(off High St.)
NN3: Moul ...4K 73
Church Mt. NN6: Guil ...7E 32
Church of the Holy Sepulchre ...3H 131
CHURCHOVER ...3B 132
Church Path Oak ...3A 138
Church Rd. NN6: Spra ...5C 34
NN7: Pid ...2F 117
NN9: Harg ...7J 49
NN11: Braun ...1A 58
NN11: Up Bod ...2B 106
NN13: B'ley ...4G 129
NN14: Pyt ...3B 44
OX17: Greatw ...3K 119
Church Row PE8: Pole ...3D 22
(off Hemington Rd.)
Church's Factory NN1: N'ton ...2J 131
CHURCH STOWE ...7E 62 (3C 137)
Church St. LE16: Cotti ...4C 12
LE16: Sibb ...3D 24
LE16: Wilb ...5H 11
MK11: Stony S ...4K 125
NN2: Bou ...5D 72
NN3: Moul ...4K 73
NN6: Brix ...2H 35
NN6: Crick ...3H 31
NN6: Long B ...1H 55
NN6: Mears A ...3A 76
NN6: Nas ...3H 33
NN6: Wat ...6D 54
NN7: Cog ...1K 97
NN7: Neth H ...5J 63
NN7: Roth ...2F 99
NN7: Weed ...4D 62
NN8: Well ...1B 78
NN9: Fine ...7G 47
NN9: Harg ...6H 49
NN9: Irth ...2B 52
NN9: Raun ...5K 53
NN9: Stanw ...1K 69
NN10: R'den ...3E 80
NN11: Byf ...2J 107
NN11: Newn ...7K 61
NN11: Stav ...4A 60
(not continuous)
NN11: Woodf H ...2D 108
NN12: Blak ...5J 109
NN12: Pat ...5H 105
NN12: Silv ...2G 121
NN13: Helm ...2B 120
NN14: Brig ...2D 20
NN14: Brou ...6G 41
NN14: Ish ...3G 45
NN14: Rin ...1F 53
NN14: Titch ...1H 49
NN14: Woodf ...7B 50
NN15: Bur L ...2K 45
NN17: Weld ...6J 15
OX17: Sulg ...6G 111
PE8: Nass ...5G 7
PE8: Oun ...5J 21
PE8: Pole ...3D 22
PE8: Warm ...2H 23
PE8: Eas H ...1C 6
Church Vw. NN2: K'thpe ...3C 84
NN3: Moul ...3K 73

Church Vw. NN4: Woot ...3F 101
NN6: Ect ...2J 87
NN6: Wal ...1H 37
NN9: Raun ...5J 53
NN12: Greens N ...1J 113
NN13: B'ley ...4H 129
NN14: Brou ...6G 41
NN15: Bur L ...1K 45
NN17: Weld ...6J 15
Church Vw. Rd. NN14: Des ...2E 26
Church Wlk. CV23: Bar ...2C 54
CV23: Kil ...6C 30
NN3: Gt Bil ...4E 86
NN7: Pid ...2F 117
NN9: Irth ...2C 68
NN11: Dav ...1H 61
NN14: Den ...7G 51
NN14: L Add ...4A 52
NN14: Rin ...1G 53
NN16: K'ing ...7D 38
NN17: Corby ...7C 14
NN17: Weld ...6J 15
NN29: Boz ...2H 103
PE8: King C ...2G 9
Church Way NN3: West F ...5A 86
NN6: Ect ...2J 87
NN6: Guil ...7D 32
NN7: D'ton ...5B 102
NN7: Gren ...2C 102
NN8: Well ...1B 78
NN12: Whit ...1A 122
Church Way NN3: West F ...6A 86
Cineworld Cinema
Northampton ...2J 93
Cinnamon Cl. NN4: N'ton ...2E 100
Circus End NN5: Dus ...5H 83
Circus Gro. PE8: Pole ...4D 22
Cirrus Pk. NN3: Moul P ...6H 73
Cissbury Rd. NN4: N'ton ...3A 94
City Bldgs. NN1: N'ton ...4J 131
Clannell Rd. NN4: N'ton ...7B 94
CLAPHAM ...3C 139
Clare Av. NN11: Dav ...1H 61
Clare Cl. NN6: E Bart ...3E 88
Clare Cres. NN12: Tow ...4B 114
Clare Dr. NN14: Thra ...3H 51
Claregate NN4: N'ton ...7C 94
Clarence Av. NN2: K'thpe ...5D 84
Clarence Ct. NN10: R'den ...5D 80
Clarence Rd. NN16: K'ing ...6E 38
Clare Rd. NN8: Well ...2H 77
Clare St. NN1: N'ton ...2K 131 (7E 84)
NN9: Raun ...6J 53
Clare Wlk. NN10: High F ...7E 68
Clark Cres. NN12: Tow ...1C 114
Clarke Cl. NN9: Irth ...7A 52
NN16: K'ing ...5C 38
Clarke Ct. NN6: E Bart ...2E 88
Clarke Ho. NN1: N'ton ...6H 85
(off Roe Rd.)
Clarke Rd. NN1: N'ton ...6H 85
NN17: Corby ...5J 13
Clarkes Way NN11: Welt ...2J 59
NN13: B'ley ...4E 128
Clarks La. NN13: F'hoe ...7G 119
Claudius Way NN8: Well ...3D 78
NN29: Irch ...3D 78
Claughton Rd. NN4: Far C ...4E 94
CLAYBROOKE MAGNA ...3A 132
CLAYBROOKE PARVA ...3A 132
CLAY COTON ...1B 136
Clay Dick NN14: Brig, Stan ...7G 19
CLAYDON ...3A 136
Claydon Cl. NN8: Well ...7K 65
Claydon Rd. NN11: Dav ...3F 59
Clayfield Cl. NN3: Moul P ...7J 73
Clayland Cl. NN29: Boz ...3G 103
Claylands, The NN7: Cog ...1H 97
Clay La. NN17: Gret ...6C 8
Claystones NN1: N'ton ...5J 93
Cleaver Ct. NN15: K'ing ...1C 42
(off Station Rd.)
Cleavers La. NN6: Old ...5E 36
Cleburne Cl. NN9: Stanw ...7F 53
Clee Ri. NN5: Dus ...6J 83
Cleeve Way NN8: Well ...4J 77
Clement Bois NN13: B'ley ...3F 129
Clevedon Cl. NN11: Dav ...3G 59
Cleveland Av. NN16: K'ing ...3D 38
Cleveland Pl. NN4: N'ton ...5B 94
CLEVELEY ...3A 140
Clickers Cl. NN5: Upton ...3J 93
Clickers M. NN5: Upton ...3J 93
Clickers Pl. NN5: Upton ...3J 93
Clifden Ter. NN6: E Had ...3C 56
Cliffe Rd. PE9: Eas H ...3C 6
CLIFFORD HILL ...1E 96
Clifford Hill Mill NN7: L Hou ...1D 96
CLIFTON ...2A 140
Clifton Cl. NN16: Long B ...1E 42
NN15: K'ing ...1E 42
Clifton Dr. PE8: Oun ...5G 21
Clifton Gro. NN15: K'ing ...1E 42

CLIFTON REYNES ...3B 138
Clifton Sq. NN17: Corby ...5K 13
CLIFTON UPON DUNSMORE ...1B 136
Cliftonville NN1: N'ton ...2F 95
Cliftonville Ct. NN1: N'ton ...1G 95
Cliftonville Rd. NN1: N'ton ...2G 95
Clinton Rd. NN4: Far C ...4C 94
CLIPSTON ...6D 24 (3D 133)
Clipstone Ct. NN14: R'ell ...7F 27
Clipston Fld. Pl. NN14: R'ell ...4F 87
Clipston La. LE16: Gt Oxe ...7H 25
Clipston Rd. LE16: Clip ...7G 25
LE16: E Far, Mar T ...3J 25
Clipston Way NN5: Dus ...5H 83
Clive Cl. NN15: K'ing ...1G 43
Clock Mdw. NN11: Byf ...2H 107
Clock Twr. Ct. NN3: N'ton ...7B 74
Cloisters, The NN8: Well ...2C 78
NN11: Dav ...1J 61
CLOPTON ...3C 135
Close, The NN2: K'thpe ...2D 84
NN7: Roa ...2C 116
NN9: Irth ...3C 68
NN12: East ...6J 105
NN15: K'ing ...2D 42
OX17: Chip W ...3D 110
OX17: Greatw ...3K 119
PE9: Eas H ...3B 6
Close Rd. NN7: Neth H ...6J 63
Cloutsham St.
NN1: N'ton ...2K 131 (7E 84)
Clovelly Ct. NN18: Corby ...2A 18
Clover Dr. NN10: R'den ...5F 81
NN14: Thra ...3H 51
Clover Fld. NN4: Gra P ...6G 101
Clover Gdns. NN16: K'ing ...5D 38
Clover La. NN2: K'thpe ...1B 84
Clover St. NN5: Upton ...2H 93
Club Diana
(Wellingborough Squash Club)
...5D 66
Club La. NN14: Woodf ...7B 50
Club St. NN16: K'ing ...6D 38
Clumber Cl. NN18: Corby ...7G 13
Clumber Dr. NN3: N'ton ...7B 86
Cluniac Cl. NN3: N'ton ...7F 75
Clun Wlk. NN17: Corby ...4H 13
Clwyd Wlk. NN17: Corby ...4H 13
Clydesdale Rd. NN17: Corby ...5H 13
Coaching Wlk. NN3: N'ton ...4A 86
Coach Yd. NN12: Pot ...6J 123
Coalport Cl. NN14: Des ...2C 26
COALVILLE ...1A 132
Cobblers Cl. NN12: Blak ...5J 109
Cobblers Pl. NN29: Boz ...3G 103
Cobblestone Cl. NN4: N'ton ...5J 93
Cobb's La. NN29: Woll ...3D 90
Cobden St. NN16: K'ing ...6C 38
Cob Dr. NN4: Swan H ...6G 93
Cobley Cl. NN11: Woodf H ...2E 108
Cockayne Cl. NN14: R'ell ...7G 27
Cockerell Rd. NN17: Corby ...5C 14
Cockerel Ri. NN14: Des ...1D 26
Cocker Wood Cl. NN18: Gt Oak ...5G 17
Cockley Rd. NN13: F'hoe ...6H 119
OX17: Greatw ...4H 119
Codlin Cl. NN3: N'ton ...5D 86
Coffee Tavern Ct. NN10: R'den ...3E 80
(off High St.)
Coffee Tavern La. NN10: R'den ...3E 80
Cogan Cres. NN14: R'ell ...7E 26
COGENHOE ...1J 97 (2A 138)
Coggins Cl. NN9: Raun ...6H 53
COLD ASHBY ...2A 32 (1C 137)
Cold Ashby Rd. NN6: Guil ...4C 32
NN6: Nas ...4F 33
NN6: Thorn ...3C 32
COLD BRAYFIELD ...3B 138
Coldermeadow Av. NN18: Corby ...2G 17
COLD HIGHAM ...6F 105 (3C 137)
COLD OVERTON ...1A 134
Coldstream Cl. NN11: Dav ...2G 61
Coldstream La. NN4: H'stone ...7F 95
Cole Ct. NN9: Raun ...7H 53
NN16: K'ing ...5D 38
Coleman Cl. NN6: Crick ...3H 31
Coleman's La. PE8: King C ...2H 9
(off Wood Rd.)
Coleman St. NN9: Raun ...6J 53
Coleraine Cl. NN2: K'thpe ...2B 84
Coleridge Wlk. NN11: Dav ...6G 59
Coleridge Way NN17: Corby ...5H 13
Coles Cl. NN15: Bur L ...2J 45
COLESDEN ...3D 139
Coles Ri. NN13: B'ley ...4E 128
Cole St. NN10: R'den ...1B 80
College Fld. Cl. NN3: N'ton ...3F 87
College Flds. OX17: Ayn ...7E 126
College La. NN12: Woode ...7F 109
College St. NN1: N'ton ...4H 131 (1D 94)
NN8: Well ...1K 77
NN9: Irth ...2B 68
NN10: High F ...6F 69

College St.—Crown Ct.

College St. NN10: R'den 3E 80
NN29: Woll 4E 90
College St. M. NN1: N'ton 4H 131
Collingcroft Cl. NN4: N'ton 1B 100
Collingdale Rd. NN3: N'ton 3A 86
Collingham Cl. NN9: Stanw 7F 53
COLLINGTREE 4D 100 (3D 137)
COLLINGTREE PARK 2D 100
Collingtree Pk. Golf Course 3C 100
Collingtree Rd. NN7: Mil M 4A 100
Collingwood Av. NN17: Corby 6F 13
Collingwood Rd. NN1: N'ton 5G 85
Collingwood Way NN11: Dav 1K 61
Collins Cl. NN12: Tow 2C 114
Collinshill NN7: Flore 1F 63
Collins St. NN1: N'ton 7G 85
Collmead Ct. NN3: N'ton 2E 86
Collswell La. NN12: Blak 4J 109
Collyns Way PE9: Colly 6C 6
COLLYWESTON 6C 6 (1B 134)
Collyweston Quarries Nature Reserve 3A 6
Collyweston Rd. NN3: N'ton 1F 87
Colmar Cl. NN11: Dav 6F 59
COLMWORTH 3D 139
Colne Cl. NN17: Corby 4H 13
Colne Way NN5: N'ton 5K 83
Colonial Dr. NN4: N'ton 3D 100
Colseed Rd. NN14: Maw 6B 40
Coltsfoot Rd. NN10: R'den 6F 81
Columbus Ct. NN11: Dav 5G 59
Columbus Cres. NN14: R'ell 6H 27
Colwell Rd. NN8: Well 1D 78
Colwyn Rd. NN1: N'ton 7F 85
Colyers Av. NN18: Corby 2G 17
Comfrey Cl. NN10: R'den 6E 80
Commercial Rd. NN16: K'ing 7C 38
NN17: Corby 7C 14
Commercial St.
NN1: N'ton 6H 131 (2D 94)
NN10: High F 7E 68
Commercial Way NN8: Well 1B 78
Compass Bus. Pk. NN4: Brack 6J 95
Compton Cl. NN6: E Bart 3D 88
Compton Grn. NN18: Corby 7F 13
Compton Ho. NN1: N'ton 4F 131
Compton Pl. NN16: K'ing 7G 39
Compton Rd. NN8: Well 7D 66
Compton St. NN1: N'ton 3F 131 (1C 94)
NN14: Des 2D 26
Compton Way NN6: E Bart 3D 88
Conduit La. NN1: N'ton 4H 131 (1D 94)
Coney Gree NN4: H'stone 7G 95
Coneygree Ct. NN3: N'ton 5E 86
Coneygree Wlk. NN3: N'ton 5E 86
Coneywell Ct. NN3: N'ton 5C 86
CONGERSTONE 1A 132
Conifer Ri. NN3: N'ton 4B 86
CONINGTON 3D 135
Coniston Av. NN3: Spin H 3J 85
Coniston Cl. NN8: Well 7H 65
NN10: High F 4E 68
NN11: Dav 1F 61
Coniston Rd. NN16: K'ing 7B 38
Connaught St.
NN1: N'ton 2J 131 (7E 84)
NN16: K'ing 6F 39
Connegar Leys NN7: Blis 2J 115
Connell Ct. NN17: Corby 1A 18
Connolly Cl. NN14: R'ell 6J 27
Connolly Dr. NN14: R'ell 6J 27
Connolly Rd. NN5: Dus 6E 82
Constable Dr. NN8: Well 5K 65
NN15: Bar S 3J 43
Constable Rd. NN18: Corby 1K 17
Constable Wlk. NN14: Woodf 6B 50
Conway Cl. NN5: N'ton 4K 83
NN8: Well 6H 65
NN10: R'den 5D 80
Conway Dr. NN14: Thra 3K 51
(not continuous)
NN15: Bur L 2H 45
Conway Wlk. NN17: Corby 4J 13
Conygar Cl. NN18: Gt Oak 7F 17
Conyngham Rd. NN3: N'ton 4C 86
Cony Wlk. NN4: Gra P 5G 101
Cook Cl. NN11: Dav 5H 59
NN14: R'ell 7H 27
Cooks Rd. NN17: Corby 5G 15
Cook's Ter. NN6: Long B 2G 55
Cook's Way NN6: Long B 2G 55
Coombes Yd. LE16: Sibb 2D 24
Coomb Rd. NN18: Gt Oak 5J 17
Co-operative Row NN10: R'den 4E 80
Cooper Cl. NN12: Tow 1C 114
Cooper Ct. NN14: Thra 4H 51
Cooper Dr. NN8: Well 4A 66
Copelands Rd. NN14: Des 2F 27
Copenhagen Rd. NN18: Corby 5E 16
COPLE 3D 139
Copperfield Cl. NN16: K'ing 3E 38
Copper Leaf Cl. NN3: Moul 7K 73
Coppertree Wlk. NN14: Thra 4H 51
Coppice, The NN14: Thra 4H 51
Coppice Cl. NN11: Dav 3H 61
NN15: Bur L 1K 45
Coppice Dr. NN3: N'ton 1H 85
COPPINGFORD 3D 135
Copse Cl. NN2: K'thpe 1A 84
NN15: Bur L 1K 45
COPSTON MAGNA 3A 132
Copymoor Cl. NN4: Woot 2H 101
Cora Rd. NN16: K'ing 5G 39
Corbieres Cl. NN5: New D 4F 83
CORBY 7K 13 (3A 134)
Corby Cube 7K 13
Corby-East Midlands International Pool 7J 13
Corby Ga. NN17: Corby 4G 15
Corby Ga. Bus. Pk. NN17: Corby 4G 15
Corby Golf Range 5D 12
Corby Indoor Tennis Cen. 3H 13
Corby Rd. LE16: Cotti 4C 12
NN14: Stan 3F 19
NN17: Corby 1E 14
NN17: Gret 7C 8
NN17: Weld 5G 15
Corby Station (Rail) 7B 14
Cordon Cl. NN3: N'ton 3E 86
Cordon Cres. NN6: E Bart 2E 88
Cordwainer Gro. NN14: Thra 4H 51
Cordwainer Ho. *NN5: N'ton 2B 94*
(off Byfield Rd.)
Cordwainers NN10: R'den 4F 81
Corfe Cl. NN18: Corby 4K 17
Cornfield Cl. NN2: K'thpe 1C 84
Cornfield Way NN15: Bur L 3K 45
Cornflower Cl. NN4: Gra P 6G 101
Cornhill Cl. NN5: Dus 3H 83
Corn Kiln Cl. NN7: Cog 1J 97
Corn La. NN8: Well 1B 78
Corn Mill Cl. NN8: Well 1D 78
Cornwall Cl. NN17: Corby 7H 13
Cornwall Rd. NN16: K'ing 6F 39
Cornwell Bus. Pk. NN4: Brack 5J 95
Corolla Way NN4: Upton 6F 93
Coronation Av. NN10: R'den 4B 80
NN14: R'ell 6G 27
Coronation Ct. NN4: N'ton 4B 94
Coronation Rd. NN11: Newn 7J 61
Corporation St. NN17: Corby 7K 13
Corran Cl. NN5: N'ton 6K 83
Cory Gdns. NN7: Harp 7B 82
COSBY 2B 132
COSGROVE 6D 122 (1D 141)
Cosgrove Rd. MK19: Old S 2J 125
NN2: K'thpe 1D 84
Cosgrove Way NN2: K'thpe 1D 84
COSSINGTON 1C 133
Cosy Nook NN14: Thra 3G 51
COTESBACH 3B 132
COTON 1C 137
Coton Manor Garden 1C 137
Coton Rd. NN6: Guil 7E 32
NN6: Rav 2B 34
Cotswold Av. NN5: Dus 6H 83
NN16: K'ing 4D 38
Cotswold Cl. NN11: Dav 5G 59
Cotswold Ct. NN5: Dus 6H 83
Cotswold Dr. NN8: Well 4J 77
Cottage Cl. NN2: K'thpe 2B 84
Cottage Gdns. NN3: Gt Bil 3E 86
NN10: R'den 6F 81
Cottagewell Ct. NN3: N'ton 5C 86
COTTARVILLE 5A 86 (2D 137)
Cottarville NN3: N'ton 5A 86
COTTERSTOCK 1K 21 (2C 135)
Cotterstock Rd. PE8: Oun 3H 21
COTTESBROOKE 1D 137
Cottesbrooke Gdns. NN4: N'ton 1E 100
Cottesbrooke Hall 1D 137
Cottesbrooke Pk. NN11: Dav 5F 59
Cottesbrooke Rd. NN6: Nas 3H 33
NN17: Corby 6G 13
COTTESMORE 1B 134
Cottesmore Av. NN15: Bar S 5J 43
Cottesmore Cl. NN5: Dus 5G 83
Cottesmore Way NN8: Well 1J 77
COTTINGHAM 4C 12 (2A 134)
Cottingham Dr. NN3: Moul 6J 73
Cottingham Rd. LE16: Rock 2E 12
NN17: Corby 7H 13
NN18: Corby 6F 13
Cottingham Way NN14: Thra 3G 51
Cottingham Way Ind. Est.
NN14: Thra 3G 51
COTTISFORD 2B 140
Cotton Ct. *NN4: N'ton 3D 94*
(off Pomfret Arms Cl.)
COTTON END 4C 94
Cotton End NN4: N'ton 7H 131 (3D 94)
NN6: Long B 1K 55
Cotton La. NN9: Stanw 1H 69 & 7D 52
Cotton Mdw. NN5: N'ton 7K 83
Cottons, The LE16: Rock 1G 13
NN8: Well 5J 65
Coughton Cl. NN11: Dav 4G 59
Coulon Cl. NN29: Irch 6H 79
Coulthard Cl. NN12: Tow 1D 114
Council St. NN29: Boz 2H 103
NN29: Woll 4E 90
Countess Ct. NN5: N'ton 7B 84
Countess Rd. NN5: N'ton 7B 84
COUNTESTHORPE 2B 132
Counties Crematorium, The
NN4: Mil M 2K 99
Countryside NN11: Braun 1A 58
Counts Farm Rd. NN18: Corby 2K 17
County Ground, The 6H 85
County Rd. NN13: B'ley 5H 129
Courier Rd. NN17: Corby 6B 14
Court Dr. NN16: K'ing 3D 38
COURTEENHALL 3D 137
Courteenhall Cl. NN2: K'thpe 1E 84
Courteenhall Rd.
NN7: Blis, Court 1H 115
Court Ho. Cl. NN6: Crea 6K 33
Court La. NN29: Boz 2H 103
Courtman Rd. NN9: Stanw 7F 53
Court M. NN8: Well 2C 78
Courtney Rd. NN10: R'den 4D 80
Court Rd. NN1: N'ton 5G 131 (2D 94)
Courtwood NN9: Stanw 1K 69
Courtyard, The NN3: N'ton 5K 85
NN6: Ect 2J 87
Court Yd. La. NN11: Badby 5D 104
Covallen Ct. NN10: R'den 2F 81
COVENTRY 1A 136
COVENTRY AIRPORT 1A 136
Coverack Cl. NN4: Del 6C 94
Coverdale NN2: K'thpe 1A 84
Covert Cl. NN2: K'thpe 7B 72
COVINGTON 1C 139
Covington Gro. NN8: Well 6B 66
Covington St. NN1: N'ton 7H 85
Cowbeck Cl. NN4: Woot 3F 101
Cowgill Cl. NN3: N'ton 3E 86
Cowley Cl. NN4: Woot 1E 100
Cowley Rd. NN11: Dav 7G 59
Cowley Way CV23: Kil 7B 30
Cowper Cl. NN6: E Bart 2F 89
NN9: Irth 3A 68
Cowper Rd. NN8: Well 1H 77
NN11: Dav 1G 61
Cowper St. NN1: N'ton 7F 85
NN16: K'ing 4D 38
Cowper Ter. NN2: N'ton 5F 85
Cowslip Cl. NN10: R'den 5F 81
NN18: Corby 4J 17
Cowslip Hill NN14: Maw 5B 40
Cow Yd. NN2: K'thpe 3C 84
Cox Gdns. NN12: Greens N 1J 113
Cox's Cl. NN6: Long B 2H 55
Cox's La. NN11: Hell 2B 104
NN14: Brou 5G 41
Crab Apple Way NN14: Thra 4J 51
Crabb St. NN10: R'den 4E 80
Crabb Tree Dr. NN3: N'ton 6C 74
Crabtree Cl. NN7: Hart 5J 117
NN8: Well 3A 78
Crabtree Ho. *NN11: Dav 1H 61*
(off Brook St.)
Crabtree La. NN6: Col A 2B 32
Craddock Ct. NN29: Irch 5J 79
Cragside NN8: Well 6H 65
Craigie NN8: Well 1H 77
Cranbrook Rd. NN2: N'ton 5D 84
Crane Cl. NN8: Well 3B 78
NN10: R'den 1E 80
NN14: Brou 5G 41
Cranesbill Cl. NN14: Des 1D 26
Crane Wlk. NN3: N'ton 7B 74
Cranford Ho. *NN2: K'thpe 3D 84*
(off Kingsland Av.)
Cranford Rd. NN2: K'thpe 3D 84
NN14: C'ord, Gt Ad 1A 52
NN15: Bar S 4K 43
NN15: Bur L 1K 45
(not continuous)
CRANFORD ST ANDREW 2G 47 (1B 138)
CRANFORD ST JOHN 2H 47 (1B 138)
Cranleigh Rd. NN15: K'ing 3D 42
Cranmere Av. NN1: N'ton 1J 95
CRANMORE 1D 135
CRANOE 2D 133
Cransley Ct. NN14: Maw 7B 40
Cransley Gdns. NN17: Corby 6G 13
Cransley Hill NN14: Brou 5G 41
Cransley Ri. NN14: Maw 6B 40
Cransley Rd. NN14: Lod 1D 40
Cransley Sailing Club 1G 41
Cransley Wlk. NN3: N'ton 7F 75
Cranstoun St. NN1: N'ton 2J 131 (7E 84)
Craven St. NN1: N'ton 1J 131 (7E 84)
Crawford Av. NN5: N'ton 7K 83
Crawford Gro. NN17: Corby 5K 13
Crawley Av. NN8: Well 5J 65
Craxford Rd. NN17: Gret 6C 8
CREATON 6K 33 (1D 137)
Creaton Rd. NN6: Crea, Holl 6G 33
Crediton Cl. NN3: West F 7A 86
Creed Rd. PE8: Oun 3G 21
Creighton Cres. NN15: Bar S 4H 43
Crescent, The NN1: N'ton 6G 85
NN3: Moul 4A 74
NN7: Flore 1G 63
NN7: Hack 1F 117
NN8: Well 5J 65
NN10: R'den 3B 80
NN12: Pat 5H 105
NN12: Whit 1C 122
NN14: R'ell 7F 27
NN15: Bur L 1K 45
NN15: K'ing 1D 42
PE9: Eas H 2B 6
Cresswell Rd. NN10: R'den 3C 80
Cresswell Wlk. NN17: Corby 4H 13
Crestline Ct. NN3: N'ton 1D 86
Crestwood Gdns. NN3: N'ton 1C 86
Crestwood Rd. NN3: N'ton 7B 74
CRICK 4J 31 (1B 136)
Crick Cl. NN17: Corby 4B 14
Cricketers Grn. NN17: Weld 5K 15
Cricklade Cl. NN3: N'ton 1A 96
Crickley Cres. NN4: N'ton 4K 93
Crick Motorway Est. NN6: Crick 3F 31
Crick Rd. CV23: Hill 1A 30
NN6: W Had 5F 29
NN6: Yel 1J 31 & 7B 28
Crimea Cl. NN4: Woot 1F 101
Crispian Ct. NN10: R'den 3D 80
Crispin Ho. NN1: N'ton 4F 131
Crispin Pl. NN16: K'ing 7D 38
Crispin St. NN1: N'ton 3G 131 (1D 94)
NN14: R'ell 6G 27
Crocket Cl. NN2: N'ton 4F 85
Crocus Way NN10: R'den 6E 80
CROFT 2B 132
Croft, The NN5: Dall 5A 84
NN6: Brix 3H 35
NN7: Weed 3D 62
NN11: Dav 3H 61
NN13: B'ley 4G 129
Croft Cl. NN8: Well 7H 65
Crofters Cl. NN4: N'ton 1C 100
Croft La. NN7: Roa 2C 116
NN11: Stav 4A 60
Croftmeadow Ct. NN3: N'ton 2E 86
Crofton Ct. NN3: Moul P 6G 73
Croft Way NN7: Weed 4B 62
NN10: R'den 2G 81
Cromarty Ct. NN17: Corby 1A 18
Cromarty Ho. *NN17: Corby 1A 18*
(off Elizabeth St.)
Crome Cl. NN8: Well 4A 66
Cromer Rd. NN9: Fine 7H 47
Cromwell Cl. NN14: Des 2D 26
Cromwell Ct. NN8: Well 7C 66
Cromwell Cres. LE16: Mkt H 1K 25
Cromwell Rd. NN10: R'den 2F 81
NN16: K'ing 7C 38
Cromwell St.
NN1: N'ton 2G 131 (1D 94)
Cronin Courtyard NN18: Corby 6F 15
Cronin Rd. NN18: Corby 6F 15
CROPREDY 1A 140
CROPSTON 1B 132
Crosby PE8: Oun 5H 21
Cross, The NN4: Gt Hou 5B 96
Crossbrooks NN4: Woot 2G 101
Cross Ct. NN16: K'ing 6C 38
Crosse Cl. NN7: Weed 3D 62
Cross Hill NN6: Brix 2H 35
Cross Keys Ct. *NN13: B'ley 4G 129*
(off High St.)
Cross Keys Dr. NN14: Thra 3G 51
Cross La. NN11: Braun 1B 58
NN13: Helm 1C 120
NN14: Ald 5A 20
Cross Rd. NN8: Well 6C 66
Cross's Grange NN7: Hart 6G 117
Cross St. NN3: Moul 4K 73
NN11: Dav 1G 61
NN14: R'ell 6H 27
NN16: K'ing 5C 38
Cross Tree Rd. MK19: Wick 6B 124
Cross Waters Cl. NN4: Woot 2G 101
Cross Way NN9: Irth 4A 68
Crouch Rd. NN9: Irth 3C 68
CROUGHTON 5B 130 (2B 140)
Croughton Cl. NN2: K'thpe 1D 84
Croughton Rd. OX17: Ayn 7F 127
Crowberry Av. NN3: Moul 6K 73
CROWFIELD 5A 120 (1C 141)
CROWLAND 1D 135
Crow La. NN3: L Bill, N'ton 6F 87
Crow La. Ind. Est. NN3: N'ton 6F 87
Crown Apartments *NN16: K'ing 7D 38*
(off Dryland St.)
Crown Ct. NN10: R'den 2B 80
NN17: Corby 1K 17

Crown La. NN6: W Had 6H 29
  NN14: R'ell 6F 27
Crown Pk. NN10: R'den 1B 80
Crownsmead NN4: N'ton 6J 93
Crown St. NN16: K'ing 6D 38
Crown Way NN10: R'den 1B 80
Crowthorp Rd. NN3: N'ton 1F 87
Croxdale Cl. NN2: K'thpe 1A 84
Croxen Cl. NN15: Bur L 2K 45
CROXTON 2D 139
Croyde Av. NN18: Corby 2A 18
Croyland Hall
  (Wellingborough Heritage Cen. & Mus.)
  . . . . .1B 78
Croyland Rd. NN8: Well 1K 77
Crucible Rd. NN17: Corby 6C 14
Crystal Cl. NN16: K'ing 6F 39
Cube, The NN1: N'ton 5K 131
Cubleigh Cl. NN3: Moul 7K 73
CUBLINGTON 3D 141
Cukow Cl. NN14: Maw 6B 40
Cullahill Ct. NN4: N'ton 5K 93
Culloden Ct. NN17: Corby 1A 18
Culloden Dr. NN15: K'ing 2G 43
Culme Cl. PE8: Oun 3G 21
Culross Wlk. NN18: Corby 3H 17
CULWORTH 7B 110 (1B 140)
Culworth Cres. NN2: K'thpe 1E 84
Culworth Rd. OX17: Chip W 3D 110
Cumberland Av.
  NN9: Stanw . . . . . . .1K 69 & 7F 53
Cumberland Cl. NN3: Spin H 3H 85
Cumbrae Dr. NN3: Gt Bil 4F 87
Cunliffe Dr. NN16: K'ing 5C 38
Cunliffe Dr. Ind. Est. NN16: K'ing . .5C 38
Cunningham Cl. NN10: High F 7E 68
  NN11: Dav 1K 61
Cupar Cres. NN17: Corby 1A 18
Curgenven Cl. NN11: Byf 2K 107
Curlbrook Cl. NN4: Woot 2H 101
Curlew Way NN11: Dav 7H 59
Currie Rd. NN2: K'thpe 5D 84
Curtis M. NN8: Well 5H 65
Curtlee Hill NN4: Woot 3G 101
Curver Way NN17: Corby 4E 14
Cut Throat La. NN29: Gt Dod 6G 77
Cuttle Mill La. NN12: Paul 6H 115
Cyclamen Cl. NN3: N'ton 1K 95
Cygnet Dr. NN4: Swan H 7H 93
Cypress Cl. NN14: Des 2C 26
Cypress Ct. NN3: N'ton 3B 86
Cyril St. NN1: N'ton 1F 95
Cytringan Cl. NN15: K'ing 3C 42

D

DADFORD 2C 141
Dadford Rd. NN12: Silv 4H 121
DADLINGTON 2A 132
Daffodil Dr. NN10: R'den 6E 80
Dag La. NN29: Boz 3H 103
Dahlia Rd. NN16: K'ing 5F 39
Daimler Cl. NN3: N'ton 2G 87
  NN11: Dav 7F 59
Dainty Gro. NN4: Gra P 5F 101
  NN6: W Had 6J 29
Dairy Cl. NN6: Brix 4G 35
  NN6: W Had 6J 29
Dairy Fld. NN6: Rav 2B 34
Dairy Ground OX17: King S 1C 126
Dairymeadow Ct. NN3: N'ton 7C 74
Dairy Way NN9: Irth 4B 68
Daisybank Av. NN14: R'ell 6E 26
Daisy Cl. NN18: Corby 4H 17
Daisy Cft. NN10: R'den 5F 81
Dakin Cl. PE8: King C 1H 9
D'Albini Cl. LE16: Stoke A 6G 11
Dalby Cl. NN16: K'ing 3C 38
Dale, The NN8: Well 7H 65
Dale Av. NN8: Well 7H 65
Dale Cl. NN6: Mears A 3B 76
  NN8: Well 7H 65
  NN11: Dav 5G 59
  NN13: B'ley 3H 129
Dale Ho. NN8: Well 1A 78
             (off Hill St.)
Dalestones NN4: N'ton 5J 93
Dale St. NN8: Well 1A 78
  NN17: Corby 6J 13
Daleswood Ri. PE8: King C 2G 9
Dalkeith Av. NN16: K'ing 7D 38
        (off British La.)
Dalkeith Pl. NN16: K'ing 7D 38
Dalkeith Rd. NN8: Well 4A 78
Dallacre Bus. Units LE16: Wilb . . .6J 11
Dallacre Dr. LE16: Wilb 6H 11
DALLINGTON 5A 84
Dallington Cl. NN14: Ged 6C 46
Dallington Ct. NN5: Dall 6A 84
Dallington Grn. NN5: Dall 6A 84
Dallington Haven NN5: Dall 6A 84
Dallington Pk. Rd. NN5: Dall 6A 84
Dallington Rd. NN5: Dall, N'ton . . .6A 84

DALSCOTE 7A 98 (3C 137)
Dalston Wlk. NN3: N'ton 2K 85
Dalton Rd. NN17: Corby 3K 13
Damherst Piece NN6: Brix 4J 35
Damson Cl. NN14: Thra 4J 51
Damson Dell NN11: Dav 6D 86
Dance Way NN8: Well 4A 66
Dando Cl. NN29: Woll 5E 90
Dands Cl. OX17: Mid C 6D 118
Dands Dr. OX17: Mid C 6D 118
Danefield Rd. NN3: N'ton 4J 85
Daneholme Av. NN11: Dav 6H 59
Daneholme Cl. NN11: Dav 6H 59
Dane Ridge NN5: Dus 1H 93
Danes Backside NN2: K'thpe 3C 84
Danes Camp Leisure Cen. 7C 94
Danes Camp Way NN4: N'ton 5J 93
Danesholme Cen. NN18: Corby 4F 17
Danesholme Rd. NN18: Corby 3E 16
Danes Way NN6: Crick 1D 30
Danetre Dr. NN11: Dav 1J 61
Danetree Gdns. NN3: N'ton 4J 85
Danewood Gdns. NN3: N'ton 4J 85
Danford Cl. PE8: Oun 5H 21
Danfords PE8: Oun 5H 21
Daniad Ct. NN13: B'ley 3F 129
Daniell Wlk. NN18: Corby 1J 17
Daniels Rd. NN8: L Irch 4D 78
Dapplestone Cl. NN4: N'ton 5J 93
Darby Cl. NN8: Well 7F 65
Dardis Ct. NN2: N'ton 5F 85
Darenth Ct. NN1: N'ton 2H 131
Darescroft LE16: Mid 4A 12
Dark La. NN9: Gt Har 2J 65
  NN11: Braun 1C 58
Darley Cl. NN16: K'ing 3E 38
Darley Dale Rd. NN17: Corby 5J 13
Darnell Way NN3: N'ton 1J 85
Dart Cl. NN17: Corby 4J 13
Dartford Cl. NN4: N'ton 5B 94
Dartmouth Row NN11: Dav 2J 61
Darwin Ct. NN17: Corby 5D 14
Darwin Ho. NN17: Corby 4G 15
       (off Corby Ga.)
Darwin Rd. NN17: Corby 4D 14
Darwin Wlk. NN5: Dus 5H 83
Dash Farm Cl. NN17: Weld 5H 15
Dave Bowen Cl. NN5: Upton 1H 93
DAVENTRY 5H 59 (2B 136)
Daventry & District Sports Club . .4H 61
Daventry Country Pk. 6J 59
Daventry Country Pk. Vis. Cen. . . .5J 59
Daventry Indoor Bowling Club 2D 60
Daventry Intl. Rail Freight Terminal
  NN6: Crick 2D 30
        (Danes Way)
  NN6: Crick 3D 30
       (Railport App.)
Daventry Leisure Cen. 1H 61
Daventry Mus. (Moot Hall) 1H 61
      (off Market Sq.)
Daventry Rd. CV23: Bar 2C 54
  CV23: Kil 7C 30
  NN11: Newn 7J 61
  NN11: Nor 7G 55
  NN11: Stav 4A 60
Davey Rd. NN17: Corby 5D 14
Davies Cl. NN15: K'ing 2B 42
Da Vinci Dr. NN5: Upton 2H 93
Davis Cl. NN14: R'ell 7H 27
Davis Ct. NN17: Corby 7B 14
Davy Cl. NN8: Well 6F 65
Dawkins Ct. NN14: Brou 6G 41
Dayrell Rd. NN4: N'ton 5K 93
Dayrell Sq. NN4: N'ton 5A 94
Dayrell Wlk. NN4: N'ton 5A 94
Dayton St. NN10: R'den 3D 80
Deacon Cl. NN10: R'den 2G 81
Deacons Ct. NN3: N'ton 2F 87
Deal Cl. NN1: N'ton 2J 131 (7E 84)
Deal St. NN1: N'ton 2H 131 (7D 84)
Dean Cl. NN9: Raun 5A 54
  NN10: R'den 5D 80
Deancourt Dr. NN5: Dus 5F 83
DEANSHANGER 5F 125 (2D 141)
Deanshanger Dr. NN12: Pot 1A 124
Deanshanger Rd. MK19: Old S . . .4J 125
  MK19: Wick 6C 124
Deans Row NN7: G'ton 6D 98
Deansway NN3: N'ton 2F 87
Dean Wlk. NN11: Dav 6G 59
Debdale Rd. NN3: N'ton 3K 85
  NN8: Well 7K 65
Deben Rd. NN17: Corby 3J 13
De Capel Cl. NN14: Woodf 7B 50
DEDDINGTON 2A 140
Deeble Rd. NN15: K'ing 1F 43
DEENE 2B 134
Deene Cl. NN17: Corby 6K 13
Deene End NN17: Weld 5J 15
Deene Pk. 2B 134
Deene Rd. NN17: Harr 2B 8
Deeneside NN17: Weld 5J 15

DEENETHORPE 2B 134
DEEPING GATE 1D 135
DEEPING ST JAMES 1D 135
Deep Side PE9: Eas H 3B 6
Deer Cl. NN4: Gra P 6G 101
Deer Pk. Rd. NN3: Moul P 7H 73
Dee Wlk. NN11: Dav 2E 60
De Ferneus Dr. NN9: Raun 5J 53
Delamere Dr. NN15: Bar S 6J 43
Delamere Rd. NN4: Del 6D 94
Delapre Abbey Gdns. 4F 95
Delapre Cl. NN4: Del 5D 94
Delapre Cres. NN4: Del 4D 94
Delapre Cres. Rd. NN4: Del 4C 94
Delapre Pl. NN4: Del 3F 17
Delapre St. NN4: Far C 4C 94
Delf La. NN7: Lwr H 5J 81
Dell, The NN6: E Bart 2D 88
Dell Cres. NN3: N'ton 1E 86
Dell Pl. NN10: R'den 3F 81
Delta Ho. NN1: N'ton 3G 131
Delta Way NN2: K'thpe 1A 84
Delves, The NN9: Raun 6H 53
De Montfort Ct. NN13: B'ley 2F 129
Dempsey Dr. NN14: R'ell 7J 27
Demswell NN6: Brix 3J 35
Denbigh Rd. NN3: N'ton 1A 96
Denby Dale NN8: Well 5J 65
Denby Dale Pl. NN17: Corby 7K 13
Dencora Bus. Pk. NN8: Well 1F 77
Dene Cl. NN8: Well 6H 65
  NN16: K'ing 4C 38
DENFORD 7G 51 (1B 138)
Denford Dr. NN15: Bar S 5H 43
Denford Rd. NN14: Rin 1G 53
  NN14: Thra 5G 51
  NN17: Corby 5G 13
Denford Way NN8: Well 5J 65
Denington Cl. NN8: Well 3B 78
Denington Ind. Est. NN8: Well 2C 78
      (not continuous)
Denington Rd. NN8: Well 3B 78
Denman Cl. LE16: Stoke A 6F 11
Denmark Cl. NN18: Corby 4E 81
Denmark Ct. NN10: R'den 4F 81
Denmark Rd.
  NN1: N'ton 4K 131 (1F 95)
  NN10: R'den 4F 81
Denne Cl. NN18: Gt Oak 5H 17
Dennetts Cl. NN11: Dav 5G 59
Denney Cres. NN11: Dav 1G 61
Denston Cl. NN4: N'ton 7C 94
Dent Cl. NN5: Dus 7E 82
DENTON
  Cambridgeshire 3D 135
  Northamptonshire . . .5B 102 (3A 138)
Denton Cl. NN10: R'den 2F 81
  NN29: Irch 5J 79
Denton Ct. NN15: Bur L 2J 45
Denton Rd. NN7: D'ton 7B 102
  NN7: Hort 2J 117
De Quincey Cl. NN13: B'ley 2F 129
Derby Rd. NN1: N'ton 7F 85
Derling Dr. NN9: Raun 6K 53
Derngate NN1: N'ton 5J 131 (2E 94)
De Roos Way LE16: Stoke A 6G 11
Derry, The NN6: Crick 4H 31
Derwent Cl. NN5: N'ton 5A 84
  NN8: Well 6H 65
  NN11: Dav 2F 61
Derwent Cres. NN16: K'ing 7B 38
Derwent Dr. NN5: Dus 5A 84
Derwent Ho. PE8: Oun 4J 21
Derwent Wlk. NN17: Corby 3J 13
DESBOROUGH 2D 26 (3A 134)
Desborough Indoor Bowls Club . . .2D 26
Desborough Leisure Cen. 3F 27
Desborough Rd.
  LE16: Bram A, Stoke A 7F 11
  LE16: Bray . . . . . . .6C 10 & 1A 26
  NN14: R'ell 5F 27
  NN14: R'ton 1A 46
DESFORD 1A 132
De Vere Rd. NN14: Thra 3H 51
Deveron Wlk. NN17: Corby 3J 13
Devon Dr. NN15: K'ing 4E 42
Devon Ox Rd. CV23: Kil 7B 30
Devonshire Cl. NN2: Bou 5D 72
  NN8: Well 6K 65
Devonshire Ho. NN5: N'ton 4F 85
      (off Alma St.)
Devon Wlk. NN10: R'den 4F 81
Devon Way NN3: N'ton 1H 85
Dewar Cl. NN17: Corby 4A 14
Dewar Dr. NN11: Dav 6F 59
Dexter Way PE8: Warm 2H 23
Diamond Cen., The 2E 68
Diamond Dr. NN9: Irth 4A 68
Diamonds Bus. Cen. NN9: Irth 1D 68
Diamond Way NN9: Irth 2D 68
Diana Ho. NN8: Well 7J 65
Diana Way NN15: Bur L 3J 45
Dibbin Cl. NN17: Weld 5J 15

Dickens Dr. MK19: Old S 3J 125
  NN16: K'ing 3D 38
Dickson Cl. NN4: N'ton 4A 94
DIDDINGTON 2D 139
Digby Cl. NN5: Dus 7H 83
Digby St. NN16: K'ing 6E 38
DILLINGTON 2D 139
Dimock Sq. NN4: N'ton 5A 94
Dingle, The NN11: Dav 3H 61
Dingle Rd. NN10: R'den 3A 80
DINGLEY 3D 133
Dingley Wlk. NN3: N'ton 1F 87
Disbrowe Ct. NN9: Chel 7K 69
Diswell Brook Way MK19: Dean . . .4F 125
Ditchford Cl. NN4: Woot 2G 101
Ditchford La. NN8: Irth, R'den 7K 67
Ditchford Rd. NN8: Well 5J 67
Dixon Rd. NN2: K'thpe 7F 73
Dixon Wlk. NN17: Corby 7B 14
      (off South Rd.)
Dobbins Cl. OX17: King S 1C 126
Dobson Cl. NN4: Gt Hou 5C 96
Dobson Wlk. NN18: Corby 1J 17
Docklewell Cl. NN12: Tow 5A 114
Doctors La. NN11: Eyd 7D 108
  NN29: Gt Dod 7K 77
Doddington Rd. NN6: E Bart 2E 88
  NN8: Well 5A 78
  NN8: Wilby 5G 77
  NN29: Woll 3C 90
Doddridge Ho. NN1: N'ton 4G 131
Doddridge St.
  NN1: N'ton 4G 131 (2D 94)
      (not continuous)
DODFORD 1A 62 (2C 137)
DOGSTHORPE 1D 135
Dolben Av. NN9: Stanw 1J 69
Dolben Cl. NN9: Fine 7G 47
Dolben Sq. NN9: Fine 7H 47
Dolver Cl. NN18: Gt Oak 4H 17
Donald Greaves Ho.
  NN17: Corby 4J 13
      (off Landor Cl.)
Donaldson Av. NN14: Brou 7G 41
Don Cl. NN17: Corby 4J 13
Donellan Grn. NN3: N'ton 7C 74
DONINGTON LE HEATH 1A 132
Donne Ct. NN10: High F 7F 69
  NN16: K'ing 3E 38
Donovan Ct. NN3: West F 6B 86
Don White Rd. NN8: Well 2C 66
Dorchester Cl. NN5: Dus 4G 83
      (off Port Rd.)
Dore Cl. NN3: N'ton 1E 86
Doris Rd. NN16: K'ing 5G 39
Dorking Wlk. NN18: Corby 3H 17
Dorman Cl. NN3: N'ton 2J 85
Dorothy Rd. NN16: K'ing 6G 39
Dorset Gdns. NN2: K'thpe 3E 84
Dorset Rd. NN2: K'thpe 3E 84
  NN17: Corby 7H 13
Doubles, The NN11: Dav 2G 61
Douglas Cl. NN15: K'ing 2G 43
Douglas Mdws. NN6: Scal 6A 36
Douglas Rd. NN5: Dus 6E 82
Doulton Cl. NN14: Des 2C 26
Dove Cl. NN12: Tow 6C 114
Dovecote, The NN6: Pits 1E 72
  PE8: King C 2H 9
      (off Park St.)
Dovecote Cl. LE16: West W 2D 10
  NN9: Raun 5K 53
  NN15: Bar S 3H 43
  PE8: Yar 2J 7
Dovecote Dr. NN7: D'ton 5B 102
  NN14: L Add 5A 52
Dovecote Rd. NN7: Roa 2A 116
Dovecote Yd. NN14: Orl 7B 44
Dovedale Gro. NN14: Des 1B 26
Dovedale Rd. NN17: Corby 6J 13
Dovehouse Cl. NN6: Welf 2H 29
  NN13: B'ley 5G 129
Dover Cl. NN10: R'den 4G 81
Dover Ct. NN5: Dus 2C 94
Dove's La. NN3: Moul 4A 74
Downing Way NN11: Dav 4H 61
Downs, The NN9: Well 3K 65
Downsway NN4: N'ton 2C 100
Downwood Cl. NN3: N'ton 3F 87
Dowthorpe End NN6: E Bart 2D 88
Dowthorpe Hill NN6: E Bart 3D 88
Drake Cl. NN11: Dav 2K 61
  NN14: R'ell 6H 27
  NN17: Corby 5G 13
Draper's Cl. PE8: Warm 2J 23
Drapery NN1: N'ton 4H 131 (1D 94)
      (not continuous)
DRAUGHTON 2E 36 (1D 137)
Draughton Rd. NN6: Maid 2B 36
DRAYCOTE 2A 136
Draycott Cl. NN3: N'ton 7A 86
Draymans Wlk. NN13: B'ley 5F 129
Drayson La. NN6: Crick 3H 31

Drayton—Everdon Pk.

DRAYTON
Leicestershire 2A 134
Northamptonshire 1F 61 (2B 136)
Oxfordshire 1A 140
Drayton Cl. NN10: R'den 5D 80
NN14: Isl 2F 51
NN18: Corby 2G 17
Drayton Flds. Ind. Est.
NN11: Dav 5E 58
Drayton Pk. NN11: Dav 5G 59
DRAYTON PARSLOW 3D 141
Drayton Pl. NN9: Irth 1C 68
Drayton Rd. LE16: Med 1K 11
NN9: Irth 1C 68
NN14: Low 7C 48
Drayton Wlk. NN2: K'thpe 2E 84
Drayton Way NN11: Dav 6E 58
Dresden Cl. NN18: Corby 4E 16
Driffield Gro. NN17: Corby 6A 14
Drift, The PE9: Colly 6C 6
Drill Hall Ct. NN15: K'ing 1C 42
Drive, The NN1: N'ton 5G 85
NN5: Dus 7F 83
NN7: Hort 2J 117
NN8: Well 2B 78
NN10: R'den 4E 80
NN15: K'ing 1D 42
Droue Ct. NN14: R'ell 6F 27
Drove, The PE8: Nass 5G 7
PE9: Colly 6C 6
Drovers Wlk. NN2: K'thpe 1B 84
Druce End NN12: Yar G 3J 123
Druids Way NN3: N'ton 1G 85
Drum La. NN1: N'ton 4H 131 (1D 94)
Drumming Well La. PE8: Oun 5J 21
Drummond Cl. NN6: Pits 1E 72
Drury La. OX17: Char 2H 127
Drydale Av. NN3: Spin H 3J 85
Dryden PE8: Oun 4H 21
Dryden Av. NN11: Dav 1G 61
Dryden Cl. NN11: Woodf H 1B 108
Dryden Rd. NN5: N'ton 7A 84
NN8: Well 7D 66
NN12: Tow 4C 114
Dryden's Cl. NN14: Titch 1H 49
Dryden St. NN9: Raun 6H 53
NN16: K'ing 6D 38
Dryden's Wlk. NN14: R'ton 2A 46
Dryden Way NN10: High F 7D 68
NN17: Corby 5H 13
Dryfield Wlk. *NN3: N'ton* 5D 86
(off Brickwell Ct.)
Dryland Rd. NN3: N'ton 4K 85
Dryland St. NN16: K'ing 7D 38
Dryleys Ct. NN3: N'ton 1E 86
Drywell Ct. NN3: N'ton 5D 86
Duchess Cl. NN16: K'ing 5D 38
Duchess End NN6: Mears A 3B 76
Duchess Gdns. NN12: Pot 6H 123
Duchy Cl. NN9: Chel 6J 69
NN10: High F 7F 69
Duck End NN13: Hin H 5A 128
NN14: C'ord 2H 47
NN14: Den 7H 51
NN29: Woll 3E 90
Duck La. NN7: Harp 1A 92
PE8: Oun 5J 21
Duck St. NN10: R'den 3E 80
Duckworth Dell NN3: N'ton 7C 74
Duckworth Rd. NN17: Corby 6G 13
DUDDINGTON 1B 134
Dugdale Cl. NN14: Thra 3H 51
Dukelands NN7: Weed 4B 62
Dukes Grn. Rd. NN7: Kisl 4B 92
Duke St. NN1: N'ton 2J 131 (7E 84)
NN8: Well 3J 77
NN15: Bur L 2J 45
NN16: K'ing 6C 38
PE8: Pole 3D 22
Dulce Rd. NN5: Dus 6H 83
Dulley Av. NN8: Well 4A 78
DULOE 2D 139
Dulverton Rd. NN3: N'ton 7A 86
Dumas Cul-de-Sac NN13: B'ley 3F 129
Dumble Cl. NN18: Corby 4H 17
Dunbar Ct. NN15: K'ing 2H 43
Duncan Cl. NN3: Moul P 6G 73
Duncan Ct. NN8: Well 3J 77
Duncan Rd. NN17: Corby 6G 13
DUNCHURCH 1A 136
DUNCOTE 3C 137
Dundee St. NN5: N'ton 1A 94
Dunedin Rd. NN18: Corby 4G 17
Dunkirk Av. NN14: Des 2D 26
Dunn Cl. NN6: Crick 3J 31
Dunnock La. NN4: Gra P 5G 101
Dunnock Rd. NN18: Corby 3K 17
Dunster St. NN1: N'ton 3K 131 (1E 94)
DUNS TEW 3A 140
DUNTON 3D 141
DUNTON BASSETT 2B 132
Durban Rd. NN16: K'ing 7F 39
Durham Cl. NN17: Corby 7G 13
Durness Cl. NN15: K'ing 2G 43
Dusthill Rd. NN14: Brig 6K 19
DUSTON 6H 83 (2D 137)
Duston Cl. NN11: Dav 7F 59
Duston Mill La. NN5: N'ton 3J 93
Duston Rd. NN5: N'ton 7J 83
Duston Wildes NN5: Dus 4F 83
Dybdale Cres. NN8: Well 7K 65
Dychurch La. NN1: N'ton 4J 131 (1E 94)
NN29: Boz 3H 103
Dyson Dr. NN16: K'ing 5C 38

E

Eady Cl. NN3: Moul 4A 74
Eady Rd. NN15: Bur L 3J 45
Eady's Row NN14: Woodf 6A 50
Eagle Av. NN14: Des 1C 26
Eagle Dr. NN4: Del 5F 95
Eaglehurst NN6: Brix 3J 35
Eagle La. PE8: King C 2G 9
Eagle Rd. NN14: C'ley, Thor M 1G 41
Eaglesfield NN11: Nor 7G 55
EAGLETHORPE 1H 23 (2C 135)
EAKLEY LANES 3A 138
Ealing Ter. NN10: R'den 2D 80
EARLS BARTON 2D 88 (2A 138)
Earls Barton Mus. 2D 88
Earls Barton Rd. NN6: Mears A 3A 76
NN29: Gt Dod 1G 89
Earlsfield Cl. NN4: Woot 2H 101
EARL SHILTON 2A 132
Earlstree Ind. Est. NN17: Corby 2A 14
(not continuous)
Earlstrees Ct. NN17: Corby 3A 14
Earlstrees Rd. NN17: Corby 2A 14
Earl St. NN1: N'ton 3J 131 (1E 94)
EASENHALL 1A 136
EASINGTON 2A 140
East Av. NN15: Bur L 1J 45
NN15: K'ing 7F 39
NN17: Corby 1A 18
East Bank NN3: N'ton 7B 74
Eastbourne Av. NN18: Corby 1G 17
Eastbrook NN18: Corby 2G 17
Eastbrook Hill NN14: Des 2F 27
E. Butterfield Ct. NN3: N'ton 1C 86
EAST CARLTON 6A 12 (3A 134)
East Carlton Countryside Pk. 5A 12
E. Carlton Pk. LE16: E Car 6A 12
EAST CLAYDON 3D 141
East Cl. NN15: K'ing 7F 39
EASTCOTE 5K 105 (3C 137)
Eastcote Rd. NN7: G'ton 7C 98
East Cres. NN10: R'den 3C 80
NN17: Weld 5K 15
East Dr. NN15: K'ing 7G 39
East End NN6: Scal 7A 36
Eastern Av. Nth. NN2: K'thpe 1E 84
Eastern Av. Sth. NN2: K'thpe 4E 84
Eastern Cl. NN2: K'thpe 1E 84
Eastern Way NN11: Dav 1H 61
EAST FARNDON 2J 25 (3D 133)
E. Farndon Rd. LE16: Mar T 2F 25
Eastfield NN7: Blis 2H 115
Eastfield Cl. NN5: Dus 5H 83
Eastfield Cres. NN9: Fine 6J 47
NN12: Yar G 4K 123
Eastfield Rd. NN4: Del 4D 94
NN5: Dus 6G 83
NN6: Brix 4H 35
NN8: Well 6C 66
NN9: Irth 2C 68
NN29: Woll 4E 90
Eastfields NN11: Braun 1B 58
Eastfields Cres. PE8: Nass 4G 7
E. Glebe Cl. NN17: Corby 5A 14
EAST GOSCOTE 1C 133
East Gro. NN10: R'den 2E 80
EAST HADDON 2C 56 (2C 137)
E. Haddon Rd. NN6: Rav 3B 34 & 1C 56
East Hill Cl. NN13: B'ley 4G 129
Eastlands Rd. NN9: Fine 6J 47
E. Langham Rd. NN9: Raun 5J 53
EAST LANGTON 2D 133
Eastleigh Rd. NN15: K'ing 3F 43
East Leys Ct. NN3: Moul 6K 73
Eastmead Ct. NN3: N'ton 5D 86
EAST NORTON 1D 133
EASTON 1D 139
Easton La. NN29: Boz 3F 103
EASTON MAUDIT 3A 138
EASTON ON THE HILL 2C 6 (1C 135)
Easton on the Hill Priest's House 1B 6
Easton Wlk. NN17: Corby 7C 14
Easton Way NN7: Gren 2C 102
East Oval NN5: N'ton 4A 84
E. Paddock Ct. NN3: N'ton 2D 86
East Pk. Pde. NN1: N'ton 6G 85
EAST PERRY 2D 139
E. Priors Ct. NN3: N'ton 2D 86
East Rising NN4: N'ton 1E 100
East Rd. PE8: Oun 5J 21
East St. NN1: N'ton 1G 95
NN6: Long B 1J 55
NN9: Stanw 1K 69
NN29: Irch 5J 79
East Vw. OX17: Greatw 2K 119
East Wlk. NN15: K'ing 7G 39
Eastwood Rd. PE8: Oun 5J 21
EATHORPE 2A 136
Eaton Ho. *NN1: N'ton* 7F 85
(off Clare St.)
Eaton Rd. NN5: Dus 5F 83
EATON SOCON 3D 139
Eaton Wlk. NN10: R'den 3E 80
Ebbw Va. Rd. NN9: Irth 3A 68
Ebenezer Pl. NN16: K'ing 7D 38
ECTON 2J 87 (2A 138)
ECTON BROOK 4G 87
Ecton Brook Rd. NN3: N'ton 3G 87
Ecton Hall NN6: Ect 2J 87
Ecton La. NN6: Syw, Ect 2G 75
Ecton La. Pk. NN3: N'ton 5G 87
Ecton Pk. Rd. NN3: N'ton 3F 87
Ecton St. NN1: N'ton 1F 95
Edale Grn. NN14: Des 1B 26
Eden Cl. NN3: N'ton 2J 85
NN11: Dav 2F 61
Eden Ct. NN6: Wat 6D 54
Eden St. NN16: K'ing 7D 38
Edgar Mobbs Way NN5: N'ton 2J 93
Edgar Rd. NN16: K'ing 6F 39
EDGCOTT 3C 141
Edgehill Dr. NN11: Dav 4H 59
Edgehill Rd. NN5: Dus 5J 83
Edgell St. NN16: K'ing 7E 38
Edgemead Cl. NN3: N'ton 6B 74
Edgemont Rd. NN3: West F 5B 86
Edges Ct. NN3: Moul 6K 73
Edgewood NN13: B'ley 2G 129
Edinburgh Cl. NN14: R'ell 7F 27
Edinburgh M. NN2: K'thpe 4D 84
Edinburgh Rd. NN2: K'thpe 4D 84
NN8: Well 4K 77
NN16: K'ing 6F 39
Edinburgh Sq. NN11: Dav 7G 59
Edison Cl. NN8: Well 6F 65
Edison Ct. NN8: Well 6F 65
Edison Courtyard NN17: Corby 2A 14
Edison Dr. NN5: Upton 3J 93
Edith Rd. NN16: K'ing 5G 39
Edith St. NN1: N'ton 1F 95
EDITH WESTON 1B 134
Edmonds Cl. NN8: Well 3B 78
Edmund St. NN16: K'ing 6F 39
Edward Cl. NN10: High F 5F 69
NN15: K'ing 3E 42
Edwardian Cl. NN4: Woot 1F 101
Edward Rd. NN15: K'ing 3E 42
NN29: Irch 6J 79
Edwards Cl. NN11: Byf 2J 107
Edwards Dr. NN8: Well 7J 65
Edward Watson Cl. NN2: K'thpe 1C 84
Edwinstowe Cl. NN3: N'ton 7B 86
Egerton Cl. NN13: B'ley 4H 129
EGLETON 1A 134
Eider Cl. NN11: Dav 7H 59
NN15: Bur L 2H 45
Einstein Cres. NN5: Dus 7H 83
Eismann Way NN17: Corby 6D 14
Ekins Cl. NN3: N'ton 4A 86
Eldean Rd. NN5: Dus 5G 83
Elderberry Ct. NN3: N'ton 3F 87
Elder Dr. NN11: Dav 6H 59
Eldon Cl. NN6: Crick 3G 31
Eldon Way NN6: Crick 3F 31
Eleonore Ho. NN3: N'ton 3K 85
Elgin St. NN5: N'ton 1A 94
Eliot Cl. NN16: K'ing 3E 38
Eliot Way NN10: High F 7D 68
Elizabeth Cl. NN6: E Bart 1D 88
NN8: Well 3J 77
Elizabeth Ct. NN10: High F 5F 69
Elizabeth Rd. NN6: W Had 5H 29
NN11: Dav 7G 59
NN14: R'ell 7F 27
NN16: K'ing 6F 39
Elizabeth St. NN1: N'ton 1G 95
NN17: Corby 7K 13
Elizabeth Wlk. NN1: N'ton 1G 95
Elizabeth Way NN6: E Bart 1C 88
NN9: Irth 4B 68
NN10: High F 4F 69
ELKINGTON 1C 137
Elkington La. CV23: Bar 2B 54
Elkington Rd. NN6: Yel 5C 28
Elkins Cl. NN6: Yel 5C 28
Ellan Cl. NN10: R'den 2B 80
Ellen Cl. NN6: Crick 3H 31
Ellesmere Av. NN5: N'ton 7K 83
NN13: B'ley 3G 129
Ellesmere Cl. NN13: B'ley 2G 129
Ellesmere Ct. NN13: B'ley 3G 129
Ellesmere Cres. NN13: B'ley 2G 129
Ellesmere Rd. NN13: B'ley 2G 129
Ellfield Ct. NN3: N'ton 3C 86
ELLINGTON 1D 139
ELLINGTON THORPE 1D 139
Ellis La. NN14: Maw 6B 40
Ellison Cl. NN9: Raun 5H 53
ELLISTOWN 1A 132
Elm Cl. NN7: Braf G 5G 97
NN9: Harg 6J 49
Elm Ct. NN14: Thra 4H 51
Elm Dr. MK19: Dean 4E 124
NN11: Woodf H 2B 108
NN13: B'ley 2G 129
ELMESTHORPE 2A 132
Elmfield Cl. NN12: Pot 6H 123
Elm Gro. NN4: Woot 2H 101
Elmhurst Av. NN3: Spin H 4H 85
Elmhurst Ct. NN3: Spin H 4H 85
Elmington Rd. NN3: N'ton 1F 87
Elm La. LE17: Catt 1A 28
Elm Rd. NN15: Bur L 1K 45
NN15: K'ing 1F 43
Elms Dyke NN11: Welt 2K 59
Elm St. NN1: N'ton 2J 131 (7E 84)
NN8: Well 6A 66
Elm Wlk. NN10: High F 6E 68
NN17: Corby 4J 13
Elm Way NN7: Hack 1H 117
Elmwood Wlk. NN5: Dus 5F 83
Elsden Rd. NN8: Well 7D 66
ELSTOW 3C 139
ELTON 2C 135
Elton Cl. NN3: N'ton 1E 86
NN14: Des 2B 26
Elton Rd. PE8: Wans 1K 7
Elwes Way NN3: Gt Bil 4E 86
Elysium Ter. NN2: N'ton 6D 84
Embankment, The NN8: Well 3D 78
EMBERTON 3A 138
Emerald Way
NN1: N'ton 5F 131 (2C 94)
Emery Cl. NN11: Welt 2K 59
Emley Cl. NN3: N'ton 5C 86
Emmanuel Cl. NN11: Dav 3H 61
EMPINGHAM 1B 134
Encon Ct. NN3: Moul P 6G 73
ENDERBY 2B 132
Enfield Cl. NN5: Dus 6E 82
Ennerdale Cl. NN3: Spin H 3H 85
NN11: Dav 1F 61
NN16: K'ing 7C 38
Ennerdale Rd. NN3: Spin H 3H 85
NN10: R'den 2G 81
NN17: Corby 4K 13
Ensleigh Cl. NN15: Bur L 3K 45
ENSTONE 3A 140
Enstone Ct. NN8: Well 4K 77
Enterprise Cl. NN16: K'ing 5B 38
Enterprise Ct. NN8: Well 6F 65
Enterprise Pk. NN17: Corby 4G 15
Enterprise Rd. NN9: Raun 5J 53
Entwood Dr. NN3: N'ton 1E 86
Epping Cl. NN15: Bar S 5J 43
Epping Wlk. NN11: Dav 6G 59
EPS Ind. Est. OX17: Chip W 1C 110
Epsom Cl. NN10: R'den 5G 81
Epsom Wlk. NN18: Corby 3H 17
EPWELL 1A 140
Equestrian Way NN7: Weed 3C 62
Ericsson Cl. NN11: Dav 5H 59
Ermine Rd. NN3: N'ton 1F 87
Ernest Wright Ho. NN17: Corby 5H 13
Erskin Wood NN6: Spra 5C 34
Esher Ct. NN3: N'ton 2A 86
Eskdaill Pl. *NN16: K'ing* 6D 38
(off Lindsay St.)
Eskdaill St. NN16: K'ing 6D 38
Eskdale Av. NN3: Spin H 3J 85
NN17: Corby 6K 13
Eskdale Cl. NN8: Well 6H 65
Esporta Health & Fitness Club
Collingtree 3D 100
ESSENDINE 1C 135
Essen La. CV23: Kil 6B 30
Essex Cl. NN17: Corby 7G 13
Essex Pl. NN15: K'ing 4F 43
Essex Rd. NN10: R'den 4F 81
Essex St. NN2: Sem 6D 84
Ethel St. NN1: N'ton 1F 95
Eton Cl. NN7: Weed 3D 62
ETTON 1D 135
Ettrick Cl. NN16: K'ing 3C 38
Euston Rd. NN4: Far C 4D 94
Evans Cl. NN11: Dav 2K 61
Eva Rd. NN16: K'ing 6G 39
Evelyn Wlk. NN9: Raun 6J 53
Evelyn Way NN29: Irch 6K 79
EVENLEY 2C 130 (2B 140)
Evenley Rd. NN2: K'thpe 1D 84
Evensford Wlk. NN9: Irth 4A 68
EVERDON 3B 136
Everdon Cl. NN2: K'thpe 2F 85
Everdon Pk. NN11: Dav 5F 59

152 A-Z Northamptonshire Atlas

Everest Ho. *NN17: Corby* 7K **13**
       (off Everest La.)
Everest La. *NN17: Corby* 7K **13**
       (not continuous)
Evergreen Dr. NN14: L Add 5A **52**
Everitt Cl. NN8: Well 3C **78**
EVERTON **3D 139**
Evesham Cl. NN8: Well 4K **77**
Evesham Ct. NN3: N'ton 6D **74**
EVINGTON **1C 133**
Evison Ct. *NN14: R'ell* 7F **27**
       (off Evison Rd.)
Evison Rd. NN14: R'ell 7F **27**
Ewenfield Rd. NN9: Fine 7H **47**
Excalibur Cl. NN5: Dus 7F **83**
Excelsior NN8: Well 1H **77**
Excelsior Cl. NN9: Irth 2B **68**
Excelsior Gdns. NN5: Dus 6F **83**
Exeter Cl. NN11: Dav 3H **61**
Exeter Pl. NN1: N'ton 7F **85**
Exeter St. NN16: K'ing 4E **38**
Exmoor Cl. NN3: N'ton 7A **86**
Exmouth Av. NN18: Corby 2A **18**
Exmouth Ct. *NN18: Corby* 2A **18**
       (off Exmouth Av.)
Express Bus. Pk. NN10: R'den . . .2A **80**
Express Cl. NN9: Irth 4B **68**
Express Pk. NN16: K'ing 6B **38**
EXTON **1B 134**
Eyam Cl. NN14: Des 3D **45**
EYDON . . . .**7D 108 (3B 136)**
Eydon Rd. NN11: Woodf H 5C **108**
EYE **1D 135**
EYE GREEN **1D 135**
Eyeletter Ho. *NN5: N'ton* 1B **94**
       (off Greenwood Rd.)
Eynard Impasse NN13: B'ley 2F **129**
EYNESBURY **3D 139**
Eynon Cl. NN3: Moul 4J **73**

F

Fairfax Ri. NN6: Nas 3H **33**
Fairfield NN7: Blis 6G **99**
Fairfield Rd. NN2: N'ton 4G **85**
  NN12: Paul 7H **115**
  NN14: Ish 3E **44**
Fairground Way NN3: N'ton 1B **96**
Fairhurst Way NN6: E Bart 2E **88**
Fair La. NN3: Thra 2J **51**
Fairlight Ct. NN18: Corby 1G **17**
Fairmead Cres. NN10: R'den 5C **80**
Fairmead Ri. NN2: K'thpe 7A **72**
Fair Mile NN2: K'thpe 7B **72**
Fairoaks, The NN3: N'ton 6C **86**
Fairoaks Dr. NN9: Raun 5H **53**
Fairway NN2: N'ton 4F **85**
Fairway, The NN9: Well 3K **65**
  NN11: Dav 1K **61**
  NN15: K'ing 2C **42**
Falcon Dr. MK19: Old S 2J **125**
Falconers Cl. NN11: Dav 7H **59**
Falconers Ri. NN4: N'ton 7B **94**
Falcon Vw. NN12: Greens N 1H **113**
Falcon Way NN13: B'ley 1E **128**
FALCUTT **3C 120**
Falcutt Way NN2: K'thpe 1E **84**
Fallowfield NN9: Well 4K **65**
Fallowfields NN6: Crick 3J **31**
Fallow Wlk. NN2: K'thpe 7B **72**
Falmer Wlk. NN18: Corby 2G **17**
Falster Cl. NN18: Corby 4F **17**
Faracre Ct. NN3: N'ton 5E **86**
Faracre Wlk. NN3: N'ton 5E **86**
Faraday Cl. NN5: Upton 2J **93**
  NN8: Well 6F **65**
  NN11: Dav 6F **59**
Faraday Ct. NN8: Well 6F **65**
  NN14: Thra 3J **51**
Faraday Gro. NN17: Corby 5B **14**
Faramir Pl. NN3: N'ton 1E **86**
FAR COTTON . . . . . .**5C 94 (3D 137)**
Farebrother Cl. NN11: Byf 2J **107**
Far End NN5: N'ton 1A **94**
Faringdon Ct. NN3: N'ton 6D **74**
Farmbrook Ct. NN3: N'ton 1C **86**
Farm Cl. NN2: K'thpe 2C **84**
  NN6: Holc 6H **37**
  NN14: Brig 2D **20**
Farmclose Rd. NN4: Woot 2F **101**
Far Mdw. Ct. NN3: N'ton 1B **86**
Farmers Cl. NN4: Woot 3F **101**
Farmers Dr. NN13: B'ley 3E **128**
Farmfield Ct. NN15: Bur L 6H **43**
Farm Fld. Ct. NN3: N'ton 1B **86**
Farmhill Rd. NN3: N'ton 7D **74**
Farm Rd. NN6: Nas 4K **65**
  NN13: B'ley 5H **129**
Farmstead Rd. NN18: Corby 1F **17**
Farm Stile NN11: Up Bod 1B **106**

FARNBOROUGH **1A 140**
Farnborough Cl. NN15: K'ing 5F **43**
  NN18: Corby 5J **17**
Farnborough Dr. NN11: Dav 4F **59**
Farndale Av. NN17: Corby 6K **13**
FARNDISH . . . .**2J 91 (2B 138)**
Farndish Cl. NN10: R'den 3C **80**
Farndish Rd. NN29: Irch 5J **79**
Farndon Cl. NN3: N'ton 7C **74**
Farndon Rd. LE16: Gt Oxe 5F **25**
  LE16: Mkt H 1K **25**
  NN11: Woodf H 3B **108**
Farnham Dr. NN10: R'den 5C **80**
Farnworth Cl. NN5: Dus 5H **83**
Farraxton Sq. NN4: N'ton 5K **93**
FARTHINGHOE . . . . .**6H 119 (2B 140)**
Farthinghoe Cl. NN13: B'ley 4E **128**
Farthinghoe Rd. OX17: Char 1H **127**
FARTHINGSTONE **3C 137**
Farthingstone Rd.
  NN7: Weed 7A **62**
  NN12: Lit 1F **109**
Faugere Cl. NN13: B'ley 3F **129**
Favell Way NN3: West F 6A **86**
FAWLER **3A 140**
Fawsley Dr. NN11: Dav 5F **59**
Fawsley Rd. NN4: Far C 5D **94**
Faxfield Wlk. NN3: N'ton 5C **86**
Faxton Cl. NN2: K'thpe 2E **84**
Faxton End NN6: Old 5E **36**
Fay Cl. NN11: Woodf H 1B **108**
Feast Fld. Cl. NN29: Woll 5E **90**
Featherbed La. NN18: L Oak 4B **18**
Federation Av. NN14: Des 3C **26**
Fegans Ct. MK11: Stony S 3K **125**
Fellmead Rd. NN3: N'ton 1F **87**
Fellows Cl. NN29: Woll 3D **90**
Fell Wlk. NN8: Well 6J **65**
FELMERSHAM **3B 138**
FENCOTT **3B 140**
Fengate Cl. NN3: N'ton 1F **87**
Fenn Cl. PE8: Nass 5G **7**
Fennel Ct. NN4: N'ton 3E **100**
Fenniston Cl. NN10: R'den 3G **81**
FENNY COMPTON **3A 136**
FENNY DRAYTON **2A 132**
Fenton Rd. NN13: B'ley 4E **128**
Ferguson's Cl. PE8: Pole 3E **22**
Fermoy Ct. NN7: L Brin 5F **57**
Fermyn Ct. NN14: Brig 1D **20**
Fermyn Pl. NN18: Corby 3F **17**
Fermynwoods Contemporary Art
  . . . .**3B 134**
Fermyn Woods Country Pk. . . .**2E 20**
Fermyn Woods Country Pk. Vis. Cen.
  . . . .**3B 134**
Fern Dale Cl. NN14: Ged 5D **46**
Ferndale Rd. NN3: N'ton 4A **86**
Fernie Cl. NN15: Bar S 5J **43**
Fernie Fld. NN3: Moul 7K **73**
Fernie Way NN8: Well 1J **77**
Fernmoor Dr. NN9: Irth 2C **68**
Fern Rd. NN10: R'den 2B **80**
Ferrers Ct. NN10: High F 5F **69**
Ferrestone Rd. NN8: Well 6B **66**
Ferris Row NN3: N'ton 7C **86**
Ferro Flds. NN6: Brix 2J **35**
Fessey Rd. NN11: Byf 1J **107**
Festival Ct. NN9: Irth 7A **52**
Festival Rd. NN12: Pat 5G **105**
Fetter St. NN1: N'ton 5J **131** (2E **94**)
Fettledine Rd. NN9: Irth 7A **52**
FEWCOTT **3B 140**
Field Cl. NN6: W Had 6H **29**
Field Cotts. NN18: Gt Oak 6G **17**
Fieldfare Cl. NN18: Corby 2K **17**
Fieldgate Cl. NN4: Woot 2G **101**
FIELD HEAD **1A 132**
Fieldmill Rd. NN3: N'ton 5E **86**
Fieldmill Sq. NN3: N'ton 5F **87**
Field Rose Sq. NN3: N'ton 4F **87**
Field St. NN16: K'ing 6D **38**
Field St. Av. NN16: K'ing 6D **38**
Fields Vw. NN8: Well 1C **78**
Field Vw. NN11: Braun 1B **58**
  NN13: B'ley 4E **128**
  OX17: Mar L 2G **119**
Field Way NN13: Helm 1C **120**
Fieldway NN3: N'ton 5J **85**
Fienesgate NN4: N'ton 6J **93**
Fiennes Ct. NN11: Dav 4H **59**
Fife St. NN5: N'ton 7A **84**
Fifth Av. NN13: Crou 6C **130**
Fifth St. NN13: Crou 7C **130**
Fifth St. E. NN13: Crou 6C **130**
Filey Cl. NN18: Corby 2G **17**
FILGRAVE **3A 138**
Filleigh Way NN3: N'ton 7K **85**
Finch Dr. NN15: Bar S 4J **43**
Finch-Hatton Dr. NN17: Gret 7D **8**
FINEDON . . . .**7H 47 (1B 138)**
Finedon Cally Banks Nature Reserve
  . . . .**1D 66**

Finedon Community Sports and
  Leisure Cen. **7H 47**
Finedon Hall NN9: Fine 7G **47**
Finedon Rd. NN8: Well 7C **66**
  NN9: Bur L, Fine 5J **45**
  NN9: Irth 1K **67**
Finedon Rd. Ind. Est. NN8: Well . .3C **66**
Finedon Sidings Ind. Est.
  NN9: Fine 6J **45**
Finedon Sta. Rd. NN9: Fine 6G **45**
Finedon St. NN15: Bur L 3J **45**
Fineshade Cl. NN15: Bar S 5J **43**
  PE8: King C 2G **9**
Fineshade Gro. NN17: Corby 5K **13**
Finland Way NN18: Corby 4F **17**
FINMERE **2C 141**
Finney Dr. NN4: Gra P 5F **101**
FINSTOCK **3A 140**
Firbank Cl. NN3: N'ton 6C **86**
Firdale Av. NN10: R'den 1E **80**
Firecrest Wlk. *NN4: N'ton* 7K **93**
       (off Bitten St.)
Fir Rd. NN16: K'ing 7F **39**
Firs, The NN11: Dav 7H **59**
Firs Ct. NN4: H'stone 7G **95**
First Av. NN8: Well 2J **77**
First La. NN5: N'ton 1A **94**
First St. NN13: Crou 7C **130**
Firsview Dr. NN5: Dus 5G **83**
Fir Tree Gro. NN29: Boz 3H **103**
Fir Tree Wlk. NN3: N'ton 4B **86**
Fish All. NN29: Boz 2H **103**
Fisher Cl. NN8: Well 5H **21**
Fisher Cl. NN14: Thra 4J **51**
Fishers Cl. CV23: Kil 7B **30**
  NN3: N'ton 5E **86**
Fishmarket **4H 131**
Fishpond Cl. NN7: D'ton 5B **102**
Fishponds Rd. NN3: Gt Bil, N'ton . . .4D **86**
Fish St. NN1: N'ton 4J **131** (1E **94**)
Fishton Cl. NN15: K'ing 3E **42**
Fitness First (for Women) Health Club
  Northampton . . . . . .**4K 131 (1E 94)**
Fitness First Health Club
  Dallington **6K 83**
Fitzroy Ct. NN6: W Had 2H **33**
Fitzroy Pl. NN1: N'ton 4F **131** (1C **94**)
Fitzroy Ter. NN1: N'ton 2H **131** (7D **84**)
Fitzwilliam Dr. NN15: Bar S 5J **43**
Fitzwilliam Rd. NN9: Irth 1C **68**
Fitzwilliam St. NN10: R'den 3D **80**
Fitzwilliam Leys NN10: High F . . .5E **68**
Five Acres Fold NN4: N'ton 4A **94**
Fjord Wlk. NN18: Corby 4F **17**
Flatford Cl. NN18: Corby 5J **17**
Flavius Ga. NN13: B'ley 4H **129**
Flaxlands Cl. NN3: N'ton 3C **86**
Flaxwell Ct. NN3: N'ton 6C **86**
FLECKNEY **2C 133**
FLECKNOE **2B 136**
Fleet St. NN16: K'ing 7C **38**
Fleetwind Dr. NN4: N'ton 1E **100**
Fleetwood Gdns. LE16: Mkt H . . .1K **25**
Fleming Cl. NN8: Well 5G **65**
Fleming Rd. NN17: Corby 3B **14**
Flensburg Cl. NN18: Corby 4G **17**
Fletcher Gdns. NN14: Thra 4H **51**
Fletcher Rd. NN10: R'den 2D **80**
Fletton Way PE8: Oun 4H **21**
Fleur Cl. NN11: Woodf H 2D **108**
Flintcomb Ri. NN3: N'ton 3E **86**
Flinters Cl. NN4: Woot 1G **101**
Flint Jetty *NN4: N'ton* 4A **94**
       (off Pitstone Rd.)
Flora Thompson Dr. NN13: B'ley . .3F **129**
FLORE . . . .**2G 63 (2C 137)**
Flore Hill NN7: Flore 3D **62**
Florence Rd. NN1: N'ton 7G **85**
Floribunda Dr. NN4: N'ton 4A **94**
Flowerhill Dr. NN8: Well 6C **66**
Flycatcher Rd. NN18: Corby 3K **17**
Flying Dutchman Way
  NN11: Dav 7F **59**
FOLESHILL **3A 132**
FOLKSWORTH **2D 135**
Folly La. NN7: Hart 7G **117**
  NN7: L Brin 5F **57**
Folly Rd. MK19: Dean 4D **124**
Fontwell Cres. NN18: L Oak 5K **17**
Ford Cl. NN9: Chel 6K **69**
Ford Dr. NN13: B'ley 3E **128**
Ford La. NN4: Brack 4J **95**
Ford St. NN16: K'ing 7E **38**
Forest App. PE8: King C 2H **9**
Forest Cl. NN15: Bur L 1K **45**
Forest Cl. NN5: R'den 2G **81**
Forest Ga. Rd. NN17: Corby 6K **13**
Forest Glade NN7: Hart 5H **117**
  NN16: K'ing 3E **38**
Forest Rd. NN4: Del 4D **94**
  NN7: Hart 6H **117**
  NN7: Pid 5H **117**
Forest Vw. NN7: Hart 5H **117**

Forfar St. NN5: N'ton 7A **84**
Forrester Dr. NN13: B'ley 2F **129**
Forrester Gro. NN14: Thra 4J **51**
Forresters, The NN9: Raun 7J **53**
       (off Thorpe St.)
Forstal Cl. NN18: Corby 3J **17**
Fort Pl. NN1: N'ton 4F **131** (1C **94**)
Fortune Cl. NN1: N'ton 1B **96**
Forum Cinema **4C 86**
  (in Lings Forum Leisure Cen.)
Fosberry Cl. NN4: Woot 2G **101**
FOSCOTE **5K 113**
Foskett Cl. NN10: R'den 2D **80**
Foskitt Ct. NN3: N'ton 6E **86**
Foskitt Wlk. NN3: N'ton 5E **86**
Fosse Cl. NN8: Well 4J **77**
Fosse Grn. NN10: R'den 2F **81**
Foster Cl. NN15: K'ing 2B **42**
Foster Ct. NN18: Corby 1K **17**
FOSTER'S BOOTH **6G 105**
Foster's Booth Rd. NN12: Pat . . .5G **105**
FOSTON **2C 133**
FOTHERINGHAY **2C 135**
Fotheringhay Castle **2C 135**
Fotheringhay Cl. NN14: Thra 3J **51**
Fotheringhay M. *PE8: Oun* 5J **21**
       (off East Rd.)
Fotheringhay Rd. NN17: Corby . . .5G **13**
  PE8: Foth, Nass 5H **7**
Foundry Cir. *NN11: Dav* 2H **61**
       (off Foundry Pl.)
Foundry Pl. NN11: Dav 2H **61**
Foundry St. NN1: N'ton . . .6H **131** (2D **94**)
Foundry Wlk. NN11: Dav 2H **61**
  NN14: Thra 4G **51**
Fourth Av. NN8: Well 2J **77**
  NN13: Crou 7C **130**
Fourth St. NN13: Crou 7C **130**
Fowey Cl. NN8: Well 6H **65**
Fox Covert Dr. NN7: Roa 3D **116**
Foxcovert Rd. NN3: N'ton 1E **86**
Fox Coverts NN14: Maw 6A **40**
Foxendale Sq. NN3: N'ton 4G **87**
Foxfield Way NN4: Gra P 6G **101**
Foxglove Av. NN11: Woodf H 2C **108**
Foxglove Cl. NN4: Gra P 6G **101**
  NN10: R'den 5F **81**
  NN18: Corby 4J **17**
Foxglove Rd. NN14: Des 1D **26**
Foxgrove Av. NN2: K'thpe 2B **84**
Fox Hill NN4: Del 6D **94**
Foxhill Rd. NN3: N'ton 4G **87**
  NN6: W Had 7G **29**
Foxholes Cl. MK19: Dean 4G **125**
Foxlands NN14: Des 3E **26**
Fox La. NN13: B'ley 5F **129**
FOXLEY **3C 137**
Fox St. NN14: R'ell 7F **27**
FOXTON **3C 133**
Foxton Cl. NN15: K'ing 2C **42**
Foxwell Sq. NN3: N'ton 6C **74**
Foxwood Cl. NN10: R'den 3B **80**
Franciscan Cl. NN10: R'den 5C **80**
Francis Ct. NN10: R'den 1B **80**
Francis Dickins Cl. NN29: Woll . . .3F **91**
Francis Jetty
  NN1: N'ton 5H **131** (2D **94**)
Francis St. NN1: N'ton 2G **131** (7D **84**)
  NN9: Raun 7G **53**
Francis Ter. *NN9: Raun* 7G **53**
       (off Stanwick Rd.)
Frank Large Wlk. NN5: Upton . . .7F **83**
Franklin Cres. NN5: N'ton 7J **83**
Franklin Flds. NN17: Corby 5B **14**
Franklin Point *NN5: N'ton* 1B **94**
       (off Weedon Rd.)
Franklin's Cl. NN6: Ect 2J **87**
Franklin St. NN5: N'ton 1A **94**
Franklin Way NN11: Dav 5G **59**
FRANKTON **1A 136**
Fraser Cl. NN11: Dav 1J **61**
Fraser Rd. NN3: N'ton 7A **74**
Freehold St. NN2: N'ton 6D **84**
Freeman Cl. NN8: Well 7C **66**
Freeman's La. NN14: Den 7G **51**
Freeman Way NN9: Fine 6K **47**
Freeschool St.
  NN1: N'ton 5G **131** (2D **94**)
Fremeaux Ter. NN2: K'thpe 4C **84**
Frencham Cl. NN4: N'ton 4A **94**
French Dr. NN15: K'ing 1G **43**
Frencher Rd. NN15: K'ing 1G **43**
Friar's Av. NN4: Del 6C **94**
Friars Cl. NN4: Del 6C **94**
  NN8: Well 2B **78**
Friar's Ct. NN4: Del 6C **94**
Friar's Cres. NN4: Del 6D **94**
Friary, The NN1: N'ton 4J **131**
Friary Cl. NN11: Dav 1J **61**
FRINGFORD **3C 141**
Frinton Cl. NN10: R'den 5C **80**
Friston Cl. NN15: Bar S 5J **43**
Frith Cl. NN18: Gt Oak 7F **17**

Fritwell—Great Addington

FRITWELL .3B 140
Frobisher Cl. NN11: Dav .1K 61
Frog Hall NN6: Brix .3G 35
NN12: Silv .2H 121
Frog La. NN11: Up Bod .2A 106
FROGNALL .1D 135
FROLESWORTH .2B 132
Frontier Cen. .7A 52
Front St. NN14: Den .7G 51
Frost Cl. NN14: Des .1E 26
Frost Ct. NN29: Gt Dod .7J 77
Frosty Hollow NN4: N'ton .2D 100
Froxhill Cres. NN6: Brix .4G 35
Froxhill Wlk. NN6: Brix .4G 35
Fuchsia Cl. NN3: N'ton .1K 95
Fuchsia Way NN10: R'den .6E 80
Fulford Dr. NN2: N'ton .3F 85
Fulleburn Ct. NN3: N'ton .3B 86
Fullen La. NN17: Gret .6D 8
Fuller Rd. NN3: Moul .5K 73
Fullers Cl. NN14: Ald .5B 20
Fuller St. NN16: K'ing .6E 38
Fullingdale Ct. NN3: N'ton .3K 85
Fullingdale Rd. NN3: N'ton .4J 85
Fullwell Rd. NN29: Boz .1H 103
Fulmar La. NN8: Well .4B 66
Fulwell Av. NN17: Gret .6D 8
Furber Ct. NN3: N'ton .2A 86
Furlong Rd. NN14: Des .2F 27
Furnace Cotts. NN9: Fine .7H 45
Furnace Dr. NN11: Dav .7F 59
NN14: Thra .4H 51
Furnace La. NN7: Neth H .7H 63
NN9: Fine, L Harr .6J 45
NN16: K'ing .4B 38
Furnells Cl. NN9: Raun .5J 53
Furtho La. NN12: Pot .6J 123
Furze Ct. NN4: N'ton .4B 94
Furze Rd. NN7: Braf G .5G 97
Furze Wlk. NN2: N'ton .4F 85
Fusilier Rd. NN11: Dav .2G 61
Fusilier Way NN7: Weed .3B 62
Fyfe Rd. NN17: Corby .5G 13
Fylingdale NN2: K'thpe .1A 84

G

Gable Cl. NN11: Dav .2G 61
Gable Ct. M. NN3: N'ton .5A 86
Gables, The NN15: K'ing .1D 42
Gables La. NN14: Brou .6H 41
GADDESBY .1C 133
Gadesby Ct. NN3: N'ton .3B 86
GAGINGWELL .3A 140
Gainage Ct. NN18: Gt Oak .5H 17
Gainsborough Av. NN15: Bar S .3J 43
Gainsborough Ct. NN18: Corby .1J 17
Gainsborough Dr. NN8: Well .5A 66
Gainsborough Rd. NN18: Corby .3F 17
Gainsborough Way NN11: Dav .4H 59
Gaiter & Spat NN1: N'ton .1F 95
Gala Bingo Club
Kettering .7D 38
Gala Casino
Northampton .5G 131
(in Sol Central)
Regent Sq. .2H 131
Galahad Ct. NN5: Dus .7F 83
Galane Cl. NN4: N'ton .6J 93
Galileo Cl. NN5: Dus .7H 83
Gallery Cl. NN3: N'ton .7D 74
Gallery Wlk. PE8: Oun .6J 21
Gallfield Ct. NN3: N'ton .6F 87
Galliard Ct. NN1: N'ton .7G 85
(off Stimpson Av.)
Gallowhill Rd. NN4: Brack .6J 95
Gambrel Rd. NN5: N'ton .1J 93
GAMLINGAY .3D 139
GAMLINGAY CINQUES .3D 139
GAMLINGAY GREAT HEATH .3D 139
Gammidge Ct. NN9: Fine .7H 47
(off Milner Rd.)
Gamston Wlk. NN18: Corby .7G 13
Gander Cl. NN17: Weld .6H 15
Gannet La. NN8: Well .4B 66
Ganton Cl. NN11: Dav .1K 61
Gap, The NN29: Woll .4F 91
Gapstile Cl. NN14: Des .1C 26
Gardenfield NN10: High F .7E 68
Gardenfields Cl. NN9: Irth .7A 52
Garden Flds. Ct. NN29: Irch .5J 79
Garden Row PE8: Oun .2K 21
Gardens, The LE16: E Car .6A 12
NN11: Whil .6D 56
NN16: K'ing .5C 38
Gardner Cl. NN9: Raun .5H 53
Gardner Ri. NN13: B'ley .4E 128
Garfield Cl. NN2: K'thpe .3D 84
Garfield St. NN2: K'thpe .3C 84
NN15: K'ing .2D 42
Garford La. PE9: Eas H .2C 6
Garners Way NN7: Harp .7B 82
Garrard Way NN16: K'ing .6B 38
Garrick Rd. NN1: N'ton .7J 85
Garrow Cl. NN9: Irth .1B 68
Garsdale NN2: K'thpe .7A 72
Garston Rd. NN18: Gt Oak .4H 17
Gas St. NN1: N'ton .5G 131 (2D 94)
Gatcombe Ho. NN10: R'den .3E 80
(off Portland Rd.)
Gateford Ct. NN18: Corby .7G 13
Gate La. NN14: Brou .5H 41
Gatelodge Cl. NN3: N'ton .7B 74
Gates Cl. NN9: Irth .1B 68
Gateway Cl. NN4: Woot .2G 101
Gaudern's La. PE8: King C .2H 9
(off Church Wlk.)
GAULBY .1C 133
Gaultney, The NN14: Des .2D 26
(off Station Rd.)
Gawaine Ct. NN5: Dus .7F 83
GAWCOTT .2C 141
GAYDON .3A 136
GAYHURST .3A 138
Gayhurst Cl. NN3: Moul .6J 73
GAYTON .6D 98 (3D 137)
Gayton Rd. NN7: Blis .1F 115
NN12: East .6J 105
GEDDINGTON .5D 46 (3A 134)
Geddington Rd.
NN18: Corby, Stan .7D 14
Gedling Cl. NN3: N'ton .6C 86
Gees Farm Cl. NN7: Yar H .7G 103
GEESTON .1B 134
Geldock Rd. NN3: N'ton .5D 86
Genner Rd. NN17: Corby .4C 14
Gentian Cl. NN10: R'den .5F 81
George Blackall Ct. NN17: Corby .5H 13
(off Keats Way)
George Nutt Ct. NN4: Far C .5D 94
George Row CV23: Kil .6C 30
NN1: N'ton .5H 131 (2D 94)
Georges Av. NN7: Bug .2K 105
Georges Cl. NN7: Bug .2K 105
Georges Dr. NN4: Gra P .5F 101
George St. NN8: Well .7B 66
NN9: Irth .3B 68
NN10: High F .5F 69
NN10: R'den .3E 80
NN15: Bur L .1K 45
NN16: K'ing .1D 42
NN17: Corby .7K 13
George Yd. MK11: S Stra .4K 125
(off High St.)
Gervase Sq. NN3: Gt Bil .5F 87
Gharana Nivas NN8: Well .7C 66
Gibbons Dr. NN14: R'ell .6H 27
Gibbsacre Ct. NN3: N'ton .5F 87
Gibbsacre Wlk. NN3: N'ton .5F 87
Gibraltar Ct. NN1: N'ton .1H 131 (7D 84)
Gibson La. NN5: Dall .6A 84
Gifford Ct. NN5: Dus .6H 83
NN5: N'ton .2B 94
Gifford La. NN5: Upton .2H 93
Gilbert Scott Ct.
NN12: Tow .3B 114
Gilbey Cl. NN9: Well .3K 65
Gilchrist Av. NN17: Corby .5B 14
Gillingham Rd. NN15: K'ing .2B 42
Gillitts Rd. NN8: Well .2K 77
Gillsway NN2: K'thpe .2B 84
GILMORTON .3B 132
Gipsy La. NN15: K'ing .6A 38
NN16: K'ing .6A 38
NN29: Irch .5D 78
PE8: Barn .4B 22
Gisburne Rd. NN8: Well .6B 66
Glade, The NN9: Well .3K 65
Glade Cl. NN3: N'ton .5E 86
NN15: Bur L .1K 45
Glades, The NN4: Gra P .6G 101
Gladiator Cl. NN4: Woot .3G 101
Gladstone Cl. NN5: Dall .6B 84
Gladstone Rd. NN5: N'ton .5B 84
Gladstone St. NN9: Raun .6J 53
NN14: Des .2D 26
NN14: R'ell .6G 27
NN14: Rin .1H 53
NN16: K'ing .7E 38
Gladstone Ter. NN9: Raun .6J 53
Glaisdale Cl. NN2: K'thpe .1A 84
Glaister Pl. NN16: K'ing .7F 39
Glamis Cl. NN10: R'den .4G 81
Glan y Mor Ter. NN2: K'thpe .1D 84
GLAPTHORN .2C 135
Glapthorn Rd. PE8: Oun .3G 21
Glapthorn Wlk. NN3: N'ton .1F 87
Glasgow St. NN5: N'ton .7A 84
Glassbrook Rd. NN10: R'den .3C 80
Glassthorpe La. NN7: Harp .1A 92
GLASTON .1A 134
Glastonbury Cl. NN15: K'ing .2H 43
Glastonbury Rd. NN4: Del .6D 94
NN18: Corby .7F 13
GLATTON .3D 135
Glebe, The NN7: Flore .2F 63
NN11: Badby .6D 104
NN11: Dav .3H 61
OX17: Ayn .7F 127
Glebe Av. NN4: H'stone .7F 95
NN14: Brou .6H 41
NN15: K'ing .2D 42
Glebe Cl. NN4: H'stone .7F 95
NN6: Holc .6H 37
Glebe Dr. NN13: B'ley .4H 129
Glebe Farm NN14: Pyt .2A 44
Glebe Farm Cl. NN4: Col .4D 100
Glebe Farm Ct.
NN29: Gt Dod .7K 77
Glebeland Cres. NN5: Dall .6A 84
Glebeland Gdns. NN5: Dall .5A 84
Glebeland Rd. NN5: Dall .5A 84
Glebelands NN6: Spra .5C 34
Glebeland Wlk. NN5: Dall .5A 84
Glebe La. NN4: Gt Hou .5B 96
NN6: Pits .1D 72
NN7: Lwr H .6D 70
NN11: Stav .4A 60
Glebe Ri. OX17: King S .1C 126
Glebe Rd. MK19: Dean .4F 125
NN6: Mears A .3A 76
NN7: Cog .1H 97
NN15: Bur L .2H 45
Glebe Way NN4: H'stone .7F 95
NN7: Cog .1H 97
Glen Av. NN7: Blis .6G 99
Glenbank NN8: Well .1B 78
Glencoe Dr. NN15: K'ing .2G 43
Glendale Ct. NN3: N'ton .5F 87
Glendale Wlk. NN3: N'ton .5F 87
Glendon Rd. NN14: R'ell .6G 27
Glendower Cl. NN11: Dav .6F 59
Gleneagles Cl. NN11: Dav .7K 59
NN15: K'ing .2H 43
Gleneagles Dr. NN8: Well .4J 65
GLENFIELD .1B 132
Glenfield Cl. NN10: R'den .2C 80
Glenfield Dr. NN29: Gt Dod .1J 89
Glengary NN3: Moul .6A 74
GLEN PARVA .2B 132
Glenshee Cl. NN15: K'ing .2G 43
Glenville NN3: N'ton .2J 85
GLINTON .1D 135
GLOOSTON .2D 133
Gloucester Av. NN4: Del .5C 94
(not continuous)
Gloucester Cl. NN4: Del .5C 94
NN7: Weed .3C 62
NN16: K'ing .7E 38
Gloucester Ct. NN14: R'ell .7F 27
Gloucester Cres. NN4: Del .5C 94
NN10: R'den .2F 81
Gloucester Pl. NN8: Well .1B 78
Glover Ct. LE16: Cotti, Mid .4B 12
Glovers Cl. NN9: Irth .4B 68
Glovers La. NN9: Raun .7H 53
OX17: Mid C .5C 118
GLYMPTON .3A 140
Glyndebourne Gdns.
NN18: Corby .2F 17
GOADBY .2D 133
Goadby's Yd. NN16: K'ing .7D 38
GODMANCHESTER .1D 139
Godwin Ct. NN13: B'ley .5F 129
Godwin Rd. NN17: Corby .2A 14
Godwin Wlk. NN5: Dus .4J 83
Goffs Yd. NN29: Boz .3H 103
Goldcrest Ct. NN3: N'ton .1D 86
Goldcrest Rd. NN13: B'ley .2E 128
Goldenash Ct. NN3: N'ton .2C 86
Golding Cl. NN11: Dav .1H 61
GOLDINGS .1D 86
Goldings Local Cen. NN3: N'ton .1D 86
(off Goldings Rd.)
Goldings Rd. NN3: N'ton .1D 86
GOLDINGTON .3C 139
Goldsmith Dr. NN17: Corby .5J 13
Goldsmith Rd. NN8: Well .1H 77
Gold St. LE16: Clip .6C 24
NN1: N'ton .5G 131 (2D 94)
NN6: Wal .1H 37
NN8: Well .7A 66
NN14: Des .2D 26
NN16: K'ing .7D 38
Gold St. M. NN1: N'ton .5G 131
Golf La. NN6: Chu B .5H 71
Goodens La. NN29: Gt Dod .7A 78
Goodhew Cl. NN15: K'ing .2B 42
Goodwin Cl. NN8: Well .4B 66
Goodwood Av. NN3: N'ton .2G 85
Goodwood Cl. NN18: L Oak .6K 17
Goodwood Rd. NN10: R'den .5G 81
Goose Grn. NN13: B'ley .5F 129
Goosemere MK19: Dean .5F 125
Gordon Rd. NN8: Well .7C 66
PE8: Oun .4J 21
Gordon St. NN2: Sem .1F 131 (6C 84)
NN10: R'den .3C 80
Gordon St. NN14: R'ell .7G 27
NN16: K'ing .7E 38
Gorse Cl. NN2: K'thpe .7C 72
Gorseholm Ct. NN9: Irth .3C 68
Gorse Rd. NN6: Spra .5B 34
NN11: Woodf H .1C 108
NN16: K'ing .5G 39
Gosforth NN8: Well .1H 77
Goslar, The NN8: Well .2G 77
Gotch Cl. NN15: Bar S .6H 43
Gotch Rd. NN15: Bar S .5H 43
Gough Cl. NN15: K'ing .1G 43
Goughs Cotts. NN5: Dus .7H 83
Gould Cl. NN11: Braun .1A 58
Gouldens Vw. NN11: Nor .7G 55
Goulsbra Rd. NN10: R'den .5G 81
Gower Cl. NN15: K'ing .4E 42
Gowerton Rd. NN4: Brack .6H 95
GP Karting .2A 94
Grace Ct. NN15: Bur L .3J 45
GRAFHAM .2D 139
Grafton PE8: Oun .5H 21
Grafton Cl. NN7: Hart .5H 117
NN8: Well .5J 65
NN12: Pot .7J 123
Grafton Ct. NN7: Pid .4F 117
Grafton Dr. NN17: Corby .5G 13
Grafton Ho. NN1: N'ton .3F 131
Grafton Pl. NN1: N'ton .2G 131 (7D 84)
GRAFTON REGIS .1D 141
Grafton Rd. NN7: Roa .2B 116
NN10: R'den .3G 81
NN12: Yar G .3K 123
NN14: Brig .4C 20
NN14: C'ord .2G 47
NN14: Ged .6D 46
Grafton Sq. NN1: N'ton .2G 131
Grafton St. NN1: N'ton .2F 131 (7D 84)
NN16: K'ing .5C 38
Grafton St. Ind. Est. NN1: N'ton .2F 131
GRAFTON UNDERWOOD .3B 134
Grafton Vw. NN4: Woot .2F 101
Grafton Way NN5: Dus .4G 83
NN7: Roth .1F 99
Graham Hill NN12: Silv .3H 121
Graham Hill Rd. NN12: Tow .1C 114
Granary Ct. NN4: N'ton .1D 100
Granary Rd. NN4: N'ton .1D 100
Granary Yd. LE16: E Far .3J 25
GRANBOROUGH .3D 141
Granby Cl. NN18: Corby .7G 13
Granby Ct. NN29: Woll .4D 90
GRANDBOROUGH .2A 136
Grandborough Cl. NN6: Brix .4J 35
GRANGE, THE .2F 61
Grange Av. NN5: Dus .5G 83
Grange Cl. NN6: E Bart .1D 88
NN7: D'ton .5B 102
NN29: Irch .6J 79
Grange Ct. NN6: Brix .3H 35
NN7: Hort .3J 117
Grange La. NN6: Pits .1E 72 & 7K 35
GRANGE PARK .5G 101
Grange Pl. NN16: K'ing .5G 39
Grange Rd. NN3: N'ton .3K 85
NN9: Stanw .1J 69
NN9: Well .3K 65
NN14: Brou .5H 41
NN14: Ged, Week .6A 46
NN14: Stan .4F 19
NN16: K'ing .6C 38
Grange Rd. Bus. Est.
NN14: Ged .6B 46
Grange Way NN29: Irch .6J 79
Grangeway NN10: R'den .5C 80
Grangewood NN4: N'ton .1B 100
Grant Cl. NN15: K'ing .3B 42
Grantham Wlk. NN18: Corby .2G 17
Grantown Cl. NN15: K'ing .2G 43
Grant Rd. NN8: Well .7C 66
Granville St. NN16: K'ing .7E 38
Grasmere Grn. NN8: Well .2G 77
Grasmere Rd. NN16: K'ing .7B 38
Grasmere Way NN10: High F .4E 68
Graspin La. NN3: West F .6A 86
Grass Cl. NN12: Tow .2A 114
Grasscroft NN2: K'thpe .1B 84
NN6: Long B .2G 55
Grassmere Av. NN3: N'ton .4B 86
Grass Slade NN6: Brix .3J 35
GRAVELEY .2D 139
Gravel Hill NN11: Mor P .3J 111
Gravely St. NN10: R'den .3C 80
Gray Cl. NN6: E Bart .2F 89
Grays Cl. NN12: Paul .6K 115
NN17: Corby .5K 13
Grays Dr. NN14: Stan .3F 19
Grays La. NN12: Paul .6K 115
NN12: Yar G .3J 123
Gray St. NN1: N'ton .1K 131 (7F 85)
NN29: Irch .6H 79
Greasley Wlk. NN18: Corby .7G 13
GREAT ADDINGTON .1A 52 (1B 138)

154 A-Z Northamptonshire Atlas

GREAT BARFORD 3D 139
GREAT BILLING 4F 87 (2A 138)
Gt. Billing Pk. NN3: Gt Bil 3E 86
Gt. Billing Way NN3: N'ton 1F 87
GREAT BOURTON 1A 140
GREAT BOWDEN 3D 133
GREAT BRINGTON 3H 57 (2C 137)
GREAT CASTERTON 1C 135
Gt. Central Way
　NN11: Woodf H 1D 108
Great Cl. NN6: Chap B 4J 71
GREAT CRANSLEY 4G 41 (1A 138)
GREAT DODDINGTON . .7K 77 (2A 138)
GREAT EASTON 2A 134
Gt. Easton Rd. LE16: Brin 1B 12
Great Fld. Ct. NN3: N'ton 1B 86
Gt. Folds Rd. NN18: Corby 5E 16
GREATFORD 1C 135
GREAT GIDDING 3D 135
GREAT GLEN 2C 133
Gt. Ground Wlk. NN4: Gra P 6F 101
Gt. Gull Cres. NN3: N'ton 7C 74
GREAT HARROWDEN 2J 65 (1A 138)
GREAT HEATH 3A 132
Gt. Holme Ct. NN3: N'ton 1B 86
GREAT HORWOOD 2D 141
GREAT HOUGHTON 5B 96 (3D 137)
Great La. NN7: Bug 2J 105
　NN7: Hack 1G 117
GREAT LINFORD 1D 141
Greatmeadow NN3: N'ton 2F 87
Greatmeadow Rd. NN3: N'ton . . .2E 86
GREAT OAKLEY 4F 17 (3A 134)
Great Oakley Meadow Nature Reserve
　. . . . . .6F 17
GREAT OXENDON 7H 25 (3D 133)
Great Pk. St. NN8: Well 7B 66
GREAT PAXTON 2D 139
GREAT RAVELEY 3D 135
Gt. Russell St.
　NN1: N'ton 2K 131 (7E 84)
GREAT STAUGHTON 2D 139
GREAT STUKELEY 1D 139
GREAT TEW 3A 140
GREATWORTH 3K 119 (1B 140)
Grebe Cl. NN11: Woodf H 2C 108
　NN14: Thra 2H 51
GREEN, THE 6A 130
Green, The CV23: Bar 2C 54
　CV23: Lil 3C 28
　LE16: Clip 6D 24
　LE16: West W 2D 10
　MK19: Cos 6E 122
　　(not continuous)
　MK19: Dean 5F 125
　NN1: N'ton 5G 131 (2C 94)
　NN2: K'thpe 3C 84
　NN4: Gra P 5F 101
　NN4: Gt Hou 5B 96
　NN4: H'stone 7G 95
　NN4: Woot 4F 101
　NN6: Crea 6K 33
　NN6: Guil 6D 32
　NN6: Holl 6G 33
　NN6: Scal 6A 36
　NN6: W Had 6G 29
　NN7: Braf G 5H 97
　NN7: Chu S 7E 62
　NN7: Dod 2A 62
　NN7: Flore 2G 63
　NN7: Gt Bri 3H 57
　NN7: Kisl 4C 92
　NN7: Roa 2C 116
　NN7: Up Harl 2C 82
　NN9: Chel 6K 69
　NN11: Badby 5C 104
　NN11: Braun 1B 58
　NN11: Byf 2J 107
　NN11: Hell 2B 104
　NN11: Lwr B 4A 106
　NN11: Newn 7J 61
　NN11: Stav 4A 60
　NN11: Whil 6D 56
　NN12: Abt 6H 113
　NN12: Blak 5J 109
　NN12: Paul 7H 115
　NN12: Weed L 2D 112
　NN13: Even 2C 130
　　(not continuous)
　NN13: Helm 2B 120
　NN13: Hin H 4A 128
　NN13: Turw 3K 129
　NN14: C'ord 3G 47
　NN14: Isl 3F 51
　NN14: L Add 4A 52
　NN14: Maw 6B 40
　NN14: Orl 7B 44
　NN14: Titch 1H 49
　NN14: Woodf 7B 50
　OX17: Cul 6B 110
Greenacre Dr. NN10: R'den 5E 80
　NN14: Stan 4F 19
Greenaway Cl. NN7: Blis 2J 115

Greenbank Av. NN15: K'ing 1F 43
Greenbank Ter. NN14: Rin 1G 53
Green Cl. NN8: Well 5H 65
　NN9: Irth 4A 68
Greendale Sq. NN3: N'ton 4F 87
GREEN END
　Bedford 3C 139
　St Neots 2D 139
Green End NN2: K'thpe 4C 84
Green Farm Cl. CV23: Lil 3C 28
Greenfield Av.
　NN3: Spin H, N'ton 3H 85
　NN15: K'ing 2B 42
Greenfield Rd. NN3: Spin H 3H 85
Green Flds. NN4: Woot 3F 101
Greenfield Way NN10: R'den 4D 80
Greenfinch Dr. NN3: Moul 7K 73
Greenglades NN3: N'ton 6K 93
Greenhill Ct. NN6: Long B 2G 55
Greenhill Cres. NN11: Dav 7G 59
Greenhill Ri. NN18: Corby 2G 17
Greenhill Rd. NN6: Long B 2G 55
　NN15: K'ing 2B 42
Greenhills Cl. NN2: K'thpe 7C 72
Greenhills Rd. NN2: K'thpe 7C 72
Greening Rd. NN14: R'ell 5F 27
Greenland Wlk. NN18: Corby 4F 17
Green La. LE16: A'ley 3H 11
　LE16: Bray 7C 10
　LE16: Stoke A 6G 11
　LE16: West W 1D 10
　NN4: N'ton 6J 93
　NN4: Woot 3F 101
　NN9: Stanw 1J 69
　NN10: Wym 7C 80
　NN12: Silv 3H 121
　NN12: Tow 4A 114
　NN14: Des 2A 26
　NN14: Ish 4G 45
　NN14: Thra 3H 51
　NN16: K'ing 7D 38
　OX17: Char, Newb 1F 127
Greenlaw NN8: Well 1G 77
Green Rd. NN7: Braf G 5H 97
Greenside NN3: N'ton 3K 85
　NN7: Blis 2H 115
　NN12: Wap 5B 112
Greenslade Cl. NN15: K'ing 2C 42
GREENS NORTON 1H 113 (1C 141)
Green St. NN1: N'ton 5F 131 (2C 94)
　NN7: Mil M 4K 99
　NN29: Woll 4F 91
Greenview Dr. NN2: N'ton 4F 85
　NN12: Tow 4B 114
Greenway NN3: West F 6K 85
　NN11: Braun 1A 58
　NN12: East 5K 105
Greenway, The NN11: Dav 3H 61
Greenway Av. NN3: N'ton 2A 86
Greenwood Cl. NN3: Moul 5K 73
　NN11: Byf 2H 107
Greenwood Rd. NN5: N'ton 1B 94
　　(not continuous)
Greenyard, The NN7: Yar H 5H 103
Greeve Cl. NN18: Gt Oak 5H 17
Greeves Cl. NN5: Dus 5E 82
Gregory Gdns. NN3: N'ton 2K 85
Gregory St. NN1: N'ton 5G 131 (2D 94)
Gregory Wlk. NN18: Corby 2J 17
Grenadier Rd. NN11: Dav 2F 61
GRENDON 2C 102 (2A 138)
Grendon Av. NN17: Corby 6G 13
Grendon Lakes Watersports Cen.
　. . . . . .5H 89
Grendon Rd. NN6: E Bart 4C 88
　NN7: Gren 6E 88
　NN7: Yar H 4H 103
　NN29: Woll 6A 90
GRENDON UNDERWOOD 3C 141
Grendon Wlk. NN3: N'ton 1G 85
　　(not continuous)
Grenville Cl. NN11: Dav 2K 61
　NN14: R'ell 7H 27
　NN17: Corby 5F 13
Gresham Dr. NN4: N'ton 5K 93
Gresley Cl. NN11: Dav 6F 59
GRETTON 6C 8 (2B 134)
Gretton Brook Rd.
　NN17: Corby 3J 13
Gretton Ct. NN8: Well 1G 65
Gretton Rd. LE16: Rock 1G 13
　NN17: Harr 2A 8
　NN17: Weld 5H 15
Gretton Rd. Ind. Est.
　NN17: Weld 5H 15
Greville Av. NN3: Spin H 2H 85
Greville Cl. NN2: Bou 5D 72
Greyfriars NN1: N'ton 4H 131 (1D 94)
Greyfriars Rd. NN11: Dav 3G 61
Greys, The NN7: Weed 3C 62
Grieg Wlk. NN16: Corby 4F 17
GRIFF 3A 132
Griffin Rd. LE16: Bray 7B 10

Griffiths Cl. NN5: Dus 6E 82
Griffith St. NN10: R'den 4E 80
Grimmer Wlk. NN9: Irth 4A 68
GRIMSBURY 1A 140
Grimsby Cl. NN18: Corby 2H 17
GRIMSCOTE 3C 137
Grimscote Rd. NN12: Grim 3K 109
Grimston Jetty NN4: N'ton 4K 93
　　(off Pitstone Rd.)
Grindleford Cl. NN14: Des 2B 26
Grizedale Cl. NN16: K'ing 3C 38
　NN17: Corby 5J 13
GROBY 1B 132
Grombold Av. NN9: Raun 6H 53
Grooms La. NN6: Crea 7K 33
Grosvenor Cen.
　NN1: N'ton 4J 131 (1D 94)
Grosvenor Ct. NN15: Bar S 5J 43
Grosvenor Gdns. NN2: K'thpe 2E 84
Grosvenor Pl. NN13: B'ley 4F 129
Grosvenor Rd. NN15: Bar S 5H 43
Grosvenor Way NN15: Bar S 4H 43
Groundwell Ct. NN3: N'ton 5C 86
Grove, The NN3: Moul 2K 73
　NN7: Roa 3D 116
　NN12: Shut 7A 116
　NN14: Lod 1D 40
　NN14: Rin 1F 53
　NN15: K'ing 1D 42
　NN18: Corby 7D 14
　NN29: Woll 5E 90
Grovebury Dell NN2: K'thpe 2B 84
Grove Farm Cl. NN6: Long B 1K 55
Grove Farm La. NN3: Moul 3A 74
Grovelands NN11: Dav 2F 61
Grove La. NN12: West 2A 112
Grove Pl. NN9: Raun 7J 53
Grove Rd. NN1: N'ton 7F 85
　NN7: Braf G 4G 97
　NN10: R'den 3F 81
　NN14: Thra 4G 51
Grove St. NN8: Well 1K 77
　NN9: Raun 7H 53
　NN10: High F 6F 69
Grove Way NN9: Fine 1F 67
Grove Works NN1: N'ton . .2K 131 (7F 85)
Grundy Ct. NN15: K'ing 2D 42
Guildhall Rd.
　NN1: N'ton 5J 131 (2E 94)
Guillemot La. NN8: Well 5B 66
GUILSBOROUGH 6D 32 (1C 137)
Guilsborough Hill NN6: Holl 2E 33
Guilsborough Rd. NN6: Rav 2B 34
　NN6: W Had 6H 29
Gullet La. LE16: A'ley 3H 11
GUMLEY 2C 133
Gunnell Cl. NN15: K'ing 2B 42
Gunning Ct. NN7: Hort 3J 117
GUNTHORPE 1D 135
Gunthorpe Pl. NN18: Corby 7G 13
Gurston Ri. NN3: N'ton 2F 87
Gynwell NN6: Nas 3H 33

H

Hachenburg Pl. NN10: High F 7F 69
HACKLETON 1G 117 (3A 138)
Hackwood Rd. NN11: Dav 3K 61
HADDON 2D 135
Haddon Cl. NN8: Well 4J 65
　NN10: R'den 5D 80
Hadrians Ga. NN13: B'ley 4H 129
Hafod Cl. NN18: Gt Oak 4H 17
Haig Dr. NN15: K'ing 1G 43
Hailsham Ct. OX17: Mid C 6E 118
Haines Rd. NN4: Far C 4D 94
Haldens Parkway
　NN14: Thra 4K 51
Halfmoon M. PE8: Oun 5J 21
Halford St. NN14: Thra 4G 51
Halford Way NN11: Welt 2K 59
Halfway Thorn NN6: Chu B 4H 71
Halifax Sq. NN18: Corby 1G 17
Hallam Cl. NN3: Moul 6J 73
HALLATON 2D 133
Hall Av. NN10: R'den 4D 80
Hall Cl. CV23: Kil 6C 30
　LE16: West W 1D 10
　MK19: Old S 3J 125
　NN5: Dus 1H 93
　NN6: Nas 2H 33
　NN7: Harp 1A 92
　NN7: Kisl 3C 92
　NN15: K'ing 2B 42
Hall Dr. NN6: Long B 1J 55
　NN9: Fine 7G 47
Halley Rd. NN17: Corby 3G 15
Hall Farm Cl. NN6: Brix 2C 56
Hall Gdns. NN6: E Had 2C 56
　NN14: Lod 1C 40
　PE8: Pole 3E 22

Hall Hill NN14: Brig 2D 20
Hall La. LE16: A'ley 3G 11
　NN6: Welf 1F 29
　NN15: K'ing 1B 42
Hall Mead Ct. NN17: Bug 3H 105
Hall Piece Cl. NN3: N'ton 3F 87
Halls Cl. NN14: Ged 5D 46
　NN17: Weld 5H 15
Hall's La. NN13: B'ley 5F 129
Hallwood Rd. NN16: K'ing 4E 38
Hall Yd. PE8: King C 2H 9
　PE9: Colly 6B 6
HALSE 1B 140
Halse Rd. NN13: B'ley 1F 129
HALSTEAD 1D 133
Halswell Ct. NN3: N'ton 2A 86
Hambledon Ri. NN4: N'ton 4K 93
Hamblin Ct. NN10: R'den 3E 80
HAMERTON 1D 139
HAMILTON 1C 133
Hamilton Ct. NN6: Chap B 4J 71
Hamilton Ho. NN18: Corby 1K 17
Hamilton La. NN7: Gt Bri 3H 57
Ham La. NN14: Rin 1F 53
Hamlet Grn. NN5: Dall 6A 84
Hammas Leys NN6: Long B 1J 55
Ham Mdw. Dr. NN3: N'ton 4F 87
Hammerstone La. NN4: N'ton 4A 94
Hampden Cres. NN16: K'ing 6F 39
Hampton Ct. Cl. NN12: Tow 4B 114
Hampton Dr. OX17: King S 1B 126
HAMPTON HARGATE 2D 135
Hampton Ho. NN10: R'den 3E 80
　　(off Portland Rd.)
Hampton St. NN1: N'ton . .1F 131 (7C 84)
Hamsterly Pk. NN3: N'ton 7D 74
Hanbury Cl. NN1: Dav 4G 59
Handcross Ct. NN18: Corby 2G 17
Handcross Way
　NN10: High F, R'den 1F 81
HANDLEY 5A 114
Handley Cl. NN5: Dus 5F 83
Hanemill Ct. NN3: N'ton 5F 87
Hanemill Wlk. NN3: N'ton 5F 87
　　(off Hanemill Ct.)
Hangerfield Ct. NN3: N'ton 3C 86
HANGING HOUGHTON 1D 137
HANNINGTON 4K 37 (1A 138)
Hanover Cl. NN15: Bar S 3H 43
Hanover Ct. NN3: N'ton 2E 86
Hanover Dr. NN13: B'ley 4F 129
Hans Apel Dr. NN13: B'ley 4E 128
HANSLOPE 3A 138
HANWELL 1A 140
Harbidges La. NN6: Long B 1G 55
HARBOROUGH MAGNA 1A 136
Harborough Rd. LE16: Bray 4A 10
　LE16: E Far 2J 25
　LE16: Gt Oxe 4J 25
　LE16: Mar T, Clip 6D 24
　LE16: Stoke A 6F 11
　NN2: K'thpe 1D 84
　NN6: Brix 3H 35
　NN6: Maid 1A 36
　NN6: Pits . . . . .1C 72 & 6H 35
　NN10: R'den 4F 81
　NN14: Des 1C 26
Harborough Rd. Nth.
　NN2: Bou, K'thpe 2C 72
　NN6: Bou 2C 72
Harborough Way NN10: R'den 4F 81
HARBURY 2A 136
Harcourt Sq. NN6: E Bart 2D 88
Harcourt St. NN9: Raun 6J 53
　NN16: K'ing 7E 38
Harcourt Way NN4: N'ton 4K 93
Hardays La. NN6: W Had 6G 29
Harden Cl. NN18: Gt Oak 6F 17
Harding Cl. NN15: K'ing 1H 43
HARDINGSTONE 7G 95 (3D 137)
Hardingstone La. NN4: H'stone . . .7E 94
Harding Ter. NN1: N'ton . .1G 131 (7D 84)
Hardlands Rd. NN5: Dus 6H 83
　　(not continuous)
HARDMEAD 3B 138
Hardwater Rd.
　NN29: Gt Dod, Woll 1H 89
HARDWICK
　Buckinghamshire 3D 141
　Northamptonshire . . .4D 64 (2A 138)
　Oxfordshire 3B 140
Hardwick Cl. NN8: Well 7K 65
Hardwick Hall Way NN11: Dav 3G 59
Hardwick Rd. NN4: N'ton 7D 94
　NN8: Well 4E 64
　　(Mnr. Farm Cl.)
　NN8: Well 6H 65
　　(Sywell Rd.)
　NN9: H'wick 4E 64
　NN9: L Harr 1G 65
　NN13: Gret 6C 8
Hardy Dr. NN4: H'stone 1G 101
Harebell Sq. NN17: Corby 4G 87

Harefield—High St.

Harefield NN4: Gra P 5G 101
Harefield Rd. NN3: N'ton 1E 86
Harefoot Cl. NN5: Dus 6G 83
Haresmoor Dr. NN12: Tow 5C 114
Hares Run NN14: Maw 5C 40
HARGRAVE 6J 49 (1C 139)
Harksome Hill NN4: N'ton 5K 93
Harlech NN18: Corby 3H 17
Harlech Ct. NN14: Thra 3K 51
HARLESTONE 7E 70 (2D 137)
Harlestone Ct. NN5: N'ton 7A 84
Harlestone Heath Nature Reserve 7G 71
Harlestone Ho. NN5: N'ton 7B 84
Harlestone Rd. NN5: Dall, N'ton 6A 84
NN5: Lwr H 7D 70
NN6: Chap B, Chu B 5G 71
NN7: Lwr H 7D 70
Harley Way NN14: Brig 2E 20
Harmans Way NN7: Weed 3C 62
Harold St. NN1: N'ton 1F 95
Harpers Cl. NN18: Gt Oak 6G 17
Harper's Ct. NN14: Brig 2D 20
HARPOLE 1B 92 (2C 137)
Harrier Pk. NN4: N'ton 7C 94
HARRINGTON 3D 133
Harrington Aviation Mus. 1D 137
Harrington Dr. NN5: Upton 3H 93
Harrington Rd. NN6: Old 5E 36
NN14: Des 2B 26
NN14: Lod 1C 40
NN14: R'ell 7E 26
HARRINGWORTH 2B 8 (2B 134)
Harringworth Rd. NN17: Gret 5D 8
Harris Cl. NN4: Woot 1G 101
NN9: Raun 5J 53
NN13: B'ley 3E 128
Harrison Cl. LE16: Mkt H 1K 25
NN8: Well 7J 65
Harrison Ct. NN7: Bug 2J 105
Harrisons Wlk. NN14: Thra 3H 51
Harris Rd. NN17: Corby 5H 13
Harrogate Ct. NN18: Corby 2G 17
HARROLD 3B 138
Harrold Rd. NN29: Boz 2H 103
HARROWDEN 3C 139
Harrowden La. NN9: Fine 1D 66
Harrowden Rd. NN4: Brack 5J 95
NN8: Well 4K 65
NN14: Orl 7B 44
Harrowick La. NN6: E Bart 1D 88
Harrow La. NN11: Dav 4J 59
Harrow Way NN2: K'thpe 7A 72
Harry Cl. NN6: Long B 2H 55
Harry Potter Ho. NN15: K'ing 1D 42
Hartburn Cl. NN3: N'ton 6F 87
HARTFORD 1D 139
Hartley Dr. NN15: Bar S 3J 43
Harts La. LE16: E Far 2G 25
HARTWELL 6H 117 (3D 137)
Hartwell Cl. NN2: K'thpe 1E 84
Hartwell Rd. NN7: A'ton 6F 117
NN7: Hart 7H 117
NN7: Hart, Roa 2C 116
Hartwood Cft. NN16: K'ing 3E 38
Harvest Cl. NN11: Dav 4J 59
NN15: Bur L 2K 45
Harvest Way NN2: K'thpe 1A 84
Harvey Cl. NN9: Raun 7G 53
Harvey La. NN3: Moul 5J 73
Harvey Reeves Rd. NN5: N'ton 2B 94
Harvey Rd. NN8: Well 2K 77
NN10: R'den 6E 80
Harwood Dr. NN16: K'ing 3C 38
HASELBECH 1D 137
Haselrig Sq. NN4: N'ton 5A 94
Hassocks Hedge NN4: N'ton 5H 93
Hastings Rd. NN2: K'thpe 2E 84
Hastings Wlk. NN18: Corby 1G 17
HATCH 3D 139
Hatfield Cl. NN4: N'ton 7D 94
NN8: Well 5H 65
NN18: Corby 3K 17
Hatherley Cl. NN6: Crick 3J 31
Hathersage Cl. NN14: Des 1B 26
Hatton Av. NN8: Well 7A 66
Hatton Cl. NN3: Moul P 7H 73
Hatton Hall NN8: Well 7A 66
Hatton La. NN17: Gret 6B 8
HATTON PARK 7K 65
Hatton Pk. Rd. NN8: Well 7K 65
Hatton St. NN8: Well 6A 66
Hautboy La. PE8: Warm 2H 23
Havelock Cotts. PE8: Oun 5J 21
Havelock Ct. NN16: K'ing 5E 38
Havelock St. NN8: Well 7B 66
NN14: Des 2D 26
NN16: K'ing 6D 38
Haven Cl. NN5: N'ton 7B 84
HAVERSHAM 1D 141
Haweswater Rd. NN16: K'ing 6A 38
Hawfinch Grn. NN14: Des 1E 26
Hawke Rd. NN11: Dav 2K 61
Hawkins Cl. NN11: Dav 1K 61
NN13: B'ley 4E 128
NN14: R'ell 6H 27
NN17: Corby 4G 13
Hawkridge NN4: N'ton 6A 94
Hawksbeard Pl. NN3: N'ton 4F 87
Hawkshead NN8: Well 2G 77
Hawksmoor Way NN5: Dus 5J 83
Hawksnest NN4: N'ton 7B 94
Hawkstone Cl. NN5: Dus 7J 83
Hawkwell Est. MK19: Old S 3J 125
Hawson Cl. NN15: K'ing 3E 42
Hawthorn Av. NN14: Maw 5B 40
Hawthorn Cl. NN15: Bur L 3J 45
Hawthorn Dr. NN11: Dav 6H 59
NN12: Tow 2C 114
NN13: B'ley 2G 129
NN14: Thra 5H 51
Hawthorne Cl. NN11: Woodf H . . . 2C 108
Hawthorne Rd. NN9: Fine 7J 47
Hawthorne Wlk. NN17: Corby 4K 13
Hawthorn Rd. NN3: N'ton 5H 85
NN15: Bur L 3J 45
NN15: K'ing 2D 42
Hawthorns, The NN10: High F 6E 68
NN12: Silv 4H 121
NN14: Des 3F 27
Hawthorn Way NN8: Well 7K 65
Hay Cl. NN10: R'den 5E 80
NN18: Gt Oak 6G 17
Haycroft Wlk. NN2: K'thpe 1B 84
Hayden Av. NN9: Fine 6J 47
Hayden Rd. NN10: R'den 3F 81
Haydock Cl. NN18: L Oak 6K 17
Haydown Grn. NN5: Dus 6J 83
Hayes Rd. MK19: Dean 5G 125
Hayeswood Rd. NN3: N'ton 2C 86
Hay La. NN9: Irth 3B 68
Hayman Rd. NN13: B'ley 4E 128
Haynes La. NN6: Spra 5C 34
Haynes Rd. NN16: K'ing 7F 39
Hayride, The NN4: N'ton 1B 100
Haystack, The NN11: Dav 4J 59
Hayway NN9: Irth 3B 68
NN10: R'den 1D 80
Hazeland Ho. NN14: Des 2D 26
Hazel Cl. NN7: Hart 5J 117
NN13: B'ley 2G 129
Hazel Copse NN4: Gra P 7G 101
Hazel Cres. NN12: Tow 4B 114
Hazel Cft. NN11: Braun 1B 58
Hazelden Cl. NN29: Woll 5E 90
Hazeldene Rd. NN2: N'ton 4F 85
Hazel Rd. NN15: K'ing 1E 42
Hazelwood NN12: Silv 3G 121
Hazelwood Ct. *NN16: K'ing 1D 42*
(off Hazelwood La.)
Hazelwood La. NN16: K'ing 1D 42
Hazelwood Rd.
NN1: N'ton 5K 131 (2E 94)
NN17: Corby 6K 13
Headingley Rd. NN10: R'den 3G 81
Headlands NN14: Des 2F 27
NN15: Brou, K'ing 4B 42
NN15: K'ing 3D 42
Headlands, The NN3: N'ton 5K 85
NN8: Well 6A 66
Headway NN18: Corby, Gt Oak 6F 17
Headway Bus. Pk. NN18: Corby 6E 16
Healey Cl. NN3: N'ton 2G 87
Hearden Ct. NN8: Well 2K 77
Heartlands Bus. Pk. NN11: Dav 5F 59
Heathcote Gro. NN14: Des 1B 26
HEATHENCOTE 1D 141
Heatherbreea Gdns. NN10: R'den . . . 2C 80
Heather Ct. NN4: N'ton 5B 94
NN10: R'den 3D 80
Heatherdale Way NN2: N'ton 3F 85
Heather La. NN3: N'ton 2B 86
Heather Rd. NN16: K'ing 5F 39
Heathers, The NN29: Woll 4F 91
Heathfield Wlk. NN18: Corby 2G 17
Heathfield Way NN5: N'ton 4B 84
Heath Grn. NN5: N'ton 5A 84
Heath Ri. NN8: Well 6J 65
Heath Ter. NN12: Tow 3C 114
Heathville NN5: N'ton 5A 84
Heath Way NN15: Bur L 1K 45
HE Bates Way NN10: R'den 3C 80
Hecham Way NN10: High F 5E 68
Hedge End NN4: N'ton 2D 100
Hedgely Ct. NN4: N'ton 5B 94
Hedgerow Dr. NN2: K'thpe 1B 84
Hedgerow La. NN14: Maw 5C 40
Hedgerow Way NN11: Dav 4H 59
Hedges, The
NN10: High F, R'den 1F 81
Hedgeway NN4: N'ton 2D 100
HELLIDON 2B 104 (3B 136)
Hellidon Cl. NN2: K'thpe 2F 85
Hellidon Rd. CV47: P Mar 4A 104
HELMDON 2B 120 (1B 140)
Helmdon Cres. NN2: K'thpe 1D 84
Helmdon Rd. NN2: K'thpe 1D 84
NN12: Wap 6B 112
NN12: West 3A 112
OX17: Greatw 2K 119
OX17: Sulg 6G 111
Helmsley Way NN18: Corby 2G 17
HELPSTON 1D 135
Hemans Rd. NN11: Dav 6G 59
Hembury Pl. NN4: N'ton 4A 94
Hemery Way NN15: K'ing 2B 42
HEMINGTON 3C 135
Hemington Rd. PE8: Pole 4D 22
Hemmingwell Lodge Way
NN8: Well 5B 66
Hemmingwell Rd. NN8: Well 5B 66
Hempland Cl. NN18: Gt Oak 6G 17
HEMPTON 2A 140
Henley Cl. NN8: Well 6H 65
NN15: Bar S 5H 43
Henley Ct. NN6: Wat 6D 54
Henry Bird Ct.
NN4: N'ton 7J 131 (3E 94)
Henry Bird Way
NN4: N'ton 7J 131 (3E 94)
Henry Smith Ho. *NN11: Dav 7G 59*
(off Queens Rd.)
Henry St. NN1: N'ton 7F 85
Henshaw Rd. NN8: Well 2J 77
Hensmans La. NN29: Boz 2H 103
Henson Cl. NN16: K'ing 4B 38
Henson Way NN16: K'ing 5A 38
Herbert Gdns. NN12: Tow 1D 114
Herbert St. NN1: N'ton . . . 3G 131 (1D 94)
Hereford Cl. NN14: Des 1F 27
Hereward Rd. NN4: Far C 5C 94
Herford Cl. NN18: Corby 4E 16
Heritage Ct. NN16: K'ing 1D 42
Heritage Way NN9: Raun 5K 53
NN17: Corby 3C 14
Hermitage Cl. LE17: Catt 1A 28
Hermitage Way NN4: Woot 2E 100
Herne Rd. PE8: Oun 6J 21
Hernhill Ct. NN4: N'ton 5K 93
Heron Av. NN14: Thra 2J 51
Heron Cl. NN8: Well 5B 66
NN11: Woodf H 2C 108
NN12: Tow 6C 114
NN15: Bur L 2G 45
Heron Ct. NN11: Dav 7H 59
Heron Dr. NN13: B'ley 2E 128
Heronsford NN4: N'ton 7K 93
Herons Wood Cl. PE8: Oun 5G 21
Heron Way NN8: Well 5C 66
Herrieffs Farm Rd. NN13: B'ley 5F 129
Herriotts Ct. *NN8: Well 7B 66*
(off Herriotts La.)
Herriotts La. NN8: Well 7B 66
Hertford Ct. NN3: N'ton 5D 86
NN11: Dav 4H 61
Hertford Rd. NN15: K'ing 4E 42
Hervey Cl. NN3: N'ton 4A 86
Hervey St. NN1: N'ton . . . 2K 131 (7F 85)
Hesketh Cres. NN12: Tow 5C 114
Hesketh Rd. NN12: Yar G 3J 123
Hesperus NN8: Well 1G 77
Hester St. NN2: Sem 1G 131 (6D 84)
HETHE 3B 140
Hever Cl. NN10: R'den 5F 81
NN14: Thra 3J 51
Hewlett's Cl. NN29: Boz 3H 103
Hexham Ct. NN4: N'ton 5B 94
Heyford La. NN7: Weed 5F 63
Heyford Rd. NN5: Dus 6E 82
NN7: Bug 1H 105
HEYTHROP 3A 140
Hiawatha NN8: Well 1G 77
Hibiscus Cl. NN3: N'ton 1K 95
Hickman Cl. OX17: Greatw 2J 119
Hickmire NN29: Woll 3E 90
Hicks Ct. NN12: Tow 5D 114
Hicks Rd. NN12: Tow 5C 114
Hidcote Cl. NN4: N'ton 1D 100
NN8: Well 3J 77
NN18: Corby 4K 17
Hidcote Way NN11: Dav 3F 59
Hield Cl. NN18: Gt Oak 5H 17
Higgins Sq. NN4: N'ton 5A 94
HIGHAM FERRERS 6E 68 (2B 138)
HIGHAM ON THE HILL 2A 132
Higham Pk. Rd. NN10: R'den 7K 81
Higham Rd. NN8: Well 4C 78
NN9: Chel 5K 69
NN9: Stanw 3H 69
NN10: R'den 2E 80
NN15: Bur L 3K 45
NN29: Irch 4F 79
High Barns Cl. NN4: Gra P 6F 101
Highbridge Rd. NN12: Wap 5B 112
Highbrook NN18: Corby 2G 17
Highcroft Cl. NN12: Yar G 3J 123
HIGH CROSS 6B 120
Highdown Cl. NN4: N'ton 4K 93
Highfield NN14: Woodf 6A 50
Highfield Ct. NN13: B'ley 5F 129
Highfield Cres. NN15: K'ing 4D 42
Highfield Gro. NN17: Corby 6A 14
Highfield Pk. NN6: Crea 6H 33
Highfield Pl. NN11: Dav 7G 59
Highfield Rd. NN1: N'ton 5H 85
NN6: Mears A 3B 76
NN8: Well 7C 66
NN9: Irth 2C 68
NN10: R'den 4B 80
NN11: Dav 7G 59
NN14: Thra 3J 51
NN15: K'ing 3D 42
Highfields NN12: Tow 5B 114
PE8: Pole 3D 22
Highfield St. NN9: Fine 6K 47
Highfield Way NN7: Yar H 6H 103
High Greeve NN4: Woot 2H 101
Highgrove Ct. NN10: R'den 3E 80
High Hill Av. NN14: R'ell 6F 27
Highlands Av. NN3: N'ton, Spin H . . 2H 85
Highlands Dr. NN11: Dav 5G 59
High Leys, The NN6: Crick 5H 31
High March NN11: Dav 3K 61
High March Cl. NN11: Dav 3K 61
High March Ind. Est. NN11: Dav . . . 3K 61
Highslade NN6: Brix 5J 35
High Stack NN6: Long B 2J 55
High St. LE16: Clip 6D 24
LE16: Cotti 4B 12
MK11: Stony S 3K 125
MK19: Dean 5F 125
NN2: K'thpe 3C 84
(not continuous)
NN3: Gt Bil 4F 87
NN3: Moul 4K 73
NN3: West F 6A 86
NN4: Col 5D 100
NN4: Gt Hou 4B 96
NN4: H'stone 7F 95
NN4: Woot 2E 100
NN5: Upton 3H 93
NN6: Brix 2H 35
NN6: Crea 6K 33
NN6: Crick 4H 31
NN6: E Bart 2D 88
NN6: Ect 2J 87
NN6: Guil 6D 32
NN6: Long B 1H 55
NN6: Nas 3H 33
NN6: Pits 1D 72
NN6: Scal 6A 36
NN6: Spra 5C 34
NN6: W Had 6H 29
NN6: Wal 1H 37
NN6: Welf 3H 29
NN6: Yel 5B 28
NN7: Blis 2G 115
NN7: Bug 2J 105
NN7: Flore 2F 63
NN7: G'ton 6D 98
NN7: Harp 1A 92
NN7: Kisl 3C 92
NN7: Mil M 5K 99
NN7: Roa 2C 116
NN7: Weed 3B 62
NN7: Yar H 5H 103
NN8: Well 7A 66
NN9: Chel 6K 69
NN9: Fine 6H 47
NN9: Irth 3B 68
NN9: Raun 6J 53
NN9: Stanw 1J 69
NN10: High F 7E 68
NN10: R'den 2E 80
(not continuous)
NN10: Wym 7E 80
NN11: Braun 1A 58
NN11: Byf 2J 107
NN11: Dav 1H 61
NN11: Eyd 7D 108
NN11: Woodf H 2D 108
NN11: Welt 2K 59
NN12: Ast 7J 105
NN12: Blak 6H 109
NN12: Greens N 1H 113
NN12: Paul 7H 115
NN12: Pot 6H 123
NN12: Shut 6A 116
NN12: Silv 3H 121
NN12: Weed L 3C 112
NN12: Wap 5C 112
NN12: West 2A 112
NN12: Whit 2C 122
NN12: Yar G 3K 123
NN13: B'ley 4G 129
NN13: Crou 5A 130
NN13: Syre 6C 120
NN14: Brig 1C 20
NN14: Brou 6G 41
NN14: C'ord 3G 47
NN14: Den 7G 51
NN14: Des 2D 26

High St. NN14: Isl 3F 51
  NN14: L Add 4A 52
  NN14: Pyt 2A 44
  NN14: R'ell 6F 27
  NN14: Rin 1F 53
  NN14: R'ton 2B 46
  NN14: Stan 4F 19
  NN14: Thra 3G 51
  NN14: Titch 1H 49
  NN14: Woodf 6B 50
  NN15: Bur L 3K 45
  NN16: K'ing 7D 38
  NN17: Corby 7B 14
  NN17: Gret 6C 8
  NN17: Weld 6J 15
  NN29: Boz 3H 103
  NN29: Gt Dod 7K 77
  NN29: Irch 5J 79
  NN29: Woll 4E 90
  OX17: Cul 6A 110
  OX17: Mid C 6C 118
  PE9: Colly 6C 6
  PE9: Eas H 2C 6
High St., The NN6: Rav 2B 34
High St. Pl. NN8: Well 1A 78
High St. Sth. NN10: R'den 4E 80
High Vw. MK19: Dean 4E 124
  NN4: Woot 2F 101
Highwoods NN6: Syw 5G 75
Hilberry Ri. NN3: N'ton 2G 87
Hilda Pl. NN16: K'ing 5G 39
HILL .2A 136
Hill, The LE16: Mid 5A 12
  NN4: Gt Hou 5B 96
  NN12: Pur E 7F 115
  NN13: Syre 5C 120
  OX17: Ayn 7E 126
Hillary Cl. NN11: Dav 5G 59
Hillary Rd. NN10: R'den 4C 80
Hill Cl. NN5: Dus 4H 83
  NN6: Wal 1G 37
Hill Crest NN7: Blis 7H 99
Hillcrest Av. NN3: Spin H 3H 85
  NN15: Bur L 3J 45
  NN15: K'ing 1F 43
Hillcrest Cl. NN14: Thra 2J 51
Hillcrest Ct. NN13: B'ley 4F 129
Hillcrest Rd. NN7: G'ton 7D 98
Hillcroft Vw. NN12: Blak 5J 109
Hilldrop Rd. NN4: N'ton 1B 100
HILLESDEN 3C 141
Hill Farm Est. NN14: L Add 5B 52
Hill Farm Ri. NN4: N'ton 1A 100
Hillfield Rd. PE8: Oun 4G 21
Hill Ho. Ct. NN12: Pat 5G 105
Hill Ho. Gdns. NN9: Stanw 1J 69
HILLMORTON 1B 136
Hillmorton La. CV23: Lil 4B 28
  NN6: Yel 6A 28
Hill Rd. NN11: Lwr B, Up Bod . . .4B 106
Hill Row NN11: Braun 2B 58
Hillside NN6: W Had 6G 29
  NN7: Hart 5H 117
  NN9: Chel 6J 69
  NN9: L Harr 7F 45
  NN9: Raun 1K 61
Hillside Av. NN12: Silv 2J 121
  NN15: K'ing 2E 42
Hillside Cl. NN29: Boz 3H 103
Hillside Cres. NN7: Neth H 6K 63
  NN17: Weld 6H 15
Hillside Rd. NN7: Flore 1E 62
  NN7: Neth H 6J 63
  NN7: Pid 3G 117
  NN8: Well 5D 66
Hillside Ter. NN16: K'ing 7C 38
(off Meadow Rd.)
Hillside Way NN3: West F 6K 85
Hillstone Ct. NN9: Stanw 1J 69
(off Chapel La.)
Hill St. NN8: Well 1A 78
  NN9: Raun 6J 53
  NN13: B'ley 4F 129
  NN16: K'ing 6C 38
HILL TOP 1E 84
Hill Top NN7: Blis 7H 99
  NN9: L Harr 7D 44
Hilltop NN7: Dod 2A 62
  NN9: L Harr 7F 45
Hilltop Av. NN14: Des 1C 26
  NN15: Bar S 5H 43
Hilltop Cl. NN6: Brix 3J 35
  NN15: Des 1C 26
Hill Vw. NN11: Eyd 7D 108
HINCKLEY 2A 132
Hind Stile NN10: High F 7E 68
HINTON 2C 108 (3B 136)
Hinton Av. NN18: Corby 2F 17
Hinton Cl. NN2: K'thpe 1D 84
  NN11: Woodf H 2C 108
HINTON-IN-THE-HEDGES
. . . . .5A 128 (2B 140)
Hinton Mnr. Ct. NN11: Woodf H . .2C 108

Hinton Rd. NN2: K'thpe 1D 84
  NN11: Woodf H 3C 108
  NN13: B'ley 5F 129
Hinton's Cl. NN13: Helm 3B 120
HINWICK 7K 91 (2B 138)
Hinwick Cl. NN15: K'ing 5F 43
Hinwick Rd. NN29: Woll 4E 90
Hirondelle Cl. NN5: Dus 5E 82
HMP Wellingborough
  NN8: Well 5B 78
Hobbs Hill NN14: R'ell 7F 27
(off Kettering Rd.)
Hobby Cl. NN4: N'ton 7C 94
Hocknell Cl. NN4: Woot 2G 101
Hockney Av. NN15: Bar S 2J 43
Hodge Cl. NN12: Ast 7J 105
Hodges La. NN7: Kisl 3C 92
Hodge Way NN16: K'ing 7F 39
Hodnet Cl. NN4: N'ton 1D 100
Hoe Way NN7: Roa 2B 116
Hogarth Cl. NN8: Well 5A 66
Hogarth Dr. NN15: Bar S 3J 43
Hogarth Wlk.
  NN18: Corby 1K 17
Hogg End OX17: Chip W 3D 110
Hogg La. OX17: Char 1H 127
Holbein Gdns. NN4: N'ton 7K 93
Holbein Wlk. NN18: Corby 1J 17
Holbush Way NN9: Irth 1B 68
HOLCOT 6H 37 (2D 137)
Holcot Cl. NN8: Well 4K 65
Holcot La. NN6: Scal 7A 36
  NN6: Syw 1G 75
Holcot Rd. NN3: Moul . . .1K 73 & 7G 37
  NN6: Brix . . . . .3H 35 & 5F 37
  NN6: Wal 4G 37
Holcutt Cl. NN4: Woot 1G 101
Holdellcrofts Ct.
  NN2: K'thpe 3C 84
(off High St.)
HOLDENBY 1C 70 (2D 137)
Holdenby NN15: K'ing 5E 42
Holdenby House Gdns. & Falconry Cen.
. . . . .1B 70
Holdenby Rd. NN2: K'thpe 2E 84
  NN6: Chu B 5H 71
  NN6: E Had, Hold, Spra
    . . . . . . .2D 56, 7A 34 & 1A 70
  NN6: Spra 6C 34
  NN15: K'ing 5F 43
Holden Gro. NN11: Dav 1G 61
Holdgate Cl. NN13: B'ley 2F 129
Holkham Cl. NN18: Corby 4J 17
Holland Ri. OX17: King S 2B 126
Hollands Dr. NN15: Bur L 2K 45
Hollies, The NN3: Moul 3J 73
  NN8: Well 1K 77
Hollingside Dr. NN2: N'ton 3G 85
Hollington Rd. NN9: Raun 6J 53
Hollow, The NN6: Rav 2C 34
  NN9: Stanw 1K 69
(off Newbridge La.)
Hollowbank NN3: Moul 1J 73
HOLLOWELL 5F 33 (1C 137)
Hollowell Cl. NN10: R'den 5G 81
Hollowell Ct. NN8: Well 1A 78
Hollowell Rd. NN6: Crea 6J 33
Hollowell Sailing Club 5F 33
Hollow Way NN11: Eyd 7C 108
  OX17: Ayn 7E 126
Hollow Wood Rd.
  NN15: Bur L 4J 45
Holly Cl. NN13: B'ley 2G 129
Hollyhill NN12: Tow 5B 114
Holly La. NN14: Des 4G 41
Holly Lodge Dr. NN2: K'thpe 1D 84
(not continuous)
Hollyoak Ter. NN3: West F 5A 86
Holly Rd. NN1: N'ton 6G 85
  NN10: R'den 2B 80
  NN16: K'ing 5E 38
Holly Wlk. NN9: Fine 7F 47
Holman Cl. NN3: N'ton 4A 86
Holm Cl. NN7: Weed 5B 62
HOLME 3D 135
Holme Cl. LE16: Wilb 5J 11
  NN9: Well 3K 65
Holmecross Rd. NN3: N'ton 1B 86
Holmes Av. NN9: Raun 7J 53
Holme Way CV23: Bar 2D 54
Holmfield Cl. NN9: L Harr 1G 65
Holmfield Dr. NN9: Raun 6K 53
Holmfield Ter. NN6: Long B 1G 55
Holmfield Way NN3: West F 6K 85
Holmfirth Wlk. NN18: Corby 2G 17
Holmleigh Cl. NN5: Dus 7H 83
Holmwood Cl. NN5: Dus 5F 83
Holyoake Rd. NN29: Woll 4E 90
Holyoake Ter. NN6: Long B 1J 55
Holyrood Cl. NN5: N'ton 7A 84
Holyrood Rd. NN5: N'ton 7A 84
Holyrood Wlk. NN18: Corby 3H 17
Home Acre NN7: L Hou 3E 96

Home Cl. NN4: Gra P 6F 101
  NN7: Blis 2H 115
  NN9: Irth 4B 68
  NN11: Stav 3B 60
  NN12: East 6J 105
  NN12: Greens N 1H 113
  NN12: Silv 3H 121
  NN18: Gt Oak 5G 17
  OX17: Mid C 6E 118
Home Ct. NN14: Thra 3H 51
Home Farm Cl. LE16: E Far 2J 25
  MK19: Dean 5F 125
  NN3: N'ton 6E 86
  NN6: Crea 5K 33
  NN7: Weed 5A 62
  NN18: Gt Oak 6G 17
Home Farm Ct. NN6: Hold 1C 70
  NN11: Nor 7G 55
Home Farm La. NN6: Pits 1D 72
Home Farm Rd. NN14: Stan 4F 19
Home Farm Yd. NN6: Holl 5F 33
Homefield NN11: Dav 3H 61
  PE8: Nass 5F 7
Homestead Ct. NN3: Moul 4A 74
Homestead Cl. NN2: N'ton 5F 85
Homestead Dr. NN7: Bug 2K 105
Homestead Ri. NN4: Woot 2F 101
Homestead Way NN2: N'ton 5F 85
  NN12: Pot 6J 123
HONEYDON 3D 139
Honey Hill Dr. MK19: Dean 4F 125
Honey Holme NN6: Brix 4G 35
Honeystones NN3: Moul 4K 73
Honeysuckle Rd. NN14: Des 1D 26
Honeysuckle Way NN3: N'ton . . .1K 95
Honister Grn. NN3: N'ton 3K 85
Honiton Gdns. NN18: Corby 2K 17
Hood Ct. NN17: Corby 5G 13
Hood Rd. NN11: Dav 1K 61
Hood St. NN1: N'ton 7F 85
Hood Wlk. NN15: K'ing 2F 43
Hookhams Path NN29: Woll 4F 91
HOOK NORTON 2A 140
Hope Ct. NN29: Boz 2H 103
Hopes Pl. NN2: K'thpe 3C 84
Hope St. NN29: Boz 1H 103
Hopmeadow La. NN3: N'ton 2E 86
Hoppet Cl. NN18: Gt Oak 6F 17
Hopping Hill Gdns. NN5: Dus . . .5J 83
Hoppner Wlk. NN18: Corby 1J 17
HOP POLE 1D 135
Hopton Cl. NN11: Dav 4J 59
HORLEY 1A 140
Hornbeam Cl. NN8: Well 7K 65
Hornbeam Ct. NN3: N'ton 3B 86
  NN14: Des 2G 27
Hornby Rd. NN6: E Bart 1D 88
Horncastle Cl. NN11: Dav 4H 59
HORNINGHOLD 2A 134
HORNTON 1A 140
Horrell Ct. NN10: R'den 3D 80
Horrocks Way NN15: K'ing 1H 43
Horse Fair La. NN4: R'ell 7G 27
Horselease Cl. NN18: Gt Oak 6F 17
Horse Mkt. NN1: N'ton . .5G 131 (2D 94)
Horsemarket NN16: K'ing 7D 38
Horsemoor Sq. NN3: N'ton 4F 87
Horsepool, The CV23: Lil 2C 28
Horseshoe Cl. NN6: Brix 3J 35
  NN6: Crea 6K 33
Horseshoe Cotts. NN6: Syw 2H 75
Horseshoe St.
  NN1: N'ton 5G 131 (2D 94)
Horse Well Ct. NN3: Moul 6K 73
Horsham Wlk. NN18: Corby 1G 17
Horsley Rd. NN2: K'thpe 5D 84
HORTON 3J 117 (3A 138)
Horton Cl. OX17: Mid C 7D 118
Horton Cres. OX17: Mid C 6D 118
Horton Dr. OX17: Mid C 6D 118
Horton Pk. NN7: Hort 3K 117
Horton Rd. NN7: Braf G 6G 97
  NN7: Hack 2H 117
  OX17: Mid C 7D 118
Hortonsfield Rd. NN12: Yar G . . .4K 123
Hortons La. NN14: Thra 3H 51
Hospital Hill NN14: R'ell 6G 27
Houghton Hill NN4: H'stone 6G 95
Houghton La. NN4: Brack 5K 95
HOUGHTON ON THE HILL 1C 133
House Martin Cl. NN14: Des 1E 26
Hove Rd. NN10: R'den 3F 81
Hove St. NN18: Corby 1G 17
Howard Av. NN17: Corby 6C 13
Howard Cl. NN14: Des 1E 26
Howard Biley Gdns. NN3: N'ton . .2K 85
Howard Cl. NN11: Dav 2J 61
Howard Ct. NN8: Well 7C 66
(off Mill Rd.)
Howard La. NN2: Bou 5D 72
Howard Rd. NN29: Woll 4E 90
Howard's Ct. NN29: Woll 4E 90
Howards Mdw. PE8: King C 2H 9
Howard St. NN16: K'ing 7C 38

Howards Way NN3: N'ton 1J 85
Howden Grn. NN14: Des 1B 26
Howe Cres. NN11: Dav 2K 61
  NN17: Corby 6F 13
Hoxton Cl. NN3: N'ton 7B 74
Hoylake NN8: Well 5H 65
Hoylake Dr. NN2: N'ton 3G 85
Hoy Wlk. NN17: Corby 4H 13
Hubble Rd. NN17: Corby 4A 14
Hudson Cl. NN11: Dav 5H 59
  NN18: Corby 3H 17
Hudson Dr. NN4: N'ton 6J 93
HUGGLESCOTE 1A 132
HULCOTE 1E 114 (3D 137)
HULCOTT 3D 141
Hulme Way NN8: Well 5K 65
Humber Cl. NN5: N'ton 4K 83
  NN11: Dav 6E 58
Humber Gdns. NN8: Well 6H 65
HUMBERSTONE 1C 133
Humber Wlk. NN17: Corby 4H 13
Humfrey La. NN2: Bou 5D 72
Humphries Dr. NN13: B'ley 3E 128
HUNCOTE 2B 132
HUNGARTON 1C 133
HUNNINGHAM 2A 136
Hunsbarrow Rd. NN4: N'ton 3K 93
Hunsbury Cl. NN4: N'ton 6K 93
Hunsbury District Cen.
  NN4: N'ton 7B 94
Hunsbury Grn. NN4: N'ton 5K 93
HUNSBURY HILL 6K 93
Hunsbury Hill Av. NN4: N'ton . . .4K 93
Hunsbury Hill Country Pk.
(Nature Reserve) 5K 93
Hunsbury Hill Rd. NN4: N'ton . . .5K 93
Hunsbury Wlk. NN4: N'ton 4A 94
Hunslet La. NN4: N'ton 6K 93
Hunt Cl. NN6: Brix 3H 35
  NN8: Well 4A 66
  NN12: Tow 2C 114
Hunter Penrose Ct. NN8: Well 7B 66
(off Great Pk. St.)
Hunters Cl. NN2: K'thpe 7E 72
Hunters Rd. NN17: Corby 4F 15
(not continuous)
Hunter St. NN1: N'ton . . .2K 131 (7E 84)
Hunters' Way NN6: Brix 3H 35
HUNTINGDON 1D 139
Huntingdon Cl. NN18: Corby 5K 17
Huntingdon Rd.
  NN14: Thra . . . . . . .3H 51 & 4F 49
Huntsham Cl. NN14: Des 7A 86
Huntsmead NN3: N'ton 2G 87
Hunt St. NN18: Corby 1J 17
Hurst Cl. NN15: Bur L 1K 45
HUSBANDS BOSWORTH 3C 133
Hussar Cl. NN11: Dav 2G 61
Hutchinson Av. NN14: Brou 7H 41
Hutts Cl. NN11: Byf 2J 107
Huxley Cl. NN8: Well 1F 77
Huxloe Pl. NN16: K'ing 7D 38
(off High St.)
Huxloe Ri. NN3: N'ton 7B 74
Hyacinth Way NN10: R'den 6E 80
Hyde Cl. NN7: Roa 2B 116
Hyde Dr. NN9: Fine 6J 47
Hyde Rd. NN7: Roa 2B 116

I

Ibsen Wlk. NN18: Corby 4F 17
IBSTOCK 1A 132
Ibstock Cl. NN3: N'ton 7D 74
Icknield Dr. NN4: N'ton 6K 93
Ickworth Cl. NN11: Dav 3G 59
Ideal Bldgs. NN1: N'ton 2H 131
Ilex Cl. NN4: H'stone 6G 95
ILLSTON ON THE HILL 2D 133
Ilmor Av. NN6: Brix 2K 35
Imperial Cl. NN10: R'den 3D 80
Independent St. CV23: Kil 6C 30
Indmere Cl. NN4: N'ton 1F 101
Ingleborough Way NN5: Dus 6H 83
Inglewood Cl. NN3: N'ton 5F 87
(not continuous)
Inglewood Wlk. NN3: N'ton 5F 87
INGTHORPE 1B 134
Inham Cl. NN18: Gt Oak 4H 17
Inkerman Way PE8: Oun 5H 21
Inlands, The NN11: Dav 2H 61
Inlands Cl. NN11: Dav 2J 61
Inlands Ri. NN11: Dav 2J 61
Inniskilling Cl. NN3: Moul 4A 74
Insignia Cl. NN4: Woot 1F 101
Interleisure Squash & Sports Club . . .7B 72
Iona Rd. NN17: Corby 5H 13
IRCHESTER 5H 79 (2B 138)
Irchester Cvn. Site NN29: Irch . . .5E 78
Irchester Country Pk. 4F 79

Irchester Country Pk. Vis. Cen. 4E 78
Irchester Narrow Gauge Railway Mus.
. . . . .4D 78
Irchester Rd. NN10: R'den 3B 80
  NN29: Farn 3H 91
  NN29: Woll 4F 91
Iron & Steel Heritage Cen. 6A 12
Irondale Cl. NN4: N'ton 4K 93
Iron Duke Cl. NN11: Dav 6G 59
Iron Pikes NN6: Brix 4J 35
Iron Pit Cl. NN18: Corby 1E 18
Ironstone Cl. NN6: Brix 2J 35
Ironstone Cl. NN9: Fine 7H 47
Ironstone Jetty NN4: N'ton 4A 94
  (off Hembury Pl.)
Ironstone La. NN4: N'ton 4K 93
Ironstone Way NN6: Brix 2J 35
Ironwood Av. NN14: Des 1D 26
IRTHLINGBOROUGH 2C 68 (1B 138)
Irthlingborough Rd. NN8: Well 2C 78
  NN9: Fine 6J 47
  NN14: L Add 6A 52
Irvine Dr. NN12: Tow 1C 114
Irving Gro. NN17: Corby 5K 13
Isabelle Ct. NN16: K'ing 6B 38
Isebrook Cl. NN15: Bur L 2H 45
Ise Rd. NN15: K'ing 1F 43
Ise Va. Av. NN14: Des 2E 26
Ise Valley Ind. Est. NN8: Well 4D 66
Ise Vw. Rd. NN14: Des 2E 26
ISHAM 4G 45 (1A 138)
Isham Cl. NN2: K'thpe 1E 84
Isham Rd. NN14: Orl 7B 44
  NN14: Pyt 2B 44
Islay Wlk. NN17: Corby 5H 13
ISLINGTON 1G 49
Islington Ct. NN12: Tow 4D 114
Islington Rd. NN12: Tow 4C 114
ISLIP 2F 51 (1B 138)
Islip Furnaces Ind. Est.
  NN14: Isl 4C 50
Ivens La. NN12: Lit 2H 109
Ivy Ct. NN11: Dav 2G 61
Ivydene Ter. NN14: Brou 5G 41
Ivy La. NN9: Fine 7H 47
Ivy Rd. NN1: N'ton 6G 85
  NN16: K'ing 5F 39
Ixworth Cl. NN3: N'ton 1C 86

J

Jackdaw Cl. NN3: N'ton 6F 87
Jackdaw Rd. NN18: Corby 3K 17
Jack English Cl. NN5: Upton 7G 83
Jacklin Cl. NN8: Well 5H 65
Jack Parnell Cl. NN5: Upton 1G 93
Jack Pin La. NN5: Upton 3J 93
Jackson Cl. NN2: K'thpe 7F 73
Jackson's La. NN8: Well 1A 78
Jackson Way NN15: K'ing 2B 42
Jacorrin Cl. NN2: K'thpe 7F 73
Jacques Rd. NN15: Bur L 3K 45
Jamb, The NN17: Corby 7B 14
James Lewis Cl. NN3: N'ton 4K 85
James Rd. NN8: Well 3A 78
James St. NN29: Irch 6J 79
James Watt Av. NN17: Corby 4B 14
James Watt Cl. NN11: Dav 6F 59
Jardine Cl. NN3: N'ton 5A 86
Jarretts Yd. NN4: Woot 2F 101
Jarvis Ct. NN13: B'ley 3G 129
  (off Burwell Hill)
Jasmine Ct. NN16: K'ing 4F 39
Jasmine Gdns. NN10: R'den 6E 80
Jasmine Rd. NN3: N'ton 1F 87
  NN16: K'ing 5F 39
Jasper Wlk. NN3: N'ton 7A 74
Javelin Cl. NN5: Dus 6H 83
Jay Rd. NN18: Corby 3K 17
Jean Rd. NN16: K'ing 6G 39
Jellicoe Cl. NN11: Dav 2K 61
Jenkinson Rd. NN12: Tow 5D 114
Jenner Cres. NN2: K'thpe 1C 84
Jennings Cl. NN10: High F 7E 68
  NN11: Dav 2J 61
Jericho PE8: Oun 5J 21
Jerome Cl. NN3: N'ton 7F 75
Jersey Cl. NN8: Well 6C 66
Jersey Cl. NN3: N'ton 5C 86
Jervis Cl. NN11: Dav 2K 61
Jesus Hospital NN14: R'ell 6G 27
Jetty, The NN6: Crea 6K 33
  NN7: Hack 2G 119
  NN12: Wap 5C 112
  NN14: Brig 1D 20
  (off High St.)
Jeyes Cl. NN3: Moul 4J 73
Jeyes Jetty NN1: N'ton 5H 131 (2D 94)
Jibwood NN14: Maw 5B 40
Jitty, The NN14: Maw 6B 40
  PE8: Nass 4H 7
Joan Pyel Cl. NN9: Irth 4B 68

Job's Yd. NN16: K'ing 7D 38
John Ashby Sports Hall, The 3J 73
John Bowen Jones Bus. Pk.
  NN7: Blis 6J 99
John Clare Cl. NN13: B'ley 2G 129
John Clare Ct. NN16: K'ing 3E 38
John Clare Hall NN17: Corby 1F 85
John Clare Way NN17: Corby 5J 13
  (off Byron Rd.)
John Clark Way NN10: R'den 2E 80
John Eagle Cl. NN9: Stanw 1J 69
John Gray Rd. NN29: Gt Dod 7J 77
John Lea Way NN8: Well 4A 78
John Pyel Rd. NN9: Well 3B 68
John Smith Av. NN14: R'ell 6H 27
Johnson Av. NN8: Well 4B 78
  NN13: B'ley 3D 128
Johnson Cl. NN11: Dav 7G 59
Johnson Ct. NN4: N'ton 7J 131 (3E 94)
Johns Rd. NN7: Bug 1K 105
John St. NN10: R'den 3E 80
  NN14: Thra 3J 51
John White Cl., The
  NN10: High F 6F 69
Jones Cl. NN13: B'ley 3E 128
Joseph Priestley Ct. NN11: Dav 2H 61
  (off New St.)
Joshua Sq. NN4: N'ton 5A 94
Jowett Cl. NN15: K'ing 2J 43
Jubilee Av. NN18: Corby 1H 17
Jubilee Cl. NN4: N'ton 4A 94
  NN6: Long B 1G 55
  NN11: Byf 2J 107
  NN14: Isl 2F 51
Jubilee Cres. NN8: Well 3A 78
Jubilee Dr. NN6: Wal 1H 37
Jubilee Gdns. NN10: R'den 5F 81
Jubilee Hill NN3: Moul 4K 73
Jubilee Ho. NN3: N'ton 4B 86
Jubilee Rd. NN11: Dav 1G 61
Jubilee St. NN9: Irth 2B 68
  NN14: R'ell 7G 27
Jubilee Ter. NN14: Ish 4G 45
  (off Park Cl.)
Jude's Ct. NN15: K'ing 1C 42
  (off Northampton Rd.)
Judges Ct. NN6: Crea 6K 33
Judith Rd. NN16: K'ing 6F 39
Julian Way NN2: K'thpe 3B 84
Junction Rd. NN2: N'ton 5F 85
Juniper Cl. NN12: Tow 5B 114
Juniper Cl. NN3: N'ton 3G 87
Juniper Thorn NN6: Brix 4J 35
Jura Cl. NN17: Corby 5G 13
  (off Denford Rd.)
Jutland Way NN16: K'ing 7C 38

K

Kane Wlk. NN17: Corby 5K 13
Kangaroo Spinney NN8: Well 2E 78
Karlstad Cl. NN18: Corby 4F 17
Kathleen Dr. NN16: K'ing 5G 39
Katrine Cl. NN17: Corby 4G 13
Kealdale Rd. NN3: N'ton 2H 85
Keating Cl. NN15: Bar S 2J 43
Keats Cl. NN3: Gt Hou 6C 96
  NN6: E Bart 2F 56
Keats Dr. NN12: Tow 4B 114
  NN16: K'ing 3E 38
Keats Rd. NN8: Well 1J 77
  NN11: Dav 7G 59
Keats Way NN10: High F 7D 68
  NN10: R'den 2B 80
  NN17: Corby 5H 13
Keble Cl. NN11: Dav 3G 61
Keble Rd. NN13: B'ley 3E 128
Kedleston Cl. NN4: N'ton 7D 94
Keebles Cl. NN14: Stan 4F 19
Keeley Green 3C 139
Keepers Cl. NN4: Gra P 5G 101
Kelburn Cl. NN4: N'ton 1C 100
Keld Cl. NN18: Corby 4J 17
KELMARSH 1D 137
Kelmarsh Hall 1D 137
Kelmarsh Rd. LE16: Clip 7D 24
  LE16: Sibb 7A 24
  NN17: Corby 6H 13
Kelmscott Cl. NN3: N'ton 1D 86
Kelsall Cl. NN5: Dus 6G 83
Kelso Cl. NN14: Gt Oak 5K 17
Kelthorpe Cl. PE9: K'ton 4A 6
Kelvin Gro. NN17: Corby 6B 14
Kemp Ho. NN17: Corby 2A 14
Kemps Cl. NN14: Maw 6B 40
KEMPSTON 3C 139
Kempston Rd. NN18: L Oak 6K 17
Kendal Cl. NN3: N'ton 2A 86
  NN8: Well 6H 65
  NN10: R'den 4G 81
Kendalls Cl. LE16: Wilb 5J 11
Kenilworth NN18: Corby 3H 17

Kenilworth Cl. NN5: Dus 6G 83
  NN10: R'den 4F 81
  NN11: Dav 2G 61
Kenilworth Dr. NN15: K'ing 2H 43
Kenilworth Gdns. NN14: Thra 3K 51
Kenmore Dr. NN14: Des 3D 26
Kenmuir Av. NN2: N'ton 4G 85
Kenmuir Cres. NN2: N'ton 4G 85
Kenmuir Gdns. NN2: N'ton 4G 85
Kenmuir Rd. NN9: Fine 7H 47
Kennedy Cl. NN11: Dav 2K 61
Kennel Hill NN14: Brig 2D 20
Kennel Rd. NN12: Whit 3C 122
Kennel Ter. NN6: Brix 3H 35
Kennet Grn. NN5: N'ton 4A 84
Kensington Cl. NN10: R'den 2B 80
  NN12: Tow 5B 114
  OX17: King S 1B 126
Kensington Gdns. NN15: K'ing 2C 42
Kensington Ga. NN3: Gt Bil 3E 86
Kensington Wlk. NN18: Corby 3H 17
Kent Cl. NN5: Dus 1H 93
  NN17: Corby 6H 13
Kentford Cl. NN4: N'ton 7C 94
Kenton Ct. NN15: Bar S 2J 43
Kent Pl. NN15: K'ing 4F 43
Kent Rd. NN5: Upton, Dus 7F 83
  NN8: Well 4A 78
  NN10: R'den 2F 81
Kentstone Cl. NN2: K'thpe 1A 84
Kent Wlk. NN5: Upton 1G 93
Kerley Cl. NN14: Brou 7G 41
Kerrfield Est. NN5: Dus 7G 83
Keston Way NN9: Raun 7G 53
Kestrel Cl. NN3: West F 5A 86
Kestrel Cres. NN13: B'ley 2F 129
Kestrel La. NN8: Well 5B 66
Keswick NN8: Well 7G 65
Keswick Dr. NN3: N'ton 2K 85
Keswick Rd. NN6: Brix 2G 81
KETTERING 6D 38 (1A 138)
Kettering Crematorium
  NN16: K'ing 5A 38
Kettering Gdns. NN1: N'ton 1F 95
Kettering Leisure Village 3C 42
Kettering Lodge Bowls Club 1D 42
Kettering Parkway NN15: K'ing 6E 42
Kettering Retail Pk. NN15: K'ing 5E 42
Kettering Rd.
  NN1: N'ton 3K 131 (1F 95)
  NN1: N'ton 1F 95
  NN3: Moul 4B 74
  NN3: N'ton, Spin H 4H 85
  NN6: Wal 1H 37
  NN9: Gt Har, L Harr . . . .1K 65 & 7F 46
  NN14: Brou 5H 41
  NN14: Ged 6C 46
  NN14: Ish 2F 45
  NN14: Isl, Twy 5A 50
  (not continuous)
  NN14: Pyt 2A 44
  NN14: R'ell 7F 27
  NN14: Stan 4F 19
  NN15: Bur L 6K 43
  NN17: Weld 6J 15
Kettering Rd. Nth. NN3: N'ton 1K 85
Kettering Station (Rail) 2C 42
Kettering Swimming Pool 1D 42
Kettering Town FC 4D 38
Kettering Venture Pk.
  NN15: K'ing 6F 43
KETTLE END 2D 112
KETTON 1B 134
Kettonby Gdns. NN15: K'ing 3D 42
Ketton Rd. PE9: Colly 4B 6
KEYHAM 1C 133
Keyham Ct. NN3: N'ton 1D 86
Keys Cl. NN11: Dav 2J 61
KEYSOE 2C 139
KEYSOE ROW 2C 139
KEYSTON 1C 139
Keystone NN4: N'ton 6J 93
Keystone Ho. NN5: Upton 7F 83
KG Bus. Cen. NN5: Dall 5A 84
KIBWORTH BEAUCHAMP 2C 133
KIBWORTH HARCOURT 2C 133
KIDDINGTON 3A 140
Kielder Ct. NN15: Bar S 6J 43
Kieldsen Cl. OX17: Mar L 3G 119
Kiel Wlk. NN18: Corby 4G 17
Kilborn Cl. NN8: Well 5K 65
Kilborn Rd. NN8: Well 6J 65
Kilborn Pl. NN10: R'den 1E 80
KILBY 2C 133
Kilby Cl. NN8: Well 2K 77
Kiln La. NN11: Welt 2K 59
  NN12: Lit 2G 109
Kiln Way NN8: Well 7J 65
KILSBY 6C 30 (1B 136)
Kilsby Rd. CV23: Bar 2C 54
  NN6: Crick 7G 31
  NN6: Crick, Wat 4B 54

Kilvey Rd. NN4: Brack 5H 95
Kimball La. NN6: Spra 5C 34
Kimball M. NN2: Bou 5D 72
Kimble Ct. NN4: N'ton 7C 94
KIMBOLTON 2C 139
Kimbolton Ct. NN14: Thra 3J 51
Kimbolton Rd. NN9: Chel 6K 69
  NN10: High F 6F 69
KIMCOTE 3B 132
Kinewell Cl. NN14: Rin 1F 53
Kinewell Lake Nature Reserve 1E 52
King Cup Cl. NN10: R'den 6F 81
King Edward Rd. NN1: N'ton 7H 85
Kingfisher Cl. NN4: N'ton 1B 100
  NN11: Woodf H 2C 108
  NN14: Rin 1F 53
  (off Carlow Rd.)
Kingfisher Ct. NN6: Syw 5F 75
Kingfisher Rd. NN13: B'ley 1F 129
Kingfisher Way NN15: Bur L 2H 45
Kingmaker Way NN4: N'ton 5B 94
King Richard Ct. NN4: N'ton 2D 100
Kings Arms Cl. NN14: Thra 3H 51
Kings Arms La. PE8: Pole 4D 22
Kings Av. NN10: High F 5F 69
Kingsbrook NN18: Corby 3G 17
KING'S CLIFFE 2H 9 (2C 135)
Kings Cl. NN4: Gra P 5G 101
Kings Cnr. Cl. NN11: Woodf H 2D 108
  (off Quinton La.)
Kings Ct. NN14: Des 2D 26
Kingscroft Cl. NN3: N'ton 5F 87
Kingscroft Wlk. NN3: N'ton 4E 86
Kingsfield Bus. Pk. NN5: N'ton 5B 84
Kingsfield Cen. NN3: Moul P 6G 73
Kingsfield Cl. NN5: Dall 5A 84
Kingsfield Piece NN12: Whit 2C 122
Kingsfield Way NN5: Dall 5A 84
King's Forest PE8: King C 2H 9
Kings Grn. NN11: Dav 4H 61
Kings Head Pas. NN14: Thra 3H 51
  (off High St.)
KING'S HEATH 4A 84
Kingshill Dr. MK19: Dean 4F 125
Kingsland Av. NN2: K'thpe 3D 84
Kingsland Cl. NN2: K'thpe 3E 84
Kingsland Gdns. NN2: K'thpe 3D 84
Kings La. NN6: Yel 5C 28
  NN7: Flore 2G 63
  NN12: Pur E 7F 115
Kingsley Av. NN11: Dav 2G 61
  NN16: K'ing 4D 38
Kingsley Dr. NN17: Corby 5J 13
Kingsley Gdns. NN2: N'ton 5F 85
KINGSLEY PARK 5G 85
Kingsley Pk. Ter. NN2: N'ton 5G 85
Kingsley Rd. NN2: N'ton 4E 84
  NN12: Silv 1J 121
  NN14: R'ell 6F 27
Kingsmead NN2: K'thpe 1B 84
  PE8: King C 1H 9
Kings Mdw. NN10: High F 4E 68
Kings Mdw. La. NN10: High F 4D 68
Kingsmead Pk. NN10: R'den 4K 81
Kingsmith Dr. NN9: Raun 6K 53
KING'S NEWNHAM 1A 136
KING'S NORTON 1C 133
Kings Pk. NN3: Moul P 7G 73
  NN7: Weed 4B 62
King's Pk. Rd. NN3: Moul P 7G 73
King's Pk. Tennis Cen. 7G 73
King's Pl. NN10: R'den 3F 81
Kings Rd. NN10: R'den 3F 81
  NN17: Weld 6J 15
  PE8: Oun 5J 21
Kings Stile OX17: Mid C 5C 118
Kings St. NN8: Well 7B 66
  NN9: L Harr . . . .—
KING'S SUTTON 1B 126 (2A 140)
Kings Sutton Station (Rail) 1A 126
Kingsthorne Pk. NN16: K'ing 5A 38
KINGSTHORPE 3D 84 (2D 137)
Kingsthorpe Av. NN17: Corby 6G 13
Kingsthorpe Bowling Club 6C 72
Kingsthorpe Gro. NN2: K'thpe 4D 84
KINGSTHORPE HOLLOW 5D 84
Kingsthorpe Ho. NN2: K'thpe 1E 84
Kingsthorpe Meadows Nature Reserve
. . . . .4B 84
Kingsthorpe Rd.
  NN2: K'thpe, N'ton 4D 84
Kingsthorpe Shop. Cen.
  NN2: K'thpe 3D 84
Kingston Cl. NN6: Long B 1J 55
  NN11: Dav 7G 59
  NN12: Blak 5J 109
  OX17: Mid C 7D 118
King St. NN1: N'ton 4H 131 (1D 88)
  NN6: E Bart 1D 88
  NN6: Long B 1H 55
  NN14: Des 2E 26
  NN16: K'ing 6D 38
King Style Cl. NN6: Crick 3H 31

Kingsway—Lime Trees Gro.

Kingsway NN2: K'thpe 2B **84**
NN8: Well 2J **77**
Kingswell Rd. NN2: K'thpe 3C **84**
Kingswell St.
NN1: N'ton 5H **131** (2D **94**)
KINGSWOOD
Kingswood 3C **141**
Northamptonshire 2G **17**
Kings Wood Nature Reserve 3F **17**
Kingswood Pl. NN18: Corby 3F **17**
Kinross Cl. NN3: N'ton 2H **85**
Kipling Dr. NN12: Tow 4B **114**
Kipling Rd. NN16: K'ing 4E **38**
NN17: Corby 5J **13**
Kipton Cl. NN14: R'ell 6H **27**
Kipton Flds. NN14: R'ell 6H **27**
Kirby Cl. NN4: Woot 1G **101**
NN18: Corby 2F **17**
Kirby Ct. NN15: K'ing 5E **42**
KIRBY FIELDS 1B **132**
Kirby Hall 2B **134**
Kirby La. NN17: Corby, Dee 1G **15**
KIRBY MUXLOE 1B **132**
Kirby Rd. NN17: Gret 6D **8**
Kirby Row *NN5: Upton 3J **93***
(off Clickers Dr.)
KIRKBY MALLORY 1A **132**
Kirkeby PE8: Oun 4H **21**
Kirkhams Cl. NN6: Yel 6D **28**
Kirkstone Wlk. NN3: N'ton 2K **85**
Kirkwall NN17: Corby 4H **13**
KIRTLINGTON 3B **140**
Kirton Cl. NN3: N'ton 1E **86**
Kirton End NN3: N'ton 2E **86**
KISLINGBURY 3C **92** (3C **137**)
Kislingbury Rd. NN7: Bug 1J **105**
NN7: Roth 1E **98**
Kitchener Cl. NN11: Dav 6G **59**
Kitchen Gdns. NN14: C'ley 4F **41**
Kites Cl. NN4: N'ton 7B **94**
KITES HARDWICK 2A **136**
Kits Cl. NN7: Hart 5H **117**
Knaphill Cres. NN4: N'ton 3A **94**
Knibb Pl. NN15: Bar S 4H **43**
Knibb St. NN16: K'ing 7E **38**
KNIGHTCOTE 3A **136**
Knightlands Rd. NN9: Irth 1C **68**
Knightley Cl. NN11: Byf 2J **107**
Knightley Rd. NN2: K'thpe 5D **84**
KNIGHTLOW HILL 1A **136**
KNIGHTON 1C **133**
Knighton Cl. NN5: Dus 3F **83**
Knightons Way NN6: Brix 5H **35**
Knightscliffe Way NN5: Dus 5J **83**
Knights Cl. NN6: E Bart 2D **88**
NN18: Corby 2F **17**
NN29: Boz 3H **103**
Knights Ct. NN3: N'ton 5E **86**
NN8: Well 7A **66**
Knights Hill NN6: Nas 3H **33**
Knights La. NN2: K'thpe 3C **84**
Knights M. NN10: R'den 4F **81**
Knob, The OX17: King S 1C **126**
Knock La. NN7: Blis 4J **115**
Knoll, The NN6: Brix 3J **35**
NN7: Gren 3C **102**
Knoll Ct. NN16: K'ing 5D **38**
KNOSSINGTON 1A **134**
Knot Tiers Dr. NN5: Upton 2H **93**
KNOTTING 2C **139**
KNOTTING GREEN 2C **139**
Knowle Cl. NN3: N'ton 1K **95**
Knowles Cl. NN10: R'den 2G **81**
Knowle Way NN11: Dav 3G **59**
Knox Ct. NN8: Well 1C **78**
Knox Rd. NN8: Well 1C **78**
KNUSTON 4B **80** (2B **138**)
Knuston Dr. NN10: R'den 3C **80**
Knuston Rd. NN29: Knus 4A **80**
Knuston Spinney NN29: Knus 4A **80**
Knutsford La. NN6: Long B 1J **55**
Kylesku Cres. NN15: K'ing 2G **43**
Kynnesworth Gdns. NN10: High F 6F **69**
Kyoto Cl. NN3: Moul P 7H **73**

L

Laburnum Cl. NN8: Well 7K **65**
NN11: Woodf H 2C **108**
Laburnum Cres. NN3: Spin H 4H **85**
NN16: K'ing 5F **39**
Laceby Wlk. NN3: N'ton 7C **74**
Lacemakers Ct. NN10: R'den 5F **81**
Lacing La. NN5: Upton 3H **93**
LADBROKE 3A **136**
Laddermakers Yd. NN7: Bug 2H **105**
Ladder Maker Yd.
NN1: N'ton 3H **131** (1D **94**)
Ladies First Health & Fitness Club
*7E **38***
(off Montagu St.)
Ladybower Cl. NN16: K'ing 6A **38**
Ladybridge Dr. NN4: N'ton 6J **93**
Lady Cl. NN11: Newn 7J **61**
Lady Cft. NN11: Dav 2G **61**
Ladyfield NN7: Blis 1H **115**
Lady Hollows Dr. NN4: Woot 2H **101**
Ladymead Cl. NN4: N'ton 6J **93**
Lady's La. NN1: N'ton 3H **131** (1D **94**)
NN6: Mears A 3A **76**
Lady Smock Cl. NN4: Gra P 6G **101**
Ladywell Ct. NN8: Well 5B **66**
(Linnet Cl.)
NN8: Well 5B **66**
(Nest Farm Way)
Ladywell M. *NN14: R'ell 6G **27***
(off Market Hill)
Lady Winefride's Wlk.
NN3: Gt Bil 4E **86**
LA Fitness
Kettering 5E **42**
Lahnstein Ct. *NN16: K'ing 7D **38***
(off Printers Yd.)
Lake Av. NN15: K'ing 2A **42**
Lake Cres. NN11: Dav 1F **61**
Lakes, The NN4: N'ton 3K **95**
Lakeside NN9: Irth 4A **68**
Lakeside Cl. NN14: Thra 2H **51**
Lakeside Dr. NN3: N'ton 3G **87**
Lakeview Grn. NN3: N'ton 2K **85**
Lake Wlk. NN4: Col 4D **100**
Lalgates Ct. NN5: N'ton 7A **84**
Lambrook Dr. NN4: N'ton 1D **100**
Lammas Cl. NN14: Orl 7B **44**
Lammas Courtyard NN17: Corby 4H **15**
Lammas Rd. NN17: Corby 4H **15**
LAMPORT 1D **137**
Lamport Cl. NN15: K'ing 5E **42**
Lamport Ct. NN11: Dav 5F **59**
Lamport Dr. NN11: Dav 5F **59**
Lamport Hall 1D **137**
Lamport Rd. NN6: Drau 2E **36**
NN6: Old 5D **36**
Lancaster Cl. NN29: Woll 3D **90**
Lancaster Dr. NN13: B'ley 3F **129**
NN14: Thra 3K **51**
Lancaster Rd. NN14: R'ell 6H **27**
NN16: K'ing 6E **38**
Lancaster St. NN10: High F 6F **69**
Lancaster Way NN4: N'ton 5B **94**
NN10: R'den 2F **81**
Lancers Way NN7: Weed 3C **62**
Lanchester Way NN11: Dav 7E **58**
Lancum Ho. NN8: Well 7K **65**
Landcross Dr. NN3: N'ton 7K **85**
Landimore Rd. NN4: H'stone 1H **101**
Landor NN8: Well 1H **77**
Landor Cl. NN17: Corby 4J **13**
Landsdown Dr. NN3: N'ton 4B **86**
Landseer Cl. NN8: Well 4A **66**
Landseer Ct. NN18: Corby 1J **17**
Lane, The LE16: West W 2D **10**
NN7: D'ton 6B **102**
NN7: Roth 2G **99**
NN12: East 5K **105**
NN12: Wap 5C **112**
PE9: Eas H 2C **6**
Lanercost Wlk. NN3: N'ton 2K **85**
Laneside Hollow NN4: N'ton 2D **100**
Langdale NN14: Des 2C **26**
Langdale Ct. NN8: Well 7J **65**
Langdale Rd. NN2: K'thpe 3E **84**
Langdon Cl. NN11: Dav 5G **59**
Langford Dr. NN4: Woot 3E **100**
LANGHAM 1A **134**
Langham Cl. NN6: Crea 5K **33**
Langham Pl.
NN2: N'ton 1H **131** (6D **84**)
NN6: Wal 1H **37**
Langham Rd. NN9: Raun 5J **53**
Langley Cl. NN4: N'ton 4K **93**
Langley Ct. NN15: Bur L 2J **45**
Langley Cres. NN9: Irth 7A **52**
Langley Wlk. NN18: Corby 1J **17**
Langley Way NN15: K'ing 4E **42**
Langport Grn. NN18: Corby 7F **13**
Langsett Cl. NN3: N'ton 5C **86**
NN16: K'ing 6A **38**
LANGTOFT 1D **135**
Langton Ct. NN18: Corby 7F **13**
Langton Pl. NN14: Ish 3F **45**
Langton Ri. NN11: Whil 6C **56**
Lansdown Cl. NN11: Dav 5J **59**
Lansom Cl. NN15: Bur L 1K **45**
Lapford Rd. NN18: Corby 2K **17**
Lapin La. NN6: Thor U 7A **26**
Lapland Wlk. NN18: Corby 4G **17**
Lapstone Ho. *NN5: N'ton 2B **94***
(off Byfield Rd.)
Lapwing Cl. NN4: N'ton 1B **100**
NN18: Corby 3K **17**
Larch Cl. NN11: Woodf H 2B **108**
NN29: Irch 6G **79**
Larch Dr. NN11: Dav 5H **59**
Larch La. NN5: Dus 4F **83**
Larch Rd. NN15: K'ing 1E **42**
NN17: Corby 4K **13**
Larchwood Cl. NN8: Well 7K **65**
Lark Cl. NN18: Corby 3J **17**
Larkhall La. NN7: Harp 1B **92**
Larkhall Way NN7: Harp 7B **82**
Larkhill NN10: R'den 1D **80**
Larkin Gdns. NN10: High F 7D **68**
Lark La. NN4: Gra P 5G **101**
Lark Ri. NN3: N'ton 2D **86**
NN13: B'ley 3F **129**
Larkwood Cl. NN16: K'ing 3D **38**
Larratt Rd. NN17: Weld 5H **15**
Larwood Cl. NN2: K'thpe 1B **84**
Lasham Ct. NN3: N'ton 5F **87**
Lasham Wlk. NN3: N'ton 5E **86**
Latham Rd. PE8: Oun 4H **21**
Latham St. NN14: Brig 2D **20**
Lathbury Rd. NN13: B'ley 3E **128**
Latimer Cl. NN15: Bur L 2K **45**
NN17: Gret 6D **8**
Latimer Rd. NN17: Corby 5K **13**
Lattimore Cl. NN6: W Had 5H **29**
Latymer Cl. LE16: Bray 7B **10**
Latymer Ct. NN1: N'ton 3H **131** (1D **94**)
Lauda Way NN12: Tow 1C **114**
Laudersdale Av. NN4: N'ton 5B **94**
Laud's Rd. NN6: Crick 4J **31**
LAUGHTON 3C **133**
Launcelot Ct. NN5: Dus 7F **83**
Laundimer PE8: Oun 5J **21**
LAUNTON 3C **141**
Laureate Ho. NN11: Dav 6G **59**
Laurel Cl. NN6: Brix 4H **35**
Laurel Ct. NN3: N'ton 3B **86**
Laurel Pl. NN12: Tow 4D **114**
Laurel Rd. NN16: K'ing 5E **38**
Laurels, The NN3: Moul 4J **73**
NN6: Ect 3J **87**
Laurel Valley NN4: Col 4E **100**
Lavant Wlk. NN3: N'ton 1G **85**
Lavender Cl. NN14: Thra 2H **51**
NN18: Corby 4J **17**
Lavender La. NN7: Hort 3J **117**
Lavender Way NN10: R'den 5F **81**
LAVENDON 3B **138**
Lavendon Ct. NN15: Bar S 5J **43**
Lavenham Cl. NN3: N'ton 1C **86**
Lavery Ct. NN18: Corby 1J **17**
Lawns, The CV23: Kil 7B **30**
NN5: Dus 6K **83**
NN16: K'ing 1C **42**
NN18: Corby 1F **17**
Lawrence Cl. NN9: Raun 7G **53**
NN15: Bar S 2J **43**
Lawrence Ct.
NN1: N'ton 1H **131** (7D **84**)
NN18: Corby 1J **17**
Laws Cft. NN13: B'ley 4E **128**
Laws La. NN9: Fine 7H **47**
PE8: King C 2H **9**
Lawson Ct. LE16: Cotti 4C **12**
Lawson Cres. NN3: N'ton 5F **87**
Lawson St. NN9: Raun 6J **53**
NN16: K'ing 6E **38**
Lawton Rd. NN10: R'den 2F **81**
Lawyers Cl. NN13: Even 2B **130**
LAXTON 2B **134**
Laxton Cl. NN17: Corby 5G **13**
Laxton Ct. NN15: Bar S 5K **43**
Laxton Dr. PE8: Oun 3K **21**
Laywood Cl. NN9: Raun 5H **53**
Laywood Way NN9: Irth 4B **68**
Leafields NN3: N'ton 6C **86**
Leah Bank NN4: N'ton 5B **94**
Leah Cl. NN18: Gt Oak 6F **17**
Lealand, The LE16: E Far 1J **25**
Leam, The NN11: Dav 2E **60**
LEAMINGTON HASTINGS 2A **136**
Leamington Way NN11: Dav 2E **60**
Lea Rd. NN1: N'ton 6G **85**
Leatherland Ct. NN16: K'ing 7D **38**
Lea Way NN8: Well 1J **77**
Leben Sq. NN3: N'ton 1F **87**
LECKHAMPSTEAD 2D **141**
Leckhampstead Rd.
MK19: Wick 6B **124**
Ledaig Way NN3: N'ton 2H **85**
Ledbury Rd. NN15: Bar S 5H **43**
LEDWELL 3A **140**
Leeds Cl. NN18: Corby 4A **18**
Lees Cl. NN12: Whit 2C **122**
Leeson Ct. *NN12: Tow 5C **114***
(off Leeson Rd.)
Leeson Cres. NN15: Bar S 4H **43**
Leeson Rd. NN12: Tow 5C **114**
Lees St. NN9: Irth 3B **68**
Lee's Way NN14: Ged 5C **46**
Lee Way NN9: Raun 5J **53**
Legion Cres. NN16: K'ing 6B **38**
LEICESTER 1B **132**
Leicester Cl. NN16: K'ing 6C **38**
NN18: L Oak 5K **17**
LEICESTER FOREST EAST 1B **132**
Leicester Pde. *NN2: N'ton 6D **84***
(off Barrack Rd.)
Leicester St. NN1: N'ton 1H **131** (7D **84**)
NN16: K'ing 6C **38**
Leicester Ter.
NN2: Sem 1H **131** (7D **84**)
LEIGHTON BROMSWOLD 1D **139**
Leighton Cl. NN8: Well 4A **66**
Leighton Pl. NN8: Well 1A **78**
Leighton Rd. NN18: Corby 1J **17**
LEIRE 2B **132**
Leith Ct. NN4: N'ton 4K **93**
Lely Ct. NN18: Corby 1J **17**
Lennox Wlk. NN5: Dus 5J **83**
Lensway NN14: Maw 5B **40**
Lenton Cl. NN14: Brou 7G **41**
Leonard La. NN3: Moul 4K **73**
Leonardo Ct. NN18: Corby 1J **17**
Lerwick Way NN17: Corby 5H **13**
Leslie Rd. NN2: Sem 1F **131** (7C **84**)
Lesson Rd. NN6: Brix 4H **35**
Letts Rd. NN4: Far C 4C **94**
Leven Way NN17: Corby 4G **13**
Levitts Rd. NN7: Bug 2J **105**
Lewin Cl. NN14: R'ell 6E **26**
Lewin Rd. NN18: Gt Oak 4G **17**
Lewis Rd. NN5: N'ton 7A **84**
NN15: K'ing 3E **42**
Lexden Cl. NN4: Woot 1G **101**
Lexton Gdns. OX17: Mid C 6D **118**
Leyland Dr. NN2: K'thpe 1B **84**
Leyland Trad. Est.
NN8: Well 1E **78**
Leyland Vw. NN8: Well 1E **78**
Leys, The NN2: K'thpe 4C **84**
NN6: Long B 1J **55**
NN6: Welf 3G **29**
NN7: Bug 3H **105**
NN7: D'ton 5B **102**
NN7: Roa 2C **116**
NN7: Yar H 6G **103**
NN11: Up Bod 1B **106**
NN14: Orl 7B **44**
NN14: Woodf 6B **50**
Leys Av. NN14: Des 2F **27**
NN14: R'ell 6F **27**
Leys Cl. NN6: Long B 1J **55**
NN7: D'ton 5B **102**
Leys Ct. NN8: Well 7C **66**
Leys Gdns. NN8: Well 6C **66**
Leyside Ct. NN3: N'ton 1E **86**
Leys La. NN4: Gt Hou 6C **96**
Leys Rd. NN6: E Bart 2C **88**
NN8: Well 7C **66**
NN12: Pat 5G **105**
Leyswell Ct. NN3: N'ton 6D **86**
Liberty Dr. NN5: Dus 5H **83**
Lichfield Cl. NN7: Kisl 4C **92**
Lichfield Dr. NN4: N'ton 1C **100**
Liddington Way NN2: K'thpe 1D **84**
LIDSTONE 3A **140**
Lightfoot La. LE16: Mid 4A **12**
Lilac Cl. NN14: Thra 3H **51**
Lilac Ct. NN8: Well 7K **65**
Lilac Gro. NN10: R'den 6E **80**
Lilac Pl. NN15: K'ing 1F **43**
LILBOURNE 3C **28** (1B **136**)
Lilbourne Rd. CV23: Clif D 3A **28**
LE17: Catt 1A **28**
NN6: Yel 5B **28**
Lilford Pl. NN16: K'ing 6F **39**
Lilford Rd. NN14: Thor W 6E **20**
Liliput Rd. NN4: Brack 4K **95**
Lilley Ter. NN9: Irth 2C **68**
LILLINGSTONE DAYRELL 2D **141**
LILLINGSTONE LOVELL 1D **141**
Lillington Ct. NN18: Corby 7G **13**
Lillycourt Ho. NN16: K'ing 6C **38**
Lime Av. NN3: N'ton 5H **85**
NN6: Long B 1J **55**
NN11: Eyd 7D **108**
PE8: Oun 3H **21**
Lime Cl. NN7: Hart 5J **117**
NN14: Brou 6H **41**
Lime Ct. NN9: Irth 2C **68**
Lime Farm Way NN4: Gt Hou 5C **96**
Limefields Way NN4: N'ton 2E **100**
Lime Gro. NN7: Bug 2K **105**
NN8: Well 5B **66**
NN10: R'den 1E **80**
Limehurst Cl. NN5: Dus 5G **83**
Limehurst Rd. NN5: Dus 6H **83**
Limehurst Sq. NN5: Dus 5H **83**
Lime Rd. NN12: Yar G 3J **123**
NN16: K'ing 5F **39**
Limes, The NN14: Thra 3J **51**
Lime St. NN9: Irth 2C **68**
NN10: R'den 1D **80**
Lime Ter. NN9: Irth 2C **68**
Lime Tree M. *NN15: K'ing 1D **42***
(off The Grove)
Lime Trees Gro. NN17: Corby 7B **14**

A-Z Northamptonshire Atlas 159

Limlow Cl. NN4: N'ton 4K 93
Limoges Ct. NN5: New D 4F 83
Linacre Cl. NN16: N'ton 7C 74
Lincoln Ct. NN13: B'ley 6G 129
Lincoln Pk. NN13: B'ley 6G 129
Lincoln Rd. NN5: N'ton 2B 94
Lincoln St. NN2: K'thpe 3D 84
Lincoln Way NN11: Dav 3H 61
  NN18: Corby 2H 17
Lindale Cl. NN3: Spin H 3J 85
Linden Av. NN10: High F 5E 68
  NN15: K'ing 1F 43
  NN16: K'ing 7E 38
Linden Cl. NN15: K'ing 1F 43
Linden Rd. NN3: N'ton 5H 85
Lindens, The NN1: N'ton 2F 95
  (off Cliftonville)
  NN12: Tow 3C 114
Lindisfarne Dr. NN15: K'ing 2H 43
Lindisfarne Rd. NN17: Corby 4H 13
Lindisfarne Way NN4: N'ton 7D 94
  NN14: Thra 3K 51
Lindrick Cl. NN11: Dav 1K 61
Lindsay Av. NN3: N'ton 4H 85
Lindsay St. NN16: K'ing 6D 38
Lindsay Ter. NN3: N'ton 4H 85
Lindsey Cl. PE8: Wood 6H 9
Lingfield Ter. NN2: N'ton 5G 85
Lingfield Wlk. NN18: Corby 3G 17
Lings Forum Leisure Cen. 4C 86
Lings Local Cen. NN3: N'ton 3C 86
  (off Billing Brook Rd.)
Lings Theatre 4C 86
Lings Way NN3: N'ton 1D 86
Lings Wood Nature Reserve 2D 86
Lingswood Pk. NN3: N'ton 3D 86
Link La. NN14: Maw 6B 40
Link Rd. NN2: K'thpe 7B 72
  NN10: R'den 6E 80
Links Rd. NN8: Well 4D 66
Link Way NN7: Bug 2K 105
  NN12: Tow 4C 114
Linley Dr. NN14: Des 1C 26
Linley Grn. NN5: Dus 6J 83
Linnell Way NN16: K'ing 5B 38
Linnet Cl. NN8: Well 5B 66
Linnet Dr. NN15: Bar S 4J 43
Linnet Rd. NN12: Tow 6C 114
Linnetts La. NN10: High F 7E 68
Lion Ct. NN4: N'ton 7J 131 (3E 94)
Lismore Cl. NN3: Gt Bil 4F 87
Lismore Wlk. NN17: Corby 4H 13
Lister Cl. NN17: Corby 4B 14
Lister Dr. NN4: N'ton 6K 93
Lister Rd. NN8: Well 7B 66
LITCHBOROUGH 2H 109 (3C 137)
Litchborough Rd. NN7: Bug 4F 105
  NN12: F'one 1F 109
  NN12: Grim 3K 109
Litchfield Cl. NN6: Brix 3H 35
  NN16: K'ing 3E 38
Litchfield La. NN6: Crea 6K 33
LITTLE ADDINGTON 4B 52 (1B 138)
LITTLE BARFORD 3D 139
LITTLE BILLING 5D 86 (2A 138)
Lit. Billing Way NN3: N'ton 4D 86
LITTLE BOURTON 1A 140
LITTLE BOWDEN 3D 133
LITTLE BRINGTON 5G 57 (2C 137)
LITTLE CASTERTON 1C 135
LITTLE CATWORTH 1D 139
Little Cl. NN6: Chap B 4J 71
  NN29: Boz 3G 103
LITTLECOTE 3D 141
LITTLE CRANSLEY 5G 41
LITTLE CREATON 7K 33
Lit. Cross St.
  NN1: N'ton 4F 131 (1C 94)
Littledale NN8: Well 6J 65
Little End NN7: Pid 2F 117
LITTLE EVERDON 3B 136
Little Fld. NN4: Gra P 4G 101
Little Fld. Cl. NN12: East 6K 105
LITTLE GIDDING 3D 135
Little Green PE8: Warm 2J 23
Lit. Greeve Way NN4: Woot 2H 101
Lit. Gull Cl. NN3: N'ton 7C 74
LITTLE HARROWDEN 1G 65 (1A 138)
Lit. Horton Ho. Dr. NN7: Hort 2K 117
LITTLE HORWOOD 2D 141
LITTLE HOUGHTON 3D 96 (3A 138)
LITTLE IRCHESTER 4D 78 (2B 138)
Little La. NN4: Gt Hou 5B 96
  NN6: Rav 2B 34
  NN7: Blis 1H 115
  NN7: Yar H 5G 103
  NN11: Dav 1H 61
  NN14: Stan 3F 19
  NN29: Woll 3E 90
  OX17: Ayn 7E 126
LITTLE LAWFORD 1A 136
LITTLE LINFORD 1D 141

Little London MK19: Dean 5F 125
  NN12: Silv 2H 121
Little Mdw. NN18: Gt Oak 5G 17
LITTLE OAKLEY 6B 18 (3A 134)
Lit. Park St. NN8: Well 7B 66
LITTLE PAXTON 2D 139
LITTLE PRESTON 3B 136
Lit. Priel Rd. NN7: Weed 3C 62
LITTLE RAVELEY 1D 139
LITTLE STAUGHTON 2D 139
Little St. NN7: Yar H 6G 103
  NN10: R'den 4F 81
  OX17: Sulg 6G 111
LITTLE STRETTON 1C 133
LITTLE STUKELEY 1D 139
LITTLE TEW 3A 140
LITTLETHORPE 2B 132
Littlewood Cl. NN5: N'ton 6B 84
Littlewood St. NN14: R'ell 6H 27
LITTLE WYMINGTON . . .6D 80 (2B 138)
Livingstone Cl. NN14: R'ell 6H 27
Livingstone Rd. NN11: Dav 6H 59
Llamas Farm Ct. CV23: Kil 7C 30
Llewellyn Wlk. NN18: Corby 1J 17
Lloyd Cl. NN8: Well 4C 66
Lloyd's Rd. NN17: Corby 6B 14
Loach Cl. NN3: Moul P 7H 73
Loake Cl. NN4: Gra P 6E 100
Loatland St. NN14: Des 2C 26
Lobelia Rd. NN16: K'ing 5E 38
Lockcroft Sq. NN5: N'ton 4G 87
Lock La. MK19: Cos 6D 122
Locks Grn. PE8: Yar 2J 7
Locktons Cl. NN12: Slapt 6G 113
Lockwood Cl. NN2: K'thpe 2D 84
Lodge Cl. NN8: Well 7C 66
  (off Mill Rd.)
LODGE FARM 4H 83
Lodge Farm Ind. Est. NN5: Dus . . .4H 83
Lodge Grn. Rd. NN17: Corby 6K 13
Lodge Pk. NN12: Whit 2C 122
Lodge Pk. Sports Cen. 4G 13
Lodge Rd. NN7: L Hou 3D 96
  NN10: R'den 5D 80
  NN11: Dav 1H 61
Lodge Way NN5: Dus 3G 83
  NN9: Irth 5A 68
Lodore Gdns. NN3: N'ton 3K 85
Logwell Ct. NN3: N'ton 5C 86
Loire Cl. NN5: New D 4F 83
Lombardy Cl. NN3: N'ton 3A 86
Lomond Cl. NN17: Corby 4H 13
Lomond Dr. NN15: K'ing 2G 43
London End NN6: E Bart 2D 88
  NN11: Up Bod 2B 106
  NN14: Titch 2J 49
  NN29: Irch 5J 79
London Rd. MK19: Old S 2J 125
  NN4: Far C, Del, Woot, Col 4D 94
  NN7: Court 1B 116
  NN8: Irch, L Irch, Well 1B 78
  NN9: Raun 4H 53
  NN11: Braun 1A 58
  NN11: Dav 2H 61
  NN12: Tow 4D 114
  NN15: K'ing 1D 42
  NN16: K'ing 7D 38
  NN29: Boz 1G 103
  NN29: Irch 1B 78
  NN29: Strix, Woll 4D 90
Lone Pine Ct. NN6: Brix 3H 35
Long Acre NN7: Braf G 4G 97
Longacres NN4: N'ton 7C 94
Long Acres Dr. NN9: Irth 1B 68
Long Barrow OX17: Chip W 2D 110
Long Breech NN14: Maw 5B 40
LONG BUCKBY 1H 55 (2C 137)
Long Buckby Rd.
  NN6: Wat . . . . .6E 54 & 1F 55
  NN11: Dav . . . . . . .7K 59 & 5F 55
Long Buckby Station (Rail) 3G 55
LONG BUCKBY WHARF 2C 137
Longburges OX17: Mid C 6E 118
Longcroft La. NN12: Paul 6J 115
Long Cft. Rd. NN14: Stan 2B 18
  NN18: Corby, Stan 2B 18
Longdown La. CV23: Bar 4C 54
Longfellow Dr. NN16: K'ing 3E 38
Longfellow Rd. NN8: Well 1G 77
Longford Av. NN3: N'ton 6D 86
Longhold Rd. LE16: Sibb 7A 24
LONG ITCHINGTON 2A 136

Longland Ct. NN3: N'ton 4J 85
Longland Rd. NN3: N'ton 4J 85
Long La. NN6: E Had . . . .1A 56 & 4A 34
  PE8: Warm 3H 23
LONG LAWFORD 1A 136
Longleat Cl. NN4: N'ton 7D 94
Longleat Gro. NN15: K'ing 5E 42
Long March NN11: Dav 3J 61
Long March Ind. Est. NN11: Dav . .3J 61
Long Marsh Sq. NN3: N'ton 7D 74
Longmead Ct. NN3: N'ton 2E 86
Long Meadow NN4: Woot 2J 101
Longmynd Dr. NN5: Dus 6J 83
Long Row NN14: Woodf 6B 50
LONG STREET 1D 141
LONGTHORPE 2D 135
Longueville Cl. NN3: N'ton 2B 86
Longwall NN13: B'ley 5F 129
Lonsborough Dr. NN15: K'ing 2A 42
Lonsdale Rd. NN15: K'ing 3D 42
Lordswood Cl. NN4: Woot 2H 101
Lorne Ct. NN17: Corby 7A 14
Lorne Rd. NN1: N'ton 1H 131 (7D 84)
Lorraine Cres. NN3: N'ton 1J 85
Lorraine Dr. NN3: N'ton 1K 85
Loseby Cl. NN10: R'den 5D 80
Lotus Cl. NN15: K'ing 1D 42
  (off Station Rd.)
LOUGHTON 2D 141
Louisa Dr. NN16: K'ing 6G 39
Louisberg Cl. NN4: Woot 1F 101
Louise Rd. NN1: N'ton 1H 131 (7E 84)
Louth Dr. NN10: R'den 5G 81
Lovap Way NN18: Gt Oak 5G 17
Lovat Dr. NN5: N'ton 7K 83
Lovell Cl. NN9: Stanw 7F 53
Lovell Ct. NN9: Irth 2C 68
Lovett Rd. NN11: Byf 1J 107
Lowbury Ct. NN4: N'ton 4K 93
Lwr. Adelaide St.
  NN2: Sem 1G 131 (7D 84)
LOWER ARNCOTT 3C 141
Lwr. Bath St. NN1: N'ton . .3F 131 (1C 94)
LOWER BENEFIELD 3B 134
LOWER BODDINGTON . . .4B 106 (3A 136)
LOWER CATESBY 3B 136
Lwr. Cross St.
  NN1: N'ton 4F 131 (1C 94)
LOWER DEAN 2C 139
Lwr. Ecton La. NN3: N'ton 5G 87
LOWER END
  Northampton 4G 97
  Wellingborough 7K 89 (2A 138)
Lower End NN7: Hart 6G 117
  NN14: Pyt 3B 44
Lwr. Farm Rd. NN3: Moul P 6G 73
Lowergrass Wlk. NN3: N'ton 5C 86
LOWER GREEN 7G 109
Lower Grn. NN6: Wal 1H 37
Lwr. Harding St.
  NN1: N'ton 3G 131 (1D 94)
LOWER HARLESTONE 7D 70
Lwr. Hester St.
  NN2: Sem 1F 131 (7C 84)
LOWER HEYFORD 3A 140
Lwr. King St. NN14: Des 2E 26
Lwr. Meadow Cl. NN3: N'ton 1B 86
LOWER MIDDLETON CHENEY 6E 118
Lower Mounts
  NN1: N'ton 3K 131 (1E 94)
Lower Pastures NN18: Gt Oak 6F 17
Lwr. Priory St.
  NN1: N'ton 2F 131 (7C 84)
Lower Rd. LE16: Stoke A 5G 11
  NN7: Mil M 4K 99
LOWER SHUCKBURGH 2A 136
Lwr. Stable Yd. NN12: Tow 4D 114
Lower Steeping NN14: Des 3E 26
Lower St. NN12: Pur E 7G 115
  NN14: Des 2D 26
  NN14: Gt Ad 2A 52
  NN16: K'ing 7C 38
  NN29: Gt Dod 7K 77
Lwr. Thrift St. NN1: N'ton 1G 95
LOWER WEEDON 4D 62
LOWESBY 1D 133
Low Farm Pl. NN3: Moul P 6G 73
Low Greeve NN4: Woot 2H 101
LOWICK 6D 48 (3B 134)
Lowick Cl. NN8: Well 5J 65
Lowick Ct. NN3: Moul 6K 73
Lowick La. NN14: Ald 7B 20
Lowick Rd. NN14: Ald 7A 20
  NN14: Isl 1F 51
Lowlands Cl. NN3: N'ton 1F 87
Low March NN11: Dav 4J 61
Low March Ind. Est. NN11: Dav . . .4J 61
Lowry Cl. NN3: N'ton 2J 85
  NN8: Well 5K 65
  NN18: Corby 2J 17
Loxton Cl. NN5: Dus 5H 83
Loyd Rd. NN1: N'ton 7H 85

LUBENHAM 3D 133
Lubenham Rd. LE16: E Far 1J 25
Lucas Cl. NN9: Irth 4B 68
Lucas La. NN7: Hack 1G 117
Lucas Rd. NN6: Long B 2G 55
LUDDINGTON IN THE BROOK 3D 135
LUDGERSHALL 3C 141
Ludlow Cl. NN3: N'ton 6D 74
Ludlow Wlk. NN18: L Oak 5K 17
Lukes Cl. NN13: Helm 1C 120
Lulworth Wlk. NN18: Corby 7F 13
Lumber La. NN12: Paul 7H 115
Lumbertubs La. NN3: N'ton 1K 85
Lumbertubs Ri. NN3: N'ton 1A 86
Lumbertubs Way NN3: N'ton 7A 74
Lunchfield Ct. NN3: Moul 4K 73
Lunchfield Gdns. NN3: Moul 4K 73
Lunchfield La. NN3: Moul 4K 73
Lunchfield Wlk. NN3: Moul 4K 73
Lundie Cl. NN9: Raun 5J 53
Lundy Av. NN18: Corby 2K 17
Lupin Cl. NN16: K'ing 5F 39
LUTTERWORTH 3B 132
Lutterworth Rd. NN1: N'ton 7H 85
LUTTON 7H 23 (3D 135)
LYDDINGTON 2A 134
Lyddington Rd. NN17: Gret 6B 8
  NN18: N'ton 3D 80
Lydia Ct. NN10: R'den 3D 80
Lyle Ct. NN8: Well 5H 65
Lyncrest Av. NN5: N'ton 7K 83
Lyncroft Way NN2: K'thpe 5C 84
LYNDON 1B 134
Lyne Wlk. NN7: Hack 1G 117
Lynford Way NN10: R'den 5C 80
Lynmore Cl. NN4: N'ton 6H 93
Lynmouth Av. NN3: N'ton 7K 85
Lynmouth Pl. NN18: Corby 2K 17
Lynton Av. NN2: K'thpe 7C 72
Lynton Gro. NN18: Corby 2K 17
Lynwood Cl. NN16: K'ing 4D 38
Lytham Cl. NN2: N'ton 3F 85
Lytham Ct. NN8: Well 5H 65
Lyttleton Rd. NN5: N'ton 7B 84
Lyveden New Bield 3B 134
Lyveden Pl. NN16: K'ing 6F 39
Lyveden Rd. NN4: Brack 6H 95
  NN14: Brig 2D 20
  (not continuous)
Lyveden Way
  NN18: Corby, Gt Oak 4H 17

M

Macadam Cl. NN11: Dav 5E 58
Macadam Rd. NN17: Corby 4B 14
McGibbon Wlk. NN9: Irth 4A 68
McInnes Way NN9: Raun 5J 53
Mackenzie Rd. NN9: Raun 7H 53
McKinlay Theatre 1E 42
  (off St Mary's Rd.)
Mackintosh Cen., The 5J 35
Mackintosh Cl. NN15: Bur L 3J 45
  (off Finedon St.)
Mackworth Dr. NN9: Fine 7G 47
Mackworth Grn. NN9: Fine 7H 47
Maclean Cl. NN3: West F 7K 85
Macmillan Way NN3: N'ton 2J 85
Macon Cl. NN5: Dus 4E 82
Madam Gdns. NN14: R'ell 6G 27
Madams Hill NN14: R'ell 6G 27
  (off Rushton Rd.)
Magdalen Cl. NN11: Dav 3G 61
  NN13: Syre 5D 120
Magdalene Cl. NN14: Ged 5D 46
Magdalen Mdws. NN13: B'ley 2F 129
Magee St. NN1: N'ton 7G 85
Magellan Cl. NN11: Dav 5H 59
  NN14: R'ell 7H 27
MAGNA PARK 3B 132
Magnolia Cl. NN3: N'ton 1A 96
Magnolia Dr. NN10: R'den 6E 80
  NN11: Dav 6H 59
Magpie Cl. NN18: Corby 3K 17
Magpie La. NN13: B'ley 5F 129
Magpie Rd. NN12: Tow 6C 114
  OX17: Sulg 6F 111
Maida Cl. NN4: Woot 1F 101
Maidencastle NN3: N'ton 3E 86
MAIDFORD 3C 137
Maidford Rd. NN12: Blak 4H 109
  NN12: Lit 2H 109
  NN17: Corby 6H 13
MAIDS MORETON 2D 141
MAIDWELL 2B 36 (1D 137)
Maidwell Rd. NN6: Drau 1D 36
Main Dr. NN12: Pot 7F 123
Main Rd. CV23: Kil 6B 30
  NN4: Far C 4B 94
  (not continuous)
  NN5: Dus 4G 83
  NN6: Crick 3G 31

Main Rd.—Melbourne Ho.

Main Rd. NN6: E Bart, Wilby 1B **88**
NN7: Gren 2C **102**
NN7: Hack 1F **117**
NN7: Up Hey 3K **63**
NN8: Wilby 5G **77**
NN12: Shut 6A **116**
NN13: F'hoe 6H **119**
NN13: Syre 6B **120**
OX17: Mid C 6C **118**
PE9: Colly . . . . .6C **6** & 4A **6**
Main St. LE16: A'ley 3G **11**
LE16: Brin 1B **12**
LE16: Dray 1A **12**
LE16: E Far 3J **25**
LE16: Gt Oxe 7H **25**
LE16: Mid 5A **12**
LE16: Rock 1G **13**
LE16: Sutt B 4C **10**
LE16: Wilb 5H **11**
MK19: Cos 6D **122**
NN6: Col A 2B **32**
NN6: E Had 2C **56**
NN6: Hann 4K **37**
NN6: Holc 6H **37**
NN6: Wat 6D **54**
NN7: Chu S 7E **62**
NN7: D'ton 5B **102**
NN7: Gt Bri 3H **57**
NN7: L Brin 6F **57**
NN9: L Harr . . . . .1G **65** & 7D **44**
NN11: Ast W 7E **106**
NN11: Badby 6C **104**
NN11: Whil 6C **56**
NN12: Abt 6H **113**
NN12: Woode 7G **109**
NN13: Turw 3J **129**
NN14: Gt Ad 1A **52**
NN14: Lod 1C **40**
NN14: Low 5D **48**
NN14: Maw 6B **40**
NN14: Sud 3B **48**
OX17: Char 1H **127**
PE8: Barn 7B **22**
PE8: Pole 3D **22**
PE8: Wood 5G **9**
PE8: Yar 2H **7**
Malabar Flds. NN11: Dav 3G **61**
Malaslea NN14: Maw 6B **40**
Malborough Way NN12: Yar G 4K **123**
Malcolm Ct. NN17: Corby 7A **14**
Malcolm Dr. NN5: N'ton 7K **83**
Malcolm Rd. NN2: N'ton 4G **85**
Malcolm Ter. NN2: N'ton 4H **85**
Malesoure Wlk. NN3: N'ton 7F **75**
Malham Ct. NN8: Well 6J **65**
Malham Dr. NN16: K'ing 4C **38**
Mall, The NN16: K'ing 7D **38**
Mallard Cl. NN4: N'ton 5A **94**
NN6: E Bart 1D **88**
NN10: High F 4F **69**
NN14: Thra 2H **51**
Mallard Dr. NN11: Woodf H 2C **108**
NN15: Bur L 2H **45**
Mallery Cl. NN10: R'den 2G **81**
Mallory Wlk. NN3: N'ton 1G **85**
Mallory Way NN11: Dav 5G **59**
Mallows Dr. NN9: Raun 5H **53**
Mallows Yd. NN29: Boz 2H **103**
Malmo Cl. NN18: Corby 4F **17**
Malpas Dr. NN5: Dus 6G **83**
Malthouse Cl.
NN4: N'ton 7K **131** (3E **94**)
NN9: Irth 2C **68**
Malthouse Ct. NN12: Tow 3C **114**
Malting La. NN14: Ged 5C **46**
Maltings, The LE16: A'ley 2H **11**
NN14: R'ell 6F **27**
NN29: Woll 3E **90**
Maltings Ct. NN17: Gret 6C **8**
Maltings La. PE8: King C 2G **9**
Maltings Rd. NN17: Gret 6C **8**
Malting Way NN7: Hart 6H **117**
Malt La. NN13: Syre 5D **120**
Malt Mill Cl. CV23: Kil 7C **30**
Malt Mill Grn. *CV23: Kil 7C 30*
(off Main Rd.)
Malton Wlk. NN18: Corby 1G **17**
Malvern Cl. NN8: Well 4J **77**
NN16: K'ing 3D **38**
Malvern Gro. NN5: Dus 6J **83**
Malzor La. NN7: Mil M 4K **99**
Manchester Rd. NN29: Woll 3D **90**
Mandarin St. NN4: N'ton 7K **93**
Mander Cl. NN5: Dus 6E **82**
Manderville Cl. NN3: N'ton 2J **85**
Manfield Health Campus
NN3: N'ton 2J **85**
Manfield Rd. NN1: N'ton 7H **85**
Manfield Way NN3: N'ton 1J **85**
Manitoba Cl. NN18: Corby 3G **17**
Manitoba Pl. NN11: Eyd 7D **108**
Manitoba Way NN11: Eyd 7D **108**
Manning Ct. NN3: Moul 6K **73**
Manningham Rd. NN9: Stanw 7F **53**
Manning Rd. NN3: Moul 6K **73**
Mannings Ri. NN10: R'den 4F **81**
Manning St. NN10: R'den 4F **81**
Mannings Yd. NN11: Eyd 7D **108**
Mannington Gdns.
NN4: N'ton 1D **100**
Mannock Rd. NN8: Well 2K **77**
Manor Cl. MK19: Cos 6D **122**
NN7: Harp 1B **92**
NN7: Roa 2D **116**
NN9: Gt Har 2J **65**
NN11: Woodf H 2C **108**
NN14: Gt Ad 2A **52**
NN14: Ish 4G **45**
NN14: Thra 3H **51**
NN29: Boz 2H **103**
NN29: Irch 5J **79**
OX17: Mid C 7E **118**
Manor Ct. LE16: Mid 4B **12**
NN2: K'thpe 3C **84**
NN7: Gren 2C **102**
NN9: L Harr 1H **65**
NN10: R'den 5F **81**
NN13: B'ley 3G **129**
Manor Dr. NN9: Irth 2D **68**
NN18: Corby 2F **17**
Mnr. Farm Cl. CV23: Bar 1C **54**
NN6: Wal 1H **37**
NN9: H'wick 4D **64**
NN14: Brou 6H **41**
Mnr. Farm Cotts. NN13: Crou 5A **130**
Mnr. Farm Ct. NN7: Cog 1K **97**
NN14: Titch 1H **49**
Mnr. Farm Rd. NN3: Gt Bil 4E **86**
NN9: Raun 6K **53**
Manorfield Cl. NN3: N'ton 6E **86**
Manorfield Rd. NN3: N'ton 6D **86**
Manorfields Rd. MK19: Old S 3J **125**
Manor Gdns. NN9: Stanw 1K **69**
NN11: Nor 7G **55**
NN14: Pyt 2A **44**
Manor Ho. PE8: Warm 2H **23**
Manor Ho., The NN14: Thra 3H **51**
Manor Ho. Cl. NN6: E Bart 1D **88**
Manor Ho. Gdns. NN7: Cog 1K **97**
NN9: Raun 6J **53**
Manor House Mus. 1D **42**
Manor La. NN6: E Bart 1D **88**
NN10: Wym 7D **80**
NN11: Newn 7K **61**
NN11: Whil 6D **56**
NN13: F'hoe 6H **119**
Manor Pk. NN7: Neth H 5K **63**
Manor Pl. NN15: K'ing 3D **42**
Manor Rd. CV23: Kil 6C **30**
NN2: K'thpe 3C **84**
NN3: Moul 5K **73**
NN6: E Bart 1D **88**
NN6: Mears A 3A **76**
NN6: Pits 1E **72**
NN6: Spra 5C **34**
NN7: Gren 2C **102**
NN7: Weed 4C **62**
NN10: R'den 5E **80**
NN11: Dav 3J **61**
NN11: Stav 4A **60**
NN11: Woodf H 1C **108**
NN13: B'ley 5F **129**
NN14: R'ell 6E **26**
NN14: R'ton 2B **46**
NN14: Stan 4F **19**
OX17: Sulg 6G **111**
Manor St. NN9: Raun 6J **53**
Manor Wlk. NN7: Neth H 5K **63**
Manor Way NN10: High F 7F **69**
NN12: Yar G 3J **123**
Manor Yd. NN14: Isl 3F **51**
Mansard Cl. NN5: N'ton 1K **93**
Mansard Ho. NN5: Upton 7F **83**
Manse Cl. MK11: Stony S 3K **125**
NN10: R'den 2F **81**
Mansefield Cl. NN14: Des 1D **26**
Mansel Cl. MK19: Cos 6C **122**
Mansell Cl. NN12: Tow 1C **114**
Mansfield Ct. NN12: Greens N 1H **113**
Mansfield St. NN9: Stanw 1J **69**
Mansfield Way NN29: Irch 5H **79**
Mansion Cl. NN3: Moul P 7H **73**
Mansion Hill OX17: Mid C 6C **118**
Mantlefield Rd. NN18: Corby 7G **13**
MANTON 1A **134**
Manton Rd. NN9: Irth 2B **68**
NN10: R'den 4F **81**
NN17: Corby 3A **14**
Manton Spinney NN29: Knus 3B **80**
Manvell Farm Pk. 1K **37**
Maple Bldgs. NN1: N'ton 2H **131**
Maple Cl. NN7: Bug 2J **105**
NN11: Braun 1C **58**
NN11: Woodf H 2B **108**
NN12: Tow 5B **114**
NN13: B'ley 1G **129**
Maple Ct. NN4: Col 4C **100**
NN17: Corby 4K 13
(off Ennerdale Rd.)
Maple Dr. NN8: Well 7K **65**
Maple Rd. NN10: R'den 3F **81**
NN16: K'ing 5F **39**
Maples, The NN11: Dav 2J **61**
Mapletoft St. NN9: Raun 7H **53**
Maple Wood NN10: R'den 6E **80**
Mapperley Dr. NN3: N'ton 6C **86**
Marble Arch NN1: N'ton . . .2H **131** (7D **84**)
Marburg St. NN3: N'ton 7F **75**
Marchwood Cl. NN3: N'ton 7C **74**
Marconi Courtyard NN17: Corby 4C **14**
Marecroft LE16: Clip 7C **24**
Mare Fair NN1: N'ton 5F **131** (2C **94**)
MAREFIELD 1D **133**
Margaret Av. NN8: Well 3K **77**
Margaret Bondfield Hall
NN2: K'thpe 1F **85**
Margaret Rd. NN16: K'ing 6G **39**
Margaret St. NN1: N'ton . . .2J **131** (7E **84**)
MARHOLM 1D **135**
Marion Sq. NN16: K'ing 6G **39**
Maritime Way NN11: Dav 2K **61**
Marjoram Cl. NN4: N'ton 2E **100**
MARKET BOSWORTH 1A **132**
Market Cross NN9: Irth 2C **68**
MARKET DEEPING 1D **135**
MARKET HARBOROUGH
. . . . .1K **25** (3D **133**)
Market Hill NN14: R'ell 6G **27**
Market Pl. NN6: Long B 1H **55**
NN13: B'ley 5F **129**
NN16: K'ing 7D **38**
PE8: Oun 5J **21**
Market Rd. NN14: Thra 3H **51**
Market Sq. MK11: Stony S 4K **125**
NN1: N'ton 4H **131** (1D **94**)
NN8: Well 1B **78**
NN10: High F 6F **69**
NN11: Dav 1H **61**
Market St. NN1: N'ton 7F **85**
(not continuous)
NN8: Well 1B **78**
NN16: K'ing 7D **38**
Market Wlk. NN1: N'ton 7F **85**
NN17: Corby 1K **17**
MARKFIELD 1A **132**
Mark Gro. Ho. NN10: R'den 2F **81**
Markham Cl. NN5: Dus 5H **83**
Markham Wlk. NN18: Corby 1G **17**
Marks Cl. NN9: Stanw 1K **69**
Marlborough Av. NN8: Well 5J **65**
Marlborough Cl. NN15: K'ing 1H **43**
OX17: King S 1B **126**
Marlborough Cft. NN13: B'ley 5G **129**
Marlborough Rd. NN5: N'ton 1B **94**
Marlow Cl. NN11: Dav 2G **61**
(not continuous)
NN14: R'ell 7F **27**
Marlow Ct. NN18: Corby 1G **17**
Marlowe Cl. NN4: N'ton 1C **100**
Marlow Rd. NN12: Tow 4D **114**
Marlstones NN4: N'ton 5J **93**
Marnock Sq. NN4: N'ton 5A **94**
Marnock Wlk. *NN4: N'ton 5A 94*
(off Marnock Sq.)
Marquee Dr. NN3: N'ton 7B **86**
Marriots Rd. NN6: Long B 2J **55**
Marriott Cl. NN9: Irth 4B **68**
Marriott St. NN2: Sem 1G **131** (6D **84**)
Marseilles Cl. NN5: Dus 5E **82**
Marsh, The NN6: Crick 4J **31**
Marshall's Rd. NN9: Raun 6H **53**
Marsh Cl. NN6: Crick 4J **31**
MARSH GIBBON 3C **141**
Marsh La. NN9: Irth 2D **68**
Marshleys Ct. NN3: N'ton 1E **86**
Marshwell Ct. NN3: N'ton 6D **86**
Marsons Dr. NN6: Crick 4H **31**
MARSTON DOLES 3A **136**
Marston Hill OX17: Mar L 1G **119**
MARSTON JABBETT 3A **132**
Marston La. LE16: E Far 2F **25**
Marston Rd. OX17: Greatw 2J **119**
MARSTON ST LAWRENCE
. . . . .2G **119** (1B **140**)
MARSTON TRUSSELL 3C **133**
Marston Way NN11: Dav 4J **59**
Martel Cl. NN5: Dus 6E **82**
Martha Wallis Ct. NN16: K'ing 7D **38**
Martial Daire Blvd. NN13: B'ley . . .3F **129**
Martin Cl. NN10: R'den 1E **80**
Martindale NN2: K'thpe 1A **84**
Martin Rd. NN15: K'ing 3E **42**
Martin's La. NN4: H'stone 7E **94**
Martins Rd. NN7: Pid 3F **117**
Martins Yd. NN5: N'ton 7C **84**
Martlet Cl. NN4: Woot 3F **101**
MARTON 2A **136**
Martyns Way NN7: Weed 4C **62**
Marvills Mill Rd. NN4: N'ton 3D **94**
Marwood Cl. NN3: N'ton 7J **85**
Masefield Cl. NN8: Well 1H **77**
Masefield Dr. NN10: R'den 3B **80**
Masefield Rd. NN16: K'ing 4E **38**
Masefield Way NN2: N'ton 4F **85**
NN17: Corby 5H **13**
Mason Cl. NN14: Thra 4H **51**
PE8: Oun 5J **21**
Masque, The 4J **43**
Massey Cl. NN4: H'stone 7F **95**
Matchless Cl. NN5: Dus 5F **83**
Matlock Way NN14: Des 1B **26**
Matson Cl. NN14: R'ell 7E **26**
Matson Ct. NN9: Raun 5K **53**
Matthews Cl. NN14: R'ton 1B **46**
Maunsell Ri. NN14: R'ell 6E **26**
Mauntley Av. NN14: Brig 2D **20**
Maurice Rd. LE16: Mkt H 1K **25**
Mawsley Chase NN14: Maw 5C **40**
Mawsley Cres. NN16: K'ing 7B **38**
Mawsley La. NN14: Lod 3C **40**
Mawsley Lodge NN14: Maw 7B **40**
MAWSLEY VILLAGE 6B **40** (1A **138**)
MAXEY 1D **135**
Maxwell Wlk. *NN18: Corby 1K 17*
(off Oakley Rd.)
May Bank NN11: Dav 3G **61**
May Cl. NN10: R'den 6F **81**
Maye Dicks Rd. NN10: R'den 5F **81**
Mayfield Dr. NN11: Dav 7G **59**
Mayfield Rd. NN3: Spin H 3J **85**
NN14: Des 2F **27**
Maylan Rd. NN17: Corby 2A **14**
Mayor Hold NN1: N'ton . . .4G **131** (1D **94**)
Mays Way NN12: Pot 6H **123**
Mazewood Ga. PE8: King C 2F **9**
Meacham Cl. NN14: Brou 7G **41**
Meadow Cl. NN5: Dus 4G **83**
NN8: Well 5E **66**
NN10: High F 6D **68**
NN11: Dav 4J **59**
NN14: Brou 5H 41
(off The Banks)
NN14: Rin 1F **53**
Meadow Ct. NN12: Tow 4C **114**
NN16: K'ing 7D 38
(off Meadow Rd.)
Meadow Dr. NN10: High F 6E **68**
Meadow Farm Cl. NN7: Flore 2G **63**
Meadow Ga. PE8: Wood 5G **9**
Meadowlands NN9: L Harr 1G **65**
Meadow La. NN7: L Hou 3D **96**
NN9: Raun 6E **52**
NN14: Den 7G **51**
NN14: Thra 2G **51**
Meadow Rd. NN14: R'ell 7F **27**
NN16: K'ing 7C **38**
(not continuous)
Meadows, The MK19: Old S 3J **125**
NN4: Gra P 7G **101**
NN9: Well 3K **65**
Meadow Sweet Rd. NN10: R'den 6F **81**
Meadowsweet Wlk. NN4: Gra P 6G **101**
Meadowvale NN9: Irth 3C **68**
Meadow Vw. NN10: High F 6D **68**
NN12: Pot 6H **123**
NN14: Gt Ad 1B **52**
Meadow Wlk. NN9: Irth 2C **68**
NN10: High F 6D **68**
Meadow Way NN9: Irth 3C **68**
Mead Rd. NN15: K'ing 2B **42**
Meads Ct. NN15: Bur L 3J **45**
Meadslade NN7: Hart 5H **117**
Meadway NN3: West F 5A **86**
NN7: Bug 2J **105**
Meadway Cl. NN15: K'ing 2F **43**
MEARS ASHBY 3A **76** (2A **138**)
Mears Ashby Rd. NN6: E Bart 4A **76**
NN8: Wilby 3D **76**
MEDBOURNE 2D **133**
Medbourne Cl. NN3: Moul 6J **73**
Medbourne Rd. LE16: A'ley 2G **11**
LE16: Dray 1K **11**
Medellin Hill NN3: N'ton 7C **74**
Medinah Cl. NN4: Col 3E **100**
Medina Rd. NN17: Corby 4H **13**
Medlicott Cl. NN18: Corby 6F **17**
Medway, The NN11: Dav 2F **61**
Medway Cl. NN5: N'ton 4K **83**
Medway Dr. NN5: N'ton 4K **83**
NN8: Well 6H **65**
Medwin NN8: Well 1G **77**
Meeting La. NN5: Dus 7H **83**
NN9: Irth 2C **68**
NN12: Tow 3C **114**
NN14: R'ell 7F **27**
NN15: Bur L 2K **45**
NN16: K'ing 7D **38**
NN17: Corby 6C **14**
Meissen Av. NN14: Des 2C **26**
Melbourne Ho. NN5: N'ton 1A **94**
NN17: Corby 4G 15
(off Corby Ga.)

Melbourne La. NN5: Dus 1H 93
Melbourne Rd. NN5: N'ton 1A 94
Melbourne St. NN1: N'ton 1G 95
Melbourne Wlk. NN1: N'ton 1G 95
Melbury La. NN3: N'ton 3E 86
Melbury Pl. NN3: N'ton 3D 86
MELCHBOURNE 2C 139
Melchester Cl. NN4: H'stone 1F 101
Meldon Cl. NN4: N'ton 7D 94
Melford Cl. NN18: Corby 4J 17
Melloway Rd. NN10: R'den 3A 80
Melrose Av. NN5: N'ton 7K 83
Melrose Cl. NN15: K'ing 2H 43
Meltham Cl. NN3: N'ton 5C 86
Melton Rd. NN8: Well 7D 66
Melton Rd. Nth. NN8: Well 7C 66
Melton St. NN16: K'ing 6D 38
Melville St. NN1: N'ton 7G 85
Membris Way NN11: Woodf H 2B 108
Memorial Grn. NN7: Roa 2C 116
Menagerie, The 3A 138
Mendip Cl. NN16: K'ing 4D 38
Mendip Ct. NN11: Dav 5G 59
Mendip Rd. NN5: Dus 6J 83
Meon Cl. NN17: Corby 4H 13
Meon Way NN5: Dus 6J 83
Mercer's Row
    NN1: N'ton 5H 131 (2D 94)
Mercia Gdns. NN3: N'ton 5K 85
Mercury Cl. NN11: Dav 6F 59
Mercury Dr. NN4: Brack 5H 95
Mere Cl. NN4: N'ton 7C 94
    NN7: Braf G 5G 97
MEREFIELD 1C 100
Merefields NN9: Irth 1B 68
Merestone Rd. NN18: Corby 3J 17
Mere Way NN4: N'ton 6C 94
Merlin Gro. NN4: N'ton 7C 94
Merrivale Cl. NN15: K'ing 3B 42
Merrycot La. NN6: Yel 5C 28
Merrydale Sq. NN3: N'ton 7D 74
Merryhill NN1: N'ton 5K 93
MERRY LEES 1A 132
Merry Tom La. NN6: Chap B 2J 71
Mersey Cl. NN4: N'ton 5B 94
Mersey Grn. NN17: Corby 4H 13
    (off Shire Rd.)
Mershe Cl. NN4: H'stone 1G 101
Merthyr Rd. NN5: N'ton 6B 84
MERTON 3B 140
Merton Cl. NN13: B'ley 3E 128
Merton Rd. NN11: Dav 4G 61
Mescalero Rd. NN2: K'thpe 2D 84
Meshaw Cres. NN3: N'ton 7J 85
Methodist Homestead NN2: N'ton 5F 85
Mews, The NN3: West F 6A 86
Michaelmas Cl. OX17: Mid C 5C 118
Michael's Wlk. LE16: Rock 1G 13
Mickleborough Cl. LE16: West W 2D 10
Micklewell La. NN3: N'ton 7C 74
MIDDLE ASTON 3A 140
MIDDLE BARTON 3A 140
MIDDLE CLAYDON 3D 141
Middlefield Cl. NN14: Rin 1G 53
Middle Grass NN9: Irth 1B 68
Middle Greeve NN4: Woot 2H 101
Middle La. LE16: Stoke A 6G 11
Middle March NN11: Dav 3J 61
Middlemarch NN3: N'ton 2E 86
Middlemead Ct. NN3: N'ton 5D 86
Middlemore NN3: N'ton 7C 74
Middle Nene Sailing Club 2G 51
Middle St. CV23: Kil 6C 30
    NN7: Neth H 5K 63
    NN14: Ish 4G 45
Middlethorpe NN12: Weed L 3C 112
MIDDLETON 5A 12 (2A 134)
MIDDLETON CHENEY . .6C 118 (1B 140)
Middleton Cl. NN2: K'thpe 1D 84
Middleton Rd. LE16: A'ley 3H 11
    LE16: Brin 1B 12
    OX17: Chac 2B 118
MIDDLETON STONEY 3B 140
Middle Way OX17: Mid C 6C 118
Middlewell Ct. NN3: N'ton 1D 86
Middlewich Cl. NN11: Dav 4H 59
Midfield Ct. NN3: N'ton 1B 86
Midland Bus. Cen. NN10: High F 6F 69
Midland Cotts. NN14: R'ton 1B 46
Midland Rd. NN8: Well 1B 78
    NN9: Raun 5K 53
    NN10: High F 6F 69
    NN10: R'den 2D 80
    NN14: Thra 3G 51
Midland Works Bus. Cen.
    NN8: Well 6D 66
Midway NN7: Blis 6G 99
    (off Oak Av.)
    OX17: Mid C 5D 118
Milburn Dr. NN5: Upton 1F 93
Milbury NN6: E Bart 3E 88
Milby La. NN14: Ged 6C 46
MILCOMBE 2A 140

Mildmay Cl. PE8: Oun 5G 21
Miles Cl. NN9: Raun 7G 53
Miles La. NN6: Long B 1J 55
Milestone M. LE16: Mid 4B 12
Mile St. NN29: Boz 2H 103
Miles Well Ct. NN3: N'ton 3A 86
Mile Wlk. NN3: N'ton 4G 87
Military Ct. NN1: N'ton 1K 131 (7E 84)
Military Rd. NN1: N'ton 1J 131 (7E 84)
Militia Cl. NN4: Woot 1F 101
Millais Rd. NN18: Corby 1K 17
Millbank NN3: N'ton 4G 87
Millbrook Cl. NN5: Dus 2B 94
Mill Cl. NN9: Raun 6H 53
    NN11: Braun 1A 58
    NN18: Gt Oak 5G 17
Milldale Gdns. NN15: K'ing 2F 43
Milldale Rd. NN15: K'ing 2F 43
Millennium Cl. NN15: K'ing 3C 42
Millennium Way NN11: Dav 1H 61
Miller Cl. NN14: Thra 4J 51
    NN15: K'ing 4E 42
Miller Hill NN4: N'ton 5K 93
Miller Rd. NN15: Bur L 3J 45
Millers Cl. NN7: Kisl 5C 92
    NN9: Fine 6J 47
    NN10: R'den 3C 80
    NN11: Lwr B 4B 106
Millers La. NN8: Well 5A 78
Millers Pk. NN8: Well 4B 78
Millers St. NN9: Raun 6J 53
Millers Way NN4: Gra P 5G 101
Mill Est. NN10: R'den 6E 80
Millfield Av. LE16: Cotti 4C 12
Mill Flds. NN10: High F 5E 68
Millfields PE8: Oun 4H 21
Millglade, The NN14: Ish 3G 45
Mill Hill NN18: Gt Oak 6G 17
Millholm Rd. NN14: Des 3E 26
Mill Ho. NN2: Sem 1G 131
    NN4: N'ton 3D 94
    (off River Vw.)
Millhouse Ct. NN5: N'ton 2C 94
    (off Byfield Rd.)
Mill La. MK11: Stony S 4K 125
    NN2: K'thpe 6A 84
    NN2: Sem 1F 131 (7C 84)
    NN5: Dall, N'ton 6A 84
    NN6: E Bart 2F 89
    NN6: Old 5E 36
    NN7: Cog 7K 87
    NN7: Kisl 4C 92
    NN9: Fine 7K 45
    NN12: Greens N 1J 113
    NN12: Grim 4F 105
    NN12: Stoke B 5D 116
    NN13: B'ley 5H 129
    NN13: Crou 6A 130
    NN14: Brig 2D 20
    NN14: Ish 3G 45
    NN14: Isl 2F 51
    NN14: Low 6D 48
    OX17: Chip W 3D 110
    OX17: King S 2B 126
    PE8: Cotte 1K 21
Mill Marina Cvn. Pk. NN14: Thra 4G 51
Mill Mdw. NN2: K'thpe 1E 84
Mill Pond Rd. NN5: Upton 3H 93
Mill Rd. LE15: Sea . . . . .1A 8 & 4A 8
    (not continuous)
    LE16: Cotti 4B 12
    NN2: Sem 1G 131 (7D 84)
    NN7: Kisl 4B 92
    NN8: Well 7C 66
    (Newcomen Rd.)
    NN8: Well 5H 67
    (Wellingborough Rd.)
    NN14: Isl 2F 51
    NN14: Woodf 6A 50
    NN16: K'ing 7E 38
    NN17: Gret 4A 8
    NN29: Boz 3G 103
    PE8: Oun 5H 21
    PE8: Yar 4H 7
Mill Rd. Ind. Est. NN8: Well 6D 66
Mill Rd. Pas. NN16: K'ing 7E 38
    (off Alexandra St.)
Mills Cl. NN6: E Bart 2E 88
Millside Cl. NN2: K'thpe 1E 84
Millstone Cl. NN4: N'ton 5J 93
Mill St. NN5: Upton 3H 93
Millway NN5: Dus 1H 93
Millwood Way PE8: King C 2G 9
Milner Rd. NN9: Fine 7H 47
MILTHORPE 3C 112 (1B 140)
Milthorpe NN12: Weed L 3C 112
MILTON 2A 140
Milton Av. NN8: Well 2H 77
Milton Bri. NN4: Woot 2H 101
Milton Ct. NN7: Mil M 5K 99
    NN16: K'ing 4E 38
MILTON ERNEST 3C 139

MILTON KEYNES 2D 141
MILTON MALSOR 4K 99 (3D 137)
Milton Rd. NN7: G'ton 6E 98
    NN8: L Irch 4D 78
    NN11: Dav 1G 61
    NN17: Corby 5H 13
    PE8: Oun 5H 21
Milton St. NN2: N'ton 5F 85
    NN10: High F 7E 68
Milton St. Nth. NN2: N'ton 4F 85
Milton Ter. PE8: Lut 7H 23
Milverton Cres. NN1: N'ton 7K 85
Mimosa Cl. NN3: N'ton 1K 95
Minden Cl. NN18: Corby 5E 16
Minehead Cl. NN18: Corby 7F 13
Minerva Way NN8: Well 7J 65
Minster Ho. NN1: N'ton 3J 131
Min St. NN14: Ald 5A 20
Minton Cl. NN14: Des 2C 26
Mirfield Cl. NN18: Corby 1H 17
MISTERTON 3B 132
Mitchell Cl. NN5: Dus 4J 83
Mitchell Rd. NN17: Corby 3C 14
Mitchell St. NN16: K'ing 3E 38
Mitchison Cl. CV23: Bar 3C 54
MIXBURY 2C 141
Mixbury Rd. NN13: Even 2C 130
Moat La. NN12: Tow 3C 114
Moat Pl. NN1: N'ton 4F 131 (1C 94)
Mobbs Miller Ho. NN1: N'ton 7H 85
Moffatt Ter. NN8: Well 7B 66
MOGGERHANGER 3D 139
MOLESWORTH 1C 139
MOLLINGTON 1A 140
Monarch Rd. NN2: N'ton 5D 84
Monarch Ter. NN2: N'ton 6D 84
Monks Hall Rd. NN1: N'ton 7G 85
MONKS KIRBY 3A 132
Monks Pk. Rd. NN1: N'ton 7G 85
Monks Pond St.
    NN1: N'ton 3F 131 (1C 94)
Monks Rd. NN29: Woll 3E 90
Monks Way NN6: Crick 3J 31
    NN8: Well 2B 78
    NN18: Corby 2F 17
    (off Manor Dr.)
Monkswood NN12: Silv 3G 121
Monmouth Cl. NN14: Thra 3K 51
Monmouth Rd. NN5: N'ton 7B 84
Monson Way PE8: Oun 3G 21
Montabaur Rd. NN13: B'ley 4H 129
Montagu Cl. NN15: K'ing 5F 43
Montague Ct. NN14: Thra 3H 51
Montague Cres. NN5: Dus 4J 83
Montague Dr. CV23: Kil 6C 30
Montague St. NN10: R'den 3D 80
Montagu St. NN16: K'ing 7D 38
Montagu Ter. PE8: Barn 6B 22
Montcalm Cl. NN15: K'ing 1H 43
Montfort Cl. NN5: N'ton 1K 93
Montgomery Cl. NN15: K'ing 1G 43
Montgomery Way NN4: Woot 1E 100
Montrose St. NN17: Corby 7A 14
Montsaye Community Sports Cen.
    . . . . .6E 26
Moonshine Gap NN9: H'wick 6C 64
Moor Cotts. NN9: Harg 6J 49
Moorcut Dr. NN5: Upton 3H 93
Moore Cl. NN15: Bar S 3J 43
    NN17: Corby 5J 13
    (off Byron Rd.)
MOOR END 3H 123
Moorend Rd. NN12: Yar G 3G 123
Moores Cl. NN7: Bug 2J 105
Moore St. NN2: N'ton 5G 85
Moorfield Grn. NN14: R'ell 7E 26
Moorfield Rd. NN14: R'ell 7E 26
Moorfield Sq. NN3: N'ton 7D 74
Moorhouse Way NN15: K'ing 2A 42
Moorings, The NN14: Woodf 7F 51
Moorland Cl. NN3: N'ton 4B 86
Moorlands NN8: Well 5H 65
Moorlands, The NN10: R'den 1E 80
Moor Rd. NN10: R'den 2D 80
Moors Cl. MK19: Dean 5F 125
Moors Dr., The OX17: Mid C 6C 118
MORBORNE 2D 135
Morby Cl. NN15: Bur L 3J 45
    (off Whitney Rd.)
MORCOTT 1B 134
Mordaunt Cl. NN14: Low 6C 48
Mordaunt La. NN5: Dus 5J 83
Morehay La. PE8: King C 3G 9
More Rd. NN11: Dav 6G 59
Moreton Av. NN8: Well 3J 77
MORETON PINKNEY 3J 111 (1B 140)
Moreton Rd. NN11: Eyd 7D 108
Moreton Way NN2: K'thpe 1D 84
Morgan Cl. NN3: N'ton 2F 87
Morgan Dr. NN6: Brix 2J 35
Morgans Cl. PE8: Pole 3E 22
Moriston Cl. NN17: Corby 4H 13
Morland Rd. NN18: Corby 1K 17

Morley St. NN16: K'ing 5E 38
Morley Wlk. NN17: Corby 5H 13
    (off Rowlett Wlk.)
Morning Star Rd. NN11: Dav 7F 59
Morris Av. NN10: R'den 4C 80
Morris Cl. NN8: Well 6F 65
Morrison Pk. Rd. NN6: W Had 5H 29
Morris Rd. NN2: K'thpe 3E 84
    NN11: Dav 7E 58
Morse Way NN14: Des 1E 26
Mortar Pit Rd. NN3: N'ton 1F 87
Mortimer Cl. NN4: N'ton 5B 94
Mortons Bush NN4: Woot 2H 101
Mosel Cl. NN8: Well 4B 78
Moss Cl. NN12: Tow 1C 114
Moss Wlk. NN18: Corby 4F 17
Motala Cl. NN18: Corby 4F 17
Motherwell Ho. NN17: Corby 5B 14
Motspur Dr. NN2: K'thpe 5C 84
Motts, The NN7: Harp 1A 92
MOULTON 4K 73 (2D 137)
Moulton La. NN2: Bou 5E 72
MOULTON LEYS 6K 73
MOULTON PARK 7G 73
Moulton Pk. Bus. Cen.
    NN3: Moul 7H 73
Moulton Pk. Ind. Est.
    NN3: Moul P 7H 73
Moulton Pk. Office Village
    NN3: Moul P 7G 73
Moulton Rd. NN3: Pits 1E 72
    NN6: Holc 7G 37
    NN6: Pits 1E 72
Moulton Sports Complex 4J 73
Moulton Way NN3: Moul P 7J 73
Moulton Way Nth. NN3: Moul 7K 73
Moulton Way Sth. NN3: Moul 7K 73
Mountbatten Dr. NN14: Rin 1H 53
Mountbatten Ho. NN11: Dav 3K 61
    (off Admirals Way)
Mountbatten Way NN9: Raun 6K 53
Mountclair Ct. NN3: West F 6B 86
Mountfield Rd. NN3: Spin H 3H 85
    NN11: Dav 1C 68
Mounthill Av. MK19: Old S 2J 125
MOUNT PLEASANT 2C 141
Mt. Pleasant NN6: E Bart 2E 88
    NN7: Harp 7B 82
    NN11: Woodf H 2E 108
    NN12: Yar G 3K 123
Mounts, The NN6: Long B 1H 55
Mounts Baths Leisure Cen., The
    . . . . .3J 131 (1E 94)
Mounts Bus. Cen. NN1: N'ton 2J 131
Mounts Ct. NN3: N'ton 3B 86
Mounts La. NN11: Newn 7K 61
MOWMACRE HILL 1B 132
MOWSLEY 3C 133
Muirfield Dr. NN11: Dav 1K 61
Muirfield Rd. NN8: Well 5H 65
Mulberry Cl. NN5: Dall 7A 84
    NN8: Well 7K 65
    NN14: Des 1D 26
Mull Dr. NN17: Corby 5H 13
Mullions, The NN4: Woot 3F 101
Mulso Rd. NN9: Fine 6J 47
Mumford Dr. NN7: Roth 1F 99
Muncaster Gdns. NN4: N'ton 1E 100
Muncaster Way NN6: W Had 5H 29
Murcott NN6: Long B 1F 55
Murray Av. NN2: N'ton 5E 84
Murray Ho. NN1: N'ton 6G 85
Murray Wlk. NN18: Corby 1K 17
MURSLEY 3D 141
Murswell Cl. NN12: Silv 3H 121
Murswell La. NN12: Silv 3H 121
MUSCOTT 2C 137
Muscott Cl. NN7: Flore 1F 63
Muscott La. NN5: Dus 1G 93
Muscott St. NN5: N'ton 7B 84
Museum Way NN3: N'ton 7C 86
Musgrave Cl. NN4: Woot 1G 101
Mushroom Fld. Rd. NN3: N'ton 4G 87
Musson Cl. NN9: Irth 2B 68
Myers Cl. OX17: Char 1H 127
Myers Way OX17: Char 1H 127
Myrtle Rd. NN16: K'ing 5F 39

N

Nags Head La. NN9: Harg 6J 49
NAILSTONE 1A 132
Nansen Cl. NN11: Dav 5H 59
    NN14: R'ell 7H 27
Nansen Wlk. NN18: Corby 4G 17
Nantwich Dr. NN11: Dav 4J 59
Naomi Cl. NN3: West F 5C 86
Napier Cl. NN8: Well 1F 77
    NN11: Dav 3J 61
NAPTON ON THE HILL 2A 136
NARBOROUGH 2B 132
Narrow La. NN1: N'ton 3G 131 (1D 94)

Narrow Toe La. NN1: N'ton 5F 131
Narvik Rd. NN18: Corby 4F 17
NASEBY 3H 33 (1C 137)
Naseby Battle & Farm Mus. 3H 33
Naseby Battlefield Monument . . .3C 133
Naseby Cl. NN8: Well 5J 65
Naseby Dr. NN11: Dav 4H 59
Naseby Rd. LE16: Clip 7C 24
LE16: Sibb 2C 24
NN6: Thorn 3E 32
NN6: Welf 2J 29
NN16: K'ing 6F 39
NN17: Corby 6H 13
Naseby St. NN2: Sem 6D 84
NASH .2D 141
Nash Cl. NN18: Corby 2J 17
Nash Ct. NN15: Bar S 2J 43
Nasmith Av. NN17: Corby 5B 14
Nasmyth Pl. NN11: Dav 5E 58
NASSINGTON 5G 7 (2C 135)
Nassington Rd. PE8: Wood 6H 9
PE8: Yar 2H 7
National Waterways Mus.
    Stoke Bruerne 6D 116
Navigation Row
    NN1: N'ton 7H 131 (3D 94)
Navisford Cl. NN14: Thra 2J 51
Neale Av. NN16: K'ing 4D 38
Neale Cl. NN3: West F 6A 86
    NN29: Woll 3D 90
Nearside NN5: N'ton 1A 94
Neaton La. NN6: Guil 6E 32
Nectar Way
    NN4: Swan H, Upton 5F 93
Needham Rd. NN9: Stanw 1J 69
Neighbourhood Shop. Cen.
    N'ton 2D 100
NEITHROP 1A 140
Nelson Av. NN11: Woodf H 2C 108
Nelson Cl. NN11: Dav 1K 61
Nelson Dr. NN14: R'ell 6H 27
Nelson Rd. NN17: Corby 5G 13
Nelson St. NN1: N'ton 1H 131 (7D 84)
    NN16: K'ing 5E 38
Nelson's Yd. NN12: Tow 3C 114
Nene Centre, The 4H 51
Nene Centre, The NN4: N'ton 2G 95
Nene Cl. NN8: Well 6H 65
    NN9: Raun 5J 53
    NN15: Bar S 6H 43
Nene Ct. NN8: Well 2D 78
    NN14: Thra 3H 51
Nene Cres. NN17: Corby 4H 13
Nene Dr. NN5: N'ton 4A 84
Nene Ent. Cen. NN2: N'ton 6D 84
Nene Ho. NN11: Dav 6F 59
Nene La. NN12: Tow 3A 114
Nene Pk. 2E 68
Nene Pl. NN5: N'ton 4B 84
Nene Ri. NN7: Cog 1J 97
Nene Rd. NN10: High F 7E 68
    NN15: Bur L 2H 45
Nene Side Cl. NN11: Badby 5C 104
Neneside Cl. NN7: Weed 4B 62
Nene Valley Bus. Pk.
    PE8: Oun 5K 21
Nene Valley Retail Pk.
    NN1: N'ton 7F 131 (3C 94)
Nene Valley Way NN3: N'ton 3J 95
    NN4: Del, N'ton 6E 94
Nene Vw. NN9: Irth 2C 68
    NN14: Isl 2F 51
    PE8: Oun 4H 21
Nene Wlk. NN5: N'ton 4A 84
    NN11: Dav 2F 61
Nene Way NN5: N'ton 4B 84
    NN7: Kisl 4B 92
    PE8: Oun 3H 21
Nene Whitewater Cen. 3H 95
Nepcote Cl. NN15: K'ing 2F 43
Nesbitt Cl. NN3: West F 7B 86
Nest Farm Cres. NN8: Well 4B 66
Nest Farm Rd. NN8: Well 4A 66
Nest Farm Way NN8: Well 5B 66
Nest La. NN8: Well 6C 66
Nether Cl. NN13: B'ley 4H 129
NETHERCOTE 2B 136
NETHERCOTT 3A 140
Netherfield Gro. NN17: Corby 5A 14
Netherfield Rd. NN15: K'ing 3E 42
Nether Grn. LE16: Clip 6D 24
NETHER HEYFORD 5K 63 (3C 137)
Nether Jackson Cl. NN3: N'ton 2E 86
Nether La. NN7: Flore 3F 63
Nethermead Cl. NN3: N'ton 2C 86
Nethertown Way NN14: Maw 6B 40
NETHER WORTON 2A 140
Nettle Gap Cl. NN4: Woot 2G 101
Neuville Way NN14: Des 2C 26
Neville Day Cl. PE9: Eas H 2B 6
Neville Ho. NN17: Corby 7K 13
    (off George St.)
Nevis Cl. NN17: Corby 4H 13

NEWARK 1D 135
Newark Dr. NN18: Corby 7G 13
NEW BARTON 1D 88
Newbery Dr. NN13: B'ley 3E 128
Newbold Cl. PE8: Oun 4G 21
NEWBOLD ON AVON 1A 136
NEWBOLD VERDON 1A 132
Newbolt Cl. NN12: Paul 6H 115
NEWBOROUGH 1D 135
NEWBOTTLE 2B 140
Newbridge La. NN9: Stanw 1K 69
Newbury Cl. NN10: R'den 2G 81
    LE16: Gt Oak 5J 17
Newbury Dr. NN11: Dav 4H 59
Newby Cl. NN3: N'ton 3K 85
Newcombe Rd. NN5: N'ton 7B 84
Newcomen Rd. NN8: Well 7C 66
New Cft. NN7: Weed 4C 62
NEW DUSTON 4G 83 (2D 137)
Newell Rd. NN14: Rin 1G 53
NEW ENGLAND 1D 135
New Forest Way NN11: Dav 6G 59
New Hall NN11: Dav 4G 61
Newham Cl. NN14: R'ell 6F 27
New Ho. PE8: Oun 6H 21
Newington Rd. NN2: K'thpe 2D 84
Newland NN1: N'ton 3H 131 (1D 94)
Newland Rd. NN6: Wal 1H 37
Newlands NN6: Brix 3H 35
    NN6: Nas 2H 33
    NN11: Dav 2H 61
    NN16: K'ing 7D 38
    OX17: King S 1C 126
Newland Sq. NN2: K'thpe 2H 84
Newlands Rd. NN6: Welf 3G 29
Newland St. LE16: Bray 7B 10
    NN16: K'ing 7D 38
Newland Wlk. NN1: N'ton 4J 131
Newlife Apartments
    NN1: N'ton 3G 131
Newman St. NN10: High F 5F 69
    NN15: Bur L 2J 45
    NN16: K'ing 7E 38
Newmarket Cl. NN18: Gt Oak 5J 17
NEWNHAM 7J 61 (3B 136)
Newnham Dr. NN11: Dav 5F 59
Newnham Rd. NN2: K'thpe 3E 84
    NN11: Badby, Newn 4D 104
Newport Pagnell Rd.
    NN4: Woot, H'stone 7E 94
    NN7: Hort 4J 117
    NN7: Pres D 7E 94
Newport Pagnell Rd. W.
    NN4: Woot 7E 94
Newport Rd. NN5: N'ton 7B 84
New Post Office Sq.
    NN17: Corby 7K 13
New Rd. NN4: Woot 2F 101
    NN12: Greens N 1H 113
    NN13: B'ley 5F 129
    NN13: F'hoe 6G 119
    NN14: Ged 6C 46
    PE8: Oun 4H 21
    PE9: Colly 6B 6
    PE9: Eas H 2C 6
New Sth. Bri. Rd.
    NN4: N'ton 7J 131 (3E 94)
Newstead Cl. NN3: N'ton 3G 87
Newstead Ct. NN15: K'ing 5E 42
Newstone Cres. NN4: N'ton 3K 93
New St. NN6: Brix 3G 35
    NN6: E Bart 2E 88
    NN7: Weed 4C 62
    NN8: Well 7B 66
    NN9: Irth 2C 68
    NN11: Dav 2H 61
    NN14: Des 2D 26
    (not continuous)
    NN14: R'ell 6G 27
    NN29: Irch 5J 79
    PE8: Oun 5J 21
New Ter. NN11: Byf 2J 107
NEWTON
    Northamptonshire 4A 46 (3A 134)
    Warwickshire 1B 136
NEWTON BLOSSOMVILLE 3B 138
NEWTON BROMSWOLD 2B 138
NEWTON BURGOLAND 1A 132
Newton Cl. NN8: Well 6F 65
    NN10: R'den 4G 81
    NN11: Dav 6F 59
Newton Gro. NN17: Corby 4B 14
NEWTON HARCOURT 2C 133
Newton La. NN14: Sud 3B 48
NEWTON LONGVILLE 2D 141
NEWTON PURCELL 2C 141
Newton Rd. NN5: Dus 5H 83
    NN10: High F 6F 69
    NN10: High F, R'den 6G 69
    NN10: R'den 3E 80
    NN14: New 4A 46
    NN15: Bar S 5H 43
    NN29: Woll 4E 90

NEWTON UNTHANK 1A 132
Newton Way LE16: Bray 6C 10
NEWTOWN 2C 139
New Town NN14: Brig 1C 20
    PE9: Eas H 2C 6
Newtown NN14: Woodf 6B 50
NEWTOWN LINFORD 1A 132
Newtown Rd. NN1: N'ton 1G 95
    NN8: L Irch 4D 78
    NN9: Raun 7K 53
Newtown St. NN14: Woodf 6B 50
New York Thunderbowl 4D 38
Nibbits La. NN11: Braun 1B 58
Nicholas Rd. NN9: Irth 3B 68
Nicholas Way NN10: R'den 2C 80
Nicholls Ct. NN3: N'ton 1B 86
Nichols St. NN14: Des 1D 26
Nichols Way NN9: Raun 5H 53
Nielson Rd. NN8: Well 4H 65
Nigel Cl. NN13: B'ley 6H 129
Nightingale Cl. NN11: Dav 4H 59
    NN13: B'ley 1F 129
Nightingale Dr. NN12: Tow 6C 114
    NN14: Des 1E 26
Nightingale La. NN8: Well 5C 66
Nine Arches Way NN14: Thra 3G 51
Niort Way NN8: Well 6G 65
Nippendale NN10: R'den 3F 81
Nithsdale Rd. NN17: Corby 6J 13
Noble Av. NN9: Irth 7A 52
Nobold Ct. LE16: Clip 6C 24
NOBOTTLE 7J 57 (2C 137)
Nook, The LE16: Cotti 4C 12
    NN17: Corby 7C 14
    PE9: Eas H 2C 6
Norfolk Cl. NN17: Corby 6H 13
Norfolk St. NN2: Sem 6D 84
Norfolk Ter. NN2: Sem 6D 84
Norlington Cl. NN14: Orl 7A 44
Normal Boot & Shoe Factory, The
    NN1: N'ton 7F 85
    (off Talbot Rd.)
NORMAN CROSS 2D 135
Norman D Gate NN1: N'ton 2F 95
Norman D Gate Ind. Est.
    NN1: N'ton 2F 95
Norman Rd. NN3: N'ton 5J 85
Norman Snow Way NN5: Dus 7H 83
NORMANTON LE HEATH 1A 132
Norman Way NN8: Well 3J 77
    NN29: Irch 5K 79
Normead Sq. NN3: N'ton 4G 87
Norris Acre NN3: Hin H 5B 128
Norris Cl. NN15: K'ing 2J 43
Norris Way NN10: R'den 2B 80
Norris Way Ind. Est.
    NN10: R'den 2B 80
Norse Wlk. NN18: Corby 4F 17
Northall NN6: Wal 1H 37
Northall St. NN16: K'ing 6D 38
Northam Ct. NN16: K'ing 5D 38
NORTHAMPTON
    . . . . .5J 131 & 2E 94 (2D 137)
Northampton & District
    Indoor Bowling Association . . .2C 84
Northampton & Lamport Railway
    Pitsford & Brampton Station . . .3A 72
Northampton Boat Club 1B 96
Northampton Central Mus. & Art Gallery
    . . . . .5H 131 (2E 94)
Northampton Ho.
    NN1: N'ton 4J 131 (1E 94)
Northampton La. Nth. NN3: Moul . . .5K 73
Northampton La. Sth. NN3: Moul . . .7J 73
Northampton Rd.
    MK19: Cos, Old S 1J 125
    NN6: Brix 4H 35
    NN6: Chap B 4K 71
    NN6: E Bart 1C 88
    NN6: Ect 2J 87
    NN6: Long B 1K 55
    NN6: W Had 6H 29
    NN6: Welf 3H 29
    NN7: Blis 7J 99
    NN7: D'ton 5A 102
    NN7: Harp 2B 92
    NN7: Roa 1C 116
    NN7: Yar H 6G 103
    NN8: Well 3H 77
    NN10: High F, R'den 2K 79
    NN12: Graf R, Yar G 1H 123
    NN12: Lit 2H 109
    NN12: Tow 3C 114
    NN13: B'ley 2H 129
    NN14: Brou 7F 41
    NN14: Orl 7A 44
    NN15: K'ing 2A 42
Northampton Sailing Club 6J 35
Northampton Saints (Franklin's Gdns.)
    . . . . .1A 94
Northampton Science Pk.
    NN3: Moul P 7G 73
NORTHAMPTON SERVICE AREA . . .1H 99

Northamptonshire County Cricket Club
    . . . . .6H 85
Northamptonshire Ironstone Railway Trust
    . . . . .5K 93
Northampton Station (Rail)
    . . . . .5F 131 (2C 94)
Northampton Town FC 2J 93
Northampton Water Ski Club 4G 95
NORTH ASTON 3A 140
North Av. NN15: Bur L 1J 45
NORTHBOROUGH 1D 135
NORTHBROOK 3A 140
Northbrook NN18: Corby 2G 17
Nth. Cape Wlk. NN18: Corby 4F 17
North Cl. NN11: Braun 1C 58
Northcote St. NN2: Sem . . .1F 131 (7D 84)
NORTHEND 3A 136
North End NN10: High F 6E 68
Northen Way NN8: Well 4K 65
Northern Cl. NN17: Gret 7C 8
Northern Way NN11: Dav 5H 59
NORTH EVINGTON 1C 133
Northfield Av. NN14: Rin 1G 53
    NN15: K'ing 1C 42
    NN16: K'ing 7C 38
Northfield Cl. NN16: K'ing 5C 38
Northfield Grn. NN6: E Had 2C 56
Northfield La. PE8: Nass 4G 7
Northfield Point NN16: K'ing 5C 38
Northfield Rd. NN5: Dus 5G 83
    NN14: C'ley 1H 41
Northfield Way NN2: K'thpe 2C 84
Nth. Folds Rd. NN18: Corby 5E 16
Northgate NN17: Tow 2C 114
Nth. Hayes Ct. NN3: N'ton 1C 86
Nth. Holme Cl. NN3: N'ton 1A 86
NORTHILL 3D 139
Nth. Kettering Bus. Pk.
    NN14: Week 1D 38
NORTH KILWORTH 3C 133
North Lea LE16: West W 2D 10
    (not continuous)
Nth. Leys Cl. NN3: Moul 6K 73
NORTH LUFFENHAM 1B 134
NORTH MARSTON 3D 141
North Mdw. Vw. NN5: Dus 1E 92
NORTH NEWINGTON 2A 140
North Oval NN5: N'ton 4A 84
Nth. Paddock Cl. NN3: N'ton 2C 86
Nth. Pk. Dr. NN16: K'ing 4E 38
Nth. Portway Cl. NN3: N'ton 6C 74
Nth. Priors Cl. NN3: N'ton 2D 86
North Rd. NN3: Moul P 7G 73
    NN6: E Bart 1D 88
North St. CV23: Kil 6B 30
    NN6: Mears A 3A 76
    NN7: Roth 2F 99
    NN8: Well 7A 66
    NN9: Raun 5J 53
    NN10: R'den 2E 80
    NN11: Dav 1H 61
    NN14: Titch 1H 49
    PE8: Oun 5J 21
Northumberland Cl.
    NN15: K'ing 4F 43
Northumberland Rd.
    NN15: K'ing 4E 42
Northumbria Gdns. NN3: N'ton 5J 85
North Way MK19: Dean 4F 125
    NN12: Pot 7J 123
Nth. Western Av. NN2: K'thpe 2B 84
Northwood Rd. NN3: N'ton 4J 85
Nortoft NN6: Guil 6D 32
Nortoft La. CV23: Kil 4A 30
NORTON 7G 55 (2C 137)
Norton Cl. NN11: Dav 1J 61
Norton Cres. NN12: Tow 3B 114
Norton Rd. NN2: K'thpe 3D 84
    NN11: Dav 1J 61
    (not continuous)
    NN17: Corby 6H 13
Norton St. NN14: R'ell 6H 27
Norway Cl. NN18: Corby 3F 17
Norwood Rd. NN5: Dus 7E 82
NOSELEY 2D 133
Notre Dame M.
    NN1: N'ton 3K 131 (1E 94)
Nuffield Cl. NN13: B'ley 3E 128
Nuffield Health Fitness & Wellbeing Cen.
    . . . . .1K 93
NUNEATON 2A 132
Nunnery Av. NN14: R'ell 6F 27
Nunn Mills Rd. NN1: N'ton 3F 95
Nuns La. NN6: Long B 1H 55
Nurseries, The NN1: N'ton 2G 95
    NN3: Moul 4K 73
    NN7: Hort 3J 117
Nursery Cl. NN6: Maid 1B 36
    NN7: L Hou 3D 96
Nursery Ct. NN6: Mears A 3A 76
Nursery Dr. NN8: Well 5C 66
Nursery Gdns. NN9: Irth 2B 68
Nursery La. NN2: Sulby 4D 84

Nutcote NN6: Nas 3H **33**
Nuthall Cl. NN3: N'ton 6C **86**
Nuthatch Cl. NN18: Corby 3K **17**

O

OADBY .1C **133**
Oak Av. NN7: Blis 6G **99**
Oak Cl. NN7: Hart 5J **117**
  NN12: Tow 5C **114**
  NN14: Brou 6H **41**
  NN29: Irch 6H **79**
Oak Dr. NN10: Woodf H 2C **108**
Oakfield NN10: R'den 1D **80**
Oak Gro. NN11: Dav 5H **59**
Oakgrove Pl. NN4: N'ton 2E **100**
OAKHAM 1A **134**
Oakham Cl. NN3: Moul 6J **73**
  NN10: R'den 5D **80**
  NN14: Des 1C **26**
Oakham La. NN11: Stav 4A **60**
Oaklands NN7: Bug 2K **105**
  NN7: Weed 5B **62**
Oaklands Dr. NN3: N'ton 5A **86**
Oak La. NN6: Crick 3H **31**
Oakleas Ri. NN14: Thra 4H **51**
Oakleigh Cl. NN9: Raun 5H **53**
Oakleigh Dr. NN5: Dus 5H **83**
OAKLEY 3C **139**
Oakley Cl. NN18: Corby 5F **17**
Oakley Dr. NN3: Moul 4A **74**
  NN8: Well 1J **77**
Oakley Hay Ind. Est. NN18: Corby . .5E **16**
  (not continuous)
Oakley Hay Lodge NN18: Corby 5F **17**
Oakley Pond NN18: Gt Oak 6G **17**
Oakley Rd. NN10: R'den 2C **80**
  NN14: Pipe, R'ton . . . .1C **46** & 7A **16**
  NN17: Corby 6F **17**
  NN18: Corby 6F **17**
Oakley St. NN1: N'ton 1J **131** (7E **84**)
  NN16: K'ing 5D **38**
Oakmont Cl. NN4: N'ton 3D **100**
Oakpits Way NN10: R'den 4F **81**
Oak Rd. NN13: B'ley 2G **129**
  NN15: K'ing 7F **39**
Oaks, The NN4: Gra P 5G **101**
Oaks Dr. NN10: High F 5E **68**
Oak St. NN1: N'ton 2H **131** (7C **84**)
  NN7: Weed 5B **62**
  NN10: R'den 1E **80**
Oak Ter. NN9: Irth 2C **68**
Oak Tree Cl. NN3: N'ton 5D **86**
  NN14: Des 1C **26**
Oak Tree Ct. NN14: Ald 6B **20**
Oaktree Ct. NN16: K'ing 1J **42**
  (off George St.)
Oak Vw. NN9: Well 3A **66**
  NN12: Pot 6H **123**
Oak Way NN9: Irth 2C **68**
Oakway NN8: Well 5A **66**
Oakwood Cl. NN14: Des 1D **26**
Oakwood Rd. NN1: N'ton 5G **85**
Oathill Cl. NN6: Brix 4H **35**
Oat Hill Dr. NN3: N'ton 4G **87**
Oathill Ri. NN15: Bur L 2K **45**
Oat Hill Rd. NN12: Tow 5C **114**
Oban Cl. NN15: K'ing 2G **43**
Obelisk Cen., The 6D **72**
Obelisk Cl. NN2: Bou 5D **72**
Obelisk Ho. NN2: K'thpe 6D **72**
Obelisk Ri. NN2: K'thpe 6D **72**
Obelisk Rd. NN9: Fine 6J **47**
Occupation Rd. LE16: Mid 2A **12**
  NN17: Corby 6K **13**
  PE8: Oun 3J **21**
Octagon, The NN17: Corby 5B **14**
Octagon Way NN3: N'ton 4B **86**
Octavian Way NN13: B'ley 5H **129**
ODELL .3B **138**
Odeon Bldgs. NN17: Corby 6B **14**
Odeon Cinema
  Kettering 6E **42**
ODSTONE 1A **132**
OFFCHURCH 2A **136**
OFFORD CLUNY 2D **139**
OFFORD D'ARCY 2D **139**
Ofield La. CV23: Kil 6B **30**
Ogee Bus. Pk. NN8: Well 2C **66**
OLD 5E **36** (1D **137**)
Old Bakehouse Yd.
  MK11: Stony S 4K **125**
Old Barn Cl. NN3: N'ton 3C **86**
Old Barn Wlk. NN3: N'ton 2C **86**
Old Bedford Rd. NN4: N'ton 3J **95**
Old Brewery Wlk. NN13: B'ley . .5G **129**
Old Brickyard, The NN6: W Had . . .6H **29**
Old Carpenters Cl. NN3: Gt Bil . . .4F **87**
Old Cl. NN4: Gra P 6F **101**
Old Dairy Farm Craft Cen. 3C **137**
Old Depot, The NN7: Weed 5C **62**

Old Dry La. NN14: Brig 1C **20**
  (not continuous)
Olde Forde Cl. NN6: Brix 4H **35**
Olde Hall Cl. NN6: Spra 5C **34**
Oldenburg Rd. NN18: Corby 3E **16**
Old End NN7: Pid 3F **117**
Oldenmead Cl. NN3: N'ton 3C **86**
Olden Rd. NN3: N'ton 1F **87**
Old Farm La. NN14: Isl 2F **51**
OLD FLETTON 2D **135**
Old Forge Dr. NN6: W Had 6H **29**
Old Gorse Way NN14: Maw 6A **40**
Old Greens Norton Rd.
  NN12: Tow 2B **114**
Oldland Rd. NN18: Corby 3J **17**
Old La. NN13: F'hoe 6G **119**
Old Manor Ct. NN11: Welt 2K **59**
Old Oak Dr. NN12: Silv 3H **121**
Old Quarry, The PE8: Oun 5K **21**
Old Quarry Ct. NN3: N'ton 2B **86**
Old Rickyard, The
  NN11: Mor P 3J **111**
Old Rd. NN6: Scal 6A **36**
  NN6: Wal 6H **29**
  NN11: Braun 2A **58**
  NN14: Stan 4F **19**
Old School La. NN12: Blak 5H **109**
Old Slipper Baths, The
  NN4: Far C 4C **94**
  (off Main Rd.)
Old Stable Yd. MK19: Old S . . .2K **125**
OLD STRATFORD 2J **125** (1D **141**)
Old Tiffield Rd. NN12: Tow 2B **114**
Old Towcester Rd. NN4: N'ton 3D **94**
OLD TOWN 4H **129**
Old Town NN13: B'ley 4H **129**
Old Vineyard, The
  NN10: High F 6E **68**
OLD WESTON 1C **139**
OLD WOODSTOCK 3A **140**
Old Woodyard, The
  NN12: Silv 3H **121**
Old Yew Ct. NN2: K'thpe 3C **84**
Oleander Cres. NN3: N'ton 2F **87**
Oliver Cl. NN10: R'den 3F **81**
Oliver St. NN2: N'ton 5F **85**
Ollerton Wlk. NN18: Corby 1G **17**
Ollis Cl. NN17: Corby 5K **13**
OLNEY .3A **138**
Olympia Cl. NN4: N'ton 7C **94**
Olympic Way NN8: Well 7H **65**
  NN15: K'ing 3B **42**
Omega Ho. NN1: N'ton 3G **131**
Onley La. CV23: Bar 1B **54**
Onslow Rd. NN5: N'ton 5B **84**
Oransay Cl. NN3: Gt Bil 4F **87**
Orbital Trade Pk.
  NN5: N'ton 5B **84**
Orchard, The LE16: Sibb 2D **24**
  NN7: Flore 2G **63**
  NN7: Kisl 4C **92**
  NN11: Stav 4A **60**
  NN11: Up Bod 2B **106**
  NN12: Pot 6G **123**
  NN29: Boz 2H **103**
Orchard Cl. LE16: Wilb 5H **11**
  NN4: Woot 2F **101**
  NN6: E Had 2C **56**
  NN6: Hann 3K **37**
  NN6: Holl 5F **33**
  NN6: Spra 6C **34**
  NN6: Yel 5C **28**
  NN7: Mil M 4K **99**
  NN7: Weed 4D **62**
  NN10: R'den 2C **80**
  NN11: Badby 5C **104**
  NN12: Tow 5C **114**
  NN12: Yar G 3K **123**
  NN14: Des 2B **26**
  NN14: Orl 7B **44**
  NN14: Rin 1H **53**
  NN17: Weld 5J **15**
  NN29: Woll 3E **92**
  PE8: Oun 4H **21**
  PE8: Warm 2H **23**
Orchard Cotts. NN7: L Hou 2D **96**
Orchard Ct. NN12: Pat 5G **105**
  NN14: Woodf 6A **50**
Orchard Cres. NN16: K'ing 5F **39**
  PE8: Wood 5G **9**
Orchard Est. NN14: Pyt 2A **44**
Orchard Fld. NN14: C'ord 3G **47**
Orchard Grn. NN3: N'ton 4K **85**
Orchard Hill NN3: N'ton 5D **86**
Orchard Ho. NN8: Well 6B **66**
Orchard La. NN7: D'ton 5B **102**
  NN17: Gret 6D **8**
  PE8: King C 2D **8**
  PE8: Wood 5G **9**
Orchard Pl. NN29: Irch 5H **79**
Orchard Ri. NN6: Long B 1K **55**
Orchard Rd. NN9: Fine 6H **47**
  NN9: Raun 7G **53**
Orchards, The NN6: Rav 2B **34**

Orchard St. NN5: N'ton 1B **94**
  NN11: Dav 1F **61**
Orchard Ter. NN6: Welf 2H **29**
  NN8: Well 1A **78**
  NN9: Fine 6H **47**
Orchard Way NN5: Dus 1H **93**
  NN7: Cog 1H **97**
  NN7: Harp 1B **92**
  NN7: Roa 2C **116**
  NN14: Thra 4J **51**
  OX17: King S 1C **126**
  PE9: Eas H 2B **6**
Orchid Cl. NN14: Des 1D **26**
Ordnance Rd. NN7: Weed 2A **62**
Oriel Rd. NN11: Dav 4H **61**
Oriel Way NN13: B'ley 3E **128**
Orient Way NN8: Well 6H **65**
Orion Way NN15: K'ing 5D **42**
Orkney Wlk. NN17: Corby 5G **13**
ORLINGBURY 7B **44** (1A **138**)
Orlingbury Rd. NN9: Gt Har 1H **65**
  NN14: Ish, Orl 6B **44**
  NN14: L Harr, Orl . . . .7B **44** & 1F **65**
  NN14: Pyt 5A **44**
Ormond Pl. NN14: Ish 4F **45**
ORTON .1A **138**
ORTON LONGUEVILLE 2D **135**
Orton Pl. NN8: Well 5J **65**
Orton Rd. NN14: Lod 1D **40**
  NN14: R'ell 7E **26**
  NN15: Bar S 5H **43**
ORTON WATERVILLE 2D **135**
ORTON WISTOW 2D **135**
Orwell Cl. NN8: Well 6H **65**
  NN9: Raun 5J **53**
OSBASTON 1A **132**
Osborn Cl. NN8: Well 2K **77**
Osborne Cl. NN10: R'den 1G **81**
Osborne Rd. NN2: K'thpe 4D **84**
Osbourne Cl. NN18: Corby 4K **17**
Osiers, The NN14: Des 3G **27**
Osier Way NN14: Thra 4G **51**
Osler Cl. NN2: K'thpe 1C **84**
Oslo Gdns. NN18: Corby 3E **16**
Osmund Dr. NN3: N'ton 1D **86**
Osprey Dr. NN11: Dav 6H **59**
Osprey La. NN8: Well 5C **66**
Osprey Ri. NN4: N'ton 7C **94**
Ostlers La. MK11: Stony S 3K **125**
Ostlers Way NN15: K'ing 2C **42**
Oswald Rd. NN10: R'den 3F **81**
Osyth Cl. NN4: Brack 5H **95**
Oulton Ri. NN3: N'ton 1G **85**
OUNDLE 5H **21** (3C **135**)
Oundle Dr. NN3: Moul 6J **73**
Oundle Rd. NN14: Thra 3H **51**
  NN17: Weld 5J **15**
  PE8: Wood 6H **9**
Oundle School Swimming Pool . . .5G **21**
Ousebank Way MK11: Stony S . .4K **125**
Ouse Cl. NN8: Well 6H **65**
Ouse La. NN12: Tow 3A **114**
Outfield Cl. NN18: Gt Oak 7F **17**
Outlaw La. NN8: Well 7A **66**
Oval, The NN15: K'ing 2D **42**
Oval Cres. NN7: R'den 3G **81**
Oval Rd. NN10: R'den 3G **81**
OVER END 2C **135**
OVER KIDDINGTON 3A **140**
Overleys Ct. NN3: N'ton 1E **86**
Overmead Rd. NN3: N'ton 4F **87**
Overslade Cl. NN4: N'ton 7B **94**
Overslade Ho. NN4: N'ton 7B **94**
OVERSTONE 3F **75** (2A **138**)
Overstone Cl. NN3: Moul 4B **74**
Overstone Cres. NN6: Over 4E **74**
Overstone Hgts. NN6: Syw 2G **75**
Overstone La. NN3: N'ton 1B **86**
  (Dore Cl.)
  NN3: N'ton 2F **87**
  (Thornapple Cl.)
  NN6: Over 4B **74**
OVERSTONE LODGE 7D **74**
Overstone Pk. 7E **74**
Overstone Rd.
  NN1: N'ton 3K **131** (1E **94**)
  NN3: Moul 4A **74**
  NN6: Syw 3F **75**
Overstone Solarium Res. Pk.
  NN6: Syw 5G **75**
OVERTHORPE 7A **118** (1A **140**)
OVER WORTON 3A **140**
Ovett Cl. NN15: K'ing 2B **42**
OVING .3D **141**
Owen Cl. NN8: Well 7G **65**
  NN7: Braf G 4H **97**
Owen M. NN8: Well 7G **65**
Owen Way NN10: High F 7D **68**
Owl Cl. NN3: Moul P 6G **73**
Owl End NN11: Lwr B 4B **106**
Owl End Way NN11: Lwr B 4B **106**
OWSTON 1D **133**
Oxburgh Ct. NN4: N'ton 7C **94**

Oxendon Rd. LE16: Bray 7A **10**
  LE16: Clip 5D **24**
  LE16: E Far 4J **25**
Oxfield Pk. Dr. MK19: Old S 2K **125**
Oxford Cl. NN6: E Bart 3E **88**
  NN11: Dav 2H **61**
Oxford La. NN11: Mor P, Can A . .1K **111**
Oxford Rd. NN13: B'ley 6F **129**
  NN17: Corby 7H **13**
Oxford St. MK11: Stony S 4K **125**
  NN4: Far C 4C **94**
  NN8: Well 1A **78**
  NN9: Fine 7J **47**
  NN10: Wym 6D **80**
  NN11: Dav 2H **61**
  NN14: R'ell 5G **27**
  NN16: K'ing 6C **38**
Oxwich Cl. NN4: Brack 6H **95**

P

Packer Rd. NN15: K'ing 2A **42**
Packwood Cl. NN11: Dav 3G **59**
PADBURY 2D **141**
Padding La. NN5: Upton 3H **93**
Paddock, The NN6: Crick 4H **31**
  NN9: Raun 7H **53**
  NN11: Lwr B 4B **106**
  NN11: Welt 2K **59**
  NN12: Weed L 3C **112**
  PE8: Wood 5G **9**
Paddock Cl. NN6: Rav 2B **34**
Paddock End NN14: Maw 6B **40**
Paddock La. NN14: Des 2D **26**
Paddock M. NN14: Des 2D **26**
Paddock Mill Ct. NN3: N'ton 2E **86**
Paddock Rd. NN6: Mears A 3A **76**
  NN14: Woodf 6A **50**
Paddocks, The NN3: Moul 4K **73**
  NN6: Brix 2H **35**
  NN6: W Had 6G **29**
  NN6: Welf 3H **29**
  NN7: Bug 2J **105**
  NN7: Gt Bri 3H **57**
  NN12: Shut 6A **116**
  NN14: Orl 7A **44**
  NN14: Stan 3G **19**
Paddocks Rd. NN10: R'den 2B **80**
Paddocks Way NN3: N'ton 5D **86**
Paddox Cl. CV23: Kil 6C **30**
Padmans Cl. NN14: Maw 6B **40**
Padwell Cl. NN3: N'ton 6D **86**
Pagent Ct. NN15: K'ing 3C **42**
Pages Wlk. NN17: Corby 7C **14**
Paget Cl. NN4: Gt Hou 5B **96**
Pagnell Ct. NN4: H'stone 1H **101**
PAILTON 3A **132**
Palace Cinema & Snooker Club . . .7B **66**
Palace Ga. NN9: Irth 2C **68**
Paling Cl. NN8: Well 6C **66**
Palk Rd. NN8: Well 1C **78**
Palmer Av. NN9: Irth 7A **52**
Palmer Cl. NN8: Well 5J **65**
Palmer Ct. NN8: Well 7A **66**
  (off Hatton Av.)
Palmer Sq. NN3: N'ton 5F **87**
Palmerston Cl. NN1: N'ton 1F **95**
Palmerston Ho. NN1: N'ton 1F **95**
  (off Palmerston Rd.)
Palmerston Rd. NN1: N'ton 1F **95**
Palm Rd. NN10: R'den 2B **80**
PAPLEY .5G **23**
Parade, The NN1: N'ton . . .4H **131** (1D **94**)
Parade Bank NN3: Moul 4K **73**
Paradise OX17: King S 1B **126**
Paradise Av. NN15: K'ing 4F **43**
Paradise La. NN15: K'ing 4F **43**
Pargeter Cl. OX17: Greatw 2K **119**
Park Av. NN3: Abing 6H **85**
  NN5: Dus 5F **83**
  NN9: Raun 7K **53**
  NN10: R'den 4C **80**
  NN16: K'ing 5D **38**
Park Av. Nth. NN3: N'ton 4H **85**
Park Av. Sth. NN3: Abing, N'ton . . .6H **85**
Park Circ. NN4: Swan H 7G **93**
Park Cl. MK19: Cos 6D **122**
  NN5: Dus 5F **83**
  NN6: E Bart 2C **88**
  NN6: Syw 3G **75**
  NN6: Wat 6D **54**
  NN7: Braf G 5H **97**
  NN11: Badby 5D **104**
  NN12: Whit 3D **110**
  NN14: Ish 4G **45**
  PE8: King C 1J **9**
Park Cnr. NN5: N'ton 1A **94**
Park Cres. NN8: Well 7B **66**
Park Cres. E. NN5: N'ton 4A **84**
Park Cres. W. NN5: N'ton 5A **84**
Park Dr. NN5: N'ton 5A **84**

Park End NN13: Crou 5B 130
Parkers Ter. NN9: Fine 7H 47
Parker Way NN10: High F 4E 68
Park Farm Ct. NN14: Titch 1H 49
Park Farm Ind. Est. NN8: Well 6G 65
    (Baird Ct.)
  NN8: Well 7F 65
    (Booth Dr.)
Park Farm Sth. NN8: Well 1E 76
Park Farm Way NN8: Well 1G 77
Parkfield Av. NN4: Del 5D 94
Parkfield Cres. NN4: Del 5D 94
Parkfield Rd. NN6: Brix 4G 35
  NN6: Long B 1G 55
Parkham Cen. NN10: R'den 2A 80
Park Hill LE16: Bray 7E 10
Park Hill Rd. NN3: N'ton 3A 86
PARKLANDS 1H 85
Parklands NN6: Crick 2E 30
  NN6: Syw 4G 75
  NN9: Stanw 1J 69
Parklands Av. NN3: N'ton 1H 85
Parklands Cl. NN14: Lod 1D 40
Parklands Cres. NN3: N'ton 1H 85
Park La. NN5: Dus 5F 83
  NN6: E Bart 2C 88
  NN6: Wat 6C 54
  NN7: G'ton 6D 98
  NN7: Harp 1B 92
  NN7: Harr 6G 117
  NN12: Paul 7H 115
  OX17: Sulg 6G 111
Park Leys NN11: Dav 3H 61
Park Lodge NN17: Corby 7K 13
Park M. NN18: Well 7B 66
Park Pl. NN10: R'den 3E 80
Park Rd. NN7: Hart 7G 117
  NN8: Well 7B 66
  NN9: Irth 3B 68
  NN9: Raun 6K 53
  NN10: R'den 3E 80
  NN14: Titch 1H 49
  NN15: Bur L 2J 45
  NN16: K'ing 5E 38
Parks, The NN17: Gret 5D 8
Parkside NN3: N'ton 4G 87
  NN5: Upton 3H 93
Park Spinney Cl. NN6: Col A 2A 32
Park Sq. NN5: N'ton 4A 84
Park St. NN6: E Bart 2C 88
  NN9: Raun 6K 53
  NN12: Tow 3C 114
  NN29: Woll 4F 91
  PE8: King C 2H 9
Park Vw. NN3: Moul 5B 74
    (not continuous)
  NN14: Thra 3H 51
  NN16: K'ing 5D 38
Park Vw. Cl. NN3: Moul 4B 74
Park Vw. Ct. NN2: K'thpe 2C 84
Park Vw. Rd. NN12: Tow 4D 114
Park Wlk. NN5: N'ton 5A 84
  NN14: Brig 2C 20
  PE9: Eas H 1C 6
Parkway NN3: West F 6A 86
  PE8: Nass 5H 7
Parkway Cl. PE8: Nass 5H 7
Parkwood St. NN5: N'ton 1C 94
Parnell Cl. NN6: W Had 5H 29
Parracombe Way NN3: N'ton 7K 85
Parsons Cl. NN6: Ect 2J 87
  NN7: Gren 2C 102
  NN7: Neth H 5K 63
Parsons Gro. NN17: Corby 5B 14
Parsons Meade NN4: N'ton 5K 93
Parsons Rd. NN11: Dav 5E 58
  NN29: Irch 5J 79
Parsons St. NN11: Woodf H 2D 108
Partridge Cl. NN2: K'thpe 1B 84
Partridge La. NN11: Eyd 7D 108
Parva Cl. NN3: N'ton 3B 86
Pascal Cl. NN17: Corby 4A 14
Pascoe Cres. NN11: Dav 6F 59
Pashler Gdns. NN14: Thra 3H 51
PASSENHAM 6K 125 (2D 141)
Pasteur Cl. NN2: K'thpe 1C 84
Pasture, The NN11: Dav 2H 61
Pasture End NN14: Maw 5C 40
Pastures, The NN2: K'thpe 1B 84
  NN9: Well 3K 65
Patenall Way NN10: High F 5D 68
Paterson Rd. NN8: Well 4C 66
Patrick Cl. NN15: K'ing 4E 42
    (off Sussex Rd.)
Patrick Ct. NN18: Corby 2J 17
Patrick Rd. NN15: K'ing 4E 42
  NN18: Corby 2J 17
Patricks La. MK19: Dean 5F 125
Patterdale Wlk. NN3: N'ton 2K 85
Patterson Rd. NN3: West F 5G 87
PATTISHALL 5G 105 (3C 137)
PAULERSPURY 7H 115 (1D 141)
PAVENHAM 3B 138

Pavilion Ct. NN1: N'ton 7G 85
  NN4: Brack 6G 95
Pavilion Dr. NN4: Brack 5G 95
  PE8: Oun 4H 21
Pavilions Way NN13: B'ley 4E 128
Paxford Cl. NN8: Well 4K 77
Paxton Rd. NN3: N'ton 2A 86
Peace Cl. NN4: N'ton 4A 94
Peace Hill NN7: Bug 3H 105
Peacock Dr. NN14: Rin 1G 53
Peacock Pl. NN1: N'ton 4J 131 (1E 94)
Peacocks Cl. OX17: Mid C 6D 118
Peak, The NN7: Neth H 6J 63
Peake Cl. LE16: Mid 5A 12
PEAKIRK 1D 135
Pearmain Av. NN8: Well 5A 66
Pearmain Ct. NN3: Well 4D 86
Pearson M. NN29: Woll 4E 90
Pear Tree Cl. NN3: N'ton 4D 86
Peartree Cl. NN11: Dav 6H 59
  NN29: Boz 2H 103
Peartree Farm Cl. NN9: L Harr . . .1G 65
Peaselands NN14: Des 1C 26
PEATLING MAGNA 2B 132
PEATLING PARVA 3B 132
Pebbleford Rd. NN15: K'ing 2F 43
Pebble La. NN8: Well 1B 78
  NN13: B'ley 4G 129
PECKLETON 1A 132
Peck Way NN10: R'den 2E 80
Pegasus Dr. NN13: B'ley 4G 129
  NN15: K'ing 6E 42
Pegasus Way NN10: R'den 1B 80
Peg's La. LE16: Clip 6C 24
Pelham Ct. NN3: N'ton 2A 86
Pell Cl. NN3: N'ton 3B 86
Pells Cl. NN6: Guil 6D 32
Pemberton Cen., The 3C 80
Pemberton St. NN16: Corby 3D 80
Pembroke Cl. NN10: R'den 4F 81
  NN14: Thra 3J 51
Pembroke Cres. NN5: N'ton 6B 84
Pembroke Gdns. NN5: N'ton 6B 84
Pembroke Rd. NN5: N'ton 6B 84
Pembroke Way NN11: Dav 4G 61
Penarth Rd. NN5: N'ton 6B 84
Pen Ct. NN1: N'ton 7J 131 (3E 94)
Pendered Rd. NN8: Well 4B 78
Pendle Av. NN16: K'ing 3C 38
Pendle Rd. NN5: Dus 6H 83
Penfold Cl. NN2: K'thpe 1B 84
Penfold Dr. NN3: Gt Bil 3E 86
Penfold Gdns. NN3: Gt Bil 3F 87
Penfold La. NN3: Gt Bil 3F 87
Pen Grn. La. NN17: Corby 5B 14
Peninsular Cl. NN4: Brack 5J 95
Penistone Rd. NN3: N'ton 3B 86
Penistone Wlk. NN3: N'ton 3B 86
    (Alexander Ct.)
  NN3: N'ton 5C 86
    (Langsett Cl.)
Pennard Cl. NN4: Brack 5J 95
Penn Gdns. NN4: N'ton 1C 100
Pennine Cl. NN11: Dav 5G 59
Pennine Way NN5: Dus 7J 83
  NN16: K'ing 4D 38
Pennycress Pl. NN3: N'ton 5F 87
Penrhyn Cl. NN18: Corby 3A 18
Penrhyn Rd. NN14: Thra 4J 51
Penrhyn Rd. NN4: Far C 4D 94
Penrith Dr. NN8: Well 6J 65
Penvale Rd. NN4: N'ton 2C 100
Peppercorn Way NN4: N'ton 2E 100
Perceval Cl. NN5: Dus 5J 83
Perch Cl. NN1: N'ton 4G 59
Percy Rd. NN1: N'ton 7G 85
  NN11: Woodf H 2D 108
Peregrine Pl. NN4: N'ton 7B 94
Perkins Ct. NN8: Well 7B 66
Perkins Rd. NN9: Irth 4B 68
Perkins Way NN11: Newn 7K 61
Perry Cl. NN15: K'ing 3C 42
Perry La. NN9: Raun 5J 53
Perry St. NN1: N'ton 7G 85
Pershore Ct. NN8: Well 5K 77
PERTENHALL 2C 139
PETERBOROUGH 2D 135
Peterborough Rd. PE8: Warm 2H 23
Peters La. NN6: Scal 7A 36
Pether Av. NN13: B'ley 3D 128
Petherton Ct. NN16: K'ing 5D 38
PETSOE END 3A 138
Petworth Gdns. NN18: Corby 1G 17
Pevensey Cl. NN10: R'den 4G 81
Pevensey Wlk. NN18: Corby 1G 17
Peverel's Way NN5: N'ton 1K 93
Peverill Cl. NN10: High F 6F 69
Peverill Rd. NN5: Dus 7G 83
  OX17: Greatw 1B 26
Pevrel Pl. NN14: Des 1B 26
Pexley Ct. PE8: Oun 5G 21
Pheasant Way NN2: K'thpe 1B 84

Philip Way NN10: High F 5F 69
Phillips Way NN6: Long B 1J 55
Phipps Rd. NN11: Woodf H 2C 108
PHIPPSVILLE 6H 85
Phippsville Ct. NN2: N'ton 5G 85
Phoenix Cl. NN8: Well 2C 78
Phoenix Parkway NN17: Corby . . .2B 14
Phoenix Parkway Ind. Est.
  NN17: Corby 5C 14
Phoenix Retail Pk. NN17: Corby . . .5C 14
Phoenix St. NN1: N'ton . .4G 131 (1D 94)
Piccadilly Cl. NN4: N'ton 5A 94
Pickering Cl. NN18: Corby 2G 17
Pickerings, The NN6: Brix 4J 35
PICKWELL 1D 133
PICKWORTH 1B 134
PIDDINGTON
  Northamptonshire . . .2F 117 (3A 138)
  Oxfordshire 3C 141
Piddington La. NN7: Hack, Pid 1F 117
Piece, The NN6: Spra 5C 34
    (off Glebelands)
  NN7: Cog 1J 97
Pie Cnr. NN6: Syw 2G 75
Pierce Cres. PE8: Warm 2J 23
Piggott's La. NN15: Bur L 2K 45
Pightles Ter. NN10: R'den 4F 81
Pightles Wlk. NN10: R'den 4F 81
Pike La. NN1: N'ton 4G 131 (1D 94)
    (not continuous)
Pikemead Rd. NN3: N'ton 2E 86
Pike Rd. NN18: Corby 5F 17
Pilgrims La. NN7: Bug 2J 105
Pilgrims Pl. NN4: Del 5D 94
Pilgrim Way NN8: Well 2A 78
Pilot Rd. NN17: Corby 6C 14
PILSGATE 1C 135
PILTON
  Northamptonshire 3C 135
  Rutland 1B 134
Pilton Cl. NN3: N'ton 1F 87
PIMLICO 7A 120
Pindar Ri. NN3: N'ton 7B 74
Pindar Rd. NN8: Well 3K 77
Pine Av. NN6: Syw 4G 75
Pine Cl. NN4: Gra P 5G 101
  NN10: R'den 5D 80
  NN14: Des 3F 27
  NN29: Irch 6H 79
Pine Copse Cl. NN5: Dus 4F 83
Pine Ct. NN7: L Brin 5G 57
  NN8: Well 1C 78
Pine Cres. NN6: Syw 4G 75
Pineham Av. NN2: K'thpe 7E 72
Pine Ridge NN3: N'ton 6C 74
Pine Rd. NN15: K'ing 1F 43
Pine Tree La. NN14: Isl 2F 51
Pine Trees NN3: N'ton 5A 86
Pinetrees Ct. NN7: Hack 1G 117
Pine Wlk. NN17: Corby 4K 13
Pinewood Cl. NN16: K'ing 3D 38
Pinewood Rd. NN3: Spin H 3H 85
Pinfold Grn. NN11: Badby 5C 104
PINLEY 1A 136
Pioneer Av. NN14: Des 3C 26
  NN15: Bur L 2J 45
Pioneer Cl. NN4: Woot 1F 101
Piper Cl. NN8: Well 4A 66
Pipers Cl. NN9: Irth 2C 68
  NN15: K'ing 1E 42
Piper's Hill Rd. NN15: K'ing 2E 42
PIPEWELL 6A 16 (3A 134)
Pipewell Rd. LE16: E Car 2A 16
  NN14: Des 1E 26
  NN14: Pipe 2A 16
Pipewell Rd. Ind. Est. NN14: Des . .1E 26
Pippin Cl. NN7: Cog 2H 97
  NN8: Well 1A 78
    (off Hill St.)
  NN10: R'den 2B 80
Pippin La. NN3: N'ton 4D 86
PITCHCOTT 3D 141
PITSFORD 1E 72 (2D 137)
Pitsford & Brampton Station
  Northampton & Lamport Railway
    . . . . .3A 72
Pitsford Rd. NN3: Moul 3G 73
  NN6: Chap B 4K 71
Pitstone Rd. NN4: N'ton 3K 93
Pittams Cl. NN6: Long B 2H 55
Pittams La. NN12: Wap 5C 112
Pittoms La. CV23: Bar 2C 54
Pitt St. NN8: Well 1K 77
Plank Ho's. NN12: Tow 4C 114
Plantagenet Cl. NN13: B'ley 3F 129
Plantagenet Sq. NN4: N'ton 5A 94
Plantagenet Wlk. NN4: N'ton 5A 94
    (off Archangel Rd.)
Playford Cl. NN14: R'ell 6J 27
Pleasant Row NN6: Woodf 6B 50
Plens Nature Reserve, The 1E 26
Plessey Cl. NN12: Tow 4D 114
Pleydell Gdns. NN4: Far C 5D 94

Pleydell Rd. NN4: Far C 5D 94
Plough Cl. NN11: Dav 4J 59
  NN14: R'ell 6G 27
Plough La. NN2: K'thpe 7B 72
Ploughmans Wlk. NN2: K'thpe . . .1C 84
Ploughmans Way NN4: Gra P 5G 101
Plough M., The NN13: B'ley 4G 129
Plover Cl. NN12: Tow 6C 114
Plowden Cl. NN11: Ast W 7E 106
Plum Pk. La. NN12: Paul 6J 115
PLUMPTON 1C 112 (1B 140)
Plumpton Ct. NN18: Corby 1G 17
PLUMPTON END 6J 115
Plumpton La. NN11: Mor P 3J 111
Plumpton Rd. NN12: Woode 7F 109
  NN12: West 3B 112
Plumtree Av. NN8: Well 5B 66
Poachers Cl. NN4: Gra P 5G 101
Poachers Way NN2: K'thpe 1C 84
PODINGTON 2B 138
Podmore Way NN14: Brou 7G 41
Poets Cl. NN2: N'ton 4G 85
Poets Way NN11: Newn 7K 61
Poitiers Ct. NN5: Dus 5E 82
Pokas Cotts. NN9: Chel 6K 69
Polar Star Cl. NN11: Chev 6F 59
POLEBROOK 3D 22 (3C 135)
Polebrook Ct. PE8: Pole 3D 22
Polegate Ct. NN18: Corby 1G 17
Pollard St. NN16: K'ing 5D 38
POLOPIT 2J 49
Polopit NN14: Titch 2J 49
Polwell La. NN15: Bar S, Bur L . . .4H 43
Pomfret Arms Cl. NN4: N'ton 3D 94
Pomfret Ct. NN4: N'ton 3D 94
    (off River Vw.)
Pomfret Rd. NN12: Tow 3C 114
Pond Bank NN7: Blis 1G 115
Ponder St. NN14: R'ell 6G 27
Pond Farm Cl. NN5: Dus 7H 83
Ponds Cl. NN9: Raun 6J 53
Pond Wood Cl. NN3: Moul P 7J 73
Pool Cl. NN12: Pat 6G 105
Poole St. NN1: N'ton 1J 131 (7E 84)
Pool Farm Ct. NN11: Woodf H 3B 108
Pool St. NN11: Woodf H 3C 108
Pope Rd. NN8: Well 2H 77
Popham Ct. NN9: Raun 5H 53
Poplar Cl. NN10: R'den 5D 80
  NN11: Dav 5H 59
  NN12: Tow 5C 114
  NN29: Irch 6H 79
Poplar Ct. NN3: N'ton 1A 86
Poplar Pl. NN8: Well 1A 78
    (off West St.)
  NN29: Woll 4F 91
Poplar Ri. NN12: Wap 5C 112
Poplar Rd. NN9: Fine 6J 47
  NN15: Bur L 1K 45
  NN16: K'ing 7F 39
  NN17: Corby 4J 13
Poplars, The NN2: N'ton 1H 131
  NN6: Guil 6D 32
  NN6: Long B 2H 55
  NN17: Weld 5H 15
Poplars Cl. NN9: Raun 6H 53
  NN12: Blak 5J 109
  OX17: Mid C 6D 118
Poplars Ct. NN6: Scal 6A 36
Poplar's Farm Rd. NN15: Bar S . . .3K 43
Poplars La. NN6: Scal 6H 37
Poplars Rd. OX17: Chac 2C 118
Poplar St. NN8: Well 7B 66
Poppy Cl. NN10: R'den 5F 81
Poppyfield Ct. NN3: N'ton 2C 86
  NN14: Thra 2H 51
Poppy Flds. NN16: K'ing 6B 38
Poppy Leys NN6: Brix 5H 35
Poreham Rd. NN14: Thra 3G 51
Porlock Cl. NN5: Dus 6K 83
Portchester Gdns. NN3: N'ton 6B 86
Porter's Cl. MK19: Dean 5F 125
Porter's La. PE9: Eas H 2C 6
Portland Cl. NN11: Dav 2J 61
Portland Pl. NN1: N'ton 7F 85
Portland Rd. NN9: Irth 1C 68
  NN10: R'den 3E 80
Portlow La. NN6: Crick 3H 31
Portree Wlk. NN17: Corby 5H 13
Port Rd. NN5: Dus 4F 83
Portstone Cl. NN5: Dus 4F 83
Portway NN13: Crou 6C 130
  OX17: Ayn 6F 127
Portway Cres. NN13: Crou 6B 130
Portway Dr. NN13: Crou 6B 130
Portway Gdns. OX17: Ayn 7F 127
Portway Rd. NN6: Brix 4J 35
Portwey Cl. NN6: Brix 4J 35
Postle Cl. CV23: Kil 7B 30
Post Office Cl. NN17: Corby 7C 14
    (off Chapel La.)
Potter Ct. NN9: Stanw 7F 53
Potters End NN11: Byf 2J 107
POTTERSPURY 6H 123 (1D 141)

Potterspury Rd.
MK19: Pux, Wick 3B **124**
POTTON **3D 139**
Pound, The NN7: Gt Bri 2H **57**
NN7: Hort 3J **117**
NN7: Neth H 6J **63**
NN13: Syre 6C **120**
Pound Cl. MK19: Wick 5B **124**
NN14: Rin 1G **53**
NN18: Gt Oak 4G **17**
Poundfield Rd. NN12: Pot 7J **123**
Pound La. NN3: Gt Bil 4F **87**
NN3: Moul 4J **73**
NN7: Bug 3J **105**
NN11: Badby 5C **104**
NN12: East 5J **105**
NN14: Woodf 7B **50**
(off The Green)
PE8: Wood 6H **9**
POUNDON **3C 141**
Powdertree Sq. NN3: N'ton 5C **86**
(off Cottagewell Ct.)
Powys Cl. NN18: Corby 4K **17**
Poyntz Gdns. NN5: Dall 6K **83**
Poyntz La. NN5: Dall 6K **83**
Pratt Rd. NN10: R'den 3F **81**
Prebendal La. PE8: Yar 2H **7**
Prebendal Manor House, The . . .5G **7**
Premier Ct. NN3: Moul P 6H **73**
Premier Way NN9: Irth 4B **68**
Prentice Ct. NN3: N'ton 1D **86**
Prentice Wlk. NN17: Corby 4H **17**
(off South Rd.)
Prescott Cl. NN3: N'ton 2F **87**
Presland Way NN9: Irth 3A **68**
Pressland Dr. NN10: High F 6F **69**
Prestbury Rd. NN5: Dus 5F **83**
Prestidge Row NN11: Mor P . . .3H **111**
PRESTON **1A 134**
PRESTON BISSETT **3C 141**
PRESTON CAPES **3B 136**
Preston Capes Rd. NN11: Newn . .7J **61**
Preston Ct. NN3: N'ton 3B **86**
NN15: Bur L 1K **45**
Preston Deanery Rd. NN7: Quin . .7J **101**
Preston Dr. NN11: Dav 4H **59**
Preston Rd. NN11: Eyd 6D **108**
NN11: Woodf H 2E **108**
Prestwold Way NN3: N'ton 1E **86**
Pretoria Cotts. NN9: Chel 6K **69**
Prices Way NN13: B'ley 2E **128**
Pridmore Cl. PE8: Wood 5G **9**
Priestwell Ct. NN6: E Had 2B **56**
PRIMETHORPE **2B 132**
Primrose Cl. NN16: K'ing 5F **39**
NN18: Corby 4H **17**
Primrose Gdns. NN9: Raun 7J **53**
Primrose Hill NN2: Sem 6D **84**
(off Kingsthorpe Rd.)
NN9: Raun 7J **53**
NN11: Dav 1H **61**
Primrose Pl. NN8: Well 7D **66**
(off Elsden Rd.)
Primrose Wlk. NN4: Gra P 6G **101**
NN11: Woodf H 2C **108**
Primula Cl. NN3: N'ton 1K **95**
Primula Ct. NN2: Sem 6D **84**
Prince Cl. NN11: Dav 7G **59**
Prince of Wales Row
NN3: Moul 4A **74**
Prince Rupert Av. NN14: Des 2C **26**
Princes Av. NN14: Des 2E **26**
Princes Cl. NN7: Weed 4B **62**
Princes Ct. NN16: K'ing 6D **38**
(off Princes St.)
Princess Cl. NN3: N'ton 1J **95**
Princess St. NN16: K'ing 6D **38**
Princess Way NN8: Well 3K **77**
Prince St. NN6: E Bart 1D **88**
Princes Wlk. NN1: N'ton 4J **131**
PRINCETHORPE **1A 136**
Prince William Rd. PE8: Oun 5G **21**
Princewood Ct. NN17: Corby 3J **13**
Princewood Rd. NN17: Corby . . .3J **13**
Printers Yd. NN16: K'ing 7D **38**
Print Works, The NN1: N'ton 7G **85**
Printworks, The NN1: N'ton 2J **131**
Priors Cl. NN10: R'den 5C **80**
Priors Ct. NN17: Corby 4G **15**
PRIORS HARDWICK **3A 136**
Priors Haw Rd. NN17: Corby 4G **15**
PRIORS MARSTON **3A 136**
Priors Marston Rd. NN11: Hell . . .3B **104**
Priory Cl. NN3: N'ton 1J **95**
NN11: Dav 3J **61**
Priory Ct. MK11: Stony S 3K **125**
NN3: N'ton 1K **95**
NN7: Weed 5B **62**
NN14: Ged 6C **46**
PE9: Eas H 2C **6**
Priory Cres. NN7: Roa 2B **116**
Priory Ho. NN1: N'ton 3F **131**
Priory M. NN14: Woodf 7B **50**

Priory Rd. NN8: Well 2A **78**
NN29: Woll 3D **90**
Pritchard Ct. NN3: N'ton 7F **75**
NN6: W Had 7G **29**
Probyn Cl. NN3: N'ton 7D **74**
Proclamation Av. NN14: R'ell 7G **27**
Promenade, The NN8: Well 7K **65**
Prospect Av. NN10: R'den 1E **80**
NN29: Irch 6G **79**
Prospect Cl. NN29: Woll 3E **90**
Prospect Ct. NN7: Blis 1J **115**
NN12: Yar G 3K **123**
Prospect Rd. MK11: Stony S . . .4K **125**
Prospect Way NN11: Dav 7E **58**
Provence Ct. NN5: Dus 5E **82**
Puddingbag La. NN29: Boz 2H **103**
Puddledock NN12: Silv 2H **121**
Pump Pl. MK19: Old S 2J **125**
Purbeck Rd. NN10: R'den 3A **80**
Purkis Ct. NN11: N'ton 6G **85**
Purvis Rd. NN10: R'den 3D **80**
PURY END . . . .**6F 115 (1D 141)**
Pury Rd. NN12: Paul 6K **115**
PUXLEY **1E 124**
Puxley Rd. MK19: Dean 4E **124**
Puzzle Ct. NN16: K'ing 7D **38**
Pyghtle, The NN6: E Bart 1D **88**
NN8: Well 6A **66**
Pyghtles, The NN11: Dav 2G **61**
NN29: Woll 5E **90**
Pyghtle Way NN4: N'ton 1B **100**
Pyket Way NN3: West F 6B **86**
Pyke Way NN6: Crick 3J **31**
Pym Cl. NN8: Well 6C **66**
Pyramid Ct. NN3: N'ton 4B **86**
PYTCHLEY . . . .**2A 44 (1A 138)**
Pytchley Cl. NN6: Brix 3H **35**
Pytchley Ct. NN17: Corby 5G **13**
(off Fotheringhay Rd.)
Pytchley Dr. NN6: Long B 1H **55**
Pytchley La. NN15: K'ing 5D **42**
Pytchley Lodge Ind. Est.
NN15: K'ing 4E **42**
Pytchley Lodge Rd. NN15: K'ing . . .4D **42**
Pytchley Ri. NN8: Well 2J **77**
Pytchley Rd. NN10: R'den 2C **80**
NN14: Orl, Pyt 6A **44**
NN15: K'ing 5E **42**
Pytchley St. NN1: N'ton 1F **95**
Pytchley Vw. NN3: Moul 4A **74**
Pytchley Way NN5: Dus 4G **83**
NN6: Brix 3H **35**
Pywell Ct. NN17: Corby 3E **14**
Pywell Rd. NN17: Corby 3E **14**

Q

QUAINTON **3D 141**
Quakers Cl. NN7: Bug 2J **105**
Quantock Cl. NN11: Dav 5G **59**
NN15: Bar S 5J **43**
Quantock Cres. NN5: Dus 6J **83**
Quarry Grn. Cl. MK19: Wick . . .6C **124**
Quarry Pk. Cl. NN3: Moul P 7J **73**
Quarry Rd. NN5: Dus 4G **83**
NN6: Brix 2J **35**
Quartercroft NN3: N'ton 4B **86**
Quarterstone NN4: N'ton 6J **93**
Quebec Cl. NN4: Woot 1F **101**
Queen Eleanor Rd.
NN4: Far C, Del 5C **94**
NN14: Ged 5C **46**
Queen Eleanor St.
MK11: Stony S 3K **125**
Queen Eleanor Ter. NN4: Del 5D **94**
Queensberry Rd. NN15: K'ing 1D **42**
Queensbridge NN4: N'ton 4J **95**
Queens Cl. LE16: Wilb 5H **11**
Queens Cres. NN2: K'thpe 4E **84**
Queensland Gdns. NN2: K'thpe . . .4D **84**
Queens La. NN8: Well 1B **78**
QUEENS PARK **4D 84**
Queen's Pk. NN7: Weed 4B **62**
Queens Pk. Ind. Est.
NN2: K'thpe 4C **84**
Queens Pk. Pde. NN2: K'thpe 4D **84**
Queens Rd. LE16: Wilb 5H **11**
NN1: N'ton 7F **85**
NN11: Dav 7G **59**
NN12: Tow 3C **114**
NN29: Woll 4E **90**
Queen's Sq. NN17: Corby 1K **17**
Queens St. NN13: F'hoe 6G **119**
OX17: Cul 7B **110**
Queen St. NN6: E Bart 1D **88**
NN7: Weed 5A **62**
NN8: Well 1H **77**
NN9: Irth 2B **68**
NN10: R'den 3E **80**
NN14: Des 1E **26**

Queen St. NN14: Ged 6C **46**
NN14: Thra 3J **51**
NN16: K'ing 7D **38**
NN29: Boz 3G **103**
OX17: Mid C 6C **118**
Queensway NN8: Well 1H **77**
NN10: High F 7F **69**
NN15: Bur L 2H **45**
Queenswood Av. NN3: N'ton 2K **85**
QUENIBOROUGH **1C 133**
Quernstone La. NN4: N'ton 4K **93**
QUINBURY END **5H 109**
QUINTON . . . .**7J 101 (3D 138)**
Quinton La. NN11: Woodf H 2D **108**
Quinton Rd. NN4: Woot 3F **101**
Quintonside NN4: Gra P 5G **101**
Quorn Cl. NN8: Well 1J **77**
NN15: Bar S 5J **43**
Quorn Rd. NN10: R'den 2C **80**
Quorn Way NN1: N'ton . . . .2F **131 (7C 84)**

R

Racecourse La. PE9: Eas H 2D **6**
Racedown NN8: Well 2G **77**
RADCLIVE **2C 141**
RADFORD SEMELE **2A 136**
Radleigh Cl. NN4: N'ton 5B **94**
Radleigh Ct. NN2: N'ton 5F **85**
Radnor Way NN15: Bar S 5H **43**
RADSTONE **1B 140**
Radstone Rd. NN13: B'ley 1G **129**
Radstone Way NN2: K'thpe 1D **84**
RADWAY **1A 140**
RADWELL **3C 139**
Raeburn Rd. NN2: N'ton 4F **85**
Raglan Cl. NN10: R'den 4G **81**
Raglan St. NN1: N'ton 1F **95**
Ragsdale Sq. NN14: R'ell 6H **27**
Ragsdale Wlk. NN3: N'ton 7A **74**
Railport App. NN6: Crick 3D **30**
Railside La. NN17: Corby 7B **14**
Railway Cotts. NN6: Chu B 6F **71**
NN18: Gt Oak 7J **17**
Railway Vw. NN16: K'ing 6C **38**
Rainbow Wlk. NN15: Bar S 5H **43**
Raincliffe Cl. OX17: Ayn 7E **126**
Rainsborough Cres. NN4: N'ton . .3A **94**
Rainsborough Gdns. LE16: Mkt H . .1K **25**
Raisins Fld. Cl. NN3: N'ton 3F **87**
Rakestone Cl. NN4: N'ton 2E **100**
Raleigh Cl. NN14: R'ell 6H **27**
NN17: Corby 5G **13**
Raleigh Ct. NN11: Dav 5G **59**
Ramsay Cl. NN9: Raun 5K **53**
RAMSEY HEIGHTS **3D 135**
RAMSEY ST MARY'S **3D 135**
Randall Cl. NN9: Irth 4B **68**
Randall Ho. NN1: N'ton 7G **85**
(off Monks Hall Rd.)
Randall Rd. NN2: N'ton 5F **85**
Randsway NN9: Raun 7K **53**
Ranelagh Rd. NN8: Well 7C **66**
Rankine Ho. NN17: Corby 5J **13**
Rannoch Cl. NN15: K'ing 2G **43**
Rannoch Way NN17: Corby 4G **13**
Ransome Rd. NN4: Far C 4E **94**
RATBY **1B 132**
Rate's La. PE8: King C 2H **9**
Rathlin Cl. NN17: Corby 5H **13**
Rathmine Ct. NN14: Brou 6G **41**
RATLEY **1A 140**
RAUNDS . . . .**6J 53 (1B 138)**
Raunds Rd. NN9: Chel 6K **69**
NN9: Stanw . . . . . .1J **69 & 7F 53**
Raven Dr. NN15: Bar S 4J **43**
Ravensbank NN10: R'den 1E **80**
Ravenscourt NN17: Corby 5A **14**
Ravens Cft. NN4: N'ton 1B **100**
RAVENSDEN **3C 139**
RAVENSTHORPE . . . .**2B 34 (1C 137)**
Ravensthorpe Rd. NN6: E Had . . .2C **56**
RAVENSTONE
Leicestershire **1A 132**
Milton Keynes **3A 138**
Ravenstone Rd. NN7: Hort 2K **117**
Ravens Way NN3: N'ton 6F **87**
Rawley Cres. NN5: Dus 5F **83**
Rawlings Cl. NN11: Dav 2J **61**
Ray Cl. PE8: Oun 3H **21**
Raymond Cl. NN29: Woll 5F **91**
Raymond Rd. NN5: N'ton 7B **84**
Raynsford Rd. NN5: Dall 5A **84**
Rea Cl. NN4: N'ton 1D **100**
Rectory Bus. Cen. NN10: R'den . . .2E **80**
Rectory Cl. CV23: Bar 2C **54**
NN4: Gt Hou 2H **101**
NN6: Crick 4H **31**
NN9: Stanw 6J **53**
Rectory Ga. LE16: E Far 3J **25**
NN10: R'den 3E **80**
RECTORY FARM **1F 87**

Rectory Farm Rd. NN3: N'ton 1F **87**
Rectory Gdns. NN9: Irth 2B **68**
Rectory Hill NN14: C'ord 1G **47**
Rectory La. CV23: Bar 2C **54**
NN6: Holc 6H **37**
NN6: Wal 2H **37**
NN7: Mil M 5K **99**
NN7: Yar H 5G **103**
NN14: Orl 7B **44**
NN14: Woodf 7B **50**
OX17: Mid C 5C **118**
Rectory Rd. NN10: R'den 2E **80**
Rectory Wlk. NN15: Bar S 3H **43**
Rectory Way NN12: Wap 5C **112**
Redbourne Pk. NN4: Brack 4J **95**
Redding Cl. NN10: R'den 6D **80**
Redgrave Cl. NN15: K'ing 3B **42**
Red Hill Cl. NN8: Well 4A **66**
Red Hill Ct. NN6: Old 5E **36**
Red Hill Cres. NN29: Woll 3E **90**
Redhill Way NN9: Well 4K **65**
Red Ho. La. NN6: Hann 3K **37**
Red Ho. Rd. NN3: Moul P 6G **73**
Redhouse Rd. NN6: Hann 1A **64**
NN14: Orl 7A **44**
Redland Dr. NN2: K'thpe 2B **84**
Red Lion St. OX17: King S 1B **126**
Red Lodge Rd. PE8: Pole 4B **22**
Redmoor NN12: Tow 5B **114**
Red Row NN9: Raun 6J **53**
Redruth Cl. NN4: Del 6C **94**
Redwell Leisure Cen. 5K **65**
Redwell Rd. NN8: Well 6A **66**
Redwing Av. NN3: Moul 7K **73**
Redwood Cl. NN14: Des 3F **27**
NN29: Irch 6H **79**
Reedham Cl. NN5: Dus 5H **83**
Reedhill NN4: N'ton 6K **93**
Reedway NN3: N'ton 2H **85**
Reffield Cl. NN12: Tow 4D **114**
Regal Cl. NN3: Moul P 7G **73**
Regal Ct. NN10: R'den 4F **81**
Regal Dr. NN16: K'ing 3E **38**
Regency Cl. NN7: Weed 3C **62**
Regency Ct. NN10: R'den 2E **80**
Regent Cl. NN15: Bur L 2H **45**
Regent Rd. NN15: Bur L 2H **45**
Regent Sq.
NN1: N'ton . . . . .2H **131 (7D 84)**
Regent St. NN1: N'ton . . . .3G **131 (1D 94)**
NN8: Well 7B **66**
NN9: Fine 7G **47**
NN14: Des 1E **26**
NN16: K'ing 6D **38**
Regent Way NN7: Hort 3J **117**
Regiment Cl. NN4: Woot 1F **101**
Regpartridge Cl. NN5: Dus 7H **83**
Reigate Wlk. NN18: Corby 3G **17**
(not continuous)
Reims Ct. NN5: New D 4F **83**
Remus Ga. NN13: B'ley 5H **129**
Rendelsham Cl. NN16: K'ing 3C **38**
RENHOLD **3C 139**
Rennishaw Way NN2: N'ton 3G **85**
Repton Cl. NN3: N'ton 2A **86**
Reservoir Cl. NN9: Irth 4B **68**
NN14: Stan 3F **19**
Reservoir Rd. NN16: K'ing 5D **38**
Resthaven Rd. NN4: Woot 2E **100**
Restormel Cl. NN10: R'den 4G **81**
Retford Cl. NN10: R'den 2C **86**
Retreat, The PE9: Eas H 2B **6**
Reynard Pk. NN13: B'ley 6F **129**
Reynard Way NN17: Corby 7E **72**
Reynolds Cl. NN8: Well 5A **66**
NN15: Bar S 2J **43**
Reynolds Ct. NN18: Corby 1K **17**
Reynoldston Cl. NN4: Brack 6K **95**
Rhodes Cl. NN11: Dav 5H **59**
Rhosili Rd. NN4: Brack 5G **95**
Ribble Cl. NN5: N'ton 4A **84**
NN8: Well 6J **65**
Ribblesdale Av. NN17: Corby 6K **13**
Richard Cl. NN15: K'ing 4E **42**
Richardsons La. NN14: Lod 1D **40**
Richardson Way NN9: Raun 5K **53**
Richmond Av. NN15: K'ing 2H **43**
Richmond Cl. NN10: R'den 4F **81**
Richmond Ct. NN12: Tow 4C **114**
Richmond Rd. NN12: Tow 3C **114**
NN17: Corby 7K **13**
Richmond St. OX17: King S 1B **126**
Richmond Ter. NN5: N'ton 1C **94**
Rickyard Rd. NN3: N'ton 3A **86**
Rickyard Wlk. NN4: Gra P 6G **101**
Ricochet Total Fitness 5D **38**
Ridding Cl. NN18: Corby 3J **17**
Ride, The NN14: Des 1E **26**
Ride La. NN6: Pits 1D **72**
Rides Ct. NN3: Moul 5J **73**
Ridge, The NN29: Gt Dod 6K **77**
Ridge Rd. NN14: Isl 2F **51**
Ridge Wlk. NN3: West F 6B **86**

Ridgewalk—St Christopher's Dr.

Ridgewalk NN3: N'ton 5C 86
(Langsett Cl., not continuous)
NN3: N'ton 3G 87
(Wimborne Cl.)
Ridgeway NN3: West F 6K 85
NN8: Well 5A 66
Ridgeway, The NN11: Welt 1K 59
Ridgeway Furlong NN7: Neth H 6J 63
Ridgmont MK19: Dean 4E 124
Ridgmont Cl. MK19: Dean 4E 124
Ridgway Rd. NN15: Bar S 2K 43
Riding, The MK19: Dean 4E 124
Riding Ct. NN13: B'ley 6G 129
Riding Rd. NN13: B'ley 6G 129
Ridings, The NN1: N'ton 4J 131 (1E 94)
NN4: Gra P 6F 101
NN6: Brix 3J 35
NN7: Roa 2B 116
(not continuous)
NN14: Des 1B 26
Ridings Arc., The NN1: N'ton 4K 131
Ridley Ct. NN11: Dav 1H 61
Ridley St. NN16: K'ing 6C 38
RIDLINGTON 1A 134
Riggall Cl. NN14: Brou 7G 41
Riley Cl. NN3: N'ton 1F 87
NN11: Dav 6E 58
Riley Rd. NN16: K'ing 5A 38
Rillwood Ct. NN3: N'ton 2B 86
Ring, The OX17: Chac 2B 118
RINGSTEAD 1G 53 (1B 138)
Ringstead Cl. NN15: Bar S 5H 43
NN17: Corby 5G 13
Ringstead Rd. NN14: Den 7G 51
NN14: Gt Ad, Rin 1B 52
Ringtail Cl. NN9: Irth 4B 68
Ring Way NN4: N'ton 4B 94
Ringwell Cl. NN9: Irth 1B 68
Ringwood Cl. NN2: K'thpe 1B 84
Ripley Rd. LE16: Cotti 4C 12
Ripley Wlk. NN18: Corby 3H 17
Ripon Cl. NN4: N'ton 5B 94
Risdene Ct. *NN10: R'den 3E 80*
(off Newton Rd.)
Rise, The NN2: K'thpe 3C 84
RISELEY 2C 139
Rivercrest Rd. MK19: Old S 3J 125
Riverside Bus. Pk.
NN3: N'ton 7B 86
Riverside Cl. PE8: Oun 6J 21
Riverside Ct. NN7: Kisl 3C 92
NN7: Weed 4C 62
Riverside Dr. NN7: Weed 4C 62
Riverside Maltings PE8: Oun 4J 21
Riverside Way NN1: N'ton 2G 95
NN14: Isl 3F 51
Riverside Way Ind. Est.
NN1: N'ton 2G 95
Riverstone Way NN4: N'ton 5J 93
(not continuous)
River Vw. NN4: N'ton 3D 94
Riverview NN15: Bur L 4J 45
Riverview Gdns. NN14: Den 7G 51
Riverwell NN3: N'ton 4G 87
Rixon Cl. NN3: West F 5B 86
Rixon Rd. NN8: Well 4C 66
ROADE 2C 116 (3D 137)
Roadins Cl. NN15: K'ing 3C 42
Roadmender 3H 131
ROAD WEEDON 3E 62 (3C 137)
Robb's La. NN14: Low 6D 48
Roberson Cl. NN12: Tow 5C 114
Roberts Cl. MK19: Dean 5F 125
Roberts Fld. NN7: Neth H 6J 63
Roberts St. NN8: Well 1K 77
NN10: R'den 3F 81
NN29: Boz 3G 103
Robert St. NN1: N'ton 2J 131 (7E 84)
Robin Cl. NN12: Tow 6C 114
NN15: Bar S 4J 43
Robinia Cl. NN4: N'ton 4K 93
Robin La. NN8: Well 5B 66
Robin Ride NN13: B'ley 2F 129
Robin Rd. NN18: Corby 3K 17
Robins Cl. NN7: Hart 6G 117
Robinson Cl. NN16: K'ing 5B 38
Robinson Dr. NN13: B'ley 4E 128
Robinson Ho. NN3: N'ton 2B 86
Robinson Rd. NN10: R'den 3F 81
Robinson Way NN4: Woot 3H 101
NN16: K'ing 5B 38
Roche Cl. NN11: Dav 3H 61
Rochelle Way NN5: New D 4F 83
Rochester Cl. NN15: Bar S 3H 43
Rochester Rd. NN18: Corby 4K 17
Roche Way NN8: Well 6A 66
Rockcroft NN4: N'ton 2E 100
Rock Hill NN14: R'ell 6G 27
Rockhill Rd. NN6: Long B 2G 55
ROCKINGHAM 1G 13 (2A 134)
Rockingham Castle 2G 13
Rockingham Castle Est.
LE16: Rock 2G 13
Rockingham Cl. NN11: Dav 6G 59
NN14: Thra 3J 51
Rockingham Ct. NN10: R'den 5D 80
Rockingham Hills PE8: Oun 3G 21
Rockingham M. NN17: Corby 6B 14
Rockingham Motor Speedway 1F 15
Rockingham Paddocks
NN16: K'ing 3D 38
Rockingham Rd. LE16: Cotti 4C 12
NN4: Del 5D 94
NN14: R'ton 1C 38
NN16: K'ing 4C 38
NN17: Corby 3H 13
NN17: Corby, Gret 7A 8
Rockleigh Cl. NN9: Fine 6J 47
Rock Rd. NN9: Fine 6J 47
PE8: Oun 4H 21
Rock St. NN8: Well 7A 66
Roderick Way NN11: Dav 6G 59
Rodney Cl. NN11: Dav 2K 61
Rodney Dr. NN17: Corby 5G 13
Roe Rd. NN1: N'ton 6G 85
Rokeby Wlk. NN5: Dus 5J 83
Roland Way NN10: High F 6E 68
Rolfe Cres. NN7: Neth H 6J 63
ROLLESTON 1D 133
Roman Cl. NN4: Woot 3G 101
NN14: Des 1E 26
NN17: Weld 5J 15
Roman Rd. NN14: Stan 3D 18
Roman Way NN4: Gra P 4F 101
NN9: Raun 6K 53
NN10: High F 5E 68
NN11: Dav 5H 59
NN13: B'ley 5H 129
NN14: Des 2D 26
NN14: Thra 2J 51
NN29: Irch 6J 79
Romany Rd. NN2: N'ton 5F 85
Romney Rd. NN18: Corby 1K 17
Romulus Cl. NN4: Woot 3G 101
Romulus Way NN13: B'ley 4H 129
Rookery, The NN4: Gra P 5F 101
Rookery La. NN2: K'thpe 1B 84
NN12: Stoke B 5E 116
Rookery Open Farm 5E 116
ROOTHAM'S GREEN 3D 139
Rose Av. NN10: R'den 4C 80
NN17: Weld 5J 15
Rosebay Rd. NN14: Des 1D 26
Rosebery Av. NN5: N'ton 1A 94
Rosebery St. NN14: Rin 1G 53
NN15: Bur L 3J 45
NN16: K'ing 7E 38
Rose Cl. NN7: Hart 5J 117
NN14: Brou 5H 41
NN14: R'ell 7H 27
NN18: Corby 4K 17
Rose Ct. NN17: Weld 5J 15
NN29: Irch 5J 79
(off High St.)
Rosedale Av. NN17: Corby 7K 13
Rosedale Rd. NN2: K'thpe 3E 84
Rose Dr. NN13: B'ley 3E 128
Rose Hall La. OX17: Mid C 6D 118
Rose Hill NN9: Fine 6H 47
Rose Hill Way NN14: Maw 5C 40
Roseholme Rd. NN1: N'ton 7H 85
Rosemoor Dr. NN4: N'ton 1D 100
Rosemount Dr. NN15: K'ing 3E 42
Rosenella Cl. NN4: N'ton 4A 94
Rose Paddock NN14: Woodf 6B 50
Roses Cl. NN29: Woll 3D 90
Rose Ter. NN14: Woodf 6B 50
(not continuous)
Rosette Cl. NN5: Dus 6H 83
Rosewood Cl. NN11: Dav 5H 59
Rosewood Pl. NN16: K'ing 5E 38
Rosgill Pl. NN3: N'ton 4J 85
Rossendale Dr. NN15: Bar S 5J 43
Rossetti Rd. NN18: Corby 1K 17
Rossiter Ho. NN13: B'ley 5F 129
Ross Rd. NN5: N'ton 1K 93
Rotherhithe Cl. NN4: N'ton 5A 94
ROTHERSTHORPE 2F 99 (3D 137)
Rothersthorpe Av. NN4: Far C 4B 94
Rothersthorpe Av. Ind. Est.
NN4: Far C 4B 94
Rothersthorpe Cres. NN4: Far C 4B 94
Rothersthorpe La. NN4: N'ton 5B 94
Rothersthorpe Rd.
NN4: Far C, N'ton 5A 94
NN7: Kisl 4C 92
Rothesay Rd. NN2: N'ton 4G 85
Rothesay Ter. NN2: N'ton 4G 85
ROTHLEY 1B 132
ROTHWELL 6H 27 (3A 134)
Rothwell Gullet Nature Reserve 5E 26
Rothwell Rd. NN14: Des 2D 26
NN16: K'ing 5A 38
(not continuous)
Rotten Row NN29: Woll 4E 90
Rotton Row NN9: Raun 5J 53
Roughton Cl. NN15: K'ing 4D 42
Round, The NN14: Maw 6A 40
Round Cl. NN11: Welt 1K 59
Roundhill Rd. NN15: K'ing 2D 42
ROUND SPINNEY 6B 74
Round Spinney Ind. Est.
NN3: N'ton 6B 74
Roundtown OX17: Ayn 7E 126
Roundway, The NN11: Dav 4J 59
Roundwood Way NN5: Dus 6E 82
ROUSHAM 3A 140
Rowallen Way NN11: Dav 6F 59
Rowan Av. NN3: N'ton 1K 85
NN14: Maw 6B 40
Rowan Cl. NN4: Gra P 6F 101
NN8: Well 7K 65
NN12: Tow 5B 114
NN13: B'ley 2G 129
Rowan Ct. *NN17: Corby 4K 13*
(off Welland Va. Rd.)
Rowans, The NN11: Dav 6H 59
Rowan Way NN11: Woodf H 2C 108
Rowell Way PE8: Oun 6K 21
Rowlandson Cl. NN3: West F 5B 86
Rowlett Cl. NN10: High F 7F 69
Rowlett Rd. NN17: Corby 5H 13
Rowley Way NN2: K'thpe 7F 73
Rowley Wood La. NN7: Hart 5G 117
ROWSHAM 3D 141
Rowtree Rd. NN4: N'ton 1A 100
ROXTON 3D 139
Roxton Cl. NN15: Bar S 5J 43
Royal and Derngate Theatres, The
5J 131 (2E 94)
Royal Cl. NN11: Dav 7G 59
Royal Gdns. NN14: Des 3C 26
Royal Oak Ind. Est. NN11: Dav 7E 58
Royal Oak La. OX17: Mid C 6D 118
Royal Oak Way Nth. NN11: Dav 6E 58
Royal Oak Way Sth. NN11: Dav 7E 58
Royal Star Dr. NN11: Dav 6F 59
Royal Ter. NN1: N'ton 2H 131 (7D 84)
Royce Cl. NN17: Corby 4A 14
Royce's La. PE8: King C 2H 9
Rubens Wlk. NN18: Corby 1K 17
Ruddington Cl. NN3: N'ton 7B 86
Rudge M. NN5: Dus 6E 82
Rudgeway NN13: Even 2C 130
Rufford Av. NN3: N'ton 7B 86
Rufford Cl. NN15: Bar S 5J 43
Rufford Wlk. NN18: Corby 7G 13
RUGBY 1B 136
Rugby & Daventry Sailing Club 4G 59
Rugby Rd. CV23: Bar 1C 54
CV23: Kil 4A 30
CV23: Lil, Clif D 3A 28
NN7: Lwr H 5B 70
Ruins, The NN12: Tow 3C 114
Runnell La. PE8: Nass 5H 7
Runnymede Gdns. NN3: N'ton 5C 86
Rush Cl. NN7: Hart 5J 117
RUSHDEN 3E 80 (2B 138)
Rushden & Diamonds FC 2E 68
Rushden & Higham Ferrers By-Pass
NN10: High F, R'den 4F 69
Rushden Cen., The *NN10: R'den 3E 80*
(off Newton Rd.)
Rushden Rd. NN10: R'den 6K 81
NN10: Wym 7D 80
Rushden Station Transport Mus. 2E 80
Rushden Town Indoor Bowls Club
7C 68
Rushes, The NN15: Bur L 4J 45
RUSHMERE 1K 95
Rushmere Av. NN1: N'ton 1J 95
Rushmere Cl. NN9: Raun 7H 53
NN14: Isl 2F 51
Rushmere Cres. NN1: N'ton 1J 95
Rushmere Rd. NN1: N'ton 3H 95
Rushmere Way NN1: N'ton 2J 95
NN10: R'den 1D 80
Rushmills NN4: N'ton 4J 95
RUSHTON 2B 46 (3A 134)
Rushton Rd. LE16: Des, Wilb 5H 11
NN14: Des 1E 26
NN14: R'ell 6G 27
Rushton Triangular Lodge 2K 27
Rushwell Cl. NN14: Gt Ad 1A 52
Rushy End NN4: N'ton 2C 100
Ruskin Av. NN8: Well 1H 77
Ruskin Rd. NN2: K'thpe 2D 84
Ruskin Way NN11: Dav 3H 61
Russell Ct. NN10: R'den 3E 80
Russell Ri. NN7: Flore 2F 63
Russell Sq. NN3: Moul 7K 73
Russell St. NN16: K'ing 7E 38
Russell Way NN10: High F 6E 68
Russet Dr. NN3: N'ton 4D 86
Rutherford Ct. NN17: Corby 4C 14
Rutherford Dr. NN8: Well 1F 77
Rutherford Way NN11: Dav 6E 58
Rutherglen Rd. NN17: Corby 6A 14
Ruth Gdns. NN16: K'ing 6G 39
Rutland Cl. NN17: Corby 6G 13
Rutland Ct. NN14: Des 1C 26
Rutland St. NN16: K'ing 6E 38
Rutland Wlk. NN3: Moul 6J 73
Rycroft Cl. NN8: Well 7J 65
Rydal NN8: Well 2G 77
Rydal Mt. NN3: N'ton 3K 85
Rydalside NN4: N'ton 4A 94
NN15: K'ing 1F 43
Ryder Ct. NN18: Corby 6E 16
Ryder Vw. NN8: Well 5H 65
Rydinghurst NN3: Moul 4J 73
Ryeburn Way NN8: Well 7K 65
Ryebury Hill NN8: Well 2F 67
Rye Cl. NN10: R'den 5F 81
NN15: Bur L 2K 45
Ryefields NN6: Spra 6C 34
Ryehill Cl. NN5: Dus 4H 83
NN6: Long B 2G 55
NN9: Irth 4B 68
NN14: Ish 3F 45
Ryehill Ct. NN5: Dus 4H 83
Ryehill Rd. NN3: N'ton 3C 86
Ryeland Rd. NN5: Dus 6F 83
Ryeland Way NN5: Dus 5F 83
RYHALL 1C 135
Ryland Rd. NN2: N'ton 4F 85
NN3: Moul 5K 73
Ryle Dr. NN8: Well 1F 77
Rylstone, The NN8: Well 2G 77
Ryngwell Cl. NN6: Brix 4H 35
RYTON 3A 132
RYTON-ON-DUNSMORE 1A 136

S

Sackville St. NN9: Raun 6J 53
NN14: Thra 3H 51
NN16: K'ing 5C 38
SADDINGTON 2C 133
Saddleback Rd. NN5: N'ton 1J 93
Saddlers, The NN4: Gra P 5G 101
Saddlers Sq. NN3: N'ton 7C 74
Saddlers Way NN9: Raun 7G 53
Saffron Cl. NN4: N'ton 3E 100
Saffron Rd. NN10: High F 5E 68
Sage Cl. NN3: N'ton 2B 86
Saimon Cl. NN13: B'ley 3F 129
St Alban's Cl. NN3: Spin H 3J 85
NN15: K'ing 1J 43
St Albans Pl. NN29: Woll 5E 90
St Alban's Rd. NN3: Spin H 3J 85
St Amandas Cl. NN15: K'ing 7H 39
St Andrews Cl. NN14: Brou 6H 41
NN14: Titch 2J 49
St Andrews Ct. NN1: N'ton 3G 131
NN14: Brou 6H 41
St Andrews Cres. NN8: Well 4K 77
St Andrews Dr. NN11: Dav 7K 59
St Andrew's Ho. *NN1: N'ton 1G 95*
(off Billing Rd.)
St Andrews La. NN14: C'ord 2G 47
NN14: Titch 1J 49
St Andrews Rd.
NN1: N'ton 5F 131 (2C 94)
NN2: Sem 5F 131 (2C 94)
NN6: E Had 2C 56
St Andrew's St.
NN1: N'ton 2G 131 (1D 94)
NN16: K'ing 7D 38
(Eden St.)
NN16: K'ing 6D 38
(off Lindsay St.)
St Andrew's Wlk. *NN17: Corby 7C 14*
(off High St.)
St Andrews Way NN14: Brou 6H 41
St Annes Cl. NN11: Dav 3H 61
NN13: B'ley 3E 128
St Anne's Rd. NN15: K'ing 1J 43
St Ann's Ct. PE8: Oun 5H 21
St Anthony PE8: Oun 5H 21
St Anthonys Cl. NN11: Dav 3G 61
St Anthony's Hill NN14: Des 3D 26
St Anthony's Rd. NN15: K'ing 2H 43
St Anthony's Wlk. NN14: Des 3D 26
St Augustine's Cl. NN15: K'ing 1J 43
St Augustin Way NN11: Dav 3J 61
St Barnabas' Cl. NN15: K'ing 1J 43
St Barnabas Ho. NN1: N'ton 3G 131
St Barnabas St. NN8: Well 1K 77
St Bartholomew's Cl. NN15: K'ing 1J 43
St Bartholomews Ho.
NN1: N'ton 3H 131
St Benedict's Mt. NN4: N'ton 6K 93
St Bernards Ct. NN15: K'ing 1H 43
St Botolph's Rd. NN15: Bar S 4H 43
St Catherines Ct. NN11: Dav 3G 61
St Catherine's Rd. NN15: K'ing 1H 43
St Cecilia's Cl. NN15: K'ing 1H 43
St Chad's Cl. NN15: K'ing 1H 43
St Christopher's Cl. NN15: K'ing 1J 43
St Christopher's Dr. PE8: Oun 6K 21

St Christopher's Wlk. NN3: N'ton . .7J 85
St Clements Ct. NN15: K'ing 3D 42
St Crispin Av. NN8: Well 3A 78
St Crispin Cl. NN15: Bur L 1K 45
St Crispin Cres. NN5: Dus 6E 82
St Crispin Dr. NN5: Dus 7F 83
  NN5: Upton 1F 93
St Crispin Retirement Village
  NN5: Upton 7F 83
  (not continuous)
St Crispin Rd. NN6: E Bart 2E 88
St Crispin Way NN9: Raun 4H 53
St Davids Cl. NN6: Brix 4H 35
  NN15: K'ing 1H 43
St David's Cl. NN13: B'ley 3H 129
St David's Rd. NN2: K'thpe 4D 84
  NN6: Brix 4G 35
  NN10: R'den 2A 80
St Dunstan's Cl. NN15: K'ing 2H 43
St Dunstans Ri. NN4: N'ton 6K 93
St Edmunds Cl. NN11: Dav 4H 61
St Edmund's Rd.
  NN1: N'ton 4K 131 (1F 95)
St Edmund's St. NN1: N'ton 1F 95
St Edmund's Ter.
  NN1: N'ton 3K 131 (1F 95)
St Emilion Cl. NN5: Dus 5E 82
St Francis Av. NN8: Well 6B 84
St Francis' Cl. NN15: K'ing 1J 43
St George's Av. NN2: N'ton 6D 84
St Georges Cl. NN12: Tow 4C 114
St Georges Ho. NN1: N'ton 3H 131
St Georges Pl. NN2: N'ton 6D 84
  (off Kingsthorpe Rd.)
St Georges Row NN9: Chel 6J 69
St George's St.
  NN1: N'ton 2G 131 (7D 84)
St George's Way NN10: R'den 2C 80
St Giles Cl. NN14: Des 2D 26
  NN15: K'ing 1J 43
St Giles' Sq. NN1: N'ton . . .5J 131 (2E 94)
St Giles' St. NN1: N'ton . . .5J 131 (2E 94)
St Giles Ter. NN1: N'ton . . .4K 131 (1E 94)
  (not continuous)
St Gregory's Rd. NN3: N'ton 3A 86
St Helens Cl. NN6: Thorn 3D 32
St Hilda's Cl. NN11: Dav 3H 61
St Hughes Cl. NN11: Dav 3H 61
ST JAMES' 2B 94
St James Cl. NN10: R'den 1E 80
  NN11: Dav 2H 61
  (off Newlands)
  NN15: K'ing 2J 43
St James' Cres. NN14: Thra 3J 51
ST JAMES' END 1B 94 (2D 137)
St James Ind. Est. NN18: Corby 1B 18
St James Mill Bus. Pk.
  NN5: N'ton 2A 94
St James' Mill Rd. NN5: N'ton 2B 94
St James' Mill Rd. E.
  NN1: N'ton 7F 131 (3C 94)
St James' Mill Rd. Ind. Est.
  NN5: N'ton 3B 94
St James Pk. 5G 129
St James' Pk. Rd. NN5: N'ton 1B 94
  (not continuous)
St James' Retail Pk.
  NN1: N'ton 6F 131 (2C 94)
St James Rd.
  NN5: N'ton 5F 131 (1B 94)
  NN13: B'ley 6F 129
  NN18: Corby 1B 18
St James St.
  NN1: N'ton 6H 131 (2D 94)
  NN11: Dav 2H 61
St John's Av. NN2: K'thpe 7D 84
  NN11: Dav 3G 61
St Johns Cl. NN1: N'ton 6J 131
St Johns Ho. NN1: N'ton 3G 131
  NN8: Well 7A 66
  (off St John's St.)
St John's La. MK19: Wick 5C 124
St John's Pl. NN17: Corby 7C 14
St Johns Rd. NN15: K'ing 2G 43
St John's Sq. NN11: Dav 1H 61
St Johns Sta. Pas. NN1: N'ton 6J 131
St John's St.
  NN1: N'ton 6H 131 (2D 94)
  NN8: Well 7A 66
St John's Ter.
  NN1: N'ton 5J 131 (2E 94)
St Johns Wlk. NN3: N'ton 5A 86
St John's Way NN7: Pid 2F 117
St Joseph's Cl. NN15: K'ing 1J 43
St Julien Cl. NN5: New D 4F 83
St Katharine's Way NN29: Irch 4H 79
St Katherine's Cl. NN1: N'ton 4G 131
St Katherine's Sq.
  NN1: N'ton 4G 131 (1D 94)
St Katherine's St.
  NN1: N'ton 5G 131 (2D 94)
St Laurence Way NN9: Stanw 1J 69

St Lawrence Ct. NN6: Long B 1H 55
St Lawrence Ho. NN1: N'ton 3H 131
St Lawrence Rd. NN12: Tow 5C 114
St Lawrence Rd. Sth.
  NN12: Tow 5C 114
St Lawrence Wlk. NN10: Wym 7E 80
  (off Church La.)
St Leonards Cl. NN15: K'ing 1H 43
St Leonards Ct. NN4: Far C 4D 94
St Leonard's Rd. NN4: Far C 4D 94
St Lukes Cl. NN5: Dus 6E 82
  NN6: Spra 6C 34
  NN15: K'ing 1J 43
St Lukes Ho. NN1: N'ton 3G 131
St Luke's Rd. NN18: Corby 1B 18
St Magdalenes Rd. NN15: K'ing . . .7H 39
St Margarets Av. NN10: R'den 4C 80
St Margaret's Gdns. NN5: Dall 5A 84
St Marks Cl. NN10: R'den 3B 80
  NN15: K'ing 1J 43
St Mark's Cres. NN2: K'thpe 7C 72
St Marks Ho. NN1: N'ton 3G 131
St Mark's Rd. NN18: Corby 1B 18
St Martins Cl. NN2: K'thpe 2D 84
St Martins Ho. NN1: N'ton 3H 131
St Mary's Av. NN9: Fine 6H 47
  NN10: R'den 4D 80
St Marys Cl. NN14: Thra 2K 51
  PE8: Nass 5G 7
  PE8: Wood 5G 9
St Marys Ct. NN1: N'ton 4G 131
  NN7: G'ton 6D 98
  NN9: Fine 6G 47
  (off Church St.)
St Mary's Hill PE8: Wood 5G 9
St Mary's Paddock NN8: Well 1D 78
St Marys Rd. NN15: K'ing 1D 42
  NN29: Boz 3H 103
  NN29: Woll 4E 90
St Mary's St. NN1: N'ton . . .4F 131 (1D 94)
St Mary's Vw. NN7: Roa 1C 116
St Mary's Way NN7: Weed 4C 62
  PE8: Nass 5G 7
St Matthew's Pde. NN2: N'ton 6G 85
St Matthew's Rd. NN15: K'ing 2J 43
St Michael's Av. NN1: N'ton 7F 85
St Michael's Gdns. NN15: K'ing . . .2E 42
St Michael's La. NN29: Woll 4E 90
St Michael's Mt. NN1: N'ton 7F 85
St Michael's Rd.
  NN1: N'ton 3K 131 (1E 94)
  NN15: K'ing 2D 42
ST NEOTS 2D 139
St Nicholas Cl. NN15: K'ing 7H 39
St Nicholas Ct. NN29: Gt Dod 7K 77
  (off High St.)
St Nicholas Rd. NN29: Gt Dod 7J 77
St Nicholas Way NN14: Isl 2F 51
St Oswalds Cl. NN15: K'ing 1H 43
St Osyths La. PE8: Oun 5J 21
St Patrick St. NN1: N'ton 2G 131
St Pauls Ct. MK11: Stony S 3K 125
  NN2: Sem 6D 84
  (off Norfolk Ter.)
  NN15: K'ing 1D 42
St Pauls Gdns. NN14: Thra 3H 51
St Pauls Rd. NN2: Sem 6D 84
St Paul's Ter. NN2: Sem 6D 84
St Peter's Av. NN10: R'den 2C 80
  NN16: K'ing 1D 42
  (not continuous)
St Peters Cl. NN11: Dav 3G 61
  NN14: Stan 4G 19
St Peters Ct. NN9: Raun 6J 53
St Peters Gdns. NN1: N'ton 5G 131
  NN3: West F 5A 86
St Peters Ga. NN13: B'ley 4H 129
St Peter's Ho. NN1: N'ton 4G 131
St Peters M. NN16: K'ing 7E 38
  (off Gladstone St.)
St Peters Rd. NN13: B'ley 3G 129
  PE8: Oun 3H 21
St Peters Sq. NN1: N'ton 5G 131
St Peter's St.
  NN1: N'ton 5F 131 (2C 94)
St Peters Wlk.
  NN1: N'ton 5H 131 (2D 94)
St Peters Way
  NN1: N'ton 5F 131 (2C 94)
  NN7: Cog 1J 97
  NN7: Weed 4C 62
  NN9: Irth 2C 68
  NN17: Corby 7B 14
St Peter's Way Retail Pk.
  NN1: N'ton 5G 131 (2D 94)
St Philip's Cl. NN15: K'ing 1J 43
St Rochus Dr. NN8: Well 4B 78
St Rumbolds Rd. NN13: B'ley 4G 129
St Rumbolds Dr. OX17: King S 1C 126
St Saviour's Rd. NN15: K'ing 1J 43
St Simon's Cl. NN15: K'ing 1J 43
St Stephens Ho. NN1: N'ton 3G 131
St Stephen's Rd. NN15: K'ing 1J 43

St Swithins Cl. NN15: K'ing 7H 39
St Theresa's Cl. NN15: K'ing 1H 43
St Thomas Rd. NN7: Braf G 4G 97
St Valentine's Cl. NN15: K'ing 1H 43
St Vincents Av. NN15: K'ing 1H 43
St Wilfrids Rd. PE8: Oun 3H 21
Salcey Av. NN7: Hart 5H 117
Salcey Cl. NN7: Hart 5J 117
  NN11: Dav 6G 59
  NN15: Bar S 5J 43
Salcey Ct. NN5: Upton 3J 93
  (off Webb Dr.)
Salcey Forest Info. Cen. 3D 137
Salcey Ri. NN7: Pid 3G 117
Salcey St. NN4: Del 5D 94
Salcombe Rd. NN18: Corby 2K 17
Salem NN6: Long B 1G 55
Salem Cl. NN6: Long B 2G 55
Salem La. NN8: Well 7A 66
Salen Cl. NN15: Bar S 5K 43
Salford Cl. NN6: Welf 2H 29
Salisbury Rd. NN8: Well 7D 66
Salisbury St. NN2: Sem . . .1F 131 (6C 84)
  NN16: K'ing 5E 38
Salisbury Wlk. NN18: L Oak 5K 17
Sallow Av. NN3: N'ton 3F 87
Sallow Rd. NN17: Corby 4F 15
Salmons La. OX17: Mid C 6E 118
SALPH END 3C 139
Salthouse Rd. NN4: Brack 5H 95
Salt Pikes NN6: Brix 5H 35
Saltwell Sq. NN3: N'ton 4F 87
Samuel Pl. NN17: Corby 5B 14
Samuels Cl. NN9: Stanw 1J 69
Samwell La. NN5: Upton 2H 93
Samwell Way NN4: N'ton 6H 93
Sandalwood Ct. NN18: Corby 3K 17
Sandby Rd. NN18: Corby 2J 17
Sanders Cl. NN8: Well 4C 66
  NN11: Braun 1A 58
Sanders La. NN12: Pot 6H 123
Sanders Lodge Ind. Est.
  NN10: R'den 2A 80
Sanderson PE8: Oun 4H 21
Sanderson Cl. NN15: K'ing 2C 42
Sanders Pk. NN8: Well 3C 66
Sanders Rd. NN8: Well 3B 66
Sanders Ter. NN6: Long B 1H 55
Sanders Wlk. PE9: Colly 6C 6
Sandfield Cl. NN3: Moul P 7J 73
SANDFORD ST MARTIN 3A 140
Sandhill Rd. NN9: N'ton 1B 94
  (not continuous)
Sandhills NN6: Spra 5C 34
Sandhills Cl. NN2: K'thpe 7C 72
Sandhills Rd. NN2: K'thpe 7C 72
Sandhurst Cl. NN4: N'ton 7C 94
Sandiland Rd. NN3: N'ton 4J 85
Sandlands Av. NN14: Brig 2D 20
Sandlands Cl. NN14: Brig 3D 20
Sandover NN4: N'ton 2E 100
Sandown Cl. NN18: Gt Oak 6J 17
Sandpiper Cl. NN15: Bur L 2H 45
Sandpiper La. NN8: Well 5B 66
Sandringham Cl. NN1: N'ton 7J 85
  NN8: Well 3J 77
  NN10: R'den 4D 80
  NN12: Tow 5C 114
  NN13: B'ley 4F 129
Sandringham Ct. NN15: K'ing 5F 43
Sandringham Rd. NN1: N'ton 7H 85
  OX17: King S 1B 126
Sandringham Wlk. NN18: Corby . . .4K 17
Sands Cl. NN12: Pat 5G 105
SANDY .3D 139
Sandy Cl. NN8: Well 6A 66
Sandy Hill La. NN3: Moul 4B 74
Sandyhome Rd. NN12: Tow 4B 114
Sandy La. NN4: Gra P 4F 101
  NN5: Dus, New D 5E 82
  NN6: Chu B 5H 71
  NN7: Harp 2D 92
Sandy La. Link Rd.
  NN7: Harp 7D 82
Saneco La. NN6: Brix 2H 35
Sansom Ct. NN3: N'ton 3A 86
Sansome Cl. NN7: Hack 1G 117
SAPCOTE 2A 132
SAPLEY 1D 139
Saplings, The NN6: K'ing 2E 38
Sapphire Cl. NN15: K'ing 1E 42
Sarek Pk. NN4: N'ton 1A 100
Sargeants La. NN4: Col 4D 100
Sargent Rd. NN18: Corby 2K 17
Sarjeant Ct. NN14: R'ell 4A 22
  (off Hospital Hill)
Sarrington Rd. NN17: Corby 5K 13
Sartoris Rd. NN10: R'den 3C 80
Saruman La. NN3: N'ton 7E 74
Sassoon Cl. NN8: Well 6G 65
Sassoon M. NN8: Well 7G 65
Saunders Cl. NN16: K'ing 1C 42
Savill Cl. NN4: N'ton 1D 100

SAWBRIDGE 2B 136
SAWTRY 3D 135
Sawyers Cres. NN9: Chel 6J 69
Saxby Cres. NN8: Well 1D 78
Saxilby Cl. NN18: Corby 2H 17
Saxon Acre NN13: B'ley 4G 129
Saxon Av. NN4: Gra P 6E 100
Saxon Cl. NN10: High F 5E 68
  NN14: Des 2D 26
Saxon Ct. NN8: Well 3B 66
Saxon Dale NN16: K'ing 3D 38
Saxon Hgts. NN6: Brix 5H 35
Saxonlea Cl. NN10: R'den 2B 80
Saxon Lodge NN6: E Bart 2D 88
Saxon Ri. NN5: Dus 7G 83
  NN6: E Bart 2D 88
  NN29: Irch 5K 79
Saxon St. NN3: N'ton 5J 85
Saxon Way NN9: Raun 6K 53
Saxon Way E. NN18: Corby 6E 16
  (not continuous)
Saxon Way W. NN18: Corby 5E 16
Sayers Cl. NN12: Silv 4H 121
SCALDWELL 7A 36 (1D 137)
Scaldwell Rd. NN6: Brix 2J 35
  NN6: Old 5C 36
Scaldwell Rd. Ind. Est. NN6: Brix . . .2J 35
  (off Scaldwell Rd.)
Scapa Rd. NN17: Corby 5H 13
Scarborough St. NN9: Irth 2B 68
Scarborough Wlk. NN18: Corby . . .2G 17
Scarletwell St.
  NN1: N'ton 3F 131 (1C 94)
Scarletwell Ter.
  NN1: N'ton 3F 131 (1C 94)
Scarplands, The NN5: Dus 1H 93
Scharpwell NN9: Irth 1B 68
Scholars Ct. NN1: N'ton . . .6K 131 (2E 94)
Scholars Row NN14: Maw 6B 40
School NN9: L Harr . . . . . .7D 44 & 1H 65
School Cl. CV23: Bar 3C 54
  NN6: Yel 5B 28
  NN11: Braun 1B 58
  NN12: Greens N 1H 113
School End OX17: Ayn 7E 126
School Farm Yd. LE16: West W . . .2D 10
School Hill LE16: Mid 5A 12
  NN11: Newn 7J 61
  NN29: Irch 5J 79
School Ho. PE8: Oun 5J 21
  (off New St.)
School La. LE16: Bray 7B 10
  LE16: Cotti 4B 12
  LE16: Wilb 5H 11
  NN3: Moul 4K 73
  NN4: Gra P 5F 101
  NN6: Hann 4K 37
  NN6: Nas 2H 33
  NN6: Scal 7A 36
  NN6: Yel 5C 28
  NN7: Harp 1A 92
  NN7: Hart 5H 117
  NN7: Kisl 3C 92
  NN7: Quin 7J 101
  NN10: High F 5E 68
  NN11: Badby 5C 104
  NN11: Eyd 7D 108
  NN12: Abt 6J 113
  NN12: Greens N 1H 113
  NN12: Wap 5C 112
  NN12: Yar G 3J 123
  NN13: Even 2C 130
  NN14: Den 7G 51
  NN14: Isl 3F 51
  NN14: R'ell 6G 27
  NN14: Titch 1H 49
  NN16: K'ing 7D 38
  NN17: Weld 2G 15
  NN29: Irch 5H 79
  PE8: Warm 2H 23
School Pl. NN18: Corby 1J 17
School Rd. NN6: Spra 5C 34
  NN12: Ast, Pat 5H 105
  NN14: Maw 6B 40
  NN17: Gret 6C 8
  NN29: Irch 5H 79
School St. NN11: Dav 1F 61
  NN11: Woodf H 2D 108
  OX17: Sulg 6G 111
School Wlk. NN8: Well 4B 78
School Way NN3: N'ton 4K 85
Scirocco Cl. NN3: Moul P 7F 73
Scotgate NN17: Harr 2B 8
Scotia Cl. NN4: Brack 5K 95
SCOTLAND END 2A 140
Scotland St. NN16: K'ing 6E 38
Scotney Cl. NN4: N'ton 7D 94
Scotney Way NN14: Thra 3J 51
Scotsmere NN9: Irth 1B 68
Scott Av. NN14: R'ell 6H 27
Scotter Cl. NN6: Rav 2B 34
  NN11: Dav 6H 59
Scotter Wlk. NN18: Corby 2H 17

Scott Rd. NN8: Well 2H 77
NN16: K'ing 4E 38
NN17: Corby 7B 14
Scott's La. LE16: Wilb 5H 11
SCRAPTOFT 1C 133
Scribers Dr. NN5: Upton 3H 93
Scribers M. NN5: Upton 3H 93
Scriveners La. NN12: Pur E 6F 115
Scrivens Hill NN11: Woodf H 2E 108
Scully Cl. NN4: Woot 1F 101
Scythe Rd. NN11: Dav 4H 59
Seaford Wlk. NN18: Corby 1G 17
Seagrave Ct. NN3: N'ton 1E 86
Seagrave St. NN15: K'ing 2E 42
Sears Cl. NN7: Flore 1F 63
Sears Ho. NN1: N'ton 7G 85
(off Lea Rd.)
SEATON 2B 134
Seaton Cres. NN18: Corby 2K 17
Seaton Dr. NN3: N'ton 5C 86
Seaton Rd. NN17: Harr 1A 8
Second Av. NN8: Well 2H 77
Second La. NN5: N'ton 1A 94
Second St. NN13: Crou 7C 130
Sedbergh Rd. NN18: Corby 2H 17
Sedge Cl. NN14: Thra 4G 51
Sedgemoor Ct. NN11: Dav 4H 59
Sedgemoor Way NN11: Dav 4H 59
Sedgwick Cl. NN3: N'ton 3C 86
Seedfield Cl. NN3: West F 5B 86
Seedfield Wlk. NN3: N'ton 6C 86
Selby Cl. NN15: K'ing 1H 43
Selby Gdns. NN29: Boz 3G 103
Selby Wlk. NN18: Corby 2H 17
Selsey Rd. NN18: Corby 1G 17
Selston Wlk. NN3: N'ton 7A 86
Selwyn Cl. NN11: Dav 4H 61
SEMILONG 6D 84
Semilong Ho.
NN2: Sem 1G 131 (7D 84)
Semilong Rd.
NN2: Sem 1G 131 (7D 84)
Senna Dr. NN12: Tow 1C 114
Sentinel Rd. NN4: N'ton 6K 93
Sentry Cl. NN4: Woot 1E 100
Senwick Dr. NN8: Well 1D 78
Senwick Rd. NN8: Well 1D 78
Sepals Way NN4: Upton 6F 93
Serve Cl. NN8: Well 4B 78
Setchell's Yd. PE8: Oun 5H 21
(off West St.)
Settlers Flds. NN15: K'ing 3C 42
Seven Sisters Cl. NN13: F'hoe 6H 119
Severn, The NN11: Dav 2F 61
Severn Cl. NN8: Well 6H 65
Severn Ct. NN15: Bur L 2J 45
Severn Dr. NN5: N'ton 4A 84
Severn Wlk. NN17: Corby 4H 13
Severn Way NN16: K'ing 4C 38
Sewter Gdns. PE8: Nass 4G 7
Sexton Cl. NN11: Dav 7G 59
Seymour Pl. PE8: Oun 3G 21
Seymour St. NN5: N'ton 1B 94
SHACKERSTONE 1A 132
Shackleton Cl. NN14: R'ell 7H 27
Shackleton Dr. NN11: Dav 5G 59
Shadowfax Dr. NN3: N'ton 1E 86
Shaftesbury Rd. NN18: Corby 7G 13
Shaftesbury St. NN16: K'ing 7E 38
Shakespeare Av. NN11: Dav 1G 61
Shakespeare Dr. NN15: Bur L 2H 45
Shakespeare Ho. NN1: N'ton 7F 85
Shakespeare Rd.
NN1: N'ton 1K 131 (7F 85)
NN8: Well 2G 77
NN10: R'den 3B 80
NN16: K'ing 4D 38
Shakespeare Way NN17: Corby 4J 13
Shale End NN5: Dus 3F 83
SHALSTONE 2C 140
SHANGTON .2D 133
Shankley Way NN5: N'ton 7B 84
Shannon Cl. NN10: R'den 2G 81
Shannon Ct. NN18: Corby 2K 17
Shannon Way NN15: Bur L 2J 45
Shap Grn. NN3: N'ton 2K 85
Shard Cl. NN4: N'ton 2D 100
Sharman Cl. NN11: Dav 5H 59
Sharman Rd. NN5: N'ton 2B 94
NN8: Well 1A 78
Sharmans Cl. NN7: Cog 1K 97
Sharman Way NN14: R'ell 5H 27
SHARNBROOK 3B 138
SHARNFORD 2A 132
Sharpes La. NN6: Long B 1H 55
Sharplands NN7: Gren 2C 102
Sharrow Pl. NN3: N'ton 4G 87
Sharwood Ter. NN29: Irch 5H 79
Shatterstone NN4: N'ton 2E 100
Shaw Cl. NN8: Well 7G 65
SHAWELL 3B 132
Sheaf Cl. NN5: Dus 4G 83
Sheaf St. NN11: Dav 2H 61

SHEARSBY .2C 133
Shearwater La. NN8: Well 5B 66
Shedfield Way NN4: N'ton 2D 100
Sheep St. NN1: N'ton 3H 131 (1D 94)
NN8: Well 1B 78
NN15: K'ing 1D 42
NN16: K'ing 1D 42
Sheerwater Dr. NN3: N'ton 3G 87
Sheffield Ct. NN9: Raun 7H 53
Sheffield Wlk. NN18: Corby 2G 17
Sheffield Way NN6: E Bart 3D 88
Sheila Pl. NN16: K'ing 5G 39
Sheldons La. NN6: Wal 1H 37
SHELFLEYS .7K 93
SHELFORD .3A 132
Shelford Cl. NN3: N'ton 1E 86
Shelley Cl. NN11: Dav 1G 61
NN12: Tow 4B 114
Shelleycotes Rd. NN6: Brix 4G 35
Shelley Dr. NN10: High F 7D 68
NN17: Corby 4J 13
Shelley Rd. NN8: Well 1G 77
NN16: K'ing 4E 38
Shelley St. NN2: N'ton 5G 85
Shelmerdine Ri. NN9: Raun 6J 53
Shelsley Dr. NN3: N'ton 2G 85
SHELTON 2C 139
Shelton Ct. NN17: Corby 3F 15
NN29: Woll 4E 90
(off St Michael's La.)
Shelton Rd. NN9: Raun 7K 53
NN17: Corby 3F 15
SHENINGTON 1A 140
SHENLEY BROOK END 2D 141
SHENLEY CHURCH END 2D 141
SHENTON 1A 132
Shepherd Cl. NN2: K'thpe 1B 84
Shepherds Hill NN29: Woll 5G 91
Shepherds Wlk. NN7: Bug 1K 105
NN7: Harp 1B 92
Sheppards Cres. NN12: Tow 4C 114
Sheppard Way NN12: Wap 5C 112
Shepperton Cl. NN3: Gt Bil 4F 87
Sheppey La. NN7: Hack 1G 117
Shepton Ct. NN18: Corby 7G 13
Sheraton Cl. NN3: N'ton 4K 85
Sheraton M. NN3: N'ton 4K 85
Sherborne Wlk. NN18: Corby 7F 13
Sherborough Way NN14: Thra 3J 51
Sheriff Rd. NN1: N'ton 7G 85
SHERINGTON 3A 138
Sherington Av. NN2: K'thpe 7A 72
Sherwood Cl. NN17: Corby 5K 13
Sherwood Dr. NN11: Dav 6G 59
NN15: Bar S 5H 43
Shetland Way NN17: Corby 5G 13
Shieling Ct. NN18: Corby 5F 17
SHILTON 3A 132
Ship La. PE8: Oun 6H 21
SHIPTON 3D 141
SHIPTON-ON-CHERWELL 3A 140
Shipton Way NN10: R'den 2K 79
Shire Bus. Pk. NN13: B'ley 5H 129
Shire Cl. NN15: K'ing 4E 42
Shire Pl. NN3: N'ton 1E 86
Shire Rd. NN17: Corby 4G 13
Shires Rd. NN13: B'ley 5H 129
Shirley Rd. NN10: R'den 2E 80
Shoal Creek NN4: Col 3D 100
Shoe Maker Cl. NN12: Ast 7J 105
Shoemakers Cl. NN6: E Bart 3D 88
Shoemakers Ct. NN10: R'den 2E 80
Shop La. NN7: Yar H 6H 103
Shoreham St. NN18: Corby 1G 17
Short Cl. PE8: Warm 2H 23
Shortlands, The NN9: Irth 7A 52
Shortlands Cl. NN13: Helm 3B 120
Short La. NN7: Cog 1K 97
NN8: Well 7A 66
Short Stocks NN10: R'den 2G 81
SHORTSTOWN 3C 139
Shortwoods Cl. NN9: Raun 7J 53
SHOTLEY 2C 8
SHOTTESWELL 1A 140
Shotwell Mill La. NN14: R'ell 3K 27
Showsley Rd. NN12: Shut 5A 116
Shrubberies, The NN14: Woodf 6B 50
Shrubfield Gro. NN17: Corby 5A 14
Shuckburgh Rd. NN11: Stav 4A 60
Shurville Cl. NN6: E Bart 3E 88
SHUTFORD .1A 140
SHUTLANGER 6A 116 (1D 141)
Shutlanger Rd. NN12: Stoke B 5B 116
Sibbertoft Rd. LE16: Clip, Sibb 5A 24
SIBBERTOFT 2C 24 (3C 133)
LE16: Mar T 1D 24
SIBFORD FERRIS 2A 140
SIBFORD GOWER 2A 140
Sibley Rd. NN9: Fine 7K 47
SIBSON
Cambridgeshire 2C 135
Leicestershire 1A 132
Siddeley Way NN11: Dav 7E 58

Siddons Cl. PE8: Oun 3G 21
Siddons Way NN3: Moul 4A 74
Sidebrook Ct. NN3: N'ton 1C 86
Sidegate La. NN8: Well 3F 67
Sidings, The NN9: Irth 4A 68
Sidings Ind. Cen., The
NN13: B'ley 3H 129
Sidmouth Wlk. NN18: Corby 1A 18
Sidney PE8: Oun 5H 21
Sidney Rd. NN11: Woodf H 2D 108
Sigma Ho. NN1: N'ton 3G 131
Silkweavers M. NN14: R'ell 6G 27
(off Well La.)
Silverdale Gro. NN10: R'den 3B 80
Silverdale Rd. NN3: N'ton 4A 86
SILVERSTONE 2H 121 (1C 141)
Silverstone Cl. NN2: K'thpe 1E 84
Silverstone Motor Racing Circuit
. . . . .7J 121
Silverstone Rally School 5G 121
Silverstone Technology Pk.
NN12: Silv 5C 121
(not continuous)
Silver St. MK11: Stony S 4K 125
NN1: N'ton 4H 131 (1D 94)
NN6: Brix 2H 35
NN6: Wal 1H 37
NN8: Well 1B 78
NN12: Abt 6H 113
NN14: Brou 5G 41
NN16: K'ing 7D 38
OX17: Chac 2B 118
Silver St. Nth. OX17: Chac 2B 118
Silverwood Ct. NN15: K'ing 2E 42
Silverwood Rd. NN15: K'ing 2E 42
Simon De Senlis Ct. NN1: N'ton 2J 131
Simon Senlis Hall NN3: K'thpe 7F 73
Simon's Wlk.
NN1: N'ton 4G 131 (1D 94)
NN12: Pat 6G 105
Simpson Av. NN10: High F 5F 69
Sinclair Dr. NN8: Well 6F 65
SINGLEBOROUGH 2D 141
Sir John Brown Ct. NN16: K'ing 1C 42
Sir John Pascoe Way
NN5: Dus 6H 83
Siskin Cl. NN18: Corby 3K 17
Sissinghurst Dr. NN14: Thra 2K 51
Siward Vw. NN5: Dus 4J 83
Six Acre Wlk. NN3: N'ton 4F 87
Sixfields Athletics Stadium 2K 93
Sixfields Leisure 2K 93
Sixfields Stadium 2J 93
Sixth St. NN13: Crou 6C 130
Skagerrak St. NN18: Corby 4F 17
Skawle Ct. NN3: N'ton 3C 86
SKEFFINGTON 1D 133
Skeffington Cl. NN14: Ged 6B 46
Skegness Wlk. NN18: Corby 2H 17
Skelton Wlk. NN3: N'ton 2K 85
SKETCHLEY .2A 132
Sketty Cl. NN4: Brack 6K 95
Skiddaw Wlk. NN3: N'ton 2K 85
Skinner Av. NN5: Upton 2J 93
Skinner's Hill NN10: R'den 3E 80
Skinyard La. NN6: Long B 2H 55
Skippon's Ct. NN6: Nas 3H 33
Skipton Cl. NN4: N'ton 1C 100
NN18: Corby 2G 17
Skittle All. OX17: Ayn 7E 126
Skye Rd. NN17: Corby 5G 13
Slade, The NN11: Dav 3H 61
NN12: Silv 2J 121
Slade Cl. NN14: Ged 5D 46
Slade Cres. NN15: K'ing 3D 42
Slade Leas OX17: Mid C 6D 118
Sladeswell Ct. NN3: N'ton 6C 86
Slade Valley Av. NN14: R'ell 4G 27
SLAPTON 6G 113 (1C 141)
Slate Drift PE9: Colly 4A 6
Slaters Cl. NN10: R'den 3G 81
SLAWSTON .2D 133
Slim Cl. NN15: K'ing 1H 43
Slip, The NN6: Brix 3J 35
Slips, The NN9: Gt Har 2K 65
SLIPTON 1B 138
Slipton La. NN14: Sud 5A 48
Slipton Wlk. NN3: N'ton 1F 87
Sloe La. NN14: Maw 5C 40
Smarts Cl. NN3: B'ley 3D 128
Smarts Est. CV23: Kil 6C 30
SMEETON WESTERBY 2C 133
Smith Cl. NN7: Pid 3F 117
Smith Ct. NN9: Raun 7J 53
Smith M. NN7: Bug 1K 105
Smithfield Pl. NN9: Raun 7H 53
Smithland Ct. NN12: Greens N 1H 113
Smiths Ct. NN4: N'ton 7J 131 (3E 94)
Smith St. NN6: Spra 5B 34
Smiths Yd. NN9: L Harr 1G 65
Smithy, The MK19: Dean 5F 125
NN3: West F 5B 86
SMOCKINGTON 3A 132

Smyth Ct. NN3: N'ton 3B 86
Snapewood Wlk. NN3: N'ton 2F 87
SNARESTONE 1A 132
Snetterton Cl. NN3: N'ton 2G 85
SNIBSTON .1A 132
Snowbell Sq. NN3: N'ton 3F 87
Snowshill Cl. NN11: Dav 3G 59
Soane Cl. NN8: Well 4H 65
Soar Grn. NN17: Corby 4H 13
(off Shire Rd.)
Sol Central 5G 131 (2D 94)
Solly's Way NN12: Tow 4C 114
SOMERBY 1D 133
Somerford Rd. NN8: Well 6K 65
Somerset St.
NN1: N'ton 2K 131 (7E 84)
SOMERTON .3A 140
Somerton Ct. NN18: Corby 7F 13
Somerville Rd. NN11: Dav 3G 61
NN13: B'ley 3E 128
Sondes Cl. PE8: Oun 3G 21
Sopers Ct. NN17: Corby 3F 15
Sopwith Way NN17: Corby 6F 59
Sorrel Cl. NN4: Woot 3F 101
NN14: Ish 3G 45
Sorrels, The NN14: Ish 3G 45
Sotheby Ri. NN3: N'ton 3G 87
Soudan Av. NN13: B'ley 3F 129
SOULDERN .2B 140
SOULDROP .2B 138
Sourton Pl. NN11: Dav 4J 59
Southall Rd. NN17: Corby 7C 14
SOUTHAM 2A 136
Southampton Rd. NN4: Far C 4D 94
South Av. NN15: Bur L 1J 45
South Bank NN13: Turw 5J 129
South Bern NN4: N'ton 4B 94
South Bri. Cl. PE8: Oun 5H 21
Southbridge Ct.
NN4: N'ton 7J 131 (3E 94)
SOUTHBROOK 1H 61
Southbrook NN18: Corby 3G 17
South Cl. NN6: Long B 2H 55
NN10: R'den 4F 81
NN11: Braun 1C 58
OX17: Greatw 3J 119
South Copse NN4: N'ton 1C 100
Southcourt NN3: Moul 6J 73
Southcrest NN4: N'ton 6K 93
SOUTH CROXTON 1C 133
Southfield Av. NN4: Far C 4E 94
Southfield Dr. NN15: Bur L 6H 44
South Fld. Rd. NN17: Gret 6D 8
Southfield Rd. NN5: Dus 7G 83
SOUTHFIELDS 6C 74
Southfields NN10: R'den 4F 81
Southfields Dr. NN6: Crick 4J 31
Southfields Ho. NN3: N'ton 7D 74
Sth. Folds Rd. NN18: Corby 5E 16
Southgate Dr. NN12: Tow 4D 114
NN15: K'ing 7F 39
South Gro. NN10: Wym 7E 80
Sth. Holme Ct. NN3: N'ton 1B 86
SOUTH KILWORTH 3C 133
Southlands NN15: K'ing 1D 42
SOUTH LUFFENHAM 1B 134
South March NN11: Dav 3J 61
Sth. Mdw. La. NN15: Upton 1F 93
South Mdw. Rd.
NN5: Dus, Upton 7F 83
Sth. Mdw. Vw. NN5: Upton 1F 93
SOUTH NEWINGTON 2A 140
SOUTHOE 2D 139
SOUTHORPE 1C 135
South Oval NN5: N'ton 5A 84
Sth. Paddock Ct. NN3: N'ton 2C 86
South Pk. NN10: R'den 4E 80
South Pl. NN11: Dav 1G 61
Sth. Portway Ct. NN3: N'ton 7C 74
Sth. Priors Ct. NN3: N'ton 3D 86
South Rd. NN17: Corby 7B 14
PE8: Oun 6H 21
South St. NN1: N'ton 1G 95
NN7: Weed 4D 62
NN11: Woodf H 2D 108
NN14: Ish 4G 45
NN29: Woll 4E 90
South Ter. NN1: N'ton 1G 95
NN12: Greens N 1H 113
South Vale NN7: Yar H 7G 103
South Vw. NN6: Brix 4H 35
NN7: Kisl 2D 92
NN7: Neth H 6J 63
NN7: Roa 2C 116
NN11: Whil 6C 56
South Way NN11: Dav 1J 61
SOUTHWICK 2C 135
Southwick Hall 2C 135
Southwick Rd. PE8: Glap 1F 21
SOUTH WIGSTON 2B 132
Southwood Hill NN4: N'ton 5A 94
Sovereign Ct. NN3: N'ton 6C 74
NN10: R'den 2E 80

Sovereigns Ct.—Stratford Ho.

Sovereigns Ct. NN16: K'ing 3E 38
Sower Leys Rd. NN18: Corby 2H 17
SPACE, THE 6G 39
Spalding Rd. NN18: Corby 2H 17
SPALDWICK 1D 139
Spanslade Rd. NN3: N'ton 5D 86
Sparke Cl. NN8: Well 5J 65
Spartan Cl. NN4: Woot 3G 101
Spectacle La. NN3: Moul 3G 73
Speedwell Rd. NN14: Des 1D 26
Speke Dr. NN11: Dav 5H 59
Spelhoe St. NN3: N'ton 7C 74
SPELSBURY 3A 140
Spencelayh Cl. NN8: Well 5A 66
SPENCER 7B 84
Spencer Bri. Rd.
NN5: N'ton 2F 131 (1B 94)
Spencer Cl. NN6: Chap B 4J 71
NN6: E Bart 2E 88
NN7: Bug 1K 105
NN13: Even 2C 130
Spencer Ct. NN10: R'den 2D 80
NN17: Corby 7K 13
Spencer Gdns. NN13: B'ley 5F 129
NN29: Boz 3H 103
Spencer Haven NN5: N'ton 7B 84
Spencer Pde. NN1: N'ton . . .4K 131 (1E 94)
NN9: Stanw 1J 69
Spencer Perceval Hall
NN3: K'thpe 7F 73
Spencer Rd. NN1: N'ton 7F 85
NN6: Long B 2H 55
NN8: Well 4A 78
NN9: Irth 3B 68
NN10: R'den 1D 80
NN14: Stan 3F 19
Spencer St. NN5: N'ton 2B 94
NN9: Raun 6K 53
NN14: R'ell 5G 27
NN14: Rin 1G 53
NN15: Bur L 3J 45
NN16: K'ing 5C 38
Spencer Wlk. NN18: Corby 1K 17
Spendlove Dr. NN17: Gret 6D 8
Spenfield Ct. NN3: N'ton 3C 86
Spenser Cres. NN11: Dav 7F 59
Spey Cl. NN8: Well 6H 65
Spiers Dr. NN13: B'ley 4D 128
Spilsby Cl. NN18: Corby 2H 17
Spinney, The NN4: Gra P 6F 101
Spinney Bank OX17: King S 1B 126
Spinney Cl. NN2: Bou 6D 72
NN10: R'den 3C 80
NN12: Tow 6C 114
NN14: Thra 4H 51
PE8: Warm 3H 23
Spinney Dr. NN4: Col 4D 100
NN15: K'ing 3F 43
Spinney Gro. NN17: Corby 6K 13
SPINNEY HILL 3H 85
Spinney Hill NN11: Braun 1C 58
Spinney Hill Cres. NN3: N'ton 2H 85
Spinney Hill Rd. NN3: N'ton 2G 85
SPINNEY HILLS 1C 133
Spinney La. NN8: Wilby 3H 77
NN15: K'ing 3F 43
Spinney Ri. NN11: Dav 2H 61
NN14: Den 7G 51
Spinney Rd. NN3: Moul P 7J 73
NN9: Irth 2C 68
NN10: R'den 4C 80
NN15: Bur L 1K 45
NN17: Weld 6K 15
Spinneyside Wlk. NN3: N'ton 2D 86
(not continuous)
Spinney St. NN9: Raun 6J 53
Spinney Ter. NN9: Irth 2C 68
Spinney Vw. MK19: Dean 4G 125
Spinney Way NN3: N'ton 1H 85
Spire Rd. NN10: R'den 1F 81
Splash Leisure Pool 2D 80
Sponne Ho. Shop. Cen.
NN12: Tow 3C 114
Sponnes Rd. NN12: Tow 4C 114
Sportsmans Cl. NN7: Cog 1G 97
Spotted Cow La. NN11: Whil 6K 55
SPRATTON 5C 34 (1D 137)
Spratton Rd. NN6: Brix 3F 35
Springbanks Way NN4: N'ton 7C 94
Spring Cl. CV23: Kil 7C 30
NN2: Bou 4D 72
NN6: Holl 6F 33
NN9: Irth 2C 68
NN11: Dav 3H 61
NN13: B'ley 4G 129
Springer Straight NN4: N'ton 4A 94
Springfield NN4: Woot 1F 101
NN7: Flore 2F 63
Springfield Av. NN14: Thra 3H 51
Springfield Cl. NN15: K'ing 3E 42
Springfield Ct. NN3: N'ton 3C 86
Springfield Gdns. MK19: Dean 5F 125
Springfield Gro. NN17: Corby 5A 14
Springfield Rd. LE16: Wilb 6H 11
NN6: Wal 1G 37
NN10: R'den 5F 81
(not continuous)
NN15: K'ing 3E 42
PE8: Oun 3H 21
Springfields NN12: Tow 4A 114
Springfield Way NN13: B'ley 3F 129
Spring Gdns.
NN1: N'ton 4K 131 (2E 94)
NN6: E Bart 2E 88
NN8: Well 1A 78
NN10: High F 6E 68
NN11: Dav 2H 61
NN12: Tow 4D 114
NN14: R'ell 6G 27
NN15: Bur L 1K 45
Spring Ho. NN8: Well 1A 78
(off Hill St.)
Spring La. NN1: N'ton 3F 131 (1C 94)
NN7: Flore 2F 63
NN8: Well 1B 78
SPRING PARK 1B 84
Spring Ri. NN15: K'ing 3E 42
Springs, The NN4: N'ton 4B 94
Spring St. NN9: Irth 2C 68
Spring Ter. NN9: Irth 2C 68
Springwell Cl. NN4: Gra P 5F 101
Springwood Ct. NN3: N'ton 1C 86
Spruce Ct. NN3: N'ton 3B 86
NN16: K'ing 5E 38
Spurlings PE8: Oun 5H 21
Spur Rd. NN8: Well 4A 78
Spyglass Hill NN4: N'ton 2C 100
Square, The NN4: Gra P 5G 101
NN5: Upton 3H 93
NN6: E Bart 2D 88
NN6: Pits 1D 72
NN6: Welf 2H 29
NN7: Yar H 6G 103
NN9: Raun 6J 53
NN11: Mor P 3H 111
OX17: Ayn 7E 126
OX17: Greatw 3K 119
OX17: King S 1B 126
Squire Cl. NN18: Corby 2F 17
Squires Hill NN14: R'ell 6G 27
Squires Wlk. NN3: Spin H 3J 85
Squirrel Cl. NN4: Gra P 6G 101
Squirrel La. NN5: Dus 7H 83
Stable Ct. NN2: K'thpe 3D 84
NN13: B'ley 4G 129
Stable Hill NN14: Brig 2D 20
Stable La. NN6: Pits 1E 72
Stables La. NN6: Chu B 5G 71
Stable Yd. NN14: Lod 1C 40
Stadtpeine Cl. NN17: Corby 6H 13
Staffa Wlk. NN17: Corby 5G 13
Stafford Cl. NN11: Dav 5J 59
Stafford Pl. NN3: Moul P 6G 73
Stafford Rd. NN17: Gret 7D 8
Staffords La. NN6: W Had 6G 29
STAGSDEN 3B 138
Stagshaw Cl. NN4: N'ton 7D 94
Stahl Theatre, The 5H 21
Staines Cl. NN5: N'ton 1K 93
Stalbridge Wlk. NN18: Corby 7F 13
STAMFORD 1C 135
Stamford La. PE8: Warm 2H 23
Stamford Rd. NN14: Ged 5C 46
NN14: Stan 3F 19
NN16: K'ing 6F 39
NN17: Dee, Weld 5J 15
NN17: Weld 1F 19
NN18: L Oak 7C 18
PE9: Eas H 3B 6
Stamford Wlk. NN18: Corby 2H 17
Standens Barn Local Cen.
NN3: N'ton 5C 86
(off Topwell Ct.)
Standens Barn Rd. NN3: N'ton 6C 86
Standing Stones NN3: Gt Bil 3E 86
Standrums PE8: Barn 7B 22
Standside NN5: N'ton 1A 94
Stanfield Rd. NN5: Dus 1H 93
Stanford Cl. NN6: Col A 2A 32
STANFORD ON AVON 1B 136
Stanford Rd. NN6: Col A 1A 32
NN6: Yel 4B 28
Stanford Way NN4: N'ton 1D 100
STANGROUND 2D 135
Stanhill Row NN12: Abt 7H 113
Stanhope Rd. NN2: N'ton 5D 84
Stanier Cl. NN16: K'ing 6C 38
Stanier Rd. NN17: Corby 4A 14
STANION 4F 19 (3B 134)
Stanion La. NN18: Corby 7C 14
Stanion Rd. NN14: Brig . . . .4J 19 & 1B 20
Stanley Boddington Ct.
NN15: K'ing 2E 42
Stanley M. NN8: Well 7C 66
Stanley Rd. NN5: N'ton 1B 94
NN8: Well 7C 66
Stanley St. NN2: Sem 6C 84
NN14: R'ell 6H 27
Stanley Way NN11: Dav 5H 59
Stannard Way NN6: Brix 3H 35
Stanton Av. NN3: Spin H 2H 85
Stanton Cl. NN8: Well 4B 66
NN14: Des 1E 26
STANTON UNDER BARDON 1A 132
Stanwell Cl. OX17: Mid C 5D 118
Stanwell Dr. OX17: Mid C 5C 118
Stanwell Lea OX17: Mid C 5C 118
Stanwell Way NN8: Well 2H 77
(not continuous)
STANWICK 1K 69 (1B 138)
Stanwick Rd. NN9: Raun 7G 53
NN10: High F 4F 69
(not continuous)
STAPLETON 2A 132
STAPLOE 2D 139
Star Cnr. CV23: Bar 2C 54
Star Ho. NN8: Well 7C 66
(off York Rd.)
Starmers La. NN7: Kisl 3C 92
Starmer's Yd. NN5: Dus 7H 83
Starvold Cl. NN6: Spra 5B 34
Station App. NN10: R'den 2E 80
(off John Clark Way)
Station Cl. NN3: Gt Bil 5F 87
NN6: Long B 2H 55
NN11: Dav 1J 61
Station Ct. NN11: Woodf H 2D 108
Station Gdns. NN11: Woodf H 2D 108
Station M. NN3: Gt Bil 4F 87
Station Rd. CV23: Kil 6C 30
CV23: Lil 1C 28
LE17: Catt 1C 28
NN3: Gt Bil 5F 87
NN6: Brix 1F 35
NN6: E Bart 2D 88
(not continuous)
NN6: Long B 3G 55
NN6: W Had 6G 29
NN6: Wat 6D 54
NN7: Blis 6G 99
(not continuous)
NN7: Cog, L Hou 1F 97
NN7: Gren 5E 88
NN9: Fine 5J 45
NN9: Irth 2C 68
(not continuous)
NN10: High F 4E 68
NN10: R'den 3D 80
NN11: Woodf H 3C 108
NN11: Welt 1K 59
NN13: Helm 3B 120
NN14: Des 2D 26
NN14: Rin 2D 52
NN14: R'ton 2B 46
NN15: Bur L, Ish 3F 45
NN15: K'ing 1C 42
NN17: Corby 7B 14
NN17: Gret 6C 8
NN29: Irch 5J 79
OX17: Ayn 7C 126
PE8: King C 2H 9
PE8: Nass 5H 7
PE8: Oun 4J 21
STAUGHTON GREEN 2D 139
STAUGHTON HIGHWAY 2D 139
Stavanger Cl. NN18: Corby 4F 17
Staveley Way NN6: Brix 2J 35
STAVERTON 4B 60 (2B 136)
Staverton Rd. NN11: Dav 3D 60
(not continuous)
STEANE 1A 128
Steane Vw. NN13: B'ley 4E 128
Steel Cl. NN14: Thra 4H 51
Steele Rd. NN8: Well 1J 77
Steel Rd. NN17: Corby 4D 14
Steene St. NN5: N'ton 1B 94
STEEPLE ASTON 3A 140
STEEPLE BARTON 3A 140
STEEPLE CLAYDON 3C 141
STEEPLE GIDDING 3D 135
STEFEN HILL 3G 61
Stefen Hill Sports Ground Track . . .4H 61
Stefen Way NN11: Dav 3E 60
Stenhouse Cl. NN6: Long B 1K 55
Stenson St. NN5: N'ton 1B 94
Stephen Bennett Cl. NN5: Dus 6H 83
Stephenson Cl. NN11: Dav 6E 58
Stephenson Ct. CV23: Kil 7B 30
NN7: Roa 2B 116
Stephenson Way NN17: Corby 5B 14
Sterling Bus. Pk. NN4: Brack 5K 95
Sterling Ct. NN14: Lod 1C 40
Sterling Ho. Bus. Cen.
NN16: K'ing 7E 38
(off Victoria St.)
Sterndale Cl. NN14: Des 2B 26
Stevens Ct. NN6: E Bart 1E 88
Stevenson St. NN4: Del 5D 94
STEVINGTON 3B 138
Stewart Cl. NN3: Moul 3J 73
Stewart Dr. NN12: Silv 3H 121
Stewarts Rd. NN8: Well 3B 66
STEWKLEY 3D 141
STEWKLEY DEAN 3D 141
Steyning Cl. NN18: Corby 1F 17
STIBBINGTON 2C 135
Stile Cl. NN11: Dav 1F 61
STILTON 3D 135
Stimpson Av. NN1: N'ton 6G 85
Stirling Cl. NN18: Corby 4K 17
Stirling St. NN5: N'ton 7A 84
Stirrup Ho. NN5: N'ton 2C 94
(off Byfield Rd.)
Stitchman Ho. NN5: N'ton 1B 94
(off Byfield Rd.)
Stockbridge Rd. NN17: Corby 4B 14
STOCKERSTON 2A 134
Stockholme Cl. NN18: Corby 4F 17
Stocking Cl. NN7: Hart 6H 117
Stockley St. NN1: N'ton 1F 95
(not continuous)
Stockmead Rd. NN3: N'ton 6D 86
Stocks, The MK19: Cos 6D 122
Stocks Ct. NN17: Corby 7C 14
(off Stocks La.)
Stocks Hill NN3: Moul 4K 73
NN9: Fine 7G 47
NN12: Silv 2H 121
Stock's La. NN17: Corby 6C 14
STOCKTON 2A 136
Stockwell Av. NN4: Woot 3E 100
Stockwell La. NN11: Hell 2C 104
OX17: Sulg 5G 111
Stockwell Rd. NN7: Mil M 4A 100
Stockwell Way NN7: Mil M 4A 100
Stockwood Dr. NN17: Corby 4A 14
STOKE .1A 136
STOKE ALBANY 6G 11 (3A 134)
Stoke Albany Rd. LE16: A'ley 3G 11
STOKE BRUERNE 6D 116 (1D 141)
Stoke Bruerne Brick Pits Nature Reserve
. . . . .7D 116
STOKE DOYLE 3C 135
Stoke Doyle Rd. PE8: Oun 7F 21
STOKE DRY 2A 134
Stoke Firs Cl. NN4: Woot 2G 101
STOKE GOLDING 2A 132
STOKE GOLDINGTON 3A 138
Stoke Hill LE16: Stoke A 6F 11
PE8: Oun 5H 21
STOKE LYNE 3B 140
Stoke Pk. Pavilions 7D 116
Stoke Rd. NN7: Blis 2H 115
NN12: Stoke B 5C 116
NN14: Des 1C 26
(not continuous)
Stokes Rd. NN18: Corby 2J 17
Stonebridge Ct. NN3: N'ton 3C 86
Stonebrig La. NN9: L Harr 2E 64
Stone Circ. Rd. NN3: N'ton 7A 74
Stone Cl. NN8: Well 4A 66
NN29: Woll 4E 90
Stone Hill Ct. NN3: N'ton 3A 86
Stonehill Way NN6: Brix 5H 35
Stonehouse Ct. CV23: Lil 3C 28
Stonehurst Cl. NN7: Hart 6G 117
Stonelea Rd. NN6: Syw 2G 75
Stoneleigh Chase NN5: Dus 5J 83
STONELY 2D 139
Stonepit Dr. LE16: Cotti 4C 12
STONESFIELD 3A 140
Stone Way NN5: Dus 7G 83
Stoneway NN7: Hart 5J 117
NN11: Badby 6C 104
Stonewold Cl. NN2: K'thpe 2B 84
Stoney Flds. NN14: Maw 5B 40
STONEYGATE 1C 133
Stoneyhurst NN4: N'ton 4A 94
Stoney Piece Cl. NN29: Boz 3G 103
STONEY STANTON 2A 132
STONTON WYVILLE 2D 133
Stony Hill NN12: Paul 6H 115
STONY STRATFORD 4K 125 (1D 141)
Stony Stratford Nature Reserve . . .2K 125
Stook, The NN11: Dav 4H 59
Stornoway Rd. NN17: Corby 4H 13
Storton's Pits Nature Reserve 2K 93
STOUGHTON 1C 133
Stour, The NN11: Dav 3F 61
Stourhead Dr. NN4: N'ton 1D 100
Stour Rd. NN5: N'ton 1A 94
NN17: Corby 4J 13
Stourton Cl. NN8: Well 4J 77
Stow Cl. NN8: Well 4J 77
Stowe Wlk. NN3: N'ton 1G 85
NN11: Dav 4G 59
STOW LONGA 1D 139
Stradlers Cl. NN4: Woot 3F 101
Stratfield Way NN15: K'ing 5F 43
Stratford Arc. MK11: Stony S 3K 125
Stratford Dr. NN4: Woot 2E 100
Stratford Ho. MK11: Stony S 4K 125

Stratford Rd. MK19: Cos 1K 125
MK19: Dean 5G 125
NN7: Roa 4B 116
Strathay Wlk. NN17: Corby 4H 13
STRATTON AUDLEY 3C 141
Stratton Cl. NN3: N'ton 7A 86
Stratton Dr. NN13: B'ley 4E 128
Strawberry Hill NN3: N'ton 3F 87
Straws Cl. NN9: Irth 3B 68
Straws Yd. NN9: Irth 3B 68
Stream Bank Cl. NN8: Well 1J 77
Streambank Rd. NN3: N'ton 7B 74
Streatfield Rd. NN5: N'ton 6B 84
Streather Ct. NN9: Raun 7H 53
Streather Dr. NN17: Corby 6K 13
Streeton Way NN6: E Bart 1D 88
Strelley Av. NN3: N'ton 6C 86
STRETTON-ON-DUNSMORE 1A 136
STRETTON UNDER FOSSE 3A 132
Stringer's Hill NN14: Pyt 2A 44
STRIXTON 6D 90 (2B 138)
Strixton Mnr. Bus. Cen.
NN29: Strix 6D 90
Strobel Dr. NN5: Upton 3H 93
Strode Rd. NN8: Well 7C 66
Stronglands Ct. PE8: Oun 4H 21
Stuart Cl. NN4: N'ton 1A 100
NN16: K'ing 7E 38
Stuart Rd. NN13: B'ley 3E 128
NN17: Corby 7K 13
Stubbing End NN18: Gt Oak 6G 17
Stubble Cl. NN2: K'thpe 7B 72
Stubbs Cl. NN8: Well 5A 66
Stubbs La. NN15: Bar S 2J 43
STUCHBURY 7J 111
Studfall Av. NN17: Corby 6J 13
Studfall Ct. NN17: Corby 5K 13
Studland Rd. NN2: K'thpe 5C 84
Sturdee Cl. NN11: Dav 2J 61
Sturgess Ct. NN15: Bur L 1K 45
Sturminster Way NN18: Corby . . .7F 13
Sturton Wlk. NN18: Corby 2H 17
Styles Pl. NN6: Yel 6C 28
Style Way NN4: Upton 6E 92
SUDBOROUGH 3A 48 (3B 134)
Sudborough Rd. NN14: Brig 2D 20
Suffolk Pl. NN15: K'ing 4F 43
Sulby Rd. NN3: N'ton 7B 74
NN6: Welf 1J 29
Sulehay Rd. PE8: Yar 1F 7
SULGRAVE 6G 111 (1B 140)
Sulgrave Dr. NN17: Corby 6H 13
Sulgrave Manor 5G 111
Sulgrave Rd. NN5: N'ton 7A 84
OX17: Cul 7C 110
Summerfield NN15: K'ing 2E 42
Summerfields NN4: N'ton 5K 93
Summerhouse Rd. NN3: Moul P . .7H 73
Summerlee Rd. NN9: Fine 7H 47
Summer Leys Local Nature Reserve
. . . . .2A 90
Summit Ri. NN4: N'ton 1E 100
Sunderland St. NN5: N'ton 1B 94
Sundew Ct. NN4: N'ton 6J 93
Sun Hill NN14: R'ell 6F 27
Sunley Ct. NN15: K'ing 1E 42
Sunningdale Cl. NN2: N'ton 4F 85
Sunningdale Dr. NN10: R'den . . .5G 81
NN11: Dav 7K 59
Sunny Side NN6: E Bart 2C 88
Sunnyside NN4: Woot 2F 101
NN6: Ect 2J 87
NN14: Woodf 6B 50
Sunny Vw. NN7: Yar H 6H 103
Sunset Cl. NN3: N'ton 4D 86
Sun Yd. NN12: Tow 4D 114
Surfleet Cl. NN18: Corby 2H 17
Surrey Cl. NN17: Corby 7H 13
Surrey Rd. NN15: K'ing 4F 43
Surtees Way NN12: Tow 2C 114
Sussex Cl. NN5: Dus 1H 93
Sussex Ct. NN1: N'ton 3H 131
Sussex Pl. NN10: R'den 1E 80
Sussex Rd. NN15: K'ing 4E 42
Sutherland NN18: Corby 2J 17
SUTTON
Bedfordshire 3D 139
Peterborough 2C 135
Sutton Acre NN7: Flore 2F 63
SUTTON BASSETT 4C 10 (2D 133)
SUTTON CHENEY 1A 132
Sutton Cl. NN2: K'thpe 7E 72
NN11: Ast W 6E 106
SUTTON IN THE ELMS 2B 132
Sutton Rd. LE16: West W 3C 10
PE8: Oun 6K 21
Sutton St. NN7: Flore 2F 63
Suttons Wlk. NN12: Ast 7J 105
(not continuous)
Swain Ct. NN3: N'ton 3B 86
SWALCLIFFE 2A 140
Swale Cl. NN7: Roa 3B 116
NN17: Corby 4H 13

Swale Dr. NN5: N'ton 4A 84
Talavera Cl. NN11: Dav 2F 61
NN8: Well 6H 65
Swallow Cl. NN4: N'ton 1B 100
NN8: Well 5C 66
NN13: B'ley 2F 129
NN15: Bar S 4K 43
Swallow Ct. NN15: K'ing 6F 43
Swallow Dr. NN10: R'den 1E 80
Swanage Ct. NN18: Corby 7F 13
Swan Av. NN14: Brig 1C 20
SWANBOURNE 3D 141
Swan Cl. NN11: Woodf H 2C 108
NN13: B'ley 1E 128
NN14: Thra 2H 51
NN15: Bur L 2H 45
OX17: Mid C 6C 118
Swann Dale NN11: Dav 2J 61
Swann Dale Cl. NN11: Dav 2J 61
Swansea Cres. NN5: N'ton 7B 84
Swansea Rd. NN15: N'ton 6B 84
Swansgate Cen., The
NN8: Well 1B 78
(off Market St.)
Swansnest NN6: Brix 3H 35
Swanspool Ct. NN8: Well 1B 78
Swanspool Pde. NN8: Well 2B 78
Swan St. NN1: N'ton . . .5J 131 (2E 94)
Swans Way NN10: High F 4F 69
SWAN VALLEY 6G 93
Swan Valley Ind. Est.
NN4: Swan H 6G 93
Swan Valley Office Village
NN4: Swan H 7H 93
Swan Valley Way
NN4: N'ton, Swan H 6G 93
Swan Yd. NN1: N'ton . . .4H 131 (1D 94)
Swedish Houses NN7: L Brin 5G 57
NN7: Up Harl 2C 82
Sweetacre Ct. NN7: Gren 3C 102
SWEPSTONE 1A 132
SWERFORD 2A 140
Swift Cl. NN4: Gra P 5G 101
NN17: Corby 7K 93
Swift Way NN13: B'ley 2E 128
Swinburne Cl. NN16: K'ing 3E 38
Swinburne Rd. NN8: Well 1G 77
SWINESHEAD 2C 139
SWINFORD 1B 136
Swinford Hollow NN3: N'ton 6D 86
Swinnertons La. NN6: Yel 1G 29
Swinneyford Rd. NN12: Tow 4C 114
SWITHLAND 1B 132
Swyncombe Grn. NN7: Hart 6G 117
Sycamore Av. NN11: Woodf H . . .2C 108
Sycamore Cl. NN10: R'den 3F 81
NN11: Dav 5H 59
NN12: Tow 5C 114
NN16: K'ing 5F 39
NN17: Corby 4K 13
PE8: Wood 6H 9
Sycamore Dr. NN6: Syw 5G 75
NN14: Des 3G 27
Sycamore Rd. NN5: Dus 7H 83
NN12: Greens N 1J 113
Sycamore Yd. NN12: Blak 5J 109
Sydney St. NN16: K'ing 7F 39
Syers Grn. NN6: Long B 1G 55
Syers Grn. La. NN6: Long B 1G 55
Syke, The NN14: Brig 2D 20
Sykes Cl. NN17: Corby 5B 14
Syles Cl. NN6: W Had 5G 29
Sylmond Gdns. NN10: R'den 5C 80
Sylvanus Ho. NN8: Well 7J 65
Symington St. NN5: N'ton 7B 84
SYRESHAM 5C 120 (1C 141)
Syresham Way NN2: K'thpe 1D 84
SYSTON 1C 133
SYWELL 2H 75 (2A 138)
Sywell Airport Bus. Pk.
NN6: Syw 1J 75
Sywell Av. NN8: Well 6J 65
Sywell Aviation Mus. 1J 75
Sywell Country Pk. 5J 75
Sywell Country Pk. Vis. Cen. 6K 75
Sywell La. NN6: Ect 1H 87
Sywell Rd. NN6: Holc 6H 37
NN6: Mears A 4K 75
NN6: Over 4C 74
NN8: Mears A, Well 6D 64
Sywell Way NN8: Well 6J 65

T

Taborley Cl. NN3: West F 5B 86
TACKLEY 3A 140
Tadcaster Cl. NN11: Dav 4H 59
TADMARTON 2A 140
Taggies Yd. NN14: Orl 7A 44
Tailby Av. NN16: K'ing 4C 38
Tailby Meadow Nature Reserve . . .3F 27
Tainty Cl. NN9: Fine 6G 47

Talan Ri. NN3: N'ton 1E 86
Talavera Cl. NN11: Dav 2F 61
Talavera Way
NN3: Moul, Moul P, N'ton . . .7J 73
Talbot Rd. NN1: N'ton 7F 85
NN8: Well 7D 66
NN10: R'den 4C 80
Talbot Rd. Nth. NN8: Well 7D 66
TALLINGTON 1C 135
Tall Trees Cl. NN4: N'ton 7A 94
Tallyfield End NN4: N'ton 4K 93
Tamar Cl. NN5: N'ton 4K 83
Tamar Grn. NN17: Corby 4J 13
Tamarisk Dr. NN3: Moul 7K 73
Tamar Sq. NN17: Dav 2F 61
Tancred Cl. NN4: Woot 1F 101
Taney Ct. PE8: Oun 5J 21
Tanfield La. NN1: N'ton 2J 95
Tanfields Gro. NN17: Corby 5J 13
Tanglewood NN4: Col 4E 100
Tanner's La. NN16: K'ing 7D 38
Tanner St. NN1: N'ton . . .6G 131 (2D 94)
Tannery Cotts. NN9: Irth 4B 68
Tann Rd. NN9: Fine 6H 47
TANSOR 2C 135
Tansor Cl. NN17: Corby 5G 13
Tansy Cl. NN4: N'ton 6J 93
Tantree Way NN6: Brix 3J 35
Tapeley Gdns. NN4: N'ton 1E 100
Taper Way NN17: Dav 7F 59
Tarn Cft. NN3: N'ton 3J 85
Tarragon Way NN4: N'ton 2E 100
Tarrant Cl. NN3: Moul 4A 74
Tarrant Way NN3: Moul 4A 74
Tarrys End NN6: Yel 5C 28
Tasman Way NN14: R'ell 7H 27
TASTON 3A 140
Tate Gro. NN4: H'stone 1F 101
TATHALL END 3A 138
Tattersall Cl. NN3: N'ton 2H 85
Taunton Av. NN3: N'ton 7K 85
NN18: Corby 7F 13
Tavern La. NN11: Dav 2H 61
Tavern Wlk. NN10: Corby 2F 17
Tavistock Cl. NN3: N'ton 4G 87
Tavistock Rd. NN15: Bar S 5J 43
Tavistock Sq. NN12: Corby 2A 18
Tay Cl. NN17: Corby 4J 13
Taylor Av. NN3: N'ton 5K 85
Taylor Cl. NN8: Well 5H 65
Taylors Grn. PE8: Warm 3H 23
Teal Cl. NN4: N'ton 7J 93
NN10: High F 4F 69
NN11: Dav 6H 59
NN15: Bur L 2G 45
Teal La. NN8: Well 6H 65
Teasel Cl. NN10: R'den 6F 81
Teasel Dr. NN14: Des 1D 26
Tebbitt Cl. NN6: Long B 1H 55
Tebbitt Cl. NN14: R'ell 6J 27
Tebbutt's Yd. NN6: E Bart 2D 88
Tees Cl. NN8: Well 6H 65
Teesdale NN3: N'ton 7C 74
Teesdale Rd. NN17: Corby 6J 13
TEETON 1C 137
Teeton La. NN6: Crea 7J 33
Teeton Rd. NN6: Guil 7E 32
NN6: Rav 2C 34
Telfords Cl. NN17: Corby 5B 14
Telfords La. NN17: Corby 5B 14
Telford Way NN5: Upton 3H 93
NN16: K'ing 4B 38
Telford Way Ind. Est.
NN16: K'ing 4B 38
(not continuous)
Temperance Cotts. NN9: Raun . . .6J 53
Temperance Ter. MK11: Stony S . .3K 125
Templar Dr. NN2: K'thpe 2B 84
Templar Rd. NN15: K'ing 1G 43
Temple Bar NN1: N'ton . . .2H 131 (7D 84)
Temple Cl. NN10: High F 5E 68
Temple Gdns. NN10: R'den 1F 81
TEMPSFORD 3D 139
Tenbury Way NN14: R'ell 6J 27
Tenby Rd. NN5: N'ton 6B 84
Tenlands OX17: Mid C 6C 118
Tennyson Cl. NN5: Dall 6A 84
NN12: Tow 4B 114
Tennyson Dr. NN17: Corby 5J 13
Tennyson Rd. NN8: Well 2C 78
NN10: R'den 3C 80
NN11: Dav 7F 59
NN14: R'ell 6F 27
NN16: K'ing 7D 38
Tenpin
Northampton 1J 93
Ten Pines NN3: N'ton 6C 74
Tenter Cl. NN10: High F 7E 68
Tenter La. NN9: Fine 6H 47
Tenter Rd. NN3: Moul P 6G 73
Tentsmuir Cl. NN16: K'ing 3C 38
Terrington Cl. NN13: B'ley 4F 129
Test Grn. NN17: Corby 4J 13

Tettenhall Cl. NN18: Corby 5F 17
Teviot Cl. NN5: N'ton 4K 83
NN17: Corby 4J 13
Tewkesbury Cl. NN4: N'ton 6B 94
NN8: Well 6J 65
Tewkesbury Dr. NN10: R'den 5G 81
TEW'S END 6H 115
Tews End La. NN12: Paul 6H 115
Tews Yd. NN11: Woodf H 2D 108
Thames Cl. NN15: Bur L 2J 45
Thames Ri. NN16: K'ing 5C 38
Thames Rd. NN4: N'ton 1C 100
NN8: Well 6H 65
NN11: Dav 2E 60
Thames Wlk. NN17: Corby 4J 13
Thatchwell Ct. NN3: N'ton 6C 86
The . . . .
Names prefixed with 'The' for
example 'The Accurate Boot' are
indexed under the main name
such as 'Accurate Boot, The'
Thebwell Rd. NN3: N'ton 5C 86
THEDDINGWORTH 3C 133
THENFORD 1B 140
Thenford Rd. OX17: Mid C 6E 118
Thenford St. NN1: N'ton 1F 95
Thetford Cl. NN18: Corby 5G 17
Third Av. NN8: Well 2J 77
Third St. NN13: Crou 7C 130
Thirlestane Cres. NN4: Far C 4C 94
Thirlestane Rd. NN4: Far C 4C 94
Thirlmere NN8: Well 7H 65
Thirlmere Av. NN3: N'ton 3K 85
Thirlmere Cl. NN11: Dav 1F 61
NN16: K'ing 6A 38
Thirsk Rd. NN18: Corby 1H 17
Thistle Cl. NN4: N'ton 4B 94
Thistle Dr. NN14: Des 1D 26
Thistleholme Cl. NN2: N'ton 3F 85
Thoday St. NN14: Brou 7G 41
Thomas Chapman Gro.
NN4: N'ton 7J 131 (3E 94)
Thomas Cl. NN6: Crick 3J 31
NN11: Byf 3J 107
NN18: Corby 2J 17
Thomas Crewe Cl. NN13: B'ley . . .4G 129
Thomas Flawn Rd. NN9: Irth 4A 68
Thomas Rippin Ct. NN14: Ged . . .6C 46
Thomas Rd. NN15: K'ing 3E 42
Thomas St. NN1: N'ton 2J 131
(not continuous)
NN8: Well 7C 66
Thomas Webb Cl. NN11: Dav 1J 61
Thompson Cl. NN5: Upton 1F 93
NN11: Braun 1B 58
Thompson Way NN15: K'ing 2B 42
Thorburn Rd. NN3: West F 6B 86
Thoresby Cl. NN18: Corby 1H 17
Thornapple Cl. NN3: N'ton 2F 87
THORNBOROUGH 2D 141
Thornbridge Cl. NN10: R'den 4D 80
THORNBY 3E 32 (1C 137)
Thornby Dr. NN2: K'thpe 3C 84
Thornby Rd. NN6: Col A 2B 32
NN6: Nas 3H 33
Thorn Cl. NN16: K'ing 3D 38
THORNCOTE GREEN 3D 139
Thorne Ct. NN18: Corby 1H 17
Thornfield NN3: N'ton 2F 87
Thorngate St. NN16: K'ing 7E 38
THORNHAUGH 1C 135
Thorn Hill NN4: N'ton 4A 94
Thornhill OX17: Chac 2B 118
THORNTON
Buckinghamshire 2D 141
Leicestershire 1A 132
Thornton Cl. NN6: Crick 3J 31
NN7: Flore 2G 63
NN11: Newn 7J 61
Thornton Hall Cl. NN2: K'thpe . . .4C 84
Thornton Rd. NN2: K'thpe 5C 84
Thoroughsale Rd. NN17: Corby . . .5K 13
THORPE BY WATER 2A 134
Thorpe Cl. NN8: Well 7H 65
Thorpe La. NN16: K'ing 7A 38
THORPE LANGTON 2D 133
THORPE MALSOR 1A 133
THORPE MANDEVILLE 1B 140
Thorpe Rd. NN4: Del 4D 94
NN6: E Bart 4D 88
NN14: Ald 6C 20
OX17: Chac 2B 118
THORPE SATCHVILLE 1D 133
Thorpe St. NN9: Raun 7J 53
THORPE UNDERWOOD 6A 26
Thorpeville NN3: Moul 6A 74
THORPE WATERVILLE 7E 20 (3C 135)
THORPLANDS 4F 17
Thor Wlk. NN18: Corby 4F 17
THRAPSTON 3H 51 (1B 138)
Thrapston Rd. NN9: Fine 6J 47
NN14: Woodf 3B 50
Three Mile Wlk. NN3: N'ton 3F 87

Thrift St. NN10: High F 7E 68
NN29: Irch 5H 79
NN29: Woll 4E 90
Thrupp Bri. NN4: Woot 2H 101
Thrupp Wharf MK19: Cos 4C 122
Thrush Cl. NN18: Corby 2K 17
Thrush La. NN8: Well 6B 66
Thruxton Dr. NN3: N'ton 2G 85
Thurburn Cl. NN14: Brou 5H 41
THURCASTON 1B 132
THURLASTON
　Leicestershire 2B 132
　Warwickshire 1A 136
THURLEIGH 3C 139
THURMASTON 1C 133
THURNBY 1C 133
THURNING 3C 135
Thursby Rd. NN1: N'ton 7J 85
Thurso Wlk. NN17: Corby 4J 13
Thurspit Pl. NN3: N'ton 4G 87
Thurston Cl. NN15: K'ing 2C 42
Thurston Dr. NN15: K'ing 3C 42
Thwaite Wlk. NN3: N'ton 5D 86
Thyme Ct. NN3: N'ton 3B 86
Tibbs Way NN7: Bug 3K 105
TICKENCOTE 1B 134
Tideswell Cl. NN4: N'ton 7A 94
　NN14: Des 1B 26
Tiffany Gdns. NN4: N'ton 2D 100
TIFFIELD 3C 137
Tiffield Rd. NN7: G'ton 7D 98
　NN12: Tow 1C 114
TILBROOK 2C 139
Tilbury Ri. NN6: E Had 2B 56
Tilbury Rd. NN6: E Had 2B 56
Tilley Hill Cl. PE8: Oun 3G 21
TILTON ON THE HILL 1D 133
Timken Cl. NN5: Dus 7J 83
Timken Wlk. NN5: Dus 7J 83
Timken Way NN11: Dav 6F 59
Timken Way Sth. NN5: Dus 7H 83
Timor Ct. MK11: Stony S 3K 125
Timpson Cl. NN16: K'ing 4E 38
Tingdene Rd. NN9: Fine 6H 47
TINGEWICK 2C 141
Tinkers Cres. NN6: Mears A 3A 76
Tinsley Cl. NN3: N'ton 3E 86
Tintagel Cl. NN10: R'den 5G 81
Tintern Av. NN5: N'ton 7B 84
Tintern Ct. NN15: K'ing 2J 43
TINWELL 1C 135
Tiptoe Cl. NN3: N'ton 2F 87
TITCHMARSH 1H 49 (1C 139)
Tithe Barn Cl. NN9: Raun 5K 53
Tithe Barn Rd. NN8: Well 1B 78
Tithe Barn Way NN4: Swan H 7G 93
Tithe Cl. NN6: Holc 6H 37
　NN14: Rin 1F 53
Tithe Rd. NN7: Weed 4B 62
Tithe Way NN7: Roa 1C 116
Titley Bawk Av.
　NN6: E Bart 7E 76
Titty Ho NN9: Raun 7H 53
Tiverton Av. NN2: K'thpe 6C 72
TIXOVER 1B 134
Todmorden Cl. NN18: Corby 1H 17
Tofts Cl. NN14: Titch 1J 49
Tollbar Rd. NN10: R'den 7E 68
Toll Bar Rd. NN14: Isl 3F 51
Toller Pl. NN15: Bar S 4H 43
Toller St. NN16: K'ing 7E 38
Tollgate Cl. NN2: K'thpe 4C 84
Toll Ga. Pl. NN18: Corby 7C 14
Tollgate Way NN5: Dus 1J 93
Toms Cl. NN4: Col 5D 100
Tonmead Rd. NN3: N'ton 2B 86
Tonmead Wlk. NN3: N'ton 3B 86
Top Cl. NN14: Thra 2K 51
Top Dysons NN14: C'ord 2F 47
Top End NN14: L Add 5A 52
　NN14: Pyt 2A 44
Top Farm Ct. NN11: Woodf H 2C 108
Top Farm La. NN29: Gt Dod 6K 77
Topgrass Wlk. NN3: N'ton 5C 86
　　　　　　　　　　　　(off Logwell Ct.)
Top Green NN6: Wal 1H 37
　NN12: Woode 7F 109
Top Mdw. Wlk. NN3: N'ton 3D 86
Topnotch Health Club 5G 131
　　　　　　　　　　　　(in Sol Central)
Top Station Rd. NN13: B'ley 3H 129
Top Station Rd. Ind. Est.
　NN13: B'ley 3H 129
Topwell Ct. NN3: N'ton 5C 86
Tordoff Pl. NN16: K'ing 7D 38
Torksey Cl. NN18: Corby 5F 17
Torridge Cl. NN16: K'ing 5B 38
Torridon Cl. NN17: Corby 4H 13
Torrington Cres. NN8: Well 6K 65
Torrington Grn. NN8: Well 6K 65
Torrington Rd. NN8: Well 6J 65
Torrington Way NN8: Well 6K 65
Torville Cres. NN15: K'ing 2B 42

TOSELAND 2D 139
Totnes Cl. NN18: Corby 2A 18
Toulouse Cl. NN4: Corby 1F 101
Touraine Cl. NN5: New D 4E 82
Tourist Info. Cen.
　Brackley 5F 129
　Corby 7K 13
　Daventry 1H 61
　Kettering 1D 42
　Northampton 5J 131 (2E 94)
　Oundle 5H 21
Tove La. NN12: Tow 3A 114
Tovey Dr. NN11: Dav 1J 61
TOWCESTER 4C 114 (1C 141)
Towcester Cen. for Leisure 4B 114
Towcester Cl. NN18: L Oak 5K 17
Towcester Dr. NN12: Pot 6F 123
Towcester Mus. 3C 114
Towcester Racecourse 4E 114 (1D 141)
Towcester Rd. MK19: Old S 2J 125
　NN1: N'ton 7F 131 (3D 94)
　NN4: Mil M, N'ton, Del, Far C
　　　　　　　　　　　　. . . . .2A 100
　NN7: Blis 3F 115
　NN8: Mil M 6K 99
　NN12: Greens N, Tow 1H 113
　NN12: Lit 2H 109
　NN12: Silv 3H 121
　NN12: Whit 1C 122
Tower Cl. NN9: Fine 7K 47
Tower Ct. NN29: Woll 3G 91
Tower Fld. Sq. NN3: N'ton 7D 74
Tower Hill Cl. NN4: N'ton 4K 93
Tower Hill Rd. NN18: Corby 1F 17
Tower Sq. NN5: N'ton 1A 94
Tower St. NN3: N'ton 3G 131 (1D 94)
Tower Works NN9: Fine 6H 47
　　　　　　　　　　　　(off Well St.)
Town Cnr. NN5: N'ton 1A 94
TOWNGATE 1D 135
Townley Way NN6: E Bart 1D 88
Towns End NN6: Long B 1J 55
Townsend NN11: Woodf H 2C 108
Townsend Cl. NN8: Well 1A 78
Townsend La. NN11: Up Bod 2A 106
Townsend Leys
　NN10: High F 5E 68
Townsend Rd. NN6: Wal 1G 37
Townson Cl. NN6: Old 5E 36
Townwell La. NN29: Irch 5J 79
Towrise OX17: Sulg 5G 141
Towton Ct. NN4: N'ton 6B 94
Trafalgar Rd. NN16: K'ing 7C 38
Trafalgar Rd. Ind. Est.
　NN16: K'ing 7C 38
Trafalgar Way NN11: Dav 2J 61
Trafford Rd. NN10: R'den 3F 81
Trailli La. NN14: Woodf 6B 50
Treen Cl. NN14: Thra 3K 51
Treetops NN3: N'ton 1D 86
Trefoil Cl. NN10: R'den 6F 81
Trenery Way NN4: N'ton . . .7J 131 (3E 94)
Trent Cl. NN5: N'ton 4K 83
　NN8: Well 6H 65
Trent Cres. NN15: Bur L 3J 45
Trentham Cl. NN4: N'ton 1D 100
Trent Rd. NN16: K'ing 4C 38
　NN17: Corby 4J 13
Trent Wlk. NN11: Dav 2E 60
Tresham Grn. NN5: Dus 5J 83
Tresham St. NN14: R'ell 6G 27
　NN16: K'ing 6E 38
Trevithick Rd. NN17: Corby 5D 14
Trevor Cl. NN5: N'ton 7K 83
Trevor Cres. NN5: N'ton 7K 83
Trimley Cl. NN3: N'ton 1A 96
Trinity Av. NN2: N'ton 5E 84
Trinity Cen. NN8: Well 5F 65
Trinity Cl. MK19: Old S 2J 125
　NN11: Dav 3G 61
Trinity Ct. NN14: R'ell 7F 27
Trinity Rd. NN14: R'ell 7E 26
Trinity Wlk. NN18: Corby 2K 17
Trinity Way OX17: Add 3A 126
Triumph Gdns. NN5: Dus 6E 82
Trojan Cen. NN8: Well 4B 66
Trojan Gym 4B 66
Tromso Cl. NN18: Corby 4F 17
Troon Cres. NN8: Well 5H 65
Troutbeck Wlk. NN3: N'ton 2K 85
Trundle Jetty NN4: N'ton 4A 94
　　　　　　　　　　　　(off Pitstone Rd.)
Trussell Rd. NN3: Gt Bil 5F 87
Tudely Cl. NN4: Woot 1G 101
Tudor Ct. NN4: Woot 2G 101
　NN16: K'ing 7F 38
　　　　　　　　　　　(off Alexandra St.)
Tudor Rd. NN1: N'ton 4H 85
Tudor Wlk. NN10: R'den 2F 81
Tudor Way NN8: Well 5K 65
　NN13: B'ley 3E 128
TUGBY 1D 133

Tulbrook Stones OX17: Mid C 7E 118
Tulip Dr. NN10: R'den 5E 80
Tunwell La. NN17: Corby 6C 14
TUR LANGTON 2D 133
Turnberry Cl. NN8: Well 5H 65
Turnberry La. NN4: Col 3C 100
Turnbrook Cl. NN9: Irth 1B 68
Turnells Mill La. NN8: Well 4B 78
Turner Cl. NN15: Bar S 2J 43
Turner Rd. NN8: Well 5A 66
　NN18: Corby 1K 17
Turners Ct. NN4: Woot 1E 100
Turners Farm Cl.
　NN6: Hann 4J 37
Turners Gdns. NN4: Woot 1E 100
Turner St. NN1: N'ton 7G 85
Turners Yd. PE8: Oun 5H 21
Turn Furlong NN2: K'thpe 1B 84
TURVEY .3B 138
TURWESTON 3J 129 (2C 141)
Turweston Rd. NN13: B'ley 2H 129
Tweed Cl. NN11: Dav 3F 61
　NN15: Bur L 3J 45
Tweed Rd. NN5: N'ton 1K 93
Twickenham Ct.
　NN18: Corby 1G 17
Twigden Rd. NN7: Kisl 4C 92
Twistle, The NN11: Byf 2H 107
Twitch Hill NN12: Shut 6A 116
TWYFORD
　Buckinghamshire 3C 141
　Leicestershire 1D 133
TWYWELL 1B 138
Twyford Av. NN9: Raun 6H 53
Twyford Cl. NN3: N'ton 6D 86
Tyebeck Ct. NN2: K'thpe 3C 84
Tyes Ct. NN3: N'ton 3C 86
Tyler Way NN14: Thra 4J 51
Tynan Cl. NN15: K'ing 2J 43
Tyne Cl. NN8: Well 6H 65
Tyne Rd. NN5: N'ton 1K 93
　NN11: Dav 3F 61
　NN17: Corby 4J 13
TYRINGHAM 3A 138
Tyringham Cl. NN3: N'ton 5A 86
Tyrrell Way NN12: Tow 2C 114
Tyson Courtyard
　NN18: Corby 6F 15
Tythings, The OX17: Mid C 4C 118

UFFINGTON 1C 135
UFFORD .1C 135
UFTON 2A 136
Uist Wlk. NN17: Corby 5H 13
ULLESTHORPE 3B 132
Ullswater Cl. NN8: Well 7H 65
　NN10: High F 4E 68
Ullswater Rd. NN16: K'ing 7A 38
Ultra Cl. NN8: Well 2D 78
Underbank La. NN3: Moul 7K 73
Underwood Rd. NN14: R'ell 6F 27
Union St. NN1: N'ton 4J 131 (1E 94)
　NN9: Fine 6J 47
　NN14: Des 2D 26
　NN16: K'ing 6C 38
Unity Cl. NN29: Woll 3D 90
Unity St. NN11: Dav 3D 26
University of Leicester
　Institute of Lifelong Learning
　　　　　　　　. . . . . .1H 131 (6D 84)
University of Northampton
　Avenue Campus 5E 84
　Park Campus 1G 85
Upland Rd. NN3: N'ton 4K 85
UPPER ARNCOTT 3C 141
UPPER ASTROP 2B 140
Up. Astrop Rd. OX17: King S 1C 126
Up. Bath St. NN1: N'ton . .4G 131 (1D 94)
　　　　　　　　　　　(not continuous)
UPPER BENEFIELD 3B 134
UPPER BODDINGTON . . .2B 106 (3A 136)
UPPER CATESBY 3B 136
Up. Cross St.
　NN1: N'ton 4G 131 (1D 94)
Upper Dane NN14: Des 2B 26
UPPER DEAN 2C 139
Upperfield Gro. NN17: Corby 5K 13
Up. George St. NN10: High F 5F 69
Up. Glen Av. NN7: Blis 6G 99
Upper Grn. NN11: Mor P 3H 111
UPPER HAMBLETON 1B 134
UPPER HARLESTONE 2C 82
Up. Havelock St. NN8: Well 7B 66
UPPER HEYFORD
　Northamptonshire 3K 63 (3C 137)
　Oxfordshire 3A 140
Up. High St. NN7: Harp 1B 92
Up. Kings Av. NN10: High F 5F 69
Upper Mounts
　NN1: N'ton 3J 131 (1E 94)

Upper Paradise OX17: King S 1B 126
Up. Park Av. NN10: R'den 4C 80
Up. Priory St.
　NN1: N'ton 2G 131 (7D 84)
Up. Queen St. NN10: R'den 2F 81
UPPER STAPLOE 3D 139
Upper Steeping NN14: Des 3E 26
UPPER STOWE 3C 137
Upper St. NN16: K'ing 7D 38
　　　　　　　　　　　　(off Northall St.)
Up. Thrift St. NN1: N'ton 1G 95
UPPER WARDINGTON 1A 140
UPPER WEALD 2D 141
UPPER WEEDON 4B 62 (3C 137)
UPPINGHAM 2A 134
Uppingham Rd.
　NN14: R'ton 7E 16
　NN17: Corby 4E 16
　NN18: Corby 4E 16
Uppingham St.
　NN1: N'ton 2F 131 (7C 84)
UPTON
　Cambridgeshire 1D 139
　Leicestershire 2A 132
　Northamptonshire . . .2J 93 (2D 137)
　Peterborough 1D 135
Upton Cl. NN2: K'thpe 7E 72
Upton La. NN5: Upton 2G 93
Upton Valley Way E.
　NN4: N'ton, Upton 6G 93
Upton Valley Way Nth.
　NN4: Upton 4E 92
　NN5: Upton 2E 92
Upton Way NN5: Upton 2J 93
Usher Ho. NN2: K'thpe 1E 84

Vale, The NN1: N'ton 5G 85
Valemead Wlk. NN3: N'ton 2D 86
Valentine Way NN3: Gt Bil 3F 87
Vale St. NN16: K'ing 6C 38
Valley Cl. NN13: B'ley 3H 129
Valley Cres. NN3: N'ton 5E 86
　NN13: B'ley 3G 129
Valley End NN12: Pat 5G 105
Valley Ri. NN13: B'ley 3G 129
　NN14: Des 3E 26
Valley Rd. LE16: West W 1D 10
　NN3: N'ton 5E 86
　NN8: Well 3A 78
　NN13: B'ley 3G 129
Valley Wlk. NN16: K'ing 7G 39
Vancouver Cl. NN18: Corby 4G 17
Vantage Mdw. NN3: N'ton 3G 87
Vara Ct. NN18: Corby 4G 17
Vardon Cl. NN8: Well 5H 65
Varley Cl. NN8: Well 4K 65
Vaux Rd. NN8: Well 3B 66
Velbert Ho. NN17: Corby 4K 13
Velocette Way NN5: Dus 5E 82
Venture Ct. NN17: Corby 4G 15
Verdant Va. NN4: N'ton 2E 100
Vernier Cl. NN11: Dav 7F 59
Vernon Cl. NN11: Dav 3J 61
Vernon Ct. NN1: N'ton 1G 95
　　　　　　　　　　　　(off Vernon Ter.)
　NN16: K'ing 4B 38
Vernon Rd. NN12: Tow 4D 114
Vernon St. NN1: N'ton 1G 95
Vernon Ter. NN1: N'ton 1G 95
Vernon Wlk. NN1: N'ton 1G 95
Verwood Cl. NN3: N'ton 1C 86
Veteran Cl. NN4: Woot 1F 101
Vian Way NN17: Corby 5G 13
　　　　　　　　　　　　(not continuous)
Vicarage Cl. NN2: K'thpe 3B 84
　NN7: Hack 2F 117
　NN8: Well 6J 65
　NN12: Whit 1C 122
Vicarage Farm Rd.
　NN8: Well 6J 65
Vicarage Hill NN11: Badby 6C 104
Vicarage La. NN2: K'thpe 3B 84
　NN6: E Had 2C 56
　NN6: Mears A 3A 76
　NN7: D'ton 6B 102
Vicarage Ri. NN12: Weed L 2D 112
Vicarage Rd. MK11: Stony S 3K 125
　NN5: N'ton 7B 84
　NN10: R'den 2F 81
　NN12: Yar G 3J 123
Vicar La. NN11: Dav 1J 61
Viceroy Cl. NN9: Raun 6K 53
Vickers Cl. NN14: R'ell 7J 27
Victoria Bus. Pk.
　NN1: N'ton 1C 94
　NN8: Well 3C 78
　　　　　　　　　　　　(not continuous)
Victoria Cl. NN6: E Bart 1D 88
　NN6: W Had 6H 29
　NN10: R'den 2E 80

Victoria Ct. NN10: R'den 2E **80**
 NN14: R'ell 6G **27**
 NN16: K'ing 7E **38**
 (off Victoria St.)
Victoria Gdns.
 NN1: N'ton 6H **131** (2E **94**)
Victoria Ho. NN1: N'ton 1F **95**
 (off Billing Rd.)
Victoria Prom.
 NN1: N'ton 6H **131** (2E **94**)
Victoria Rd. NN1: N'ton 1F **95**
 NN7: Cog 2H **97**
 NN8: Well 1B **78**
 NN9: Fine 6H **47**
 NN10: R'den 2E **80**
 PE8: Oun 4J **21**
Victoria St. NN1: N'ton . .3J **131** (1E **94**)
 NN6: E Bart 1E **88**
 NN9: Irth 3B **68**
 NN14: Des 2D **26**
 NN15: Bur L 2J **45**
 NN16: K'ing 7D **38**
Vienne Cl. NN5: Dus 6E **82**
Viking Cl. NN16: K'ing 3E **38**
Viking Way NN18: Corby 4E **16**
Villa Gdns. NN15: Bur L 3J **45**
Villagers Cl. NN4: Woot 3F **101**
Villa La. NN9: Stanw 1J **69**
Villa Ri. NN10: High F 5E **68**
Villa Way NN4: Woot 3G **101**
Vincent Cl. NN5: Dus 6E **82**
Vine Cl. PE8: Oun 5J **21**
Vine Hill Cl. NN10: High F 6D **68**
Vine Hill Dr. NN10: High F 6E **68**
Violet Cl. NN14: Des 1D **26**
 NN18: Corby 4J **17**
Violet La. NN6: Crea 6K **33**
Virgin Active Health Club
 Northampton **1C 96**
Viscount Rd. NN3: N'ton 7F **75**
Vivian Rd. NN8: Well 7C **66**
Vokes Cl. NN3: N'ton 5D **86**
Volunteer Cl. NN4: Woot 2F **101**
Vue Cinema
 Northampton **5G 131**
 (in Sol Central)
Vulcan Cl. NN11: Dav 6F **59**
Vyse Rd. NN2: Bou 6C **72**

W

Wadcroft NN16: K'ing 7D **38**
Wadd Cl. La. NN11: Whil 6D **56**
WADDESDON **3D 141**
Wade Mdw. Ct. NN3: N'ton 2C **86**
Wade Mdw. Wlk. NN3: N'ton 3C **86**
WADENHOE **3C 135**
Wadenhoe Rd. NN14: Ald 5A **20**
Wades Cl. PE8: Wood 6H **9**
Wadham Ct. NN11: Dav 4H **61**
Waendel Leisure Cen. **7C 66**
Waggoners Way NN7: Bug 2K **105**
Wagtail Cl. NN3: Moul 6K **73**
Wagtail Wlk. NN18: Corby 3K **17**
Waingrove NN7: Ect 2E **86**
Wainwright Av. NN14: Thra 4H **51**
Wake Cl. NN8: Well 4A **78**
Wakefield NN8: Well 1H **77**
Wakefield Dr. NN6: Welf 3G **29**
Wakefield Rd. NN2: K'thpe 2E **84**
Wakefield Way NN7: Neth H 6K **63**
Wakehurst Dr. NN4: N'ton 1D **100**
WAKERLEY **2B 134**
Wakerley Cl. PE8: Oun 5F **21**
Wakerley Rd. NN17: Harr 2B **8**
Wake Way NN4: Gra P 6F **101**
Walcot Cl. PE8: Oun 3G **21**
WALCOTE **3B 132**
Wales St. NN14: R'ell 6F **27**
 OX17: King S 1A **126**
WALGRAVE . . . .**1H 37 (1A 138)**
Walgrave Cl. NN3: N'ton 6E **86**
Walgrave Rd. NN6: Hann, Wal 2H **37**
 NN6: Holc 6H **37**
 NN6: Old 5E **36**
Walk, The NN6: Spra 6C **34**
Walker Dr. NN12: Tow 1C **114**
Walkers Acre NN6: Wal 1H **37**
Walkers Fld. PE8: King B 1H **9**
Walkers La. NN6: Chu B 5G **71**
 NN16: K'ing 7D **38**
Walker Sq. NN8: Well 5H **65**
Walkers Way NN4: Woot 3F **101**
 NN9: Fine 7H **47**
Walks, The PE9: Colly 6C **6**
Wallace Gdns. NN2: N'ton 4G **85**
Wallace Rd. NN2: N'ton 4G **85**
Wallace Ter. NN2: N'ton 4G **85**
Wallbeck Cl. NN2: K'thpe 2D **84**
Walledwell Ct. NN2: N'ton 5C **86**
Wallingford End NN3: N'ton 6D **86**
Wallis Cl. NN8: Well 1F **77**

Wallis Cres. NN15: K'ing 2E **42**
Wallis Rd. NN15: K'ing 2E **42**
Wallwin Cl. NN7: Roa 3B **116**
Walmer Cl. NN10: R'den 4G **81**
Walnut Cl. NN11: Braun 1C **58**
 NN12: Silv 3H **121**
 NN13: B'ley 2G **129**
 NN17: Weld 5J **15**
 OX17: Cul 7C **110**
Walnut Cres. NN16: K'ing 5F **39**
Walnut Tree Cl. NN14: Woodf 7B **50**
Walnut Tree Rd. NN10: High F 5E **68**
WALSGRAVE ON SOWE **3A 140**
Walsingham Av. NN15: K'ing 2H **43**
Walter Tull Way NN15: K'ing 2J **93**
Waltham Cl. NN17: Corby 4J **13**
WALTON
 Leicestershire **3B 132**
 Peterborough **1D 135**
Walton Heath Way NN2: N'ton 3F **85**
Walton Pl. NN18: Corby 7G **13**
WANLIP **1C 133**
Wansell Rd. NN17: Corby 5G **15**
WANSFORD **2C 135**
Wansford Pl. NN17: Corby 5G **13**
Wansford Rd. PE8: Yar 2H **7**
Wansford Wlk. NN3: N'ton 7B **74**
Wantage Cl. NN3: Moul 4B **74**
 NN7: Hack 1G **117**
Wantage Pl. NN29: Irch 5J **79**
Wantage Rd. NN1: N'ton 6H **85**
 NN29: Irch 5J **79**
Wappeham Rd. NN12: Abt, Slapt . .7F **113**
WAPPENBURY **2A 136**
WAPPENHAM . . . .**5C 112 (1C 141)**
Wappenham Rd. NN13: Helm 2B **120**
 NN13: Syre 5C **120**
Wardens Lodge NN11: Dav 1H **61**
 (off North St.)
WARDINGTON **1A 140**
Wardington Ct. NN2: K'thpe 2C **84**
Wardington Rd. OX17: Chac 1A **118**
Wardle Ct. NN16: K'ing 6D **38**
 (off Princes St.)
Wardle's Cl. NN7: Gt Bri 2G **57**
WARDLEY **1A 134**
Wardlow Cl. NN4: N'ton 7A **94**
Ward Rd. NN13: B'ley 6H **129**
Wards La. NN6: Yel 6D **28**
Wareham Grn. NN18: Corby 7G **13**
 (off Taunton Av.)
Wareing La. NN7: D'ton 6B **102**
Ware Orchard CV23: Bar 1C **54**
Ware Rd. CV23: Bar 1C **54**
WARESLEY **3D 139**
WARKTON . . . .**5J 39 (1A 138)**
Warkton La. NN15: Bar S, K'ing 3J **43**
 NN16: K'ing, Warkt 3J **43**
Warkton Rd. NN14: Warkt 5K **39**
 NN16: Warkt 5K **39**
Warkton Way NN17: Corby 5G **13**
WARKWORTH **1A 140**
Warkworth Rd.
 OX17: Mid C, Warkw 7A **118**
 (not continuous)
WARMINGTON
 Northamptonshire . . .**2H 23 (2C 135)**
 Warwickshire **1A 140**
Warminster Rd. NN18: Corby 6F **13**
WARMONDS HILL **1D 80**
Warmonds Hill NN10: High F 7E **68**
Warners Hill NN29: Boz 3H **103**
Warnham Rd. NN8: Well 7G **65**
Warren, The NN4: H'stone 1G **101**
Warren Bri. PE8: Oun 5G **21**
Warren Cl. NN29: Irch 6K **79**
Warren End NN14: Des 1E **26**
 NN14: Maw 6A **40**
Warren Hill NN16: K'ing 6A **38**
Warren Rd. NN5: N'ton 7A **84**
 NN12: Yar G 3J **123**
 NN14: Stan 3F **19**
Warrens Cl. NN9: Irth 1C **68**
WARRINGTON **3A 138**
Warth Ho. NN9: Raun 5G **53**
Warth Pk. Way NN9: Raun 5G **53**
Warwick Av. NN14: Stan 3F **19**
Warwick Cl. NN5: Dus 6G **83**
 NN9: Raun 7J **53**
Warwick Ct. NN11: Dav 2G **61**
 (off Warwick St.)
 NN15: K'ing 2H **43**
Warwick Gdns. NN14: Thra 3K **51**
Warwick Rd. NN8: Well 3B **78**
 NN11: Up Bod 2A **106**
Warwick St. NN11: Dav 2G **61**
Warwick Way NN17: Corby 7H **13**
Washbrook Cl. NN3: N'ton 5E **86**
Washbrook La. NN6: Ect 1J **87**
Washbrook Rd. NN10: R'den 2D **80**
Washingley La. PE7: Wash 6K **23**
Washington Ct. NN14: Thra 2J **51**
 NN16: K'ing 6F **39**

Washington Sq. NN16: K'ing 6F **39**
Washington St. NN2: K'thpe 3C **84**
Washle Dr. OX17: Mid C 6E **118**
Water Cl. MK19: Old S 2J **125**
Waterfowl Wlk. NN3: N'ton 5E **86**
Waterhouse Gdns.
 NN15: Bar S 3J **43**
Watering La. NN4: Col 4D **100**
Water La. LE16: Cotti 5C **12**
 NN4: Woot 2F **101**
 NN9: Chel 7J **69**
 NN12: Shut 6A **116**
 NN12: Tow 4C **114**
 NN13: B'ley 4H **129**
 NN17: Weld 5H **15**
Waterlee Furlong NN6: Brix 4J **35**
Waterloo NN11: Dav 2H **61**
Waterloo Way NN9: Irth 4B **68**
Waterloo Yd. NN8: Well 1A **78**
Waterlow Bri. NN9: Fine 6H **47**
Water Mdw. Cl. NN18: Gt Oak 5G **17**
Watermeadow Dr. NN3: N'ton 1C **86**
Watermill Cl. NN14: Des 2G **27**
WATER NEWTON **2D 135**
Water Pike NN6: Brix 3J **35**
Waterpump Ct. NN3: N'ton 1B **86**
Waterside Way NN4: N'ton 5J **95**
Waters La. OX17: Mid C 4E **118**
Watersmeet NN1: N'ton 1K **95**
WATER STRATFORD **2C 141**
Water St. NN16: K'ing 7E **38**
Waterview Wlk. NN3: N'ton 1B **86**
Watervill Way NN14: L Add 4A **52**
Waterworks La. NN8: Well 5H **65**
Watery La. NN7: Neth H 5K **63**
 NN13: B'ley 4H **129**
WATFORD . . . .**6D 54 (2C 137)**
WATFORD GAP SERVICE AREA . . .**7D 54**
Watford Rd.
 NN6: Crick, Wat . . . . . .6H **31** & 4C **54**
 NN6: W Had 7F **29**
 NN11: Welt 7A **54**
Watkin Ct. NN1: N'ton 1K **131**
Watkin Ter. NN1: N'ton . . .1J **131** (7E **84**)
Watling St. CV23: Kil 6C **30**
 CV23: New, Clif D . . .3A **28** & 1C **30**
 MK19: Old S 1G **125**
 NN6: Wat 7B **54**
 NN7: Chu S, Up St, Weed 1C **62**
 NN11: Broc, Nor, Weed 4H **55**
 NN12: Fos B, Grim, Pat 4F **105**
 NN12: Old S, Pot 4F **123**
 NN12: Paul 4H **115**
 NN12: Tow 1A **114**
Watling St. E. NN12: Pat 5G **105**
 NN12: Tow 5D **114**
Watling St. W. NN12: Fos B 5G **105**
 NN12: Tow 3C **114**
Watson Av. LE16: Mkt H 1K **25**
Watson Cl. NN8: Well 5H **65**
 NN17: Corby 3K **13**
 PE8: Oun 3G **21**
Watson Rd. NN6: Long B 3H **55**
Watt Av. NN17: Corby 5B **14**
Watts Cl. NN7: Cog 1J **97**
Watts Way NN6: Long B 2J **55**
Wavell Cl. NN15: K'ing 1G **43**
Waveney Cl. NN11: Dav 3F **61**
Waveney Way NN5: N'ton 5A **84**
Waver Cl. NN18: Corby 3J **17**
Waverley Av. NN17: Corby 7B **14**
Waverley Cl. OX17: King S 1B **126**
Waverley Rd. NN2: N'ton 5F **85**
 NN15: K'ing 2F **43**
Waynflete Av. NN13: B'ley 4F **129**
Waynflete Cl. NN13: B'ley 4F **129**
Waypost Cl. NN3: N'ton 3C **86**
Wayside NN7: Roa 3D **116**
Wayside Acres NN4: N'ton 7C **94**
Weaver Cl. NN16: K'ing 3D **38**
Weavers, The NN4: N'ton 1D **100**
Weavers Leisure Cen. **1J 77**
Weavers Rd. NN8: Well 1J **77**
Webb Cl. PE8: Oun 5K **21**
Webb Rd. NN9: Raun 5H **53**
Webbs Factory NN2: N'ton 5E **84**
Webbs La. NN6: Syw 2F **75**
Webster Cl. NN9: Raun 5J **53**
Weddell Way NN4: Brack 5K **95**
WEDDINGTON **2A 132**
Wedgwood Cl. NN14: Des 2C **26**
Wedmore Cl. NN5: Dus 7J **83**
Wedmore Ct. NN18: Corby 7G **13**
WEEDON **3D 141**
WEEDON BEC . . . .**3B 62 (3C 137)**
Weedon La. NN7: Dod 1A **62**
 NN11: Nor 1D **56**
WEEDON LOIS . . . .**3D 112 (1C 141)**
Weedon Rd.
 NN5: Upton, Dus, N'ton 2H **93**
 (not continuous)
 NN7: Chu S 7F **63**
 NN7: Kisl, Up Hey 3A **92**

Weedon Rd. NN7: Neth H 4H **63**
 NN11: Newn 7K **61**
Weedon Rd. Ind. Est. NN5: N'ton . .1K **93**
WEEKLEY . . . .**3H 39 (3A 134)**
Weekley Glebe Rd. NN16: K'ing . . .4F **39**
Weekley Wood Av. NN14: Week . . .1D **38**
Weekley Wood La. NN16: Week . . .3G **39**
Weekly Cl. NN14: L Add 4A **52**
Weggs Farm Rd. NN5: Dus 6E **82**
Weighbrigde Way NN9: Raun 7H **53**
Weinahr Cl. LE16: Wilb 5H **11**
Weir, The NN11: Dav 3G **59**
 (off Buscott Pk. Way)
Weir Cl. NN8: Well 6A **66**
Welbeck Cl. NN15: K'ing 2H **43**
 NN18: Corby 1H **17**
Welbourne Cl. NN9: Raun 6H **53**
WELDON . . . .**6J 15 (3B 134)**
Weldon Cl. NN8: Well 5J **65**
Weldon Nth. Ind. Est.
 NN17: Corby 4H **15**
 (not continuous)
Weldon Rd. NN17: Corby 7B **14**
Weldon Sth. Ind. Est.
 NN18: Corby 6F **15**
Weldon St. NN16: K'ing 6E **38**
Weldon Woodland Pk. **6H 15**
WELFORD . . . .**3H 29 (3C 133)**
Welford Av. NN9: Irth 7A **52**
Welford Cl. NN9: Irth 7A **52**
Welford Gro. NN17: Corby 6H **13**
Welford Rd. NN2: Chap B, K'thpe . .6A **72**
 NN6: Chap B 6A **72**
 NN6: Chap B, Crea, Spra
 . . . . .4H **33**, 4B **34** & 1H **71**
 NN6: Nas 2H **33**
 NN6: Sibb, Sulb 2H **33**
 NN6: Thorn 2D **32**
WELHAM **2D 133**
Welham Rd. LE16: West W 1C **10**
Welland Cl. NN9: Raun 5H **53**
 NN11: Dav 2E **60**
 NN17: Gret 7C **8**
Welland Ct. NN14: Des 2D **26**
 NN15: Bur L 2J **45**
Welland Grn. NN5: N'ton 4A **84**
Welland Ri. LE16: Sibb 2C **24**
Welland Rd. NN16: K'ing 4C **38**
Welland Va. Rd. NN17: Corby 4J **13**
Welland Vw. Rd. LE16: Cotti 4C **12**
Welland Wlk. NN5: N'ton 4A **84**
Welland Way NN5: N'ton 4A **84**
Well Hill Cl. NN6: Crick 4H **31**
WELLINGBOROUGH . . . . .**7B 66 (2A 138)**
 NN8: Well 3C **78**
Wellingborough Bus. Cen.
 NN8: Well 3C **78**
Wellingborough Heritage Cen. & Mus.
 (Croyland Hall) **1B 78**
Wellingborough Indoor Bowls Club
 . . . .**7K 65**
Wellingborough Mus. **1C 78**
Wellingborough Rd.
 NN1: N'ton 3K **131** (1F **95**)
 NN3: Abing, N'ton 6J **85**
 NN6: E Bart 1E **88**
 NN6: Ect 2J **87**
 NN6: Mears A 3B **76**
 NN6: Syw 2H **75**
 NN8: Well 4E **66**
 NN9: Fine 1F **67**
 NN9: Gt Har, Well, L Harr 1G **65**
 (not continuous)
 NN9: Irth 5J **67**
 NN10: R'den 2A **80**
 NN14: Brou, Pyt 6G **41**
 NN14: Ish 4F **45**
 NN29: Woll 3D **90**
Wellingborough Station (Rail) **7D 66**
Wellington Pl. NN1: N'ton 2H **131**
Wellington Rd. NN9: Raun 7H **53**
Wellington St.
 NN1: N'ton 4J **131** (1E **94**)
 (not continuous)
 NN16: K'ing 6D **38**
Wellington Ter. NN14: Is'l 3F **51**
Wellington Works NN16: K'ing 6E **38**
 (off Wellington St.)
Well La. NN6: Guil 7E **32**
 NN11: Stav 4A **60**
 NN11: Welt 1K **59**
 NN14: R'ell 6G **27**
 PE8: Barn 5B **22**
Wells, The NN9: Fine 6H **47**
WELLSBOROUGH **1A 132**
Wells Cl. NN15: K'ing 2B **42**
Wells Ct. NN3: Moul 5K **73**
Wells Grn. NN18: Corby 7G **13**
Wellspring NN7: Blis 2H **115**
Well Yd. NN2: K'thpe 3C **84**
Welsh Rd.
 NN11: Ast W, Chip W, Up Bod
 . . . . .1B **106**
 OX17: Greatw, Mar L 1H **119**

WELTON 2K 59 (2B 136)
Welton La. NN11: Dav, Welt 5J 59
Welton Pk. NN11: Welt 1J 59
Welton Rd. CV23: Bar 3B 54
   NN11: Braun 1B 58
   NN11: Dav 6H 59
Welton Station (Rail) 7C 54
WENDLEBURY 3B 140
Wenlock Way NN5: Dus 6J 83
WENNINGTON 1D 139
Wensleydale NN2: K'thpe 1A 84
Wensleydale Pk. NN17: Corby . . .5J 13
Wentin Cl. NN18: Gt Oak 5H 17
Wentworth Av. NN8: Well 6H 65
Wentworth Ct. NN11: Dav 7K 59
Wentworth Dr. PE8: Oun 3G 21
Wentworth Rd. NN9: Fine 6J 47
   NN10: R'den 3D 80
Wentworth Way NN2: N'ton 3F 85
   NN12: Stoke B 6C 116
WERRINGTON 1D 135
Weskers Cl. NN16: Clip 7D 24
Wesley Ct. *NN14: R'ell* 6G 27
                 (off Well Dr.)
Wesley Pl. OX17: Chac 2B 118
Wessex Cl. NN16: K'ing 3D 38
Wessex Way NN3: N'ton 5J 85
West Av. NN15: Bur L 1J 45
West Bank NN3: N'ton 7B 74
West Brook NN7: Blis 1H 115
   NN11: Newn 7J 61
Westbrook NN8: Well 1G 77
Westburgh Sq. NN11: Dav 3H 61
WESTBURY 2C 141
Westbury Cl. NN5: Dus 7J 83
Westbury Wlk. NN18: Corby 2H 17
WESTCOTT 3D 141
WESTCOTT BARTON 3A 140
W. Cotton Cl. LE16: Clip 3D 94
Westcott Way NN3: N'ton 7A 86
   NN18: Corby 7J 13
West Ct. NN6: Welf 2H 29
   NN11: Dav 2H 61
West Cres. NN10: R'den 3B 80
WEST DEEPING 1D 135
WEST END 3B 138
West End NN6: Scal 7A 36
   NN6: W Had 5G 29
   NN6: Welf 4G 29
   NN7: Bug 2H 105
   NN12: Silv 4G 121
Westerdale NN2: K'thpe 1A 84
Western Av. NN7: Neth H 6J 63
   NN11: Dav 1G 61
   PE9: Eas H 2B 6
Western Cl. NN11: Dav 1G 61
Western Vw. NN1: N'ton . . .5F 131 (2C 94)
Western Way NN8: Well 2J 77
W. Farm Cl. NN6: Hann 3K 37
WEST FARNDON 5A 108 (3B 136)
Westfield Av. MK19: Dean 4E 124
   NN9: Raun 7G 53
   NN10: R'den 3B 80
Westfield Cl. NN6: W Had 6H 29
Westfield Cres. NN6: Welf 2H 29
Westfield Dr. NN9: Raun 7G 53
Westfield Ho. NN16: K'ing 7C 38
Westfield Pl. NN8: R'den 3C 80
Westfield Rd. NN5: Dus 6G 83
   NN5: N'ton 1A 94
   NN8: Well 1K 77
Westfields NN9: L Harr 1G 65
   PE9: Eas H 2B 6
Westfields Av. NN10: High F 7E 68
Westfields Rd. NN17: Corby 5K 13
Westfields St. NN10: High F 7E 68
Westfields Ter. NN10: High F 7E 68
West Furlong NN15: K'ing 1B 42
Westgate Ind. Est. NN5: N'ton . . .1J 93
Westgate Rd. NN5: N'ton 1J 93
W. Glebe Rd. NN17: Corby 5A 14
WEST HADDON 6H 29 (1C 137)
W. Haddon Rd. NN6: Col A 3A 32
   NN6: Crick 3J 31
   NN6: Guil 5A 32
   NN6: Rav 2A 34
   NN6: Wat 6E 54
Westhaven PE9: Eas H 2C 6
Westhill Av. NN13: B'ley 4E 128
Westhill Cl. NN13: B'ley 4F 129
   NN15: K'ing 1B 42
Westhill Dr. NN15: K'ing 1B 42
Westhill Gdns. NN13: B'ley 4E 128
WESTHORP . . . . . . .3B 136 & 2H 107
Westhorp OX17: Greatw 2K 119
Westhorpe LE16: A'ley 3G 11
   LE16: Sibb 2C 24
Westhorpe La. NN11: Byf 2H 107
Westhorpe M. NN11: Byf 3H 107
Westlea Rd. NN6: Syw 2G 75
Westleigh Cl. NN1: N'ton 6G 85
Westleigh Office Pk. NN3: Moul P . .7F 73
Westleigh Rd. NN3: Bar S 2K 43

Westley Cl. NN15: Bur L 3J 45
W. Leys Cl. NN3: Moul 6K 73
West Lodge Rural Cen. 3A 134
West March NN11: Dav 4J 61
W. March Ind. Est. NN11: Dav . . .3J 61
W. Mead Ct. NN3: N'ton 5C 86
West Mill PE9: Eas H 3B 6
Westminster Cl. NN13: B'ley 4H 129
Westminster Cres. NN13: B'ley . . .4G 129
Westminster Cft. NN13: B'ley 4G 129
Westminster Dr. NN15: Bar S 3H 43
Westminster Rd. NN8: Well 6J 65
   NN13: B'ley 5G 129
Westminster Wlk. NN18: Corby . . .2H 17
Westmoreland Dr. PE8: Nass 5G 7
Westmorland Dr. NN14: Des 1F 27
WESTON 3B 112 (1B 136)
WESTON BY WELLAND . . .2D 10 (2D 133)
Westone Av. NN3: N'ton 5A 86
WESTON FAVELL 6A 86 (2D 137)
Weston Favell Shop. Cen.
   . . . . .4C 86
WESTON IN ARDEN 3A 132
Weston Mill La. NN3: West F 7B 86
WESTON-ON-THE-GREEN 3B 140
Weston Rd. LE16: A'ley 2F 11
   LE16: Sutt B 4C 10
   NN11: Mor P 3H 111
             (not continuous)
   NN13: Helm 1B 120
   OX17: Sulg 5H 111
WESTON UNDER WETHERLEY . . .2A 136
WESTON UNDERWOOD 3A 138
Westonville PE9: Colly 6C 6
Weston Wlk. NN18: Corby 7H 13
Weston Way NN3: West F 6K 85
Weston Wharf
   NN1: N'ton 6G 131 (2D 94)
West Oval NN5: N'ton 5A 84
Westover Rd. NN15: K'ing 1B 42
W. Paddock Ct. NN3: N'ton 2C 86
WEST PERRY 2D 139
West Pl. *NN11: Dav* 1H 61
                (off West Ct.)
W. Priors Ct. NN3: N'ton 2C 86
W. Puxley Cl. MK19: Dean 4E 124
West Ridge NN2: K'thpe 3E 84
West Rising NN4: N'ton 1E 100
West St. NN1: N'ton 1G 95
   NN3: Moul 4J 73
   NN6: E Bart 2C 88
   NN6: Ect 3J 87
   NN6: Long B 1G 55
   NN6: Welf 3H 29
   NN7: Weed 4C 62
   NN8: Well 1A 78
   NN9: Raun 6J 53
   NN9: Stanw 1H 69
   NN10: R'den 3E 80
   NN14: Brou 5G 41
   NN14: Ged 6C 46
   NN14: Woodf 6A 50
   PE8: King C 2G 9
   PE8: Oun 5H 21
   PE9: Eas H 1B 6
West St. M. *PE8: Oun* 5H 21
               (off West St.)
West Vw. NN8: L Irch 4D 78
   NN11: Dav 2G 61
   NN17: Corby 6C 14
West Vw. Ct. *NN8: Well* 1A 78
               (off West St.)
Westvilla Cotts. NN8: Well 1A 78
W. Villa Rd. NN8: Well 1A 78
West Way NN6: E Bart 1C 88
   NN7: Weed 4C 62
Westway NN15: K'ing 1B 42
Westway, The NN11: Dav 3J 61
WESTWOOD 2D 135
Westwood Wlk. NN18: Corby 1H 17
Westwood Way NN3: N'ton 5A 86
West Yd. NN14: Isl 2F 51
Westy Rd. NN12: Pur E 6F 115
Wetenhall Rd. NN9: Stanw 7F 53
Wetheral Ct. NN3: N'ton 2K 85
Weymouth Cl. NN18: Corby 7G 13
WHADDON 2D 141
Whaddon Cl. NN4: N'ton 6K 93
Whaddon Fld. NN6: Brix 4J 35
Whalley Gro. NN7: Cog 1J 97
WHARF, THE 3H 105
Wharf, The NN11: Braun 2A 58
Wharf Cl. MK19: Old S 2J 125
Wharfedale Rd. NN17: Corby 4K 13
Wharf Grn. NN5: N'ton 4A 84
Wharf La. MK19: Old S 2K 125
Wharf Rd. NN10: High F 6D 68
Wharton Cl. NN11: Dav 4H 59
Wheat Cl. NN11: Dav 4H 59
Wheatcroft Gdns. NN10: R'den . . .3E 80
Wheatens Cl. NN6: Brix 5J 35
Wheatfield Dr. NN15: Bur L 2K 45

Wheatfield Gdns. NN3: N'ton 5J 85
Wheatfield Rd. NN3: N'ton 5J 85
Wheatfield Rd. Nth. NN3: N'ton . . .4J 85
Wheatfield Rd. Sth. NN3: N'ton . . .5J 85
Wheatfield Ter. NN3: N'ton 5J 85
Wheatley Av. NN17: Corby 7A 14
Wheeler's Ri. NN13: Crou 5A 130
Wheelwright Cl. NN9: Raun 5K 53
Wheelwrights Way MK19: Old S . .2J 125
Wheelwrights Yd. NN29: Boz 3H 103
Whernside NN8: Well 6J 65
Whernside Way NN5: Dus 6H 83
WHETSTONE 2B 132
Whilton Locks NN11: Whil 6J 55
Whilton Locks 6D 56 (2C 137)
Whilton Mill Go-Karting 6A 56
Whilton Rd. NN2: K'thpe 2E 84
   NN7: Gt Bri 2F 57
Whistlets Cl. NN4: N'ton 6J 93
WHISTON 7C 88 (2A 138)
Whiston Rd. NN2: K'thpe 2E 84
   NN7: Cog . . . . . .1K 97 & 7K 88
   NN7: D'ton 5B 102
Whitby Cl. NN15: K'ing 2H 43
WHITCHURCH 3D 141
Whitecroft Gdns. NN11: Woodf H . .1C 108
Whitecroft La. NN11: Byf 2J 107
White Delves NN8: Well 5K 65
White Doe Dr. NN3: Moul 6K 73
Whitefield Rd. NN5: Dus 5G 83
Whitefield Way NN9: Raun 5H 53
Whiteford Dr. NN15: K'ing 3E 42
Whitefriars NN10: R'den 4B 80
Whitegates NN4: N'ton 6J 93
Whiteheart Cl. NN9: Raun 4E 86
Whitehill Rd. NN14: Des 2B 26
WHITE HILLS 7C 72
White Hills Cres. NN2: K'thpe 7C 72
White Hills Way NN2: K'thpe 7C 72
White Horse Yd. NN12: Tow 3C 114
Whitehorse Yd. *MK11: S Stra* 4K 125
                (off High St.)
White Ho. Ct. *NN10: R'den* 4F 81
             (off Denmark Rd.)
White Ho. Ind. Est. NN6: E Bart . . .7C 76
Whiteland Rd. NN3: N'ton 4K 85
Whiteman La. NN14: R'ell 6F 27
White Post Ct. NN17: Corby 3K 13
Whitesands Way NN4: N'ton 5H 93
Whites La. NN5: Lwr H 3F 83
Whites Ri. NN9: Irth 3B 68
White Way NN6: E Bart 1D 88
WHITFIELD 2C 141
Whitfield Way NN2: K'thpe 1E 84
Whiting Ct. NN3: Moul 5K 73
Whitney Cl. NN9: Raun 7H 53
Whitney Rd. NN15: Bur L 3J 45
Whitsundale Cl. NN9: Fine 7H 47
Whittall St. OX17: King S 1B 126
Whittam Cl. NN9: Raun 5H 53
Whittemore Rd. NN10: R'den 2G 81
WHITTLEBURY 1C 122 (1C 141)
Whittlebury Cl. NN2: K'thpe 1E 84
Whittlebury Ct. NN12: Whit 1C 122
Whittlebury Rd. MK19: Wick 2A 124
   NN12: Pot, Wick 2A 124
   NN12: Silv 2H 121
Whittle Cl. NN8: Well 6G 65
   NN11: Dav 5F 59
Whittle Rd. NN17: Corby 5C 14
Whittles Cross NN4: Woot 2H 101
Whittlesea Ter. NN14: Woodf 7B 50
Whitton Cl. OX17: Greatw 2K 119
Whittons La. NN12: Tow 3C 114
WHITWELL 1B 134
Whitwell Cl. PE8: Oun 5G 21
Whitworth Av. NN17: Corby 4B 14
Whitworth Cres. NN6: E Bart 1D 88
Whitworth Rd. NN7: Flo 7G 85
   NN8: Well 7D 66
Whitworth Way NN8: Well 3C 78
   NN9: Irth 4B 68
Whytewell Rd. NN8: Well 6A 66
WIBTOFT 3A 132
Wick Cl. NN18: Corby 3J 17
WICKEN 6C 124 (2D 141)
Wicken Pk. Rd. MK19: Wick 6C 124
Wicken Rd. MK18: Leck 7A 124
   MK19: Dean 6D 124
Wickery Dene NN4: Woot 2H 101
Wicksteed Cl. NN15: K'ing 4E 42
Wicksteed Ct. *NN5: Upton* 3J 93
              (off Clickers Dr.)
Wicksteed Pk. 3G 43
WIGGINTON 2A 140
WIGSTHORPE 3C 135
WIGSTON 2C 133
WILBARSTON 5H 11 (3A 134)
Wilbarston Rd. LE16: Stoke A 6G 11
Wilberforce St. NN1: N'ton 1F 95
WILBY 4G 77 (2A 138)
Wilby Cl. NN17: Corby 5G 13
Wilbye Grange NN8: Well 3J 77

Wilby La. NN29: Gt Dod 6J 77
Wilby Pk. Mobile Home Pk.
   . . . . .3H 77
Wilby Rd. NN6: Mears A 4A 76
Wilby St. NN1: N'ton 1G 95
Wilby Way NN8: Well 3J 77
Wilce Av. NN8: Well 4B 78
Wildacre Rd. NN10: R'den 3B 80
Wild Cherry Cl. NN11: Woodf H . .2C 108
WILDEN 3C 139
Wildern La. NN4: N'ton 3D 100
Wilford Av. NN3: N'ton 6C 86
Wilkie Cl. NN15: K'ing 2B 42
Wilkie Rd. NN8: Well 4A 66
Wilks Wlk. NN4: Gra P 5F 101
WILLENHALL 1A 136
Willetts Cl. NN17: Corby 5K 13
WILLEY 3A 132
William Carey Hall NN3: K'thpe . .7F 73
William Lee Cl. NN6: Col A 2A 32
William Rd. NN6: Long B 2H 55
WILLIAMSCOT 1A 140
William Steele Way NN10: High F . .7F 69
Williams Ter. NN11: Dav 1G 61
William St. NN1: N'ton 2J 131 (7E 84)
   NN9: Fine 7J 47
   NN15: Bur L 2J 45
   NN16: K'ing 5D 38
Williams Way NN4: Gra P 5F 101
   NN10: High F 1F 68
   NN29: Woll 5F 91
William Trigg Cl. NN9: Irth 4B 68
WILLINGTON 3D 139
Willison Cen. 3B 116
Willis Way NN12: Tow 4C 114
Williton Cl. NN3: West F 7A 86
Willmott Rd. NN10: R'den 5F 81
WILLOUGHBY 2B 136
Willoughby Cl. NN11: Dav 7G 59
Willoughby Rd.
   CV23: Bar, Kil . . . . .3C 54 & 7C 30
WILLOUGHBY WATERLEYS 2B 132
Willoughby Way NN7: Pid 3F 117
Willowbrook E. Ind. Est.
   NN17: Corby 3E 14
Willow Brook Rd. NN17: Corby . . .5H 13
Willow Brook Sq. NN3: N'ton 3G 87
Willow Cl. NN6: Spra 6B 34
   NN11: Woodf H 2B 108
   NN12: Tow 5C 114
   NN14: Des 2F 27
Willow Ct. NN1: N'ton 7H 85
Willow Cres. NN4: Gt Hou 5B 96
Willow Gro. MK19: Old S 3J 125
Willow Herb Cl. NN10: R'den 6F 81
Willow Herb Wlk. NN14: Des 1D 26
Willow Ho. *NN1: N'ton* 7G 85
                (off Lea Rd.)
Willow La. MK11: Stony S 4K 125
   NN4: Gt Hou 5B 96
   NN14: Stan 4F 19
   PE8: King C 1G 9
Willow Pl. NN17: Corby 1K 17
Willow Ri. NN3: N'ton 6E 86
Willow Rd. NN13: B'ley 5H 129
   NN15: K'ing 1E 42
Willows, The NN4: N'ton 4J 95
   NN9: L Harr 1G 65
   NN11: Dav 7H 59
   NN12: Silv 2G 121
   NN14: Thra 4G 51
   OX17: King S 1C 126
Willow Vw. NN7: Kisl 4B 92
Wills Cl. NN6: Guil 6D 32
Wilmington Wlk. NN18: Corby 1G 17
Wilson Cl. NN11: Dav 6F 59
Wilson Cres. NN9: Irth 3B 68
Wilson Rd. NN10: R'den 3D 80
Wilson Ter. NN16: K'ing 5D 38
Wilson Way NN6: E Bart 3D 87
WILSTHORPE 1C 135
Wilton Cl. NN14: Des 3D 26
Wilton Rd. NN15: K'ing 2H 43
Wimbledon St. NN5: N'ton 1B 94
Wimborne Cl. NN3: N'ton 3G 87
Wimborne Pl. NN11: Dav 5H 59
Wimbourne Wlk. NN18: Corby 6F 13
Wimpole Rd. NN8: Well 1H 77
Wincanton Ct. NN18: Corby 7G 13
Wincely Cl. NN11: Dav 4D 59
Winchester Cl. NN4: Del 6D 94
Winchester Rd. NN4: Del 6D 94
   NN10: R'den 4F 81
Winchilsea Dr. NN17: Gret 6C 8
Windermere Cl. NN11: Dav 1G 61
Windermere Dr. NN8: Well 7H 65
   NN10: High F 4E 68
Windermere Rd. NN16: K'ing 7B 38
Windermere Way NN3: N'ton 2K 85
Windflower Pl. NN3: N'ton 4G 87
Windingbrook La.
   NN4: Col, N'ton 3D 100
Winding Way NN14: Thra 3J 51

Windmill Av. NN7: Blis 2H **115**
  NN9: Raun 6J **53**
  NN15: K'ing 6F **39**
  NN16: K'ing 6F **39**
Windmill Banks NN10: High F 5E **68**
Windmill Bus. Cen. NN10: R'den . . .3C **80**
Windmill Cl. LE16: Cotti 4C **12**
  NN8: Well 3K **77**
  NN14: Woodf 6A **50**
  NN29: Woll 4F **91**
Windmill Ct. NN16: K'ing 6F **39**
  (off Edmund St.)
Windmill Gdns. NN11: Stav 4B **60**
Windmill Glade NN6: Brix 4G **35**
Windmill Gro. NN9: Raun 6J **53**
Windmill La. NN7: D'ton 6B **102**
  NN9: Raun 5H **53**
  NN11: Stav 4B **60**
Windmill Ri. LE16: Cotti 4C **12**
Windmill Rd. NN9: Irth 3B **68**
  NN10: R'den 3D **80**
Windmill Ter. NN2: K'thpe 1E **84**
Windmill Wlk. NN15: K'ing 1F **43**
Windmill Way NN12: Greens N . . .1H **113**
Windrush Rd. NN4: H'stone 7G **95**
Windrush Way NN5: N'ton 5B **84**
Windsor Av. NN14: Des 3C **26**
Windsor Cl. LE16: Wilb 6H **11**
  NN6: Long B 2H **55**
  NN7: Weed 3C **62**
  NN11: Dav 2G **61**
  NN12: Tow 4B **114**
  OX17: King S 1B **126**
Windsor Ct. NN3: Gt Bil 4F **87**
Windsor Cres. NN5: N'ton 1K **83**
Windsor Dr. NN13: B'ley 3F **129**
  NN14: Thra 3J **51**
Windsor Gdns. NN16: K'ing 6C **38**
Windsor Ho. NN5: Dus 6H **83**
  (off Limehurst Rd.)
Windsor Pl. NN17: Corby 1K **17**
Windsor Rd. NN8: Well 4K **77**
  NN10: R'den 2F **81**
Windyridge NN2: K'thpe 3E **84**
WING 1A **134**
Wingate Cl. NN15: K'ing 1G **43**
Winnington Cl. NN3: N'ton 1F **87**
Winsford Way NN3: N'ton 7A **86**
Winsland Ct. NN6: Holc 6H **37**
WINSLOW 3D **141**
Winstanley Rd. NN8: Well 1C **78**
Winston Cl. NN3: N'ton 1K **85**
  NN7: Neth H 6J **63**
  NN11: Woodf H 2D **108**
Winston Cres. NN13: B'ley 5G **129**
Winston Dr. NN14: Ish 3E **44**
Winterbourne Ct. NN18: Corby 7G **13**
Winterburn Cl. NN16: K'ing 6A **38**
Winthorpe Way NN18: Corby 7G **13**
WINWICK
  Cambridgeshire 3D **135**
  Northamptonshire 1C **137**
Winwood Cl. MK19: Dean 4F **125**
Wisley Cl. NN4: N'ton 1D **100**
Wisteria Cl. NN10: R'den 6E **80**
Wisteria Way NN3: N'ton 1K **95**
Witham, The NN11: Dav 2E **60**
Witham Grn. NN5: N'ton 4K **83**
Witham Wlk. NN5: N'ton 4A **84**
Witham Way NN5: N'ton 5A **84**
Witheys, The NN4: Gra P 6G **101**
WITHYBROOK 3A **132**
WITTERING 1C **135**
Wittlich Rd. NN8: Well 6C **66**
Witton Rd. NN5: Dus 6H **83**
Woburn Ct. NN10: R'den 5D **80**
Woburn Ga. NN3: N'ton 3G **87**
Wodhams Dr. NN13: B'ley 2F **129**
Wold Rd. NN15: Bur L 1K **45**
Wolfe Cl. NN15: K'ing 1H **43**
WOLLASTON 4E **90** (2B **138**)
Wollaston Ind. Est. NN29: Woll 5F **91**

Wollaston Mus. 4E **90**
Wollaston Rd. NN29: Boz 1G **103**
  NN29: Irch 7G **79**
Wollaton Gdns. NN3: N'ton 6C **86**
Wollongong Ho. NN17: Corby 5A **14**
Wolsey Cl. NN6: Crick 3J **31**
WOLSTON 1A **136**
WOLVERTON 1D **141**
WOLVEY 3A **132**
WOLVEY HEATH 3A **132**
Wood Avens Cl. NN4: N'ton 6K **93**
Woodborough Gdns. NN3: N'ton . . .6B **86**
WOOD BURCOTE 7C **114** (1C **141**)
Woodcock St. NN15: Bur L 1K **45**
Woodcote Av. NN3: N'ton 2G **85**
Woodcroft Cl. NN12: Tow 6C **114**
Woodcroft Way NN15: K'ing 2E **42**
WOOD END 2C **139**
WOODEND 7G **109** (1C **141**)
WOODEND GREEN 7F **109**
WOODFIELD 3B **140**
Woodfield PE9: Colly 7C **6**
Woodfield Gro. NN17: Corby 6K **13**
Woodfields Wlk. NN3: N'ton 1B **86**
WOODFORD 6B **50** (1B **138**)
Woodford Chase NN6: Syw 3F **75**
Woodford Cl. NN15: Bar S 5H **43**
Woodford Glebe NN6: Welf 3H **29**
WOODFORD HALSE 2D **108** (3B **136**)
Woodford La. NN14: Low 6C **48**
Woodford Rd. NN11: Byf 2J **107**
  NN11: Eyd 6C **108**
  NN14: Gt Ad, Woodf 1A **52**
  NN14: L Add 3B **52**
Woodford St. NN1: N'ton 1F **95**
Woodford Wlk. NN1: N'ton 1F **95**
  (off Woodford St.)
Woodgate Rd. NN4: Woot 2G **101**
Woodhall Cl. NN4: N'ton 6J **93**
Wood Hill NN1: N'ton 5J **131** (2E **94**)
Woodhill Rd. NN5: Dus 5G **83**
Woodland Av. NN3: N'ton 5H **85**
  NN6: Over 4E **74**
  NN15: Bar S 5J **43**
Woodland Cl. NN5: Dus 4G **83**
Woodland Dr. NN15: Bur L 1K **45**
Woodland Rd. NN10: R'den 2D **80**
Woodlands NN4: Gra P 7F **101**
Woodlands, The NN9: Stanw 1K **69**
  NN11: Stav 4A **60**
  NN12: Silv 3H **121**
  NN14: Ged 5C **46**
Woodlands Av. NN17: Corby 4A **14**
Woodlands Cl. NN14: Brig 2D **20**
Woodlands Ct. NN6: Wat 6D **54**
  NN16: K'ing 5E **38**
Woodlands Grange NN6: E Bart 2F **89**
Woodlands La. NN18: Gt Oak 6G **17**
Woodlands M. NN14: Brig 2D **20**
  (off Stable Hill)
Woodlands Rd. NN17: Weld 6K **15**
  NN29: Irch 6G **79**
Woodland Wlk. NN3: N'ton 7E **74**
Wood La. NN7: Hart 5J **117**
  PE8: King C 1F **9**
  PE8: Oun 6F **21**
Woodlark Ct. NN4: N'ton 7K **93**
Woodleigh Pl. NN17: Corby 7K **13**
Woodley Chase NN5: Dus 5G **83**
Woodmans Cl. MK19: Dean 5F **125**
WOODNEWTON 5G **9** (2C **135**)
Woodnewton Rd. PE8: Nass 7F **7**
Woodnewton Way NN17: Corby 6H **13**
Woodpecker Cl. NN13: B'ley 2E **128**
Woodpecker Way NN4: N'ton 1A **100**
Wood Rd. PE8: King C 2G **9**
Woodrush Way NN3: Moul 6K **73**
Woods Ct. NN13: B'ley 4E **128**
Woodsfield NN6: Brix 3G **35**
Woodside NN6: Syw 4G **75**
Woodside Av. NN3: N'ton 2A **86**
Woodside Cres. NN3: N'ton 2A **86**

Woodside Grn. NN5: N'ton 5A **84**
Woodside Pk. NN17: Weld 6K **15**
Woodside Vs. NN14: Low 6D **48**
Woodside Wlk. NN5: N'ton 5K **83**
Woodside Way NN5: N'ton 5K **83**
Woods La. NN12: Pot 6J **123**
WOODSTOCK 3A **140**
Woodstock NN1: N'ton 1F **95**
Woodstock Cl. NN8: Well 5K **65**
WOODSTON 2D **135**
Wood St. NN1: N'ton 4J **131**
  NN8: Well 1A **78**
  NN10: High F 7F **69**
  NN14: Ged 6D **46**
  NN16: K'ing 6D **38**
  NN17: Corby 7K **13**
Woodville Cres. NN12: Yar G 3J **123**
WOODWALTON 3D **135**
Woodward Cl. NN11: Dav 2K **61**
Woodwell Hill NN14: Des 3C **26**
Woodyard Cl. NN14: Brig 1D **20**
Wooldale Rd. NN4: Woot 3E **100**
WOOLLEY 1D **139**
Woolmonger St.
  NN1: N'ton 5H **131** (2D **94**)
WOOLSCOTT 2A **136**
Woolston Cl. NN3: N'ton 2J **85**
Woolston Ct. NN17: Gret 7D **8**
Wooton Rd. NN7: Gra P, Quin 4G **101**
WOOTTON
  Northamptonshire . . .2F **101** (3D **137**)
  Oxfordshire 3A **140**
Wootton Brook Cl. NN4: N'ton 2D **100**
Wootton Ct. NN12: Tow 4C **114**
Wootton Flds. Cen. NN4: Woot 2G **101**
Wootton Hall Pk. NN4: N'ton 7D **94**
Wootton Hill Farm NN4: N'ton 7A **94**
Wootton Hope Dr. NN4: Woot 1G **101**
Wootton Rd. NN7: Hart 4K **117**
Wootton Trad. Est. NN4: Woot 2G **101**
Worcester Cl. NN3: N'ton 4E **86**
  NN6: W Had 5H **29**
  NN18: L Oak 5K **17**
Worcester Way NN11: Dav 4H **61**
Wordsworth Av. NN17: Corby 4J **13**
Wordsworth Cl. NN12: Tow 4B **114**
  NN13: B'ley 2G **129**
Wordsworth Rd. NN8: Well 2G **77**
  NN11: Dav 7G **59**
  NN16: K'ing 4E **38**
Works, The NN1: N'ton 1F **95**
  (off Ethel St.)
Worksop Gdns. NN18: Corby 7G **13**
  (off Clumber Ct.)
WORMLEIGHTON 3A **136**
Wormleightons Way NN14: Ged 5C **46**
  (off West St.)
Worthing Rd. NN18: Corby 1G **17**
WOTHORPE 1C **135**
WOTTON UNDERWOOD 3C **141**
Wrekin Cl. NN4: N'ton 4K **93**
Wrenbury Rd. NN5: Dus 6E **82**
Wren Cl. NN4: Gra P 5G **101**
  NN12: Tow 6C **114**
  NN13: B'ley 2E **128**
  NN15: Bar S 4J **43**
  NN18: Corby 2K **17**
Wrightons Hill NN13: Helm 2B **120**
Wright Rd. NN6: Long B 2H **55**
Wrights La. NN7: G'ton 4D **98**
Wroe, The NN10: High F 5E **68**
Wroe Cl. NN18: Gt Oak 5H **17**
WROXTON 1A **140**
Wyatt PE8: Oun 4H **21**
Wyatt St. NN16: K'ing 7E **38**
Wyatt Way PE8: Oun 4G **21**
WYBOSTON 3D **139**
Wychwood Cl. NN5: Dus 5F **83**
Wyckley Cl. NN9: Irth 1B **68**
Wycliffe Rd. NN1: N'ton 7H **85**
Wye, The NN11: Dav 3F **61**
Wye Cl. NN8: Well 6H **65**

Wykeham Rd. NN10: High F 5F **69**
WYKEN .3A **132**
WYKIN 2A **132**
Wyman Cl. NN29: Boz 3H **103**
Wymersley Cl. NN4: Gt Hou 5C **96**
WYMINGTON 7E **80** (2B **138**)
Wymington Pk. NN10: R'den 7G **81**
Wymington Pk. NN10: R'den 4E **80**
Wymington Rd. NN10: R'den 6E **80**
Wyndham Way NN16: K'ing 5A **38**
Wysall Rd. NN3: N'ton 1D **86**

Y

Yaffle Cres. NN14: Des 1E **26**
Yardley Cl. NN17: Corby 5J **13**
Yardley Dr. NN2: K'thpe 7E **72**
YARDLEY GOBION 3K **123** (1D **141**)
YARDLEY HASTINGS . . .5G **103** (3A **138**)
Yardley Rd. MK19: Cos 5B **122**
  NN7: Gren 4B **102**
  NN12: Pot 6J **123**
Yarrow NN8: Well 2G **77**
Yarrow Cl. NN10: R'den 6F **81**
Yarrow Gallery 5H **21**
YARWELL 2J **7** (2C **135**)
Yarwell Ct. NN15: K'ing 4E **42**
Yarwell Mill Cvn. & Camping Pk.
  PE8: Yar 3J **7**
Yarwell Sq. NN4: N'ton 5A **94**
Yateley Dr. NN15: Bar S 5J **43**
YAXLEY .2D **135**
YELDEN .2C **139**
Yelden Cl. NN10: R'den 3C **80**
Yeldon Ct. NN8: Well 4C **66**
YELVERTOFT 5C **28** (1B **136**)
Yelvertoft Rd. CV23: Lil 3C **28**
  NN2: K'thpe 3D **84**
  NN6: Crick 3H **31**
  NN6: W Had 5G **29**
  NN6: Yel 4B **28**
Yeoman Cl. NN14: Rin 1F **53**
Yeoman Dr. NN2: K'thpe 1C **84**
Yeoman Mdw. NN4: N'ton 7A **94**
Yeomanry Cl. NN11: Dav 2G **61**
Yeomanry Way NN11: Dav 1F **61**
Yeomans Cl. NN13: B'ley 3H **129**
Yeomans Ct. NN15: Bur L 2K **45**
Yew Cl. NN17: Corby 4K **13**
Yew Tree Cl. NN15: K'ing 2E **42**
  OX17: Mid C 6D **118**
Yewtree Ct. NN3: N'ton 1A **86**
Yew Tree Gdns. NN7: Flore 2F **63**
Yew Tree Gro. NN11: Dav 3G **61**
Yew Tree La. NN6: Spra 5C **34**
Yew Tree Ri. NN13: Crou 5B **130**
York Av. NN7: Cog 1J **97**
York Cl. NN10: High F 5F **69**
  NN12: Tow 4C **114**
York Ct. NN12: Tow 4C **114**
York Dr. NN13: B'ley 3F **129**
Yorke Cl. NN9: Fine 6G **47**
York Ho. NN1: N'ton 1G **95**
  (off Cliftonville)
York Ride NN7: Weed 3C **62**
  (off Gloucester Cl.)
York Rd. NN1: N'ton 4K **131** (1E **94**)
  NN8: Well 7C **66**
  NN10: High F 5F **69**
  NN10: R'den 4F **81**
  NN16: K'ing 7D **38**
  NN18: Corby 1G **17**
  NN29: Woll 3D **90**
York Way NN9: Raun 5H **53**
  NN11: Dav 4K **61**

Z

Zion Hill NN6: Wal 1H **37**

HOSPITALS, TREATMENT CENTRES and HOSPICES
covered by this atlas.

N.B. Where it is not possible to name these facilities on the map,
the reference given is for the road in which they are situated.

BERRYWOOD HOSPITAL 6F **83**
Berrywood Drive
NORTHAMPTON
NN5 6UD
Tel: 01604 596340

BRACKLEY COTTAGE HOSPITAL 4G **129**
Pebble Lane
BRACKLEY
NN13 7DA
Tel: 01280 702388

CORBY COMMUNITY HOSPITAL 7J **13**
Cottingham Road
CORBY
NN17 2UN
Tel: 01536 400070

CRANSLEY HOSPICE 1E **42**
St. Mary's Hospital
Pippers Hill Road
KETTERING
NN15 7RJ
Tel: 01536 493041

CYNTHIA SPENCER HOSPICE 2J **85**
Manfield Health Campus
Kettering Road
NORTHAMPTON
NN3 6NP
Tel: 01604 678030

DANETRE HOSPITAL 3H **61**
London Road
DAVENTRY
NN11 4DY
Tel: 01327 708800

ISEBROOK HOSPITAL 2C **78**
Irthlingborough Road
WELLINGBOROUGH
NN8 1LP
Tel: 01933 440099

KETTERING GENERAL HOSPITAL 7B **38**
Rothwell Road
KETTERING
NN16 8UZ
Tel: 01536 492000

KETTERING TREATMENT CENTRE 7B **38**
Rothwell Road
KETTERING
NN16 8UZ
Tel: 01536 492000

LAKELANDS DAY HOSPICE 4J **17**
Butland Road
CORBY
NN18 8LX
Tel: 01536 747755

NHS WALK-IN CENTRE (LAKESIDE PLUS) 7H **13**
Cottingham Road
CORBY
NN17 2UR
Tel: 01536 204154

NORTHAMPTON GENERAL HOSPITAL 2F **95**
Cliftonville
NORTHAMPTON
NN1 5BD
Tel: 01604 634700

PRINCESS MARINA HOSPITAL 1G **93**
Kent Road
Upton
NORTHAMPTON
NN5 6UH
Tel: 01604 752323

RUSHDEN HOSPITAL 5E **80**
Wymington Road
Rushden
NORTHAMPTON
NN10 9JS
Tel: 01933 440666

ST ANDREW'S HEALTHCARE (NORTHAMPTON)
......................................2H **95**
Billing Road
NORTHAMPTON
NN1 5DG
Tel: 01604 616000

ST MARY'S HOSPITAL 1E **42**
77 London Road
KETTERING
NN15 7PW
Tel: 01536 410141

THREE SHIRES BMI HOSPITAL 2G **95**
The Avenue
Cliftonville
NORTHAMPTON
NN1 5DR
Tel: 01604 620311

The representation on the maps of a road, track or footpath is no evidence of the existence of a right of way.

The Grid on this map is the National Grid taken from Ordnance Survey® mapping with the permission of the Controller of Her Majesty's Stationery Office.

Copyright of Geographers' A-Z Map Company Ltd.

No reproduction by any method whatsoever of any part of this publication is permitted without the prior consent of the copyright owners.

SAFETY CAMERA INFORMATION

Safety camera locations are publicised by the Safer Roads Partnership who operate them in order to encourage drivers to comply with speed limits at these sites. It is the driver's absolute responsibility to be aware of and to adhere to speed limits at all times.

By showing this safety camera information it is the intention of Geographers' A-Z Map Company Ltd., to encourage safe driving and greater awareness of speed limits and vehicle speed. Data accurate at time of printing.